P9-CNC-447

Vietnam

100 miles

100 km

CENTRAL VIETNAM

SOUTH TO QUY NHON

NHA TRANG AND SURROUNDINGS

NHA TRANG AND DALAT

DALAT AND SURROUNDINGS

AROUND HO CHI MINH CITY

HO CHI MINH CITY

SOUTHERN VIETNAM

THE MEKONG DELTA

BIEN DONG

Quy Nhon
Mui Ong Dien
Tuy Hoa
Mui Nay

Phan Rang-Thap Cham

Cu Lao Thu

Da Lat
(Dalat)
Duc Trong
Mui Ne
Phan Thiet
Khe Ga

(Chu Yang Sin
National Park)

Vung Quoc Gia
Nam Cat Tien
(Cat Tien National Park)

Vuon Quoc Gia Yok Don
(Yok Don National Park)

Dat
au

Ho Chi Minh
Thu Dau Mot
Tan An
Tay Ninh
Prey Veng
Svay Rieng

Bac Lieu
Ca Mau

Vuon Quoc Gia
Con Dao
(Con Dao National Park)

Con Dao

Long Xuyen
Can Tho
Rach Gia
Chau Doc
Tien Giang
Hau Giang
Ben Tre
Mui Ca Mau

Ha Tien
Hon
Chong
Hon Rai
Kampot

Vuon Quoc Gia Phu Quoc
(Phu Quoc National Park)
Dao Phu Quoc

Kampong Saom

Phnum Penh
(Phnom Penh)

C A M B O D I A

Mekong
Kampong Cham
Kracheh
Kampong Thum
Stoeng Sen
Kampong
Chhnang
Pouthisat
Tonle
Sab
Siemreab
Battambang
Pailin
Sisophon

Phumi
Samraong
Phumi
Mlu Prey
Sbeng Trenb
Phumi
Stoeng Trenb

Srepok
Srepok
Krong Kaon Kong

Ko Kut
Ko Chang

Attapu
Virochey
Pakxe
Champasak

Anlong Veng

Mekong

Trat
Chanthaburi
Prachin Buri
Nakhon
Ratchasima
Buriram
Surin
Sisaket
Ubon
Ratchathani

Mae
Nang Khong

INSIGHT ⊙ GUIDES

VIETNAM

⊙ Walking Eye App

YOUR FREE DESTINATION CONTENT AND EBOOK AVAILABLE THROUGH THE WALKING EYE APP

Your guide now includes a free eBook and destination content for your chosen destination, all for the same great price as before. Simply download the Walking Eye App from the App Store or Google Play to access your free eBook and destination content.

HOW THE WALKING EYE APP WORKS

Through the Walking Eye App, you can purchase a range of eBooks and destination content. However, when you buy this book, you can download the corresponding eBook and destination content for free. Just see below in the grey panels where to find your free content and then scan the QR code at the bottom of this page.

Destinations: Download your corresponding essential destination content from here, featuring recommended sights and attractions, restaurants, hotels and an A–Z of practical information, all for free. Other destinations are available for purchase.

Ships: Interested in ship reviews? Find independent reviews of river and ocean ships in this section, all available for purchase.

eBooks: You can download your free accompanying digital version of this guide here. You will also find a whole range of other eBooks, all available for purchase.

Free access to travel-related blog articles about different destinations, updated on a daily basis.

HOW THE DESTINATION CONTENT WORKS

Each destination includes a short introduction, an A–Z of practical information and recommended points of interest, split into 4 different categories:

• Highlights
• Accommodation
• Eating out
• What to do

You can view the location of every point of interest and save it by adding it to your Favourites. In the 'Around Me' section you can view all the points of interest within 5km.

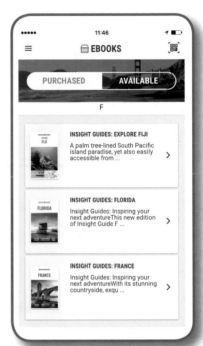

HOW THE EBOOKS WORK

The eBooks are provided in EPUB file format. Please note that you will need an eBook reader installed on your device to open the file. Many devices come with this as standard, but you may still need to install one manually from Google Play.

The eBook content is identical to the content in the printed guide.

HOW TO DOWNLOAD THE WALKING EYE APP

1. Download the Walking Eye App from the App Store or Google Play.
2. Open the app and select the scanning function from the main menu.
3. Scan the QR code on this page – you will then be asked a security question to verify ownership of the book.
4. Once this has been verified, you will see your eBook and destination content in the purchased ebook and destination sections, where you will be able to download them.

Other destination apps and eBooks are available for purchase separately or are free with the purchase of the Insight Guide book.

CONTENTS

Travel Tips

Maps

LEGEND
🔎 Insight on
📷 Photo story

THE BEST OF VIETNAM: TOP ATTRACTIONS

△ **Halong Bay**. The Unesco World Heritage Site of Halong Bay is a magical landscape of more than 3,000 limestone crags and outcrops riddled with caves and half submerged in the indigo-coloured bay. Spend the night on a sailing junk and visit one of the floating fishing villages. See page 175.

△ **Mui Ne**. Ancient Cham towers, Chinese assembly halls, whale temples and Vietnam's largest reclining Buddha are all located near Mui Ne, but it's the sprawling beach and kite-boarding that draw crowds to Vietnam's fastest-growing resort destination. See page 313.

▽ **Sa Pa**. The town of Sa Pa is perched amid stunning highland scenery and is home to numerous ethnic minorities with thriving cultures. The Sunday-morning market in Bac Ha hosts merchants from the Nung, Dao, Tay, Thai, Flower Hmong and other hill tribes, clad in their colourful traditional dress. See page 154.

▽ **Ho Chi Minh City**. This is Vietnam's economic powerhouse, with all the best that an international city has to offer. Downtown District 1 has trendy bars and cafés, superb restaurants, plus lots of shopping opportunities and historic sites galore. See page 279.

△ **Nha Trang**. This area has a lively nightlife with a plethora of bars and restaurants around the beach. The main reason to visit, however, is found in the bay, where divers and snorkellers head out to the surrounding islands for a close-up view of the country's finest coral reefs. See page 249.

△ **Con Dao Archipelago**. Once home to Vietnam's most notorious prison, the Con Dao Archipelago is now the country's finest marine reserve, known for its sea turtle conservation programme and secluded resorts on remote beaches. See page 316.

▷ **My Son**. The ancient religious capital of the Indianised Champa kingdom (5th to 15th centuries) is located at My Son, central Vietnam; it is a Unesco World Heritage Site. The ruined temples and towers, severely damaged in the war – as well as by the weather – are a concentrated sample of the many Cham towers scattered along the country's long coastline. See page 228.

◁ **Hue**. The city of Hue sits at the heart of the country, straddling mazes of moats and canals, lotus lakes and the sleepy Perfume River. The Imperial City, a Unesco World Heritage Site, was home to the Nguyen dynasty, whose kings and queens now rest in elaborate mausoleums nearby. See page 199.

▽ **Hoi An's Old Town**. Stroll the Unesco World Heritage Site of Hoi An's Old Town, along the banks of the Thu Bon River, and experience the old-world ambience of the Japanese Covered Bridge, ancient Chinese assembly halls and old merchant homes built in a fusion of Vietnamese, Chinese, Japanese and French architectural styles. See page 223.

△ **Hanoi**. This vibrant city is both the political and cultural capital of Vietnam. One of its highlights is the Old Quarter, nicknamed "36 Streets" after the 36 merchant guilds located along their respective streets. This and other pockets of nostalgia make for a charming, French-influenced city. See page 111.

THE BEST OF VIETNAM: EDITOR'S CHOICE

Magical, mysterious Halong Bay.

VIETNAM FOR FAMILIES

Water puppets: Hanoi and Ho Chi Minh City (HCMC). Only in Vietnam can you enjoy a musical puppet theatre performance with an aquatic twist. See pages 117, 289.

Vinpearl Land and Underwater World: Hon Tre Island, Nha Trang. Ride the world's longest ocean-crossing cable car to this island amusement park for exciting rides, games, a water park and an aquarium. See page 256.

Oceanographic Institute: Nha Trang. A splendid aquarium with lots of bizarre sea creatures and live sea turtles. See page 255.

Hang Nga's Crazy House: Dalat. Any tree-house-lover will enjoy exploring this whimsically imaginative house full of hidden corridors and secret rooms. See page 267.

Thap Ba Hot Springs: Nha Trang. Take a therapeutic mineral mud bath and then frolic in the hot-spring pools at this family-friendly site. See page 251.

Traditional dance performance.

TOP BEACHES

Jungle Beach. The Hon Heo Peninsula north of Nha Trang shelters one of Vietnam's finest beaches, backed by rocky mountains and washed by clear, emerald waters. See page 258.

Mui Ne Beach. An all-time favourite that is easily accessible from Ho Chi Minh City, with a burgeoning water-sports scene. See page 313.

Nha Trang. The hottest nightlife in central Vietnam spills out onto its finely manicured city beach. See page 249.

China Beach. One of the longest uninterrupted stretches of beach in Vietnam also has the best surfing. See page 218.

Cua Dai Beach. Its easy accessibility from Hoi An makes this the perfect beach to relax on and chill out by day. See page 227.

Sao Beach. Located at the southeastern end of Phu Quoc Island, this stretch of paradise is difficult to get to but well worth the effort. See page 334.

Hanoi's famous Temple of Literature.

BEST OUTDOOR ACTIVITIES

Kiteboarding and windsurfing: Mui Ne. Vietnam's premier water-sports and dune-surfing capital. See page 313.

Golf: Dalat and Mui Ne. Play a round at a highland course or a few holes among the ocean dunes. See page 265.

Snorkelling and diving: Nha Trang. Some of Vietnam's best reefs are found in its surrounding waters. See page 256.

Kayaking and trekking:

Cat Ba Island. Explore this beautiful location from the water or on dry land. See page 178.

Abseiling: Dalat. Experience Datanla waterfall and others in the central highlands up close. See page 270.

Trekking: Sa Pa. Hike to the minority villages of the northern highlands. See page 157.

Caving: Phong Nga. Experience the world's largest cave passage in the seldom-visited Tonkin region. See page 193.

TOP TEMPLES AND RELIGIOUS SITES

Temple of Literature: Hanoi. The city's most important temple is devoted to Confucian teaching. See page 124.

Cao Dai Great Temple: Tay Ninh. Part cathedral and part pagoda, the headquarters of this curious indigenous religion attracts many visitors. See page 305.

My Son. Champa's ancient capital in central Vietnam is a mini, albeit crumbling, counterpart

to Cambodia's Angkor Wat. See page 228.

Perfume Pagoda: near Hanoi. Built into limestone cliffs, this is one of northern Vietnam's most important religious sites. See page 137.

Van Thuy Thu Temple: Phan Thiet. This is the oldest temple devoted to the worship of whales in Vietnam. The whale and dolphin skeletons are a fascinating sight. See page 312.

Kitesurfing on the beach.

The wide, sandy expanse of China Beach.

BEST HOTELS AND RESORTS

The Nam Hai Resort: Cua Dai Beach. Combining minimalist chic with tasteful Vietnamese accents, this beachfront luxury hotel is a designer's dream resort located near Hoi An (tel: 510 394 0000; www.fourseasons.com/hoian).

Park Hyatt Saigon: HCMC. Built in faux colonial style, this chic luxury hotel is easily the city's most stylish, and also most expensive, accommodation (tel: 83 824 1234; www.saigon.park.hyatt.com).

Sofitel Metropole Hotel: Hanoi. The grande dame of colonial hotels in Vietnam still has heaps of old-world charm despite extensive renovations to its interior (tel: 4/3 826 6919; www.sofitel.com).

Caravelle Hotel: HCMC. Headquarters for journalists and diplomats during the Vietnam War, today it's one of the city's most luxurious hotels (tel: 83 823 4999; www.caravellehotel.com).

Dalat Palace. Enjoy authentic French colonial atmosphere with modern comforts in Dalat's original lakefront hotel (tel: 63 382 5444; www.dalatpalacehotel.com).

Six Senses Hideaway Ninh Van Bay: Nha Trang. Accessible only by speedboat, this all-villa hotel offers the highest level of luxury (tel: 58 352 4268; www.sixsenses.com).

Life Wellness Resort: Quy Nhon. A stylish beachside spa resort inspired by ancient Cham architecture. Represents style at a good price (tel: 56 384 0132; www.avanihotels.com/quynhon).

Ana Mandara Villas: Dalat. Ensconced within snug and refurbished French colonial villas dating from the 1920s and 30s, you will find little reason to venture out to downtown Dalat (tel: 63 355 5888; www.anamandara-resort.com).

Pick from three pools at the Nam Hai.

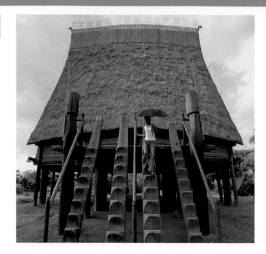

Bahnar communal house at the Vietnam Museum of Ethnology.

TOP MUSEUMS

Museum of Vietnamese History: HCMC. Stroll through halls exhibiting artefacts from all the ancient cultures of Vietnam. See page 293.

Ho Chi Minh Museum: Hanoi. The most thorough and definitive showcase of the man behind the Vietnamese communist revolution for independence. See page 127.

Museum of Cham Sculpture: Danang. This unmatched collection of artefacts tells the other half of the story found at the ancient Cham sites along coastal Vietnam. See page 215.

War Remnants Museum: HCMC. A controversial museum documenting atrocities suffered by the Vietnamese during the war with America. See page 289.

Lam Dong Museum: Dalat. Lat gongs, Ma longhouses and Funan relics are interspersed among an outstanding taxidermy collection. See page 268.

Quang Trung Museum: Quy Nhon. Dedicated to emperor Quang Trung and the Tay Son brothers, leaders of the infamous rebellion. See page 239.

Vietnam Museum of Ethnology: Hanoi. This museum offers a superb introduction to the culture and lifestyles of Vietnam's 54 ethnic minorities. See page 131.

Hoi An's Old Quarter. This Unesco World Heritage town is itself a living museum, but several merchant homes have also been turned into remarkable showcases for culture, local folklore and crafts. See page 223.

BEST NATURE EXPERIENCES

Halong Bay. Myriad rock formations hide enchanting caves to explore and solitary beaches for swimming. See page 175.

Bach Ma National Park. Vietnam's rainiest rainforest contains countless waterfalls, wild rhododendrons and the rare saola antelope. See page 220.

Mount Fansipan. A guide is necessary for the exhilarating climb up Vietnam's highest peak. The hike will take three days. See page 158.

Tam Coc. Jagged limestone outcrops sticking out from flooded rice paddies make for some spectacular scenery. See page 185.

Endangered Primate Rescue Centre: Cuc Phuong National Park. See some of the rarest primates in the world, including langurs, gibbons and snubnosed monkeys. See page 188.

Cat Tien National Park. Spend the night at Crocodile Lake and catch a glimpse of Siamese crocodiles, and animals like the sambar deer and peafowl. See page 309.

Con Dao Archipelago. Go snorkelling to find sea turtles in the reefs, or watch them nesting on shore. See page 316.

Dragonfruit in the Mekong Delta.

VIETNAMESE EATS

Pho. Served with beef or chicken, pho noodle soup is available throughout Vietnam. Diehards swear that Hanoi's version is the best. See page 88.

Banh khoai and banh beo: Hue. The best taroand-rice-batter pancakes and steamed rice-flour dumplings are served at the city's Lac Thien, Lac Thanh and Lac Thuan eateries. See page 91.

Imperial Banquet: Hue. Dine like royalty at Phuoc Thanh on a large variety of local dishes created for emperors.

For more on Hue's cuisine see page *349*.

Cao lau: Hoi An. This rice noodle dish with pork and sesame crackers is served at all the local eateries in the Old Town. See page 223.

Goi cuon. A southern speciality also known as "summer rolls", with vermicelli, prawns, pork and herbs. See page 91.

Fresh fruit: Mekong Delta. Vietnam's fertile southern delta is the best place to sample the country's tropical fruits. See page 320.

Vietnam's most famous dish – pho.

TOP CULTURAL EXPERIENCES

Cham Villages: Phan Rang. Visit villages populated by minority Cham people who live a lifestyle little changed by modernity. See page 258.

Fish sauce: Phan Thiet and Phu Quoc. See how fish sauce *(nuoc mam)* is made and, more importantly, sample the cuisine based around it. See page 310.

Market shopping. For an insight into local culture, shop at markets like those in Dalat and Ho Chi Minh City (Benh Thanh). See pages 265.

Ao Dai. Women can visit a local tailor and get fitted for a silk *ao dai*, the national dress of Vietnam. Hanoi, HCMC and Hoi An are the best places for tailored clothes. See page 222.

Homestays. Spend a night in a wooden stilt house in a hill-tribe village or Mekong Delta backwater. Book via a tour agency. See page 345.

Mekong Delta. Take a boat through the mighty Delta to see how the deep south lives. See page 320.

Water puppetry is a northern Vietnamese art form.

Button and sequin portrait
of Ho Chi Minh.

Radish farm, Dalat.

Ethnic clothing for sale, Bac Ha.

Evening market in Hanoi's Old Quarter.

TRIUMPH OVER ADVERSITY

Having overcome war and deep divisions, today's Vietnam is now better known for its breathtaking scenery, beaches and vibrant cities.

Motorbikes aplenty.

Modern yet traditional, communist yet capitalist, cosmopolitan yet quaint – calling Vietnam diverse doesn't even begin to tell the story. Its associations with war may still be present, but today the tunnels are tourist traps, the tanks are displayed in museums and the divisions are all but healed.

The sheer range of landscapes and attractions makes Vietnam something of a challenge. The long, sandy beaches and the turquoise seas are tempting, but then so are its forested mountains and verdant countryside. Vietnamese cities are dynamic, full of life and colour.

Back in 1975 when the last US troops fled Vietnam, things were not so rosy. The country was reunified but faced a new battle – economic stability. As the government clung firmly to its Marxist–Leninist blueprint, the country floundered. By the mid-1980s, Vietnam was on the brink of bankruptcy; some people were starving, and inflation topped 800 percent. The economic revolution known as *doi moi* began in 1986 and opened up the country to foreign investment – and foreign visitors. From 2000 to 2007 Vietnam was one of the world's fastest-growing economies and the darling of foreign investors. Global recession hit the export-oriented Vietnamese economy hard with GDP growth falling to 5 percent in 2013. However, by the end of 2017 it had rebounded to reach an estimated 6.2 percent.

Vietnam is home to many tropical beaches.

Today's ruling communist government still keeps a tight reign on cultural and political affairs, and the sheer pace of development means major cities are packed to bursting point. Despite this, there has never been a better time to visit Vietnam as much of the progress is aimed at attracting tourism. The result is that travelling is simpler, the hotels are more luxurious and the restaurants of higher quality than ever before. Vietnam doesn't forget its past – that's why many visitors come, after all – but it is keen to move forward and showcase its natural beauty and its people's friendly nature.

GEOGRAPHY AND LANDSCAPE

From the jagged slopes of the northern mountains to the waterways of the Mekong Delta in the deep south, Vietnam is a land endowed with startling physical beauty and a rich biodiversity.

Resembling an elongated letter S, Vietnam runs along the length of the Indochinese Peninsula, bordering the Bien Dong (literally Eastern Sea), better known as the South China Sea, to the east. Its 3,730km (2,320-mile) frontier borders China to the north, and Cambodia and Laos to the west. Covering some 331,000 sq km (127,799 sq miles), Vietnam's territory also encompasses a lengthy coastline and thousands of islands reaching from the Gulf of Tonkin to the Gulf of Thailand. These include the disputed Spratly (Truong Sa) and Paracel (Hoang Sa) islands, which China and a number of Southeast Asian nations lay claim to, mostly due to the islands' rich oil and gas deposits.

Vietnam is a long, narrow country. Broadest at its northern and southern ends, it tapers to a mere 50km (30 miles) in the centre. Mountains and forests make up more than three-quarters of the total land area, with roughly 25 percent of the land under cultivation. The 3,000km (1,850-mile) coastline is dotted with beautiful beaches.

A traditional Chinese-style junk, Halong Bay.

THE LIE OF THE LAND

The northern mountains and steeply carved valleys that separate Vietnam from China and northern Laos include the mighty Hoang Lien Son range, an eastern extension of the Himalayas. This includes Vietnam's highest mountain, Mount Fansipan (3,143 metres/1,030ft), which can be climbed on a three-day trek.

To the south and east of these highlands are the extensive plains of the Song Hong, or Red River, which is home to 90 percent of northern Vietnam's population. The Red River flows from its source in the Yunnan region of China across the north of Vietnam and then southeast via the city of Hanoi to its coastal mouth near Haiphong. The coastline is mostly muddy in the delta area

and rocky around Halong Bay, where a stunning archipelago of thousands of limestone outcrops (or karsts) and isles of various sizes and shapes lies scattered in the Gulf of Tonkin.

There are several other areas with karst formations in the far northeast as well as the north-central area of Vietnam, notably in Tam Coc and Hoa Lu, and the area south from Dong Hoi that contains the remarkable Phong Nha Caves. Not yet fully explored, the caves at Phong Nha extend over 35km (20 miles) of underground passages: in 2003, this area became Vietnam's fifth Unesco World Heritage Site.

Central Vietnam, formerly known as Annam, forms a long convex curve within which are narrow plains wedged between the South China Sea and the high plateaux of the Truong Son mountains. This terrain is characterised by coastal dunes and lagoons, and terraces of alluvial deposits towards the mountains.

The narrow coastal strip of central Vietnam is home to much of the region's population, its towns and villages linked by the main north–south railway and Highway 1. The imperial capital of Hue, the large city of Danang and the attractive old town of Hoi An are located here.

Further south, the Central Highlands between Danang and Dalat are rich in volcanic basalt soil and contain some of Vietnam's most extensive forests, in addition to vast tea- and coffee-growing plantations. There are various ethnic minority groups in the hills, but many areas are politically sensitive and access is restricted in some areas. The colonial hill station of Dalat is the main tourism hub.

The long stretch of coastline south from Hoi An to Nha Trang has some of the country's most beautiful beaches, largely undeveloped except around Nha Trang, itself Vietnam's leading resort.

The deep south is characterised by extensive lowlands around Ho Chi Minh City (Saigon), one of Vietnam's main rice-growing areas, and more sandy beaches around Mui Ne, Phan Thiet and Vung Tau. To the southwest is the extensive delta of the Mekong River, a maze of waterways and marshes unlike anywhere else in the country. Beyond, in the turquoise waters of the Gulf of Thailand, is the large island of Phu Quoc.

FLORA AND FAUNA

Despite the damage inflicted by American chemical defoliants in the war, and the inevitable decline due to population pressure and logging, Vietnam has retained a significant amount of forest cover and its wildlife has held up relatively well. Yet things are changing rapidly, and the environment is increasingly under threat as habitats continue to vanish and enforcement continues to be slack.

Vietnam's complex climate (see page 346) and varied geography provide a wide range of habitats for its remarkable variety of plants and animals – both tropical and temperate species – some of which are unique to the country.

VIETNAM'S FORESTS

The country's forests are a valuable resource and contain more than 1,200 identified plant species, providing a rich source of oils, resins, timber and medicines. The tropical forests host more than 800 types of wood, including hardwoods such as teak and mahogany.

There are small populations of tigers, leopards and elephants and larger numbers of various primate species, small carnivores such as marbled cats and civets, numerous deer species, wild pigs, pangolins and dozens of rodent species. There are also several reptile species including numerous venomous snakes as well as crocodiles, and over 800 bird species. The

Limestone crags amid rice fields at Tam Coc.

⊘ BUSHMEAT

Vietnam's increasing affluence, coupled with an appetite for wildlife meat, is driving some species to extinction. Eating certain animal body parts is often falsely believed to have medicinal or aphrodisiacal effects. Some animals are killed for their skin and teeth, while others are kept in illegal private zoos, but most, over 75 percent, end up in the cooking pot. A 2010 survey of more than 7,000 Ho Chi Minh City residents revealed that about half the respondents admitted using wild animal products, whether it be for food, health or just as ornaments. The most popular meats were snake, wild boar, deer, porcupine and monitor lizard.

forests occasionally throw up some surprises. In 1989, a Javan rhinoceros thought to be extinct in mainland Asia was rediscovered in Vietnam. Sadly, scientists declared the animal extinct in Vietnam in 2011 following the discovery of a dead individual in Cat Tien National Park, thought to have been killed by poachers.

In the northern mountains, the forests are temperate rather than tropical, and shelter Eurasian species such as black bears, squirrels, civets, otters and foxes. In terms of plant life, the highland areas are home to a wide range of

A slow loris at the Primate Rescue Center, Cuc Phuong National Park.

temperate, subtropical and evergreen species, some of which produce timber.

ENDANGERED MARINE LIFE

Although the offshore waters contain some 2,000 species of fish, overfishing is a major problem. The government has spoken of creating sustainable breeding programmes for the more economically important species and creating alternative livelihoods for those who depend on the sea to make a living.

Numerous islands are, however, still rich in underwater species and popular with divers, particularly in the south around Nha Trang and the Con Dao archipelago. Species include moray eels, green turtles, various sharks and manta rays.

THE WILDLIFE TRADE

Fewer than 100 tigers and 100 wild elephants are believed to survive in the wilds of Vietnam, their gene pools already too small to ensure their long-term survival. While the country has been famous over the past two decades for the discovery of new species, it is now on the verge of becoming infamous for the extinction of numerous species.

Exacerbating the problem is the highly lucrative – and illegal – wildlife trade. According to sources, every year nearly 3,300 tonnes of illegal live wildlife and animal products are shipped in and out of Vietnam. Commonly traded creatures include tigers and bears.

Scientists and environmental agencies have voiced concern over Vietnam's lax environmental laws. If someone is caught with an endangered species at a private farm, they merely have to pay an administrative fine, which is usually a tiny fraction of the animal's value on the illegal wildlife market, and agree to keep the animal housed in "suitable conditions". What that means, no one really knows, so in reality there is no effective environmental protection at all. The international community is starting to put pressure on the Vietnamese government to be more proactive: in 2010 the Convention on International Trade in Endangered Species of Wild Fauna and Flora (CITES) cited Vietnam as one of the worst offenders.

The only way for protection groups to confiscate wildlife is when the animals are caught while in transit. To get around this, smugglers have been known to create fake permits or use wedding cars or funeral hearses as cover. In one case, a bear was reported to have been smuggled in a hospital ambulance. Fuelling this illicit trade is the Vietnamese affinity for consuming exotic wildlife meat.

The animal trade is so accepted in Vietnam that traders openly sell animals on city streets. Inspectors do occasionally perform raids, but the traders are adept at packing up and disappearing into the crowds whenever an official is nearby. In 2014, the government adopted a firmer stance on the issue by passing a directive aimed at halting the illicit cross-border wildlife trade in Vietnam.

CONSERVATION EFFORTS

The urgent task of protecting rich biodiversity is a major challenge in a rapidly developing nation such as Vietnam.

Vietnam's rapid development has put new pressures on an already fragile environment. A growing population – now estimated to be over 95 million – brings ever greater demands on the land. Much of the country's lowlands are already intensively farmed, while the forests of the central highlands and the northern mountains continue to be threatened by traditional slash-and-burn farming techniques practised by the hill tribes.

It's a familiar story. The country's forests, according to some estimates, more than halved in area between 1945, when it accounted for some 45 percent of the land, to around 17% in the late 1970s (the use of toxic chemical defoliants during the Vietnam War led to around 5 percent being wiped out). Precious hardwoods were being felled in industrial quantities as timber for export, and minerals were also heavily extracted. The cost of this destruction could have been severe, and not just for the animals whose habitat was being lost.

REFORESTATION PROGRAMME

The government has tried to reverse this alarming trend by spearheading a reforestation programme. Yet the 5 million-hectare (12 million-acre) project, started in 1998, involved planting fast-growing cash-crop trees (usually non-native species) that actually masks the ongoing loss of primary and natural forest – and does little to protect wildlife. Therefore, despite more trees being planted than cut in recent years, the fragile ecosystems and biodiversity are finding themselves under even greater stress.

There is now a move to reintroduce native trees to the forests, but these take far longer to mature than cash-crop trees. Logging is illegal, but a black market trade inevitably continues. Logging in the north is a particular problem, and there have been several reports of violence against officials when illegal activity has been unearthed. In 2010, four rangers were killed while trying to stop the loggers.

Several independent groups are working towards improving the situation, including the Vietnam Conservation Fund, an organisation which helps local communities find sustainable and practical ways to earn a living that do not involve damaging the biodiversity of an area.

There are some successes. The Green Corridor project, an international effort, protected 1,340 sq km (500 sq miles) of forest in the central Thua Thien Hue province and led to the discovery of 11 new species of animals and plants. Two hours outside Ho Chi Minh

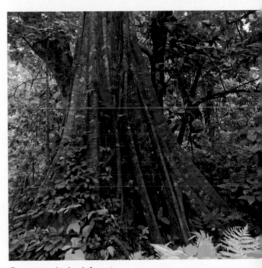

Dense tropical rainforest.

City, the Wildlife Rescue Station (www.wildlifeatrisk.org) has rescued and released more than 5,500 animals since its launch in 2006. The station has become a popular tourist destination. Among animals recovered from illegal traders and poachers and transferred to the rescue station are many rare species including Tibetan bears, Malayan bears, black yellow-cheek gibbons, pig-tailed monkeys, water rats, Java pangolins and mountain tortoise.

The government has also set aside large swathes of the country as protected areas, in the form of national parks and nature reserves. But most environmentalists claim these are, in reality, half-hearted measures and not backed up with adequate legislation and enforcement.

DECISIVE DATES

13th-century Cham tower at Po Klong Garai.

1st millennium BC
Bronze Age. Dong Son culture flourishes in the Red River basin and Tonkin coast.

258 BC
Kingdom of Au Lac.

208 BC
Kingdom of Nam Viet.

AD 39–42
Trung sisters lead an unsuccessful rebellion against the Chinese. Viet people are placed under Chinese rule.

542–4
Ly Bon leads an uprising against China.

545–938
Vietnam languishes under periodic Chinese rule.

939–1009
A succession of three short dynasties: Ngo, Dinh and Tien Le.

1010–1225
Hanoi established as Thang Long by Ly Thai To.

1225–1400
Further consolidation under Tran dynasty.

1400–28
Ho dynasty.

1428–1527
Le dynasty.

1471
Le dynasty takes over the southern Champa territory.

1527–92
Short-lived Mac dynasty.

1624
Jesuit priest Alexandre de Rhodes translates Vietnamese into a Romanised system of writing.

1672
The country is divided by rival Trinh and Nguyen lords.

1771–92
Tay Son Rebellion.

1802–1945
Nguyen dynasty.

1802
Capital moved to Hue.

1861
French capture Saigon and within six years take over southern Vietnam.

1883–1907
Various anti-French movements are crushed.

1919
Ho Chi Minh presents an anti-colonial petition at the Versailles Peace Conference.

1926
Emperor Bao Dai ascends the throne.

1930
Ho Chi Minh rallies communist groups; becomes founder of Indochinese Communist Party.

1942–3
Ho Chi Minh imprisoned in China. He is released and recognised as the chief of the Viet Minh.

1945
Japan overthrows the French and renders Vietnam "independent" but under Japanese "protection". Japanese later surrender to the Allies, and the Viet Minh takes over the country. Ho Chi Minh declares Vietnam's independence. Emperor Bao Dai abdicates.

1946
Hostilities against French begin after the latter try to reclaim Vietnam.

1951
Ho Chi Minh consolidates Viet Minh and announces the formation of the Workers' Party.

1954
The French are defeated at Dien Bien Phu. Geneva Accord divides Vietnam at 17th parallel. Democratic South Vietnam is led by Ngo Dinh Diem; North Vietnam comes under the communist Ho Chi Minh.

1955
Escalation of hostilities between North and South

Vietnam. Direct US aid to South Vietnam begins.

1959
North Vietnam infiltrates South Vietnam via the Ho Chi Minh Trail.

1960
North Vietnam forms the National Liberation Front (NLF) in the war against the south.

1963
Ngo Dinh Diem is overthrown and assassinated.

1965
US bombs military targets in North Vietnam. First American ground combat troops land in Vietnam at Danang.

1968
The Viet Cong launch the Tet Offensive, the turning point in the Vietnam War. Peace talks begin in Paris.

1969
Ho Chi Minh dies, aged 79.

1973
Paris Peace Agreement ends hostilities. Last US troops depart.

1975
North Vietnamese troops enter Saigon. The South Vietnamese government surrenders. Saigon is renamed Ho Chi Minh City.

1976
Vietnam is officially reunified as a communist country.

1976–85
A period of severe economic hardship. Millions of refugees, or "boat people", flee from persecution by the new government.

1977
Vietnam admitted to the UN.

1978–9
Vietnam signs friendship treaty with the Soviet Union. Hostilities with Cambodia and China.

1986
Programme of socio-economic renovation called *doi moi* is launched.

1994
US lifts trade embargo.

1995
Diplomatic ties are restored with the US. Vietnam is admitted to the Association of Southeast Asian Nations (ASEAN).

1997
Asian economic crisis; investors leave Vietnam.

2000
Bill Clinton becomes the first US president to visit Vietnam since the war.

2001
The US and Vietnam enter a trade agreement. Foreign investment picks up.

2007
Vietnam joins the WTO.

2008
The economy suffers as food and fuel prices skyrocket.

2011
Inflation rises and the currency is devalued.

2014
Dispute over Paracel Islands intensifies as China introduces a drilling rig into nearby waters, leading to violent protests and several collisions between Vietnamese and Chinese ships.

2016
Ha Tinh Steel causes the death of millions of fish and other marine life on the central coast by dumping toxic waste into the sea.

2017
A record number of storms cause the death of around 400 people.

South Vietnamese troops during the Vietnam War.

Ed-brick Cham tower at My Son,
near Hoi An.

EARLY HISTORY

Dynasties quickly rose and fell as Vietnam fused into a nation.
Having initially been influenced by China in the north, Vietnam
later faced a fresh threat – from French colonialists.

Vietnam's ancient history is steeped in the mists of myth, and only by melding Chinese and Vietnamese historical annals with Vietnamese folklore and recent archaeological discoveries have historians managed to piece together the country's origins.

The story of Vietnam begins in the northern Red River Delta, nearly 5,000 years ago, where legend has it that a powerful dragon lord called Lac Long Quan and a mountain fairy named Au Co sired exactly 100 sons. The eldest of these sons was later crowned king of the Lac Viet, naming himself Hung Vuong (Brave King) and his kingdom as Van Lang.

It should be pointed out that the Vietnamese state is generally considered to have started in the north of the country: further south, power lay with the Hindu Cham in the centre and various Khmer kingdoms in and around the Mekong Delta, and these areas were only assimilated into the Vietnamese state much later in its history.

French colonialists later dismissed the story of Van Lang, claiming they were mere myths. But we now know this kingdom was well organised and powerful, encompassing most of present-day northern and central Vietnam. It is said to have prospered under the rule of 18 successive Hung kings during the 1st millennium BC until Thuc Phan, king of neighbouring Au Viet, defeated the Lac Viet in 258 BC. He then renamed himself An Duong Vuong (Peaceful Sun King) and established the new kingdom called Au Lac, establishing his capital at Phuc An. The remains of his citadel are located in the present-day village of Co Loa, to the north of Hanoi.

A matriarchal society, which is sometimes referred to as the Dong Son culture, is thought to have prevailed at this time. At its peak around

Bronze Dong Son tomb figure of a kneeling lamp bearer.

Extending from northern Vietnam into Cambodia, Laos and even Indonesia, the Dong Son culture, named after a small village in northern Vietnam, produced exquisite bronze works as early as 300 BC.

500–200 BC, Dong Son is best known for its ornately carved wooden drums and fine bronze ornaments.

CHINA'S INFLUENCE

Around 200 BC, the Au Lac kingdom fell to the northern hordes led by an ambitious general called Trieu Da from the south of China. He founded the independent kingdom of Nam Viet, which included much of present-day southern China, and established the Trieu dynasty in 208 BC. His capital was located near present-day Guangzhou (Canton).

Nam Viet gradually came under the Chinese sphere of influence as the Han dynasty unified China. By 111 BC, the plains of northern Vietnam had become a colonial province of China called Giao Chi (Jiaozhi). Administrators from China were appointed as governors to rule the country, but their efforts to impose Chinese culture on the Viet people were met with fierce resistance.

Frustrated by decades of Chinese influence and culture, the Vietnamese not only guarded their national identity but fought fiercely to preserve it. One dauntless woman called Trung Trach, a member of an indigenous elite class, sparked the leap from protest to revolt. In AD 39, together with her sister Trung Nhi, she led a swift rebellion that forced the Chinese authorities to flee. Trung Trach was made queen but her reign was short-lived. Three years later,

The big cat (China) receives tribute from servile mice (Vietnam).

⊘ RISE AND FALL OF THE CHAM CIVILISATION

The earliest records of the Cham civilisation date back to the end of the 2nd century AD. The Cham grew in strength on the basis of maritime trade and became more Indianised through commercial relations with India and Southeast Asia. By the 4th century, Hinduism had been adopted and Sanskrit was the language of communication. At the height of its power, Champa controlled the entire central coast from the Hoanh Son Pass in the north to the area around Vung Tau in the south.

The Cham civilisation is best known for its brick temples and towers, remnants of which are scattered along the south-central coast where the Cham kingdom once dominated. While the Cham ruins cannot compare with the similarly Indian-influenced Angkor in Cambodia or Pagan in Burma, their masterful masonry and exquisite sculpting are still apparent in the ruins of Po Nagar at Nha Trang and My Son near Hoi An.

The territorial ambitions of later Viet kings would eventually reduce Champa to a sliver of territory near Nha Trang by the end of the 15th century. In 1720, the last Cham king and his subjects fled to neighbouring Cambodia. Today, only about 100,000 Cham people are left in southern Vietnam. Most converted to Islam centuries ago, but there are still small communities of Hindu and Buddhist Cham people. For more on the Cham, see page 242.

the better-equipped Chinese army brought the country again under their control. The two sisters, known to Vietnamese as Hai Ba Trung (Two Trung Ladies), committed suicide. Today, they are honoured as national heroes.

KHMER AND CHAM KINGDOMS

Direct Chinese control did not extend into present-day central and southern Vietnam, which were heavily influenced by maritime trade with India and Southeast Asia. The far south was part of the Khmer Funan kingdom, and later the Chen La kingdom which led on to the foundation of Angkor. From the second century AD, much of the centre was ruled by the powerful Cham kings (see page 30).

REBELS WITH A CAUSE

After the Trung sisters' rebellion was crushed, Nam Viet was administered as a Chinese province known as Giao Chau (Jiaozhou) until the 6th century, when a scholar named Ly Bon led an armed revolt and succeeded in routing the Chinese. Ly Bon was declared emperor and he renamed the empire Van Xuan (Eternal Spring), changing his own name to Ly Nam De (the Southern Emperor) in AD 544. His kingdom was short-lived, however; the Chinese quickly regained supremacy in the area in 545. Ly Nam De fled to Laos where he died in exile. His successor, Triet Viet Vuong, an accomplished general, managed to drive the Chinese out of Van Xuan in 550, but eventually the Chinese returned and resumed occupation in 603.

The Chinese, now under the prosperous Tang dynasty, again made concerted efforts to impose their culture and civilisation on Nam Viet, which they renamed An Nam. Nonetheless, armed revolts by the Vietnamese remained a thorn in their side. Rebel leaders such as Mai Hac De in 722 and Phung Hung in 791 successfully rallied locals and managed to overthrow the Chinese rulers. Their brief reigns ended when China inevitably sent reinforcements. However, with each revolt a new folk hero was born, inspiring more shrines and more legends, which only served to fuel the desire to remove the Chinese.

THE EARLY DYNASTIES

Disorder accompanied the decline of the Tang dynasty in China, giving the Vietnamese the chance to stake their claim for independence.

In a protracted war a general called Ngo Quyen defeated the Chinese reinforcements and founded the first Vietnamese dynasty in 939. He renamed the country Dai Viet and moved the capital back to Co Loa. After his death in 967, the kingdom fell into chaos and remained fragmented for more than 20 years, while the threat from China's Song dynasty loomed large to the north.

The most powerful of the feudal lords, Dinh Bo Linh, eventually reunified the fragmented country under the name of Dai Co Viet and took the imperial title of Dinh Tien Hoang De (The First

Temple of Literature, Hanoi.

August Emperor Dinh). He wisely negotiated a non-aggression treaty in exchange for tributes payable to the Chinese every three years.

Dinh Tien Hoang established his royal court in the new capital of Hoa Lu in Ninh Binh province, 100km (62 miles) south of Hanoi. He instated a rigorous justice system and introduced the death penalty to anyone who threatened his rule. Security and order were progressively re-established, inaugurating a new era of peace. However, the emperor was assassinated in 979 by a palace guard. The heir to the throne was only six years old, so the court's commander, Le Hoan, seized power and proclaimed himself Emperor Le Dai Hanh. He succeeded in warding off the Chinese but also continued paying them tribute.

With relative peace assured on the northern border, Le Dai Hanh sought to pacify the south. In 982, a military expedition was launched

> *In the 16th century, Ho Chi Minh City was a Khmer village called Prei Kor. When the Viet settled this area in later years, ethnic Khmers were resettled in the Mekong Delta, where today they are a minority race.*

Long (Ascending Dragon) after seeing the apparition of an ascending dragon on the proposed site.

During the Ly dynasty, Buddhism flourished as the national religion. Buddhist masters assisted the Ly kings as advisers. Several Ly kings also led Buddhist sects. Confucian studies were also encouraged under the Ly dynasty. In 1070, the Temple of Literature dedicated to Confucius was constructed in Thang Long.

The Ly dynasty consolidated the monarchy along Confucianist principles. It established a centralised government, a tax system, a judi-

Old print of traditional village in the Hue area.

against the Champa kingdom, which would gradually be absorbed over the following centuries. The emperor also sought to consolidate the Viet nation. He developed a road network in order to administer the country better. However, a succession of local revolts assured 24 years of difficult rule until Le Dai Hanh died.

LY DYNASTY

The Ly dynasty (1009–1225), which reigned over the country for more than two centuries, was the first of the more enduring national dynasties. Ly Cong Uan was a disciple of a monk, Van Hanh, who helped him rise to power. After assuming the name Ly Thai To, the new sovereign moved the capital to present-day Hanoi, naming it Thang

ciary and a professional army. Important public works, including the building of dykes and canals in the Red River Delta region, were undertaken to develop agriculture.

TRAN AND HO DYNASTIES

An ambitious commoner, Tran Canh, married into the Ly dynasty royalty and shrewdly manoeuvred his way to power to found the Tran dynasty (1225–1400). During this period the Viet armies repelled three invasions – in 1257, 1284 and 1288 – by the Mongols under Kublai Khan, who had occupied China and founded the Yuan dynasty. The mastermind behind the latter two victories was Tran Quoc Toan (better known as Tran Hung Dao), one of Vietnam's greatest military heroes. The key to his success was to avoid the Mongols' strength in open field battles and city sieges (the Tran court abandoned the capital and the cities), then counter them at their weak points in swampy areas and on rivers. The Mongols retreated only to be routed at the Bach Dang River in 1288.

The country's territorial ambitions to the south also continued. The king's sister married the king of Champa in 1307, thus extending the territory southwards with the peaceful annexation of the Hue region through a diplomatic marriage.

Towards the end of the 14th century, the Tran dynasty went into swift decline. A political opportunist called Le Quy Ly shrewdly manoeuvred his way to power and founded a dynasty under his ancestral name of Ho. While successful for initiating many economic, financial and educational reforms, his reign prompted another attack from China. Aware that the new king had usurped the throne, the Chinese Ming dynasty emperor sent 5,000 soldiers under the pretext of helping the faithful followers of the deposed Tran dynasty. The Ming intervention led to the fall of the Ho dynasty in 1407. During the short period of Chinese occupation that followed, the Vietnamese suffered inhumane exploitation. The Chinese strove to destroy the Vietnamese national identity – Vietnamese literature, artistic and historical works were burnt or taken to China, and in schools, books were replaced with Chinese classics. The Chinese style of dress and hair was imposed on Vietnamese women, local religious rites and festivals were replaced or banished by the Chinese and private fortunes were confiscated.

LE DYNASTY

It took a man called Le Loi, renowned for his courage and generosity, to organise a resistance movement from his village and wage a guerrilla war against the Chinese. Through surprise attacks, Le Loi weakened the enemy and at the same time avoided combat with the superior Chinese forces. His strict military discipline ensured that no pillaging was carried out by his troops in the regions under his control, making him a popular military hero.

Le Loi founded the Le dynasty in 1428 and became king under the name of Le Thai To. He renamed the country Dai Viet and immediately began the task of its reconstruction after the devastation caused by the war. He reduced his army from 250,000 to 10,000 men and adopted a rotation system that enabled soldiers to return to the countryside to work and help boost food production. The legal system was reorganised and the penal system revised. A new college was founded to educate future administrators, with admission based entirely on merit and not on social or family status.

Le Thai To died in 1443, leaving the throne to his son, Le Thai Tong, whose sudden death not long after was followed by a decade of confusion

Vietnamese court officials.

and plots within the royal court. This troubled period ceased when Le Thanh Tong began his 36-year reign in 1460 and the country prospered as never before. He revised the fiscal system, encouraged agriculture and placed great emphasis on customs and moral principles. He penned the first volume of Vietnamese history.

Le Thanh Tong's reorganised army also won an easy victory over the southern Champa army in 1471. His farmer-soldiers excelled not only on the battlefields but also in the fields where they set up militarised agricultural communities wherever they went. In this way the national territory gradually expanded southwards, until finally the Champa kingdom was completely absorbed and assimilated.

SECESSION WARS

The increasing decadence of the Le dynasty in the late 16th century and the corrupt and idle kings who succeeded Le Thanh Tong led to the country's division into two rival principalities. Mac Dang Dung, a shrewd and scheming adviser at the court, seized control of the north (including Hanoi) and founded the short-lived Mac dynasty in 1527. Meanwhile, descendants of the Le dynasty rallied around Nguyen Kim, a former official in the Le court, and his son-in-law Trinh Kiem founded the southern court near Thanh

Depiction of French troops entering Hung Hoa in 1884.

Hoa, 120km (75 miles) south of Hanoi, in 1543. A protracted civil war continued indecisively until the death of the Mac dynasty's last king, Mac Mau Hop, in 1592.

In an effort to restore law and order to the territory controlled by the Mac dynasty, Trinh Kiem left the southern court under the temporary control of Nguyen Kim's nephew, Nguyen Hoang, and set out for the north. After pacifying the region, Trinh Kiem returned to find Nguyen Hoang well entrenched in the southern court as lord and master of all.

This led to a drawn-out standoff. Between 1627 and 1672, the Trinh Lords of the north and the Nguyen Lords of the south battled indecisively for over 40 years. Eventually, the Trinh

Lords consented to the partition of the country just north of Phu Xuan (Hue).

Relative peace between both sides lasted for a century, during which time the Nguyen Lords made further inroads into the Mekong Delta. In 1771 revolution broke out in Quy Nhon province, south of Phu Xuan. Provoked by corruption within the imperial court and the north–south feud, a man named Nguyen Hue (no relation to the Nguyen Lords), along with his two brothers, led a peasant uprising known as the Tay Son Rebellion, which overthrew the Nguyen Lords. The Tay Son brothers took control of the south of Vietnam before defeating the Trinh Lords in the north and, most audaciously, the Chinese forces occupying Thanh Long. A peasant uprising had, incredibly, unified Vietnam.

NGUYEN DYNASTY

Nguyen Hue pronounced himself Emperor Quang Trung in 1788 and devoted his energies to rebuilding the country. Sadly, his promising reign was cut short by his premature death in 1792.

In the meantime, one of the surviving Nguyen Lords, Nguyen Anh, had not given up hope of securing power for himself. He befriended a French Catholic, Pigneau de Behaine, the Bishop of Adran. De Behaine saw an opportunity to expand the Catholic Church's influence and negotiate a promise of military aid for Nguyen Anh from the French government in exchange for territorial and commercial rights in Vietnam. However, the French were busy with other internal disputes and the promised aid never materialised. Undaunted, the bishop organised funds and recruited troops himself. Training in Western military techniques proved invaluable to Nguyen Anh and his army, and it facilitated victory in 1801 when he defeated the last of the Tay Sons. In 1802, he proclaimed himself Emperor Gia Long, the founder of the Nguyen dynasty.

Nguyen Anh may have owed his accession to the French, but he was suspicious of France's designs. Therefore, he relied more on the assistance of Confucian mandarins than the Catholic missionaries in the consolidation of his empire. The reunified and renamed Viet Nam extended from the Chinese frontier to the Ca Mau Peninsula at the country's southernmost tip. Serious efforts were made to codify the law and develop the national administration along Confucian principles. Hue became the country's new administrative capital, and elaborate palaces, mausoleums, temples and pagodas were built.

The Nguyen kings extended Vietnam's border into Laos and Cambodia, incorporating parts of these two kingdoms as vassal states. They closed the country off to Western penetration from the seas, fearing that the expansion of trade links would undermine the inherent structure of the Nguyen monarchy.

THE FRENCH CONNECTION

Prince Canh, Nguyen Anh's eldest son, accompanied de Behaine to France during his negotiations with the French government. The prince was later educated at a missionary school in Malacca and converted to Catholicism. This made Canh the first Viet prince to be given a Western education. Military leaders within Nguyen Anh's army realised the superiority of modern Western military technology and so wanted to utilise Prince Canh's knowledge to rebuild the country after the war. Canh was seen as the one who could modernise Vietnam.

But after Gia Long died in 1820, court ministers from the Chinese faction supported Canh's younger brother, Mien Tong, to take the throne. Prince Canh, supported by the French faction, reportedly died of measles at the age of 21, though missionaries close to the court claimed he had been poisoned. Once Mien Tong was crowned as Emperor Minh Mang, the French-Chinese divide officially ended. Most of Canh's followers were demoted or executed.

In the meantime, Catholic missions began to accelerate their proselytising efforts, provoking Emperor Minh Mang into taking a vigorous anti-Catholic stance, "lest they spread darkness in the kingdom".

This gave the French the perfect excuse to intervene in Vietnam. The old cycle of invasion and occupation began anew, but this time from afar. The landing of a French party in Danang in 1858 heralded the beginning of colonial occupation that would last almost a century. The French government wanted a strategic and religious sphere of influence in Indochina (present-day Vietnam, Laos and Cambodia), but their demands for a French consulate and commercial attaché in Danang

were rejected by the Vietnamese imperial court in Hue. The French responded to the affront by seizing Danang.

Alexandre de Rhodes, a French Jesuit priest, arrived in Vietnam in 1619 and began work on the first Portuguese-Latin-Vietnamese dictionary. This was later used to develop the Romanised Vietnamese alphabet called quoc ngu.

The young Prince Canh received a Western education.

⊘ FROM NAM VIET TO VIETNAM

In the early 19th century, the Nguyen Emperor Gia Long sent his ambassador to China to seek approval for the reunification of the old land of An Nam and the new land of Viet Thuong, and to change the country's name to Nam Viet. But the Chinese emperor was advised that the name Nam Viet would bring to mind the ancient kingdom of Nam Viet Dong, which had included two Chinese provinces, and might also conceal territorial ambitions on the part of Gia Long. Therefore, the two words *Viet* (people) and *Nam* (south) were simply reversed to give the country the name it bears to this day.

The Ho Chi Minh Mausoleum in Hanoi.

THE ROAD TO WAR

A century of French colonialism culminated in a bloody war of independence, swiftly followed by the catastrophic Vietnam War. The country emerged from these conflicts battered but unified.

In 1861 the French took Saigon and within six years the entire southern part of the country had been annexed as a French colony and rechristened Cochinchina. In the 1880s, central and northern Vietnam became French protectorates under the nominal rule of the Nguyen dynasty. Central Vietnam was renamed Annam, while the north became Tonkin.

The Vietnamese were no happier under French domination than they had been under the Chinese. Resistance movements took shape in occupied areas, some led by former court officers, others by peasants. Even the teenage Nguyen emperor Ham Nghi started an anti-French movement, only to be captured and exiled to Algeria.

One influential resistance movement, composed mainly of aristocrats, intellectuals and young people, was led by the radical Confucian scholars Phan Boi Chau and Phan Chau Trinh, who embraced the idea of democracy. This movement had been inspired by the Japanese victory over Russia in 1904–5, which convinced them that Western powers were not invincible.

Phan Boi Chau established the Eastward Movement (Dong Du) in 1907 and secretly sent students to learn from the Japanese. The French authorities discovered the scheme and negotiated with Japan to extradite the Vietnamese students. However, Japanese officials helped some escape to China, where they witnessed the 1911 revolution led by Sun Yat-sen. This convinced them that Vietnam was ready for a similar kind of coup.

But the revolutionaries were not united. A rift widened between the Westernised reformer Phan Chu Trinh and the nationalist Phan Boi Chau. The latter created the Vietnam Quang

The legendary Ho Chi Minh in the 1950s.

Phu Hoi Party and planned armed resistance against the French, while Phan Chu Trinh maintained that Vietnam could regain independence through the democratic process. In 1915, he went to Paris to rally Vietnamese exiles and radical French politicians into supporting the struggle against colonial rule.

A YOUNG LEADER IN THE MAKING

The Russian Revolution of 1917 had a tremendous impact on shaping Vietnamese history, primarily because of its influence on a young revolutionary called Nguyen Tat Thanh, later known as Ho Chi Minh.

Under the alias Nguyen Ai Quoc, Ho submitted an anti-colonial petition at the Versailles

Conference in 1919. He became involved with French intellectuals who formed the French Communist Party in 1920, and then went to Moscow to be trained as an agent of Communist International (Comintern).

In 1924, Ho was sent to China where he contacted young Vietnamese revolutionaries and founded the Association of Vietnamese Youth. Emperor Khai Dinh died in 1925, and his son Bao Dai ascended the throne in 1926, aged just 12. Bao Dai (see page 40) was sent to France for his education and would not return to Vietnam until 1932.

a military revolt while communist groups staged several peasant uprisings. The French took severe measures against the fledgling movements, but the apparent calm that reigned after the reprisals was shattered with the first battles of World War II.

COMMUNISM CONSOLIDATES

For Vietnam, the onset of World War II in 1939 was a landmark event as significant as the French occupation of Danang in 1858. The pro-Nazi Vichy government of France accepted the

A Hanoi street view from the early 20th century.

In 1945 members of the US Office of Strategic Services, the predecessor of the CIA, parachuted into Vietnam to train members of the Viet Minh, including Ho Chi Minh and General Vo Nguyen Giap.

The Vietnamese waited to see if the French would adopt more liberal politics, but it soon became clear they would make no real concessions. In 1930, Ho rallied several communist groups and founded the Indochinese Communist Party. In the same year, under the leadership of the revolutionary Nguyen Thai Hoc, the Quoc Dan Dang (Vietnam Nationalist Party) launched

Japanese military occupation of Indochina, but on condition that it could continue administering Vietnam. In 1941, the Central Committee of the Indochinese Communist Party had met in China and announced the formation of the Revolutionary League for the Independence of Vietnam, later known as the Viet Minh.

At the end of World War II in 1945, Vietnam faced a political void as Japan overthrew the French, imprisoned their civil servants and rendered Vietnam "independent" under Japanese "protection", with Bao Dai as head of state. By the middle of August, following the Japanese defeat, chaos and uncertainty reigned. Using the clandestine Indochinese Communist Party and the Viet Minh as intermediaries, Ho tried to become the dominant political force by occupying as much territory as possible.

THE AUGUST REVOLUTION

On 16 August 1945, the Viet Minh announced the formation of a National Committee of Liberation for Vietnam. Three days later, Ho's guerrilla forces took Hanoi. Hue's turn came four days later when Bao Dai's government was besieged and "asked" to hand over the royal seal. After Bao Dai's abdication, Ho announced the forma-

relations between the French and the Viet Minh deteriorated. Hostilities reached a peak with the French bombing of Haiphong port, east of Hanoi. In December 1946, Ho ordered an offensive against the French in Hanoi and at the French garrisons in northern and central Vietnam. A war for independence had begun that would rage for 30 years.

WAR OF RESISTANCE

Thousands of Vietnamese took up arms against the French, yet few knew the identity

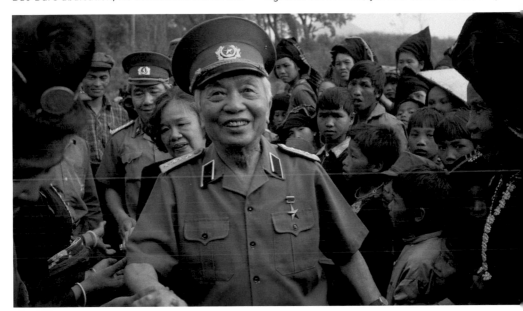

General Vo Nguyen Giap on the 40th anniversary of the French defeat.

tion of a provisional government in Hanoi, and proclaimed himself president of the new Democratic Republic of Vietnam.

However, the situation was precarious. The British arrived in Saigon looking to disarm the Japanese and restore order, while the French tried to reclaim their former colony. From the north, the Chinese entered Vietnam looking to disarm the Japanese.

In the general elections, organised in early 1946, the Viet Minh won a majority in the first National Assembly. The country's first national constitution was approved, and the French were allowed to stay for five years in return for recognising the Democratic Republic of Vietnam as a free state within the French Union. However,

and allegiance of their new leader and his party. On Ho's orders, his principal collaborator, General Vo Nguyen Giap, launched a general offensive against the colonial forces, but in the face of superior firepower the Vietnamese troops retreated to the countryside. They adopted Mao Zedong's guerrilla strategy of a "people's war and people's army" by attacking and sabotaging isolated French units, rather than becoming embroiled in large-scale battles, a tactic reminiscent of that used by Le Loi against the Chinese in the 15th century.

After Ho's guerrillas had wiped out several French posts on the Chinese border, China and Vietnam established direct contact for the first time. China, the old aggressor, was now an

VIETNAM'S LAST EMPEROR

A pawn in the power struggle between the French and Ho Chi Minh, Bao Dai was an enigmatic figure who lived most of his life in exile.

Emperor Bao Dai.

The last ruling monarch of Vietnam, Prince Nguyen Vinh Thuy, was born in 1913 and spent his youth in France where he was educated according to Western principles. On becoming emperor in 1926, when he took the name Bao Dai (Keeper of Greatness), he was just 12 years old. Too young to take up his royal duties, the young monarch returned to France to continue his studies. A council of regency, made up of French loyalists, ruled Vietnam in his absence. When he turned 20, Bao married a Vietnamese Catholic, Marie-Thérèse Nguyen Hu Thi Lan, better known as Empress Nam Phuong. Also educated in France, she combined – in Bao's words – "the graces of the West and the charms of the East". But this didn't stop him, however, from also having four other wives.

When Bao Dai returned home to the imperial city of Hue in 1932, he tried to reform the judicial and educational systems, but soon became better known as the "Playboy Emperor" thanks to his lavish lifestyle. He is said to have devoted weeks at a time to hunting tigers in the Vietnamese rainforests. But when faced with political peril he was less brave. After the Japanese swept across Southeast Asia and occupied Vietnam during World War II, he was allowed to retain his throne, as the Japanese hoped his presence would demonstrate some continuity. After the Japanese departed in 1945, the Viet Minh quickly "persuaded" Bao Dai to abdicate. He famously explained his decision by saying that he preferred "to be a citizen of an independent country rather than Emperor of an enslaved one".

Despite his face-saving offer to be Ho Chi Minh's supreme adviser, the communists had no intention of sharing power with the former emperor. With war on the horizon, Bao Dai left for Hong Kong and China, but in 1949 he was coaxed back to Vietnam by the French, who needed a recognised figurehead as head of state. As before, Bao Dai left the major decisions to his French-backed advisers, preferring to spend time with his mistress at his hunting lodge in the central highlands.

When the 1954 peace accord between the French and the communists resulted in the division of Vietnam into North and South, Bao Dai and his advisers tried to assume true power in South Vietnam. In response, the American-backed premier, Ngo Dinh Diem, organised a referendum on the issue of monarchy versus republicanism. The corrupt Ngo won 98.2 percent of the votes in a remarkable election which saw 605,000 votes cast in the Saigon-Cholon area, where only 450,000 voters were registered.

Even though the fraudulent election was discredited and Ngo was later assassinated, the monarch returned to France where he remained until his death. In a rare public statement, made in 1972, he appealed to the Vietnamese people for national reconciliation. That same year, his mother, who remained in Vietnam, reportedly sold the family porcelain to help her only son survive in exile. He spent the final years of his life in a modest Paris apartment before his death in 1997.

ally, supplying the young republic with military equipment and substantial provisions.

On his side, Ho attempted to shore up the nationalist support. In 1951, he merged the Viet Minh with the Lien Viet, or Patriotic Front, into the National Union of Vietnam. He also announced the formation of the Workers' Party (Lao Dong), a disguise for the Communist Party that had officially disbanded but in reality was still active. The nationalists and non-communists were forced to choose between the new regime and the French colonialists.

THE GENEVA AGREEMENT

In May 1954, the French base at Dien Bien Phu suffered a humiliating and historic defeat after a heavy artillery attack from General Vo Nguyen Giap's forces, which famously used bicycles to carry supplies. The French forces in northern Vietnam evacuated to below the 16th parallel at Danang. The war officially ended on 20 July, after long negotiations in Geneva.

In finally gaining national independence, however, Vietnam lost its unity. The Geneva Agreement signed in August divided the country at the

The battle of Dien Bien Phu.

⊘ THE BATTLE OF DIEN BIEN PHU

The battle of Dien Bien Phu in 1954, masterminded by General Vo Nguyen Giap, marked a turning point in Vietnamese history. The French strategy was to force the Viet Minh into a large-scale battle which France would, presumably, win. In December 1953, a defensive complex was built at Dien Bien Phu, which would block the route of the Viet Minh forces trying to return to camps in neighbouring Laos.

General Vo's first task was to dig a trench that encircled the French fortification. From the outer trench, more tunnels were dug inwards towards the centre. In this way the Viet Minh could close in on the French troops while escaping fire. Meanwhile, reinforcements arrived. Soon General

Vo had 70,000 soldiers surrounding Dien Bien Phu, five times the number of French troops. Employing recently obtained anti-aircraft guns and howitzers from China, he severely restricted the ability of the French to supply their forces in Dien Bien Phu.

On 13 March 1954, General Vo launched his offensive and for 56 days the Viet Minh pushed the French forces back until they only occupied a small area of Dien Bien Phu. The French surrendered on 7 May, after 13,000 of their men and another 25,000 of the Viet Minh had died. Shortly after, the war ended with the 1954 Geneva Accord, under which France agreed to withdraw from its former Indochinese colonies in Asia.

17th parallel, pending general elections scheduled for 1956. The north of the country became the Democratic Republic of Vietnam – communist North Vietnam – under the leadership of Ho Chi Minh; and the south became the Republic of South Vietnam.

By this time, the last French troops had left Vietnam and Indochina. Bao Dai, who had been persuaded to return from exile by the French after his abdication, appealed on behalf of the royalists and asked Ngo Dinh Diem, a former minister at Bao Dai's court, to

A Viet Cong base camp being burnt by the Marines.

become prime minister of what would become South Vietnam. Ngo was a curious choice, a Catholic in a predominantly Buddhist country who had been away from Vietnam for two decades. In a subsequent fraudulent referendum, Bao Dai was deposed by Ngo Dinh Diem, marking the beginning of the Republic of South Vietnam. But rather than creating stability, it set the stage for Vietnam's next, and bloodiest, conflict.

THE NORTH–SOUTH DIVIDE

The elections stipulated by the Geneva Agreement to take place in 1956 never occurred. From 1954 to 1974, the two Vietnams had no diplomatic, cultural or commercial relations

with each other. Immediately after the Geneva Agreement, a virtual state of war existed between the two divided parts of the country. North Vietnam's intensified armed and revolutionary activities made the prospect of reunification increasingly unlikely.

Meanwhile, the US saw the conflict in Vietnam as part of a larger global fight against communism. It reinforced Ngo's troops, in effect turning South Vietnam into an American military protectorate. In December 1960, North Vietnam formed the National Liberation

> *By the time the dust settled on the Vietnam War, some 2 million civilian Vietnamese, along with 1 million soldiers from North Vietnam, 250,000 soldiers from South Vietnam and 57,605 Americans had perished.*

Front (NLF), which began revolutionary activities against Ngo's increasingly repressive and unstable regime. Its communist ally in South Vietnam, dubbed the Viet Cong, which fought against Ngo's government and the US, grew stronger in the early 1960s. To bolster the Viet Cong, North Vietnam sent additional reinforcements in the form of North Vietnamese Army (NVA) troops.

Facing mounting pressures from his own people, Ngo, himself a devout Roman Catholic, ordered oppressive measures against the Buddhist establishment, provoking a wave of suicides by Buddhist monks, who set fire to themselves. In June 1963, Thich Quang Duc, a 66-year-old monk, immolated himself on a street corner in Saigon.

This signalled the end for Ngo's regime. He and his brother, Ngo Dinh Nhu, head of the security forces, were murdered five months later by Ngo's own officers following a US-backed coup.

AMERICAN INVOLVEMENT

The beginning of 1965 marked the escalation of direct American involvement in Vietnam, when US President Lyndon Johnson sent in large numbers of troops. By the end of 1967, there were more than 500,000 American and 100,000

Allied troops (mostly from Korea, Australia and New Zealand) in Vietnam.

What many consider the war's turning point came in 1968, when the Viet Cong launched surprise attacks on Saigon and other cities throughout the south during the Lunar New Year, or Tet. The "Tet Offensive" included a raid on the American embassy in Saigon that stunned and embarrassed the US. Domestic opposition in the US increasingly took on political and social legitimacy as the American public got wind of atrocities like the My

crumbled, the US Congress refused to offer additional military aid, in effect ending South Vietnam's ability to continue the war.

The north launched its final offensive, and on 30 April 1975 the Northern Vietnamese Army (NVA) entered Saigon as the very last American troops and diplomats fled by helicopter from the American embassy. The Communist Party's long struggle for power had finally ended in victory. Vietnam was now independent of foreign troops and control, and it could set its sights on unification.

Troops enter Saigon, 1975.

Lai massacre. Eventually, Johnson announced he would not run for re-election. His successor, Richard Nixon, had promised a secret plan to end the war during the election campaign, but this turned out to be nothing more than turning the bulk of fighting over to the South Vietnamese.

In 1969, Ho Chi Minh died without seeing his work completed, and peace negotiations dragged on in Paris between 1968 and 1973. Eventually Americans troops left in 1973, as part of the Paris Peace Agreement, although the US continued funding the Southern Vietnamese military efforts. In 1975, when the communist forces from North Vietnam steadily moved south and the Saigon regime finally

⊘ THE MY LAI MASSACRE

The My Lai massacre of 16 March 1968 was a turning point in the public perception of the Vietnam War. In just three hours more than 500 Vietnamese civilians were killed in cold blood by US troops. The soldiers had been on a "search and destroy" mission to root out communist fighters in what was fertile Viet Cong territory. However, there had been no firefight with the enemy. In fact not a single shot was fired at the American soldiers. When the story of My Lai was exposed, it tarnished the name of the US army, as well as adding momentum to the anti-war movement that was spreading across the US at the time.

MODERN HISTORY

Vietnam's journey towards unity and development has been long, and often painful, but since the 1990s the nation has made rapid economic progress. Freedom of speech may take a little longer.

Following the unification of Vietnam in 1975, it looked as though years of oppression and suffering were at an end. Yet the dreams for national rehabilitation never fully materialised. Several strategic errors, later admitted by Hanoi's communist leaders, destroyed any hopes that this may have been the dawning of a progressive new era.

In July 1976, Vietnam was officially reunified into one country, and a radical programme of socialist construction was put forward by the Communist Party government. It called for the rapid socialisation of the southern economy, with the forced collectivisation of agriculture, small industry and commerce. The South's intellectual and government leaders were also sent to so-called "re-education camps". This policy quickly resulted in an unprecedented economic disaster, prompting more than a million refugees (or "boat people"), many of whom were southerners facing political persecution by the new government, to flee the country.

Refugees in 1975.

WAR WITH CAMBODIA AND CHINA

Just a few years after reunification, Vietnam found itself fighting again – this time with neighbouring Cambodia's Khmer Rouge and its leader Pol Pot. This led to a clash with China in the north in 1979 in a brief but bloody battle (to this day, both sides of the conflict claim victory). The invasion of Cambodia (then known as Kampuchea) and the subsequent entanglement with China absorbed most of Vietnam's post-war energies and delayed its long-overdue recovery.

For the next decade, the presence of Vietnamese troops in Cambodia remained a central issue in the international arena. China, the US and the members of ASEAN (Association of Southeast Asian Nations) managed to garner international

support to isolate Vietnam, which in turn had lost most of its hard-earned international sympathy. At the Fifth Party Congress in 1982, the old guard, under the guidance of party secretary-general Le Duan, stubbornly maintained Vietnam's course, hoping that, against all odds, it could consolidate its political and military edge in Cambodia, and at the same time stabilise Vietnam's own economic and social situation. It was a policy that would drive the country to the brink of disaster.

ECONOMIC SHIFTS AND DOI MOI

The 1980s are remembered bitterly by most Vietnamese as a time of wretched poverty. People were starving, there wasn't enough rice to go around and meat was rationed. People had to stand in line for monthly and weekly allotments of food. It was only in 1986, following the Soviet example of *glasnost* and *perestroika*, that the party decided to reinvent the country with an ambitious programme of socio-economic renovation called *doi moi*.

Under the new leadership of Nguyen Van Linh, the motto of the party was "to change or to die". A new contract system was implemented in 1988 to encourage Vietnamese farmers to cultivate their land, and, as a result, rice production witnessed an immediate upsurge in 1989. Progress was also recorded in the sector of manufactured goods and commodities exports.

Until the end of 1988, socialist Vietnam followed the path of Soviet *perestroika*, but the Vietnamese leaders were soon aghast to see the direction of Mikhail Gorbachev's "new thinking" and its social and political consequences. Hastily, while reaffirming the Communist Party's commitment to reform, Nguyen Van Linh repeatedly rejected any idea of political pluralism in Vietnam.

Vietnamese forces withdrew from Cambodia in 1989. With the fall of the Soviet Union in 1991, a valued ally, Vietnam changed tack and adopted a new course in foreign affairs: it started to court China. By the early 1990s, European and Asian companies started flooding into Vietnam seeking investment opportunities in what many saw as the last economic frontier. Hanoi and Ho Chi Minh City were soon buzzing with developments. Hotels were renovated and new ones built, international airline services increased, and telecoms and other infrastructures upgraded. In 1993, the American administration led by Bill Clinton allowed the release of International Monetary Fund loans to Hanoi. Foreign investment in Vietnam leapt. In early 1994, the US lifted its trade embargo, and in the following year Clinton restored diplomatic ties between Vietnam and the US, and an embassy opened in Hanoi. In 1995, Vietnam became a full member of ASEAN, ending an era of costly international ostracism.

A GROWING ECONOMY

The Asian financial crisis in the late 1990s slowed the pace of economic growth that marked the earlier part of the decade. However, from 2000 onwards, the economy picked up, primarily as the result of ongoing economic and trade liberalisation. In 2001, a bilateral trade pact was signed with the US, and investors returned in large numbers.

The subsequent period of rapid economic growth transformed the country from an economic backwater into one of the world's hottest economies. US president George W. Bush arrived in 2006 to strengthen economic ties at an Asia-Pacific summit hosted in Hanoi. In 2007, the country joined the World Trade Organization, further cementing its position as a dynamic player in the global economy. Vietnam had become a "poster child" of the benefits of market-oriented reforms. In Ho Chi Minh City and Hanoi, where real-estate prices are among the highest in Asia, a frenzy of construction

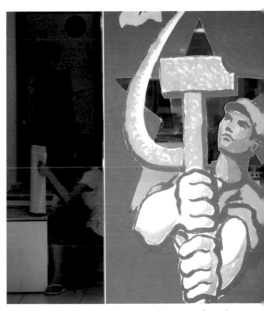

Sign of the times in Hanoi: propaganda posters for sale as souvenirs.

has brought a rash of luxury apartments, shopping malls and five-star hotels.

RECENT DEVELOPMENTS

In 2008, against the backdrop of an impending global recession, Vietnam's economy started to lose its fizz. Compounded by a looming trade deficit, a widening urban–rural income gap and a major rise in food and oil prices that caused inflation levels to hit 25 percent, workers at many of Vietnam's factories went on strike, demanding higher salaries in order to survive. This led to panic in the local stock market and rumours of a currency depreciation. In 2009 exports plunged by 10 percent, prompting the government to respond with lending schemes and stimulus spending. Help came in part from foreign donors who promised US$8 billion in investments. The result was that growth turned the corner in 2010 and returned to healthy levels. The same year Vietnam became the official negotiating partner in the Trans-Pacific Partnership (TPP), a regional regulatory and investment treaty still being negotiated by twelve countries of the Pacific rim.

However inflation rates began creeping up in 2011, the country's credit rating was downgraded and state-run companies began to face difficulties.

In a five-year plan ending in 2015, the government predicted gross domestic product to grow annually by around 7 percent, but the forecast proved too optimistic as GDP growth slowed to 5 percent in 2013 – the worst result since 1999. However, it rose to 5.98 percent in 2014 as the economy started to show signs of recovery.

CHALLENGES FOR THE FUTURE

Accompanying the doubts about the economy's staying power, an array of other issues hinders Vietnam's progress. Corruption has always been

Soldiers at Hanoi's Museum of the Vietnamese Revolution.

⊘ THE "BOAT PEOPLE"

In 1979 alone, more than 270,000 refugees left Vietnam, the vast majority taking to the seas as other routes were impractical. The exodus became a global issue as images of crowded fishing boats packed with Vietnamese became commonplace. Thousands died at sea and countless others were robbed by pirates, while those that did find refuge were often poorly treated. Camps were set up in Hong Kong, Malaysia, the Philippines, Indonesia and Thailand. When ethnic Chinese started to be persecuted in Vietnam in 1979, Hong Kong gave them refuge. The US, meanwhile, accepted more than 800,000 Vietnamese and set up a resettlement programme, while the Catholic Church, with its long-standing connections to Vietnam,

also played a major role. Others were granted asylum in Great Britain and elsewhere in Europe. Hong Kong later began to view some Vietnamese as economic migrants and, controversially, started forcible repatriation. The final camp closed in June 2000 and its residents were offered residency in Hong Kong.

By the late 1980s there were fewer and fewer refugees, while financial rewards to return to Vietnam and a growing economy through the 1990s meant many people did come back. In 2008 a final group of 200 refugees who had been living in the Philippines were accepted into the US, Norway and Canada, bringing to an end the Boat People's long journey.

rampant in business – foreigners and Vietnamese alike complain that they are nickel-and-dimed to death, with bureaucrats at all levels demanding "tokens" in order to get paperwork completed, licences approved and offices opened. Following a number of high-profile trials, there are signs that the government is trying to confront this issue. In 2014 it launched the third stage of the Vietnam Anti–Corruption Initiative Program 2014 (VACI). However, in the last available Transparency International Corruption Perceptions Index, Vietnam occupied the 119th position out of 175 countries – far behind the least corrupt countries in the world.

Almost as bad as the corruption is the glacial speed of legislative and bureaucratic processes. Although the press enjoys much more freedom of speech these days, and the internet provides the public with access to the world at large, domestic coverage of the government and its leaders is strictly censored. "Dissident voices" are swiftly silenced, while overseas anti-government websites are firewalled. All this is proof that the government remains nervous at the thought of losing its firm grip on society.

Despite the impressive economic turnaround of the past 25 years, Vietnam remains an agricultural country, with around 50 percent of its people still engaged in this sector. Income levels nationwide have been steadily rising for the past few years but are still relatively low – the average per capita income in 2016 was just US$2,185.7 a year – and large swathes of rural areas are mired in poverty. Unemployment during non-harvest periods routinely hits 25 to 35 percent. The presence of a new urban class of unskilled workers who have left the countryside for work in the cities, and the increasing visibility of Vietnam's nouveaux riches, is already causing some social friction.

> *When a local paper, Tuoi Tre (Youth), conducted a survey asking young people to name their idols, Microsoft's Bill Gates nearly outpolled Ho Chi Minh, much to older generations' dismay.*

Ho Chi Minh City is experiencing an economic boom.

⊘ ISLAND DISPUTE

Long-standing tension between China and Vietnam has been heating up in recent years over a disputed group of islands. The Paracel and Spratly island chains, rich in oil and natural gas, are claimed by several countries: China claims that the islands have been under its sovereignty for 2,000 years, Vietnam says it has ruled them for 400 years, while the Philippines feels it has a legitimate claim because the islands lie closer to its territory than any other country's. Taiwan, Indonesia, Malaysia and Brunei have also staked claims.

Violent clashes flare up from time to time, with China allegedly scuppering a Vietnamese expedition, while Vietnam has angered Beijing with live-firing exercises.

Following alleged damage to a Vietnamese vessel's cables by the Chinese, hundreds of residents in Hanoi and Ho Chi Minh City held peaceful protests in June 2011. Tensions between the countries rose again in 2014, when China introduced an oil rig – since removed – into the waters off Paracel Islands, causing widespread protests in Vietnam.

The islands are minuscule: if grouped together, Spratly's 750 reefs and seamounts would comprise a mere 5 sq km (2 sq miles), but they are spread out over 425,000 sq km (160,000 sq miles). France held the islands until World War II, when Japan used them as a submarine base. Today most of the countries that stake a claim have soldiers or some form of base on several of the islets.

Enjoying a mineral mud bath at Nha Trang.

PEOPLE

Vietnam is trying to balance rapid economic and population growth rates with a fiercely traditional culture – all the while under the watchful eye of a communist government.

Around 5,000 years ago in the foothills and valleys of the Red River Delta, a distinctive culture emerged that can be traced to the people who now call themselves Vietnamese. This is where the kingdom of Van Lang came into being, considered the cradle of Vietnamese culture. Its line of kings, known as the Hung, were the forefathers of the Vietnamese people.

Studies on the origins of the Vietnamese show that the people who settled in the Indochinese Peninsula and its bordering regions most likely came from southern and eastern China, the high plateaux of Central Asia, islands in the South Pacific and also other parts of the world. Vietnam can thus be considered the proverbial melting pot into which the major Asiatic and Oceanic migrations converged.

THE MAIN ETHNIC GROUPS

Almost 87 percent of Vietnam's 92.7 million-strong population lists its ethnicity as Kinh (or Viet) – the commonly accepted term – but in reality, most Vietnamese have evolved from a mixture of ethnicities over thousands of years. That mixture is the result of repeated invasions from outside Vietnam, particularly from China, along with continual migrations within the country, most commonly from north to south. As a result, you will find in Vietnam today the predominant Kinh as well as distinct ethnic minority groups, like the hill tribes (see page 60) of the northern and central highlands, and small pockets of Cham and Khmer people in the south, whose kingdoms were vanquished by Vietnamese armies from the north.

The Cham people mainly inhabit the Phan Rang and Phan Thiet regions in southern Vietnam. Today they number about 100,000 – but the

Flower Hmong ethnic minority in Sa Pa.

Champa kingdom was once home to a distinctive culture that lasted for several centuries. Ethnic Khmers, part of the same ethnic stock as Cambodians, number around 900,000 and are concentrated in the Mekong Delta area.

Minority groups have been among the last to reap the rewards of Vietnam's new-found prosperity – with one exception. Ethnic Chinese, who as recently as the late 1970s were ostracised – if not run out of the country – because of tensions arising from the northern border clash with China, have not only benefited from Vietnam's economic progress but, in many ways, fuelled the country's economic growth. This is particularly pronounced in Ho Chi Minh City, the country's main economic hub.

Most of Vietnam's 860,000 Chinese, known as Hoa, have adopted Vietnamese citizenship. Most are shopkeepers and businesspeople who settled in Ho Chi Minh City's Cholon district, which has long flourished as the Chinese community's primary commercial centre in southern Vietnam.

VILLAGE AND FAMILY BONDS

Much of Vietnamese culture has been heavily influenced by the Chinese, who colonised Vietnam over 2,000 years ago. Among their number were the usual tyrants and exploiters, but also administrators and teachers who brought with them religions, philosophies, organisational skills, and a written language, the *chu han*.

In Vietnam, the family is considered to be a small world unto itself. Deeply influenced by Confucian principles, children are taught the importance of *hieu* (filial piety) – respecting one's elders, in fact, was once enshrined by the law. The family in turn is duty-bound to pay homage to its ancestors. A traditional family home would typically have as many as three generations under the one roof: grandparents,

Locals at a trendy Hanoi bar.

⊘ VIETNAMESE NAMES

All Vietnamese names follow a simple structure: family name, middle name and given name. When a Vietnamese hands you a business card you should address the person with the name on the far right (their given name; these often have a literal meaning). A man named Nguyen Manh Hung, for example, should be addressed as Hung.

There are roughly 140 Vietnamese family names in use today. The most common is Nguyen, which was also the name of the last royal dynasty. Other royal surnames still in use today include Tran, Trinh and Le. The name was probably acquired to show loyalty to the monarch in power, or taken on as a mark of respect when a new dynasty rose to power.

Only around 30 of the 140 or so family names used in Vietnam are actually of Vietnamese origin. For the most part, family names are of Chinese (Khong, Luu, Truong, Lu, Lam), Cambodian (Thach, Kim, Danh, Son), or ethnic minority origins (Linh, Giap, Ma, Deo).

The most common middle names are Van for men and Thi for women. The middle name is traditionally used to indicate a person's generation, or the separate branches of a big family, or a person's position within the family – for instance, Ba is for the first son of the first wife, Manh for the first son of the second wife, and Trong for a second son.

parents, married sons with wives and children, and unmarried children. In the event that one member needed money for an investment or for university studies, the entire family would chip in to help. Family connections are strong and the family tree can have dozens of branches.

Traditionally, having a boy in the family was a "must" as the eldest son would assume the duties of his father as head of the family when the latter died. Women were generally brought up for domestic duties, and were less educated than men. Despite growing affluence and gender equality today, especially in urban areas, there is a still a clear preference for boys, as witnessed by the number of sex-selective abortions in the country. Vietnam had an official two-child policy for years; while this is no longer officially the case, local penalties and sanctions may still be applied for a further pregnancy.

Greater prosperity, as well as the inevitable rise in materialism brought by television and the internet, has spurred a desire for personal independence and individualism among younger Vietnamese. Increasingly, young married couples are buying apartments and moving out of the family home. While the older generation, especially in the north, may cling to Ho Chi Minh's ideals, Vietnam's younger generation is far more interested in their iPods than ideology. This shift has caused annoyance among some of Vietnam's elderly population, who can remember the bombs and destruction. As younger people start to outnumber the old and more and more look for careers in the cities, this divide becomes ever greater. Young Vietnamese now are more confident and embrace fashion, won't be told whom to date and are more outgoing than their predecessors.

Overall, though, this is still a conservative and traditional country where the new-found wealth has created a gulf between rich and poor. Changing demographics mean that it is Vietnam's youthful population – 72 percent of its citizens are under 35 years of age – which dominates society, despite the collective influence of the state and that of older generations raised on Confucianist principles during less privileged times.

Many of those who emigrated during and after the war, mainly to the US, Australia, Canada and France, have now returned. Known as Viet Kieu, they were once seen as privileged and the elite, but today they are generally accepted.

VIETNAMESE SOCIETY

Although the country is now technically united, there are plenty of divisions that are clear to see. North and south view each other with some cynicism. Northerners tend to see Ho Chi Minh City dwellers as business-orientated and keen on displaying their new wealth; southerners claim northerners are tough and lack any sense of fun. Maybe that shouldn't be a surprise, given that each region took entirely separate paths for so long, yet it would be too simplistic to say the north hangs on to its communist roots while the south

Vietnamese children now pick up English from an early age.

⊘ KEEP SMILING

Vietnamese often smile when embarrassed, confused or when they are being scolded by an older person or their boss. They also smile when they do not understand what a foreigner is asking, which can be rather disconcerting. Some tourists lose their temper when this happens because they believe the situation is not being taken seriously. However, this is not necessarily the case, but rather that he or she is embarrassed for you. Likewise, when a traffic accident is averted, Vietnamese often crack into a wide smile, especially if you are a foreigner. It means, "I'm sorry!" or "Aren't we lucky nothing serious happened!"

retains capitalist dreams. Vietnam may still officially be communist, but the hammer and sickle have been all but forgotten and replaced by the dollar and dong.

Along with an increasing desire for Western ideals of wealth has come a desire to speak English. Older generations may speak French, Russian or even German, but today's young people are far more likely to want to learn English; it is the language of business, after all.

Children in urban areas learn English at school and at private language schools. Their confidence

Modern wedding ceremony.

with the language and easy interaction with foreigners are noticeable. Teenagers will commonly listen to English songs and watch Hollywood movies on DVD, while everyday speech and online chats are liberally sprinkled with English words and slang. Students are quite likely to approach tourists in major cities for the opportunity to practise their English skills.

But whatever language they use, almost no subject is taboo (the major exception is political reform in Vietnam). So at your very first encounter with a Vietnamese, you are likely to be asked where you're from, whether you are married, how much you earn, what car you drive, and so on, in whatever fractured English the speaker can muster. This curiosity should not be

misinterpreted as nosiness. There is a genuine fascination with foreigners, especially in the less visited areas of Vietnam.

The Vietnamese are proud of what their country has achieved. When it comes to China, there is a guarded welcome to improved relations. Trade links are strong and there is talk of economic corridors and economic zones. But old habits die hard, and old wounds still fester, with the disputed Spratly islands (see page 47) a particularly emotive issue.

SEX AND MARRIAGE

Marriages were once seen as a form of business transaction between two families. Spouses were screened and selected by parents and other senior family members rather than by the prospective partners. These days, it is more common for couples to court each other before the wedding, though family approval is still a symbolic part of the process. Wedding rituals include the bride and her family bringing an odd number of gifts to the groom's family. Given the tight family structure, a wedding is a huge event in any community. In order to demonstrate this, families often spend far more than they can afford to ensure everyone sees just how lavish their family's wedding is.

Even today the wife is expected to move to the husband's house upon marriage. This is a stressful and daunting prospect for any young bride as she is expected to please the whole family and follow the rules of the house.

Vietnam is still a very traditional country, though not necessarily a prudish one. Pre-marital sex is taboo for the older, more conservative generations, but attitudes are changing rapidly. Internet chat rooms, websites, blogs and columns in the state-run media have become forums for young people to discuss subjects like love, sex and sexual orientation. The past few years have seen an upsurge in short stories or novels written by female writers on female sexuality and in 2015, the government lifted the ban on same-sex marriage.

SOCIALISING

Vietnamese people of all ages love to *di choi* (go out to play). This means going out to have fun, hanging out with friends at a bar or café, singing karaoke, etc. When Vietnamese *di choi*, it's often a case of the more the merrier. Whether it's celebrating a birthday or a job promotion, they will invite all their friends and partners/spouses out for a meal. Vietnamese typically drink with a meal, so local restaurants are often filled with boisterous

While Vietnam doesn't have a reputation for sex tourism like Thailand or Cambodia, prostitution is more widespread than it appears. Often, karaoke bars and massage parlours serve as fronts for illicit activities.

boys, not to mention the constant and chaotic flow of traffic, will assail your senses. Even in quieter residential areas, families often gather in the lanes to gossip with neighbours or buy fruit from passing vendors.

With a lot more cars, motorbikes and people than ever before, Vietnam's major cities suffer from chronic congestion, leading the government to impose restrictions on street activity. Street vendors, shopkeepers and food stalls are perpetually playing hide and seek with local police and district authorities who will confiscate goods – plas-

Almost everyone rides motorbikes in Ho Chi Minh City.

drinkers shouting *"Tram phan tram"* (literally 100 percent) before downing a glass of beer or shot of *ruou* (rice liquor).

It's customary for the person who extended the invitation to pick up the tab. In fact, Vietnamese rarely split the bill, even if it isn't a special occasion. Friends are forever trying to grab the bill in cafés and restaurants or surreptitiously bribing the waiter in an attempt to be presented with the bill first.

STREET LIFE

Living in cramped houses filled with extended three-generation families means that life often spills onto the streets. Itinerant vendors on bicycles and on foot, streetside barbers, shoeshine

Vietnamese can come across as quite blunt; being called beo (fat) can be a well-intentioned remark that someone's just looking well and happy rather than overweight.

tic stools, baskets, whatever – if these items are deemed to be blocking traffic or pushing pedestrians onto the road.

CUSTOMS AND ETIQUETTE

Face, and not losing it, is an important part of nearly every Asian culture. In Vietnam it is particularly crucial. People will go to all sorts of lengths to avoid causing embarrassment to others, and visitors should be particularly mindful of this. Direct criticism and raised voices are ideal ways to lose any argument. When things do go wrong, they can go wrong in spectacular fashion as the Vietnamese have a fiery temperament and public arguments occur far more frequently than in other Southeast Asian countries.

As tourist numbers increase, some values are changing. Vietnamese sometimes have no qualms about overcharging visitors, and no amount of complaining will stop this. If visitors do feel they have been ripped off, polite but firm discussions are the best way to proceed. In some areas, a particularly resolute approach is required. The northwestern town of Sa Pa is one such place, as here the Hmong people will follow tourists relentlessly around town in a bid to sell them souvenirs, and polite refusals often fall on deaf ears.

Other customs include never touching somebody on the head, not pointing, passing items with both hands and not touching members of the opposite sex. When eating, be sure not to leave chopsticks poking up in a rice bowl as this resembles

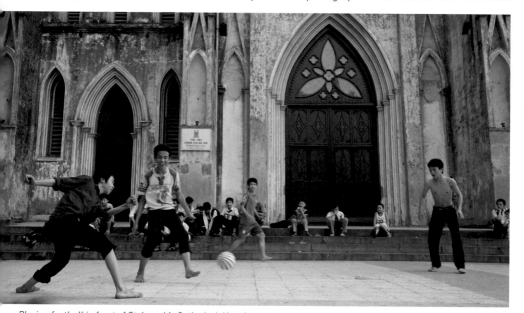
Playing football in front of St Joseph's Cathedral, Hanoi.

⊙ THE VIETNAMESE LANGUAGE

The country shares one common tongue, a blend of several languages – ancient and modern – that has evolved from a mixture of the Austro-Asiatic, Austronesian and Sino-Tibetan sources. Yet there are distinct dialects across the country, and northerners and southerners often find it impossible to understand each other. Some letters of the alphabet are pronounced differently, and the vocabularies of northerners and southerners contain distinct words. Even the syntax is different. In addition to Vietnamese, the country's many ethnic minorities speak their own languages and dialects. In the Mekong Delta, for example, a large number of people speak the Khmer language of Cambodia.

Thousands of words in contemporary Vietnamese – as much as 70 percent – are derived from Chinese. There is a touch of French too, with words that entered the lexicon during the colonial period. Several food items are recognisably French – ca phe (café), pho mat (fromage), ga to (gâteau) and bia (bière).

Learning to speak Vietnamese is challenging. Despite the Romanised alphabet, the use of tones alters the sounds of words. The city of Hue, for example, is pronounced "whey", not "Hugh", and the popular beef noodle soup pho bo is pronounced "fuh baw", not "foe bow".

incense sticks at a funeral, an extremely offensive sign. If you are invited to a person's home, it is customary to bring a small gift, such as a basket of fruit – but never wrap it in black or white paper. When eating with Vietnamese, wait until the oldest member of the party begins to eat before starting to feast. If people do constantly ask your age, they aren't being rude – they are simply trying to ascertain how to address you, as hierarchy is an important part of Vietnamese culture.

EDUCATION

Children begin primary education aged around six and remain there for five years. After this time, students will sit a test, which determines the kind of secondary school they will attend.

At the end of grade 12, students take one more test, which they need to pass to gain their high-school diploma. Getting into university is an important first step towards almost any successful career. Most universities are state-run, though the number of private and foreign-run establishments is increasing.

Vietnam has a literacy rate of more than 90 percent, but the quality of teaching is questionable. Rote-learning and teacher-centred classrooms are the norm. In order to pass classes, many students study after school and so it is not uncommon to be walking home at night and hear a chorus of English coming from a crowded room-full of students.

COMPETITIVE SPIRIT

Once the working day is done, Vietnamese tend to pull on their fitness gear and head outside. Many towns and cities have open areas where locals play badminton, practise t'ai chi or join in mass aerobics.

Tennis and golf are now the sports of choice for the well-heeled, but football is by far the most popular working-class sport. Vietnamese men play (and watch) the game with great enthusiasm. In the height of summer, matches are played early in the morning as it would be too hot by the afternoon. It is not uncommon for Vietnamese men to stay up all night to watch European football matches – and then go to work the next day bleary-eyed.

UNDER THE TABLE

Corruption is an entrenched part of Vietnamese society. Palms are greased to skip bureaucratic

hurdles, win contracts and invite preferential treatment from people in positions of authority, such as traffic police and teachers.

There are occasional reports of protests and

> *With 57 percent of its people under the age of 35, Vietnam has one of the youngest populations in the world, a powerful engine for driving the country's growth.*

Smiling boy, Can Tho.

even riots from disgruntled locals, but little changes. The pro-democracy movement Bloc 8406 (so called as it was formed on 8 April 2006) has had some impact, but authorities continue to crack down on those who speak out of line. Catholic priest Nguyen Van Ly was jailed for eight years in 2007 for supporting the group. Released in 2010 to receive better medical care, he was returned to prison in 2011 and finally granted early release, ending his sentence in May 2016.

The government is trying to root out corruption, but it is an uphill task given the fact that it is so deeply ingrained. In the past, Vietnamese would have blamed the war for the country's poverty; these days, corruption is often cited as the main reason for any perceived ills.

THE LEGACY OF WAR

The war may be over, but its aftermath is omnipresent. From rusty bullets for sale on street corners to the politics of international relations, the war's impact can still be felt.

In the years following the war with the US, Vietnam survived largely in isolation from the West. From 1975 until 1994 it was illegal for US firms to trade

Tourist on the firing range at Cu Chi Tunnels.

with Vietnam, with the only form of help coming from Soviet quarters (until the late 1980s). But by the early 1990s relations with America were thawing and in 1995 formal diplomatic relations were restored by the then US president Bill Clinton. In 2000 Clinton became the first US head of state to visit the country since the war; this played a large part in normalising relations. A raft of trade deals has since been signed that has catapulted Vietnam's economy forwards. In 2016 the US Census Bureau estimated that bilateral trade had reached US$52.2 million, with Vietnam's export amounting to US$42 million.

In addition to economics, it is in the USA's strategic interests to have Vietnam close, even if only to help keep rivals China in check. In turn, Vietnam values its relationship with the US for financial reasons, but it walks a fine line as it must be careful not to allow its growing US links to damage its ties with China. Vietnam therefore views links with the US as a useful buffer against any Chinese aggression while paradoxically looking to repair relations with China. This delicate balancing act, amid US calls for improved human rights, has placed limits on how far the relationship with the USA can progress.

INTEREST IN THE WAR

Nonetheless, despite the healthy trade relations and Vietnam's welcoming attitude to tourists – be they American, British or French – it would be a mistake to think that all is forgotten and forgiven. The war is still within living memory of many Vietnamese and Americans and there are scars on both sides that will take generations to heal. Still, most Vietnamese have few qualms about discussing the war and tourists should not consider it a taboo subject. Indeed, it would be virtually impossible to visit Vietnam and not have a conversation about the country's recent history.

The war has an influence on nearly everyone. Its effects on the physical landscape are clear, from the devastating impact of Agent Orange on the country's fields to the still-visible bomb craters and, more significantly, the thousands of landmines that still lie undiscovered. For some, the war remnants offer an entrepreneurial edge as they sell allegedly genuine war medals and memorabilia to tourists – and some war sites (notably the Cu Chi Tunnels near Ho Chi Minh City) are full-scale tourist attractions.

Interest in the war is inevitable and Vietnam does its best to oblige, even toning down some of the jingoistic propaganda. A case in point is the museum in Ho Chi Minh City originally known as "The House for Displaying War Crimes of American Imperialism and the Puppet Government". This was later changed to the slightly less inflammatory "Museum of American War Crimes" and today it's known far more euphemistically as the War Remnants Museum.

Another factor is the inevitable change as the country develops and new generations grow up. Younger citizens seem happy to embrace Western ideals. Many are now pushing traditional boundaries in terms of lifestyle choices, while the number of English-language schools is proof of how important the tourist industry is now. Maybe the biggest post-war change has come in terms of attitudes to the West. Ask Vietnamese teenagers whom they most admire today and they are more likely to name an English Premier League footballer than Uncle Ho (Chi Minh).

THE WAR IN LITERATURE AND FILM

Among the numerous books on the war, several stand out. *A Bright Shining Lie* by Neil Sheehan tells of this journalist's conversations with Lt Col on the Fourth of July details the memoirs of Ron Kovic, who was paralysed by a bullet. The book was later made into a movie of the same name. *Vietnam: Rising Dragon* by Bill Hayton gives a comprehensive overview of contemporary Vietnamese history while *The Quiet American*, a classic by Graham Greene, (made into a film twice) is a fascinating tale of love, innocence and morality in Vietnam. See also Further Reading on page 358.

Perhaps the ultimate Vietnam War movie is actually based on a book about Africa. *Apocalypse Now* is Francis Ford Coppola's seminal film, and is heavily influenced by Joseph Conrad's *Heart of Darkness*. Marlon Brando plays Kurtz, a colonel who has lost his mind due to the horrors of war. *Full Metal Jacket*, director Stanley Kubrick's tale of a teenage recruit who ends up in Hue during the 1968 Tet Offensive, is

My Lai Massacre exhibit at the War Remnants Museum in Ho Chi Minh City.

John Paul Vann, who was so appalled by the incompetence of the South Vietnamese and US generals that he started briefing reporters on what was really happening. *Dispatches* by Michael Herr details the hundreds of notes that Herr, a former journalist, amassed after front-line reporting in Vietnam. The result is a part-fictitious, part-factual narrative that brilliantly captures the swirling, horrific mess of war. Robert Timburg's *The Nightingale's Song* looks at the experiences of several notable veterans, including author Oliver Stone and US politician John McCain, while *Born* a gripping, no-holds-barred vision of war, while *Platoon* is a violent, gripping tale that tells things from a soldier's perspective. *Hamburger Hill* is based on the 101st Airborne Division's battle for survival in the heart of Vietnam's dense jungle while Brian De Palma's *Casualties of War* narrates a true story of an American soldier, an outsider who stands up to his colleagues in defence of an enslaved Vietnamese girl. *Good Morning Vietnam* features an iconic role by the late Robin Williams, and offers a wonderfully nuanced insight into the absurdities of the Vietnam War.

HILL TRIBES

Living in remote mountainous regions with little fertile ground for agriculture, Vietnam's hill tribes inhabit a world far removed from the bustle of the country's urban centres.

There are 54 ethnic minority groups in Vietnam, the bulk of which comprise those hill tribes that inhabit the mountainous areas that extend through much of the length of the country. Each has its own language, lifestyle and heritage. Collectively referred to as the Montagnards (or mountain people) by the French, the hill tribes live in the most remote and inaccessible parts of Vietnam. Although the government has tried to reduce poverty and provide access to education and other facilities, the hill tribes have been left behind in Vietnam's race towards modernisation.

Fully aware of the lucrative potential of tourism, the government has encouraged the hill tribes to preserve their traditional identity and heritage. Northern hill tribes such as the Hmong, Dao and Tai in particular have successfully tapped into Vietnam's growing tourism industry, offering homestay accommodation and producing handicrafts for sale. The hill tribes living in the central highlands, however, do not feature on many tourist itineraries. Much of this region is sensitive, and there have been uprisings over land disputes and accusations by international human rights groups of religious oppression.

The following text identifies the major groups.

NORTHERN HIGHLANDS

DAO

The Dao (pronounced "Zao") first arrived from China in the 18th century. Part of the Hmong-Dao language group, they number about 620,000 and are found all across Vietnam's northern provinces, living in large villages or small isolated hamlets and cultivating rice using the slash-and-burn method. The Dao can

Red Dao woman from a village near Sa Pa.

also be broken up into subgroups based on customs and the women's clothing. These include the Dao Quan Trang (White Trousers Dao), Dao Ao Dai (Long Tunic Dao), Dao Dau Troc (Shaven-Headed Dao) and Dao Do (Red Dao). The Red Dao wear a striking scarlet turban decorated with tassels or bells.

The Dao are expert artisans and highly skilled at making their own paper. For centuries they have used Chinese characters to record their genealogies, popular songs and rhymes, as well as folk tales and fables. The women plant cotton, which they weave and then dye with indigo. Dao embroidery is worked directly onto the cloth from memory, the traditional designs fixed in the weavers' minds.

HMONG

The Hmong, or Meo, who number about 800,000, are found in villages known as *giao* throughout the highlands of northern Vietnam. Unrest and warfare encouraged the Hmong to migrate to Vietnam from the southern Chinese kingdom of Bach Viet at the beginning of the 19th century.

The Hmong minority group has been sub-divided into branches classified by women's costume, dialect and customs. For example, the Hmong of Sa Pa are called Black Hmong because of their predominantly black clothing.

MUONG

Numbering around 1.2 million, the Muong people inhabit the mountainous parts of Hoa Binh

Since the mid-1990s the former French hill station of Sa Pa has become one of the main tourist attractions in the country, and villagers have benefited from selling various handicrafts to tourists.

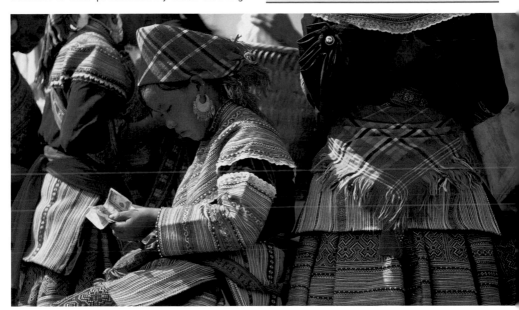

A Flower Hmong trader at Bac Ha market.

The most colourful sub-group are the Flower Hmong, found in large numbers around Bac Ha in Lao Cai province, who wear bright-coloured clothes with embroidery.

Corn is the main staple of Hmong people, but rice is often grown on terraces watered with the aid of irrigation. Hemp is grown to be woven into textiles, and cotton is also cultivated in some villages. As skilled artisans, the Hmong produce a variety of items, including handwoven indigo-dyed cloth, paper, silver jewellery, leather goods, baskets and embroidery. The Hmong have no written language. Their legends, songs, folklore and proverbs have been passed down from one generation to the next through the spoken word.

and Thanh Hoa provinces. They are most closely related to the Kinh majority. Ethnologists believe that the Muong remained in the mountains and developed independently, while the majority Kinh moved to the lowlands and became influenced by Chinese culture after the 11 BC invasion led by the Han emperor Wu Ti.

NUNG

The Nung share the same language, culture and customs as the Tay. Numbering about 870,000, they live in Cao Bang and Lang Son provinces in the northeast bordering China. They are known for their rich folk-art traditions, including music and poetry, as well as a variety of handicrafts.

SAN CHI

There are almost 150,000 San Chi living in villages, most of them in Ha Giang, Tuyen Quang and Bac Tai provinces, but they are also found in certain regions of Lao Cai, Yen Bai, Vinh Phu,

> *Vietnamese hill tribes often serve sweet rice liquor called ruou can in a communal jar with a bunch of bamboo shoots for straws.*

A patriarchal society, the Tays cultivate a variety of crops, including rice, tobacco, spices and a variety of fruit on the steep mountainsides. Although the influence of Vietnam's dominant Kinh culture is evident in their customs and traditions, the Tay prefer to speak in their own indigenous language.

TAI

There are more than 1.4 million Tai living along the Song Hong (Red River), in the northwest of Vietnam, often together with other ethnic minor-

Drinking ruou can, sweet rice liquor, in Mai Chau.

Ha Bac and Quang Ninh provinces. They are of the Tay-Tai language group and arrived from China at the beginning of the 19th century. San Chi ritual dances are elaborate: boys and young girls perform traditional love songs in festivities that can last all night.

TAY

The highlands of northern Vietnam are home to the 1.5 million-strong Tay, Vietnam's largest minority group. Tay villages are found in the provinces of Cao Bang, Lang Son, Bac Tai, Quang Ninh, Ha Giang and Tuyen Quang, and also in the Dien Bien Phu region. Their villages, or *ban*, are located in valleys near flowing water, where they build their houses, usually on stilts.

ities. Their bamboo or wooden stilt houses are constructed in two distinct styles. The Black Tai build homes shaped like tortoise shells, while the White Tai construct rectangular dwellings. The women wear long, black sarongs and short tops with silver buttons. They are skilled weavers and produce beautiful embroidery using motifs of flowers, birds, animals and dragons.

SOUTHERN AND CENTRAL HIGHLANDS

BAHNAR

The Bahnar (also spelt Ba Na), one of Vietnam's poorest ethnic groups, live primarily in the central highland provinces of Gia Lai and Kon Tum as well as the coastal provinces of Binh Dinh and Phu Yen. There are around 180,000 Bahnar people, for whom life revolves around a traditional calendar, in which 10 months are set aside for cultivation and the remaining two months for social and personal duties such as marriage, weaving, ceremonies and festivals. One of their unique traditions is the ear-piercing ceremony. When babies turn a month old, their ear lobes are pierced, signifying the official acceptance of the child as a member of the village. Those who die without ear piercings are believed to be banished to a land of monkeys headed by a black-eared goddess called Duydai.

JARAI (GIA RAI)

The Jarai, or Gia Rai, numbering around 320,000, live in the central highland provinces of Gia Lai, Kon Tum and Dak Lak. They belong to the Malay-Polynesian language group and arrived in the Tay Nguyen highlands around 2,000 years ago. They live a sedentary lifestyle in villages known as *ploi*, or sometimes *bon*. Jarai villages, with at least 50 homes, are built around a central *nha rong*, a communal house. The community has small matriarchal families.

Young Jarai girls take the first step in choosing a marriage partner, making their approach through an intermediary. The promise of marriage is sealed with the exchange of bronze bracelets, with the ceremony proceeding in three steps. First, the bracelet-exchanging rite is performed in front of the two families and the intermediary. Then the young couple's dreams are interpreted, a ritual that predicts their future prospects. Finally, the wedding ceremony is held at the home of the groom's parents.

RHADE (EDE)

The Rhade, or Ede, found mainly in Dak Lak province in the central highlands, number more than 270,000. Like the Jarai, they belong to the Malay-Polynesian language group. They live in wooden longhouses built on stilts in villages known as *buon*. Each longhouse shelters a large matriarchal family under the authority of a *koa sang*, the most senior and respected woman. She directs community affairs, settles internal conflicts, and is also responsible for the safekeeping of all the communal heirlooms, especially the bronze gongs and ancient jars used for preparing rice beer for important festivals. The village's autonomous organisation is run by the *po pin ea*, the chief who is elected to take care of its communal affairs.

The Rhade employ slash-and-burn techniques to clear the land for agriculture. Rice, the main crop, is cultivated along with sugar cane, melons, cotton and tobacco. Nearly every village has its own forge to produce and repair metal farming implements. Basketry, pottery and indigo cloth are produced by the Rhade for their own use.

Rice terraces surrounding Sa Pa.

⊘ LOWLAND MINORITIES

Numbering around 1.1 million people, the Khmer Krom are ethnic Cambodians who live around the Mekong Delta. Reports claim that the Khmer Krom are one of the more persecuted groups, forced to speak Vietnamese and adopt local names. Authorities allow some limited television programmes to be broadcast in Khmer, but there are reports that those who try to privately access Cambodian channels end up in trouble.

There are around 130,000 Cham still in Vietnam, the remnant of a once-great empire brought into the Vietnamese polity in the 15th century. There are some 860,000 Ethnic Chinese (Hoa), mostly clustered in the main urban centres.

Buddhist statuette, Long Khanh
Pagoda, Qui Nhon.

RELIGIOI

Nearly every religion can be found in Vietnam, including Buddhism, Confucianism, Taoism, Animism, Christianity, Islam, and the unique fusion of the Cao Dai faith.

When the government started relaxing its grip on organised religion in 1986 as part of the country's *doi moi* (economic renovation) policy, it sparked a religious revival. Across the country, thousands of pagodas were resurrected as centres of spiritual life. Temples which had been closed or turned into schools or granaries returned to their original use. Rituals and festivals were revived, and congregations at Roman Catholic and Protestant masses were suddenly spilling out onto the streets. Suppressed for decades, religion was back in vogue.

Organised religion in Vietnam has long been a thorn in the side of the Communist Party. Although the government's decision to permit religion has filled a spiritual and ideological void, religious practice is still closely monitored.

> *Astrological charts are often consulted to select an auspicious date for ceremonies, such as weddings, and other important events.*

RELIGIOUS FUSION

Vietnam is often regarded as a Buddhist country. The reality is rather more complex. Although up to 85 percent of the population regularly visits Buddhist pagodas, only 16 percent would be considered strictly Buddhist if you go by the book.

Over the centuries, Taoism, Buddhism and Confucianism have become simplified, intertwined and Vietnamised to constitute – along with other indigenous animistic beliefs – a core religion that is shared to some extent by all Vietnamese. This religion is sometimes referred to as *tam giao* (triple religion). There is no sense of contradiction for

Lat people singing in a village church.

a Vietnamese person to make offerings to Buddha at a pagoda, a national saint at a temple and a deceased grandparent at the family altar. Even some church-going Christians practise ancestor worship at home, while Vietnamese who regard themselves as non-religious routinely visit temples on festival days. The everyday behaviour and attitude of the typical Vietnamese is shaped by a complex synthesis of Asian religious traditions.

To complicate matters, Vietnam also has its own indigenous spirituality. Together, the gods of the earth, water and mountains define and transform the geomantic structures and rules that determine – in the same way that the Chinese use *feng shui* – the orientation of houses, businesses, cities, graves and temples, and configure the good and bad luck of families, communities and nations. Between heaven and earth, but never separate from them, are humans, both male and female, the dead and the living, the ancestors and the descendants.

Each of the realms – heaven, earth and human – has its own rules, regulations, elements of good, bad, ugly and beautiful, and, above all, its own deities. These deities are found everywhere – in stones, trees, lakes and animals – and they are praised, fed, housed and revered with ritual offerings and prescribed modes of behaviour.

CHINESE INFLUENCE

When the Chinese imposed their rule on Vietnam, they brought along their agricultural know-how and their books on religion, philosophy and

> *The small mirrored octagonal disc with the Yin Yang symbol fixed above the front door of houses and shops throughout the country is believed to bar wandering spirits and ghosts from entering.*

Altar, Temple of Literature in Hanoi.

☉ CAO DAI

In 1921 a former civil servant of the French colonial administration called Ngo Minh Chieu received a message from a "superior spirit" called Cao Dai, meaning High Spirit or Supreme Being. Disillusioned by existing religions, Ngo was urged to create a new religion that meshed the world's main creeds together.

Today, the Cao Dai religion has an estimated 4 million followers in Vietnam. Cao Dai incorporates the teachings and philosophies of Buddhism, Taoism and Confucianism. Before God existed, there was the Tao, that nameless, formless, unchanging and eternal source referenced in the *Tao Te Ching*. Then a Big Bang occurred, out of which God was born. The

universe could not yet be formed and to do so, God created *yin* and *yang*. He took control of *yang* and shed a part of himself, creating the Goddess to preside over *yin* as Mother Buddha.

The religion's three original prophets were a disparate bunch of people: French novelist Victor Hugo, Chinese Nationalist Party leader Sun Yat-sen and Vietnamese poet Trang Trinh, while the extensive list of Cao Dai saints includes William Shakespeare, Joan of Arc, Julius Caesar, René Descartes and Thomas Jefferson. British author Graham Greene described the Cao Dai faith as "a game that had gone on too long".

other ideas, written in one of the most complicated scripts ever devised. While a new Vietnamese written language replaced Chinese script in the 13th century, the Vietnamese are still attached to the old Chinese characters, which visually and stylistically represented the meaning and feeling attached to each word.

Although the Vietnamese fought against Chinese cultural hegemony, they selectively screened and assimilated what they considered the best aspects. Chinese teachers, some of whom were administrators, were usually accompanied by Confucian scholars, Buddhist masters and Taoist diviners. The Vietnamese absorbed much of what they had to offer, and these religious influences persist in Vietnam today, as do the religions introduced later – Hinduism and Islam brought from India, and Christianity from Europe and America.

CONFUCIANISM

Confucianism is based on the teachings of Confucius, who was born in northern China around 550 BC and lived at a time of great political turmoil. As a teacher and unsolicited adviser to kings, he compiled rules and ideas to define the relationships between ruler and subject, parents and children, husband and wife, student and teacher. Confucius was more of a moral and ethical guide than a spiritual leader. He refused to discuss life after death, as well as the unseen or the mystical, and he was primarily interested in a social order based upon compassion, etiquette, loyalty, knowledge and trust.

Confucianism reached Vietnam over 2,000 years ago and it has remained a pillar of the Vietnamese moral and spiritual establishment ever since. Officially, and pragmatically, the Vietnamese imperial dynasties adopted Confucianism because of its ability to sustain a system of social order without much repression, and for its code of social mobility based on merit. It became the official doctrine of the imperial government examinations, the first of which was held in 1706. The Vietnamese monarchy recruited its high officials according to the results of these competitive examinations, which were in theory open to all men, except (for some reason) actors.

Those who earned their degrees received a hat and tunic from the emperor and were welcomed home as wise scholars by the entire population.

Those who failed the examinations would most likely have returned home and made a living as teachers. In this way, whole villages were indirectly introduced to the teachings of Confucianism.

BUDDHISM

Vietnamese Buddhism is a fascinating blend of several branches of Buddhism. Introduced across the sea from India and overland from China, Buddhism extended the question of knowledge from the social order and rules of Confucianism to the general human condition.

Devotees at Dien Huu Pagoda in Hanoi.

⊘ THE POWER OF ASTROLOGY

Vietnamese people believe there are good days and bad days. A person's future welfare could therefore rest on choosing the most propitious date and time for any significant event. Divination by astrology is the main way of working out when to move house, apply for a job or get married: in each case, the fortune teller's decision is final and instructions are closely followed.

Naturally, such services come at a cost, sometimes hundreds of dollars. In addition, the decision may not always be convenient – the spirits may decide that you need to move house in the middle of the night, for instance.

From the 2nd to the 10th century, two popular Buddhist sects – the A-Ham (Agama) and the Thien (Dhyana in Sanskrit and Zen in Japanese) – competed peacefully for followers and believers in Vietnam. Eventually Thien prevailed, despite its exacting practice that requires continual training in self-discipline and in mastering the techniques of breathing, meditation and concentration.

> *While travelling in Vietnam, you will hear locals exclaim, either in excitement or exasperation, "Oi Gioi oi"! (pronounced "oi zoi oi"), which means, "Oh my God"!*

Thien is one of the many sects of Mahayana Buddhism widely observed in China, Japan, Korea and Vietnam. Less dogmatic than others, it is more receptive to the diverse cultural and social conditions of different countries. The other branch of Buddhism, the Hinayana or Theravada (found in Sri Lanka, Burma, Thailand, Laos, Cambodia and parts of southern Vietnam),

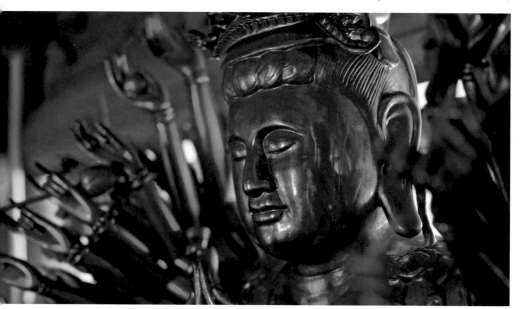

Gilded Buddha statue at Tay Phuong Pagoda.

⊘ CATHOLICS IN VIETNAM

There are 5.7 million Catholics in Vietnam, the secondlargest group in Southeast Asia after the Philippines, and the religion is enjoying an upswing in popularity; in heavily Catholic areas the countryside is scattered with churches which have experienced something of a rebuilding frenzy in recent years. The Church's relations with Vietnam's leaders has often been fractious, but the situation has steadily improved since 2007. After their meeting in Rome in 2014, both Pope Francis and the Vietnamese Prime Minister Nguyen Tan Dung announced that they were committed to restoring diplomatic relations.

is more orthodox yet co-exists with Mahayana. The main doctrinal division between the two schools is that the Mahayana sect maintains that lay people can attain nirvana, whereas the Theravada school believes that only ordained monks and nuns can do so.

Few Vietnamese outside the clergy, however, are acquainted with Buddhism's elaborate cosmology. What appealed to them at the time it was introduced was the ritual and imagery of Mahayana Buddhism. Mahayana ceremony easily conformed to indigenous Vietnamese beliefs, which combined folklore with Confucian and Taoist teachings, and Mahayana saints were often venerated alongside various animist spirits.

HOA HAO

Hoa Hao is a religious tradition based on Buddhism founded in 1939 by Huynh Phu So. Adherents consider Huynh to be a prophet and Hoa Hao a continuation of a 19th-century Buddhist ministry known as Buu Son Ky Huong (Strange Perfume from Precious Mountains, referring to the That Son range on the Vietnamese–Cambodian border).

The religion has an estimated 2 million followers in Vietnam. In some provinces around the Mekong Delta, the religion's birthplace, some 90 percent of the population practises Hoahaoism. Hoa Hao puts great emphasis on the practice of Buddhism by laypeople in the home, rather than at the temple. Aid to the poor is favoured over pagoda-building or expensive rituals. Religious ceremonies are simple and modest, and do not include food offerings or divination services.

TAOISM

The *tao* is the highest and most active level of an otherwise static consciousness, the general law of the motion of the universe and of all things. It is both energy and matter, and the moment when the contradictory forces of yin and yang fuse in temporary harmony. In Chinese writing, it is represented by a character meaning "way" or "path".

In Vietnamese villages where Buddhism, Confucianism, animism and other forms of worship co-existed, Taoist priests were also welcomed. Introduced to Vietnam about the same time as Confucianism, Vietnamese Taoism does not have the hierarchy of schools and systems typical of China.

ANCESTOR WORSHIP

A French Jesuit priest, Léopold Cadière, who spent decades in Vietnam studying religion, wrote in 1944 that Europeans were deluded about the importance of Buddhism in Vietnam. He believed that if there was one uniform religion, it was "the cult of spirits". Ancestor veneration is one of the most unifying aspects of Vietnamese culture, as practically all Vietnamese, regardless of religious affinity, usually have an altar dedicated to ancestors in their home or business place. This concept of filial piety has roots in the teachings of

Confucianism. Failing to worship one's ancestors is considered sinful, and condemns the ancestors to a life of hellish wandering.

Vietnamese believe that burning votive objects will help their loved ones settle into a comfortable afterlife. On the anniversary of the person's death, the extended family will gather together to feast and pay their respects by burning incense and votive offerings at the tomb or shrine of the ancestor. In the past, typical offerings were paper replicas of household goods, clothes and fake money. Nowadays, the offer-

Prayerful Catholic nuns.

ings can be more ostentatious – real houses, cars, iPods and credit cards.

WHALE WORSHIP

If there is one place where whales can swim safely, it is off the coasts of Vietnam. That is because of a religious practice that worships these giants of the sea. Ngu Ong is a whale god that is feared and revered by followers, while living whales are given special respect. In 2010 a dead 15-tonne individual was found in Bac Lieu province and was buried in a giant glass tomb. In Danang province an annual festival is held in the third lunar month of the year where boats are brightly coloured and special thanks are given to the whales for protecting the community's fishermen.

CHRISTIANITY

The first Western missionaries set foot in Tonkin, in northern Vietnam, in 1533, and more arrived in central Vietnam in 1596. But their stay was brief. It was not until 1615 that the first permanent Christian missions were founded – in Hoi An, Danang and Hanoi – by the Portuguese Jesuits. The introduction of this organised and culturally alien religion generated, unavoidably, misunderstanding and conflict.

Many Vietnamese from all classes of society converted to Catholicism. This development

Muslim men attending a prayer meeting at Jamiul Azhar Mosque near Chau Doc.

worried the mandarins and ruling classes, who saw the new religion as a threat to the traditional order of society and its rites, particularly the belief in *nam giao* and ancestor worship. Between 1712 and 1720, a decree forbidding Christianity was enforced in the north. In the south, foreign missionaries were sent packing in 1750 when Christianity became forbidden.

Levels of tolerance towards Christianity varied among leaders. Under Emperor Minh Mang, who viewed Christianity as "the perverse religion of Europeans" that "corrupts the heart of men", a decree was enforced forbidding the entry of Christian missionaries to Vietnam. Thieu Tri was more tolerant, but his successor,

Tu Duc, reinforced the prohibition of Christianity. This period of persecution lasted until the mid-1860s, when a treaty ceded territory and commercial rights to the French and granted freedom for Christians to practise their faith. Between 1882 and 1884, another wave of persecution hit the Catholic Church, and many followers paid with their lives. The persecution ended in 1885 with the French conquest of the entire country.

After the signing of the Geneva Agreement in 1954 and the division of the country, over half a million Catholics fled North Vietnam for the tolerance of the former South Vietnam. Since the reunification of Vietnam in 1975, the Catholic Church has operated under the written law of the Socialist Republic of Vietnam, which guarantees the freedom of religion or non-religion under an official Marxist-Leninist ideology. All Catholic schools in the country have been nationalised.

While there is significantly more freedom of religion for the Catholic Church, the government remains cautious of Protestant hill tribes in the central highlands and followers of Hoa Hao Buddhism. Protestantism is the country's fastest-growing religion. Thanks to a six-fold increase in the past decade, there are now nearly one million followers practising in over 400 churches in Vietnam. Local authorities keep an eye on proceedings. The Saigon Protestant Church in Ho Chi Minh City, for instance, one of the biggest in the country, has to submit a list of its event schedules, financial records and appointments of Church leaders to government officials for their prior approval.

ISLAM

Vietnam's small Muslim community consists mainly of ethnic Chams and South Asians. A 10th-century stela inscribed in Arabic, found near the central coastal town of Phan Rang, provides the earliest record of Islam's presence in Vietnam. Although they consider themselves as Muslim, their religious practices are not fully orthodox. They don't make the pilgrimage to Mecca, and although they avoid eating pork, Vietnamese Muslims drink alcohol and observe Ramadan for only three days instead of a full month. Their rituals also co-exist with other animistic and Hindu-based worship.

TET: THE LUNAR NEW YEAR

Similar to its Chinese counterpart, Vietnam's colourful New Year festival is a time of parades, fireworks and family gatherings.

Tet Nguyen Dan (Festival of the First Morning of the Year), often called simply Tet, is Vietnam's most important festival and marks the beginning of the lunar year. It is celebrated in either January or February, depending on the lunar calendar.

Tet rites begin a week before Mung Mot (the first day of the Lunar New Year). This is when the Kitchen God (Ong Tao) returns to the Kingdom of Heaven and presents his annual report on the state of earthly matters to the Jade Emperor before returning to earth on New Year's Eve. During his week-long journey to heaven, the Vietnamese guard themselves against bad spirits. In the countryside, you will often find a *cay neu* (signal tree), a bamboo pole with a clay tablet and a piece of yellow cloth attached, in front of the home. Another indispensable feature in the north is a branch of peach blossom, or *cay dao*. In southern and central Vietnam, *cay mai*, a branch of yellow apricot blossom, is more common. The kumquat tree is another popular decorative feature in the north. This tree is carefully selected to ensure it has both golden-orange ripe fruit and unripe green fruit, representing prosperity now (ripe fruit) and prosperity to come (green fruit).

During the holiday the family table will be laden with food. There will be plenty of *banh chung*, glutinous rice cakes stuffed with pork beans and onion, *xoi* (sticky rice) with pork and pickled onions as well as a variety of *mut*, or candied sweets.

The Vietnamese traditionally lit firecrackers to scare off bad spirits. However, firecrackers had turned the cities and countryside into a battle zone, and in 1995 they were outlawed. Today, extravagant fireworks displays are organised in every major city to celebrate the start of the New Year.

TET RITUALS

The first day of Tet is for the worship of ancestors, who are ceremoniously welcomed back from heaven on New Year's Eve during the Giao Thua, the transition as one year passes to the next. It is also considered to be the first day of spring, which is why the festival is sometimes called Hoi xuan (spring festival). Elaborately prepared food offerings, together with burning incense, await the ancestors at the altar. All events – whether favourable or unfavourable – that take place on the first day of Tet are believed to affect the course of one's life for the year ahead. Homeowners will also consider carefully who should be the first person to walk through their door after

New Year wishes at a temple.

the New Year begins, a custom known as *xong nha*. It must be a person who has had a prosperous year or a person with a reputation for bringing good luck.

The rest of the week will be spent visiting relatives, family friends, temples and pagodas. Children will receive *mung tuoi* (or *li xi*), meaning lucky money, in slim red envelopes from elders. Employees will often visit their boss, sometimes bearing lavish gifts to curry favour for the working year ahead.

Traditionally, people would have stopped working for at least a week. Now in most cities many businesses only close for three days, forcing reluctant staff back to work prematurely. Still, during Tet, tourists should anticipate services to be running more sluggishly than usual, if at all.

📷 VIETNAMESE TEMPLES AND PAGODAS

Pagodas and temples reflect the cultural diversity of religious practice in Vietnam and are a focus of social, political and religious life.

Most Vietnamese villages have their own complex of temple buildings, including the *dinh* (communal house), where the village founder is venerated and the village council, an assembly of male leaders, traditionally meets to debate local affairs and conduct important meetings. The *chua* (pagoda) is regarded as an important social centre for women and is generally devoted to the worship of the Buddha. The *den* (temple) and *mieu* are shrines to the ancestors of individual families. Temples often have Taoist and Confucian elements, dedicated to other gods, national heroes or guardian spirits.

Vietnamese religious practice is eclectic, and this is reflected in the layout of the temple buildings. Large temple complexes may include a *phuong dinh* (front hall), a *ngoai cung* (central hall), a *noi cung* or main altar hall, and a *cay tien huong*, which acts as a gate to the main temple complex. The choice of temple gods also varies from one village to the next. In some temples, statues of Confucius sit alongside Taoist or Buddhist images. In the north, it is common to find Vietnam War heroes joining the statue line up. Many offer the chance to burn joss sticks before a life-size statue of the national hero Ho Chi Minh.

After 1945, religious activity was discouraged, but since the 1980s there has been a revival and many Vietnamese have donated money towards temple renovations in their villages.

Every temple gate has its *quan bao ve*, or guardian soldier, one malevolent and one benevolent, as pictured here at the Co Tien Temple near Sam Son Beach in north Vietnam.

First built in wood in 1049, Hanoi's Chua Mot Cot (One Pillar Pagoda) was destroyed in 1954 and has since been reconstructed in sturdy concrete.

Hanoi's Tran Quoc Pagoda, near West Lake, is one of Vietnam's oldest.

Making incense in the Mekong Delta.

The importance of incense

Worship in pagodas is informal, as people come and go, chat with the monks, drink tea and present offerings. But nobody visits a pagoda without burning incense. On festival days, packets of joss sticks can be bought outside the pagoda building. One may burn the whole packet or a small number of sticks, depending on the occasion. But the total burnt must add up to an odd number – it is taboo to burn an even number of sticks.

After lighting the incense, worshippers stand in contemplation before the altar for a few moments. They then make respectful bowing movements before placing the burning sticks in a small urn filled with ash.

The rising smoke from the joss sticks symbolises communication with the other world. It allows people to maintain contact with ancestors, ask for wishes to be granted, or act as a thanksgiving to one of the many gods in the Vietnamese religious pantheon.

Chinese influence on Vietnam's culture is reflected in temple architecture, and Chinese characters are common features of religious buildings. Pictured here is the Fujian Assembly Hall in Hoi An, central Vietnam.

Incense offerings are made in the form of joss sticks. They are an essential part of all worship, both in the home and, as here, in temples and pagodas.

A folk music and dance performance in Hoi An.

PERFORMING ARTS

After decades of neglect, Vietnam's traditional performing arts must now compete with more modern forms of entertainment to survive.

The ancient Dong Son bronze drums, which depict dancers performing to the accompaniment of musical instruments, testify to the long-standing importance of musical and dance traditions in Vietnam. For a long time, however, music played an integral part in religious ceremonies and not as a means of public entertainment. It wasn't until much later that music became part of the cultural landscape in a broader sense.

A MUSICAL TRADITION

The majority Kinh or Viet population, and many of Vietnam's 54 ethnic minorities, have a rich musical heritage. Generally Vietnamese music falls into two groups: *dieu bac*, literally northern mode, which exhibits more of a Chinese influence, and *dieu nam*, southern mode, which features the slower tempo and sentimentality of ancient Cham culture.

Folk music takes the form of tunes sung by villagers illustrating their life in the countryside. There are several categories: lullabies, known as *hat ru* in the north, *ru em* in the centre and *au o* in the south; work songs or *ho*; and mushy love songs, known as *ly*.

Perhaps the most important catalyst in the development of contemporary Vietnamese folk entertainment was the appearance of the call-and-response dialogue song, a genre found widely throughout Southeast Asia. Most ethnic minorities have a version of a flirtatious male–female courting game in which boys and girls sing poetic dialogue that tests each other's skills.

QUAN HO

Among the Kinh majority, the call-and-response dialogue song developed into various forms, including the unique Red River Delta art form

Enjoying the music at a traditional house.

known as *quan ho*, a complex and technically demanding style of romantic folk singing. *Quan ho* has close links to the custom of *ket cha* (establishing friendship between villages) in which male and female singers, accompanied by a small traditional music ensemble and sometimes by a small chorus, perform songs interspersed with improvised repartee.

Quan ho is sung a cappella and is characterised by a special vibrato technique called *nay hat*. More than 180 different *quan ho* songs are still performed in around 40 villages in Bac Ninh and Bac Giang provinces. Various *quan ho* festivals are held throughout the region after the Tet festival, the largest and most important being the Hoi Lim Quan Ho festival in Bac Ninh province.

COURT MUSIC

Despite the establishment of an independent Viet kingdom in the 10th century, successive Vietnamese rulers continued to mimic the courtly traditions of their powerful Chinese neighbour. In subsequent centuries, Confucian music and dance traditions were increasingly appropriated from the Chinese imperial court. Court music was also influenced by the music of the old Hindu kingdom of Champa, in the southern part of present-day Vietnam.

Giving a lesson in traditional music.

During the Le dynasty (1428–1527), a system of court music was established. A number of musical categories was invented for different religious and social occasions, although the majority of royal dances functioned as a means to wish the sovereign and his family happiness, prosperity and longevity.

From the turn of the 20th century onwards, the royal court at Hue became increasingly Westernised and, during the reign of French-educated Bao Dai (1926–45), the last of the Nguyen kings, traditional royal music and dances were rarely performed. Since the late 1980s, court music has been revived in the old imperial capital by the Thua Thien Hue Provincial Traditional Arts Company and the Hue Royal Palace Arts Troupe.

CA TRU

One traditional Vietnamese folk art enjoying a revival is *ca tru*, which scholars trace back to a form of music widely performed as an expression of worship during the Ly dynasty (1010–1225). *Ca tru* is often described as sung poetry, but the accompanying music is an integral part of the performance.

A group usually consists of three performers. The singer, always a woman, plays the *phach*, an instrument made of wood or bamboo beaten with two wooden sticks. A musician called *kep* accompanies the singer on the *dan day*, a long-necked lute with three silk strings and 10 frets. There is also a drummer, *trong chau*, who moves with the rhythm of the singer or the songs.

Traditionally, before enjoying the music at a communal house, private home or inn, guests would purchase a stack of bamboo cards. These cards were given to the singers in appreciation of the performance, each singer receiving payment in proportion to the number of cards received. This explains how the name *ca tru* was born. Literally, *tru* means card in Chinese, *ca* means song in Vietnamese, hence the name *ca tru*, or card songs.

Although *ca tru* flourished during the French colonial period, it had shady implications as a geisha-style form of entertainment. Attractive young singers known as *co dau* were assigned to help rich male listeners relax while plying them with drinks and opium.

Because of this sleazy reputation, *ca tru* was suppressed after the August Revolution

⊘ FUNERAL MUSIC

Some genres of Vietnamese music originally evolved as a means of celebrating or marking major life and social events such as marriage, birth and death. Of these, only funeral music is still commonly heard – and it came close to dying itself when the government clamped down on religious and superstitious beliefs in the 1960s.

Now revived as an art form, musicians and singers are hired by grieving families to perform laments at their loved ones funerals. This service is known as khoc thue, which literally means "rented tears". Traditionally only men are allowed to perform, but all-female bands are emerging.

in 1945. In recent years, *ca tru* has been rediscovered and performed at a number of clubs, foremost among which is the Hanoi Ca Tru Club. Besides hosting regular performances, the club organises an annual *ca tru* festival to help promote this traditional art form, which was recognised by UNESCO in 2009 as an Intangible Cultural Heritage.

THEATRE

Vietnam's oldest recorded theatrical performance is *tro he*, a farce created during the Tien Le dynasty (980–1009). During the Tran period (1225–1400), two new types of theatre emerged: *hat giau mat*, masked performances, and *hat coi tran*, coat-less performances. These archaic forms of theatre no longer exist today. Today's varieties – *cheo, hat tuong* and *cai luong* – are a blend of court theatre and folk performances with some foreign influences.

CHEO

Cheo is as old as the Vietnamese nation itself and has been depicted on the engravings of Bronze Age drums and urns. The word "*cheo*" is a distortion of *tieu*, the Chinese word for laughter. Although it hails from and is performed almost exclusively in the north of the country, *cheo* is promoted as a national art form. Generally presented in accordance with conventions laid down in 1501 by a theorist called Luong The Vinh, *cheo* dramas provide a framework within which the players improvise; the troupe is judged according to its ability to vary and reinvent a familiar theme.

Musicians sit to the right of the stage area with drums, gongs, rattles, stringed instruments and a flute. To start the play, someone from the audience beats a large drum. When a performer sings well, this drum will be beaten by a member of the audience to register approval; when the performance is poor, the drum's wooden barrel is struck instead.

Costumes and make-up are simple, in marked contrast to that of *hat tuong*. Characterisation (of stock character types such as the drunk old man, the Confucian scholar, the coquette and the clown) has much in common with that of Italian commedia dell'arte, with interaction between the performers and the audience always an important feature of the action.

In addition to restoring and performing ancient *cheo* classics, the Cheo Theatre in Hanoi also sponsors the writing of new works aimed at rural audiences, many of which relate to contemporary issues such as drug abuse and Aids. Unfortunately, as with their counterparts from other branches of Vietnamese traditional theatre, *cheo* artists have seen their audiences decline significantly in recent years. Many of the country's professional *cheo* companies have been obliged to diversify their activities into more commercial forms of entertainment to survive.

Xylophone at the Temple of Literature, Hanoi.

⊘ RISE AND FALL OF THE CIRCUS

Travelling acrobatic troupes were once a prominent feature of village entertainment in Vietnam. During the French colonial period, professional circus companies from Europe inspired the establishment of local circus troupes, and in the post-war period in the 1950s a number of prestigious Vietnamese groups were established with Soviet aid. In recent years, many provincial troupes have been disbanded and the remaining companies have struggled due to a lack of funds. In areas with strong Chinese connections acrobatic groups still exist, while lion and dragon dances continue to draw crowds, especially during festivals as they are seen as harbingers of good fortune.

HAT TUONG

Unlike *cheo*, which is uniquely Vietnamese, *hat tuong* arrived from China in the 13th century

> *While traditional performing arts have struggled to survive, there is no shortage of willing participants for talent shows, cabaret nights and beauty pageants, all extremely popular with modern audiences.*

Preparation for a cai luong performance.

during the Tran dynasty. An individual named Ly Nguyen Cat – a prisoner of war captured after the defeat of the Mongols – was a master of Chinese theatre who later became a Vietnamese citizen and taught Chinese drama to the Vietnamese court. From China also came make-up, ceremonial costumes, masks, stylised gestures, percussion and wind-instrument music, and the emphasis on heroic and noble themes.

Hat tuong originated as a theatre for the elite. It begins with a song introducing the drama's story-line. Each player describes his character and role. The stage is nearly empty save for symbolic props: a branch represents a forest, a painted wheel stands for a cart. The dramatic action is guided by Confucian moral virtues and concepts – for example, loyalty to kings or devotion to parents. The orchestra sits on the stage's side, accompanying not only the singing but also details of the activity and movement on stage. *Hat tuong* was adapted to the Vietnamese character, with women replacing men in the female roles, and the orchestra was enlarged, incorporating Indian influences from the Cham culture.

Today, the *hat tuong* orchestra includes cymbals, gongs, drums, tambourines, flutes and an arsenal of stringed instruments, including the *dan nhi*, a violin with a high register played by drawing two strings tight over a drum skin, and the *dan bau*, whose single string, stretched over a long lacquered sound box, is both bowed and plucked to produce vibrato effects and long resonances of great subtlety.

CAI LUONG

Cai luong made its first appearance in southern Vietnam in 1920. It interprets classical Chinese stories in a more accessible style. Influenced by the European stage, *cai luong* has evolved into its present spoken-drama form, abandoning the cumbersome epic style in favour of shorter acts, emotional and psychological themes, and free dialogue.

Whilst audiences for other traditional Vietnamese theatre genres have declined over the years, *cai luong* has to a certain extent retained its appeal by continually appropriating elements from contemporary culture, including popular characters, plot scenarios and hit songs.

Today, *cai luong* continues to develop in tandem with Vietnamese spoken drama; indeed many of its leading practitioners are active in both fields. Nowadays the musical accompaniment to *cai luong* takes the form of a mixed ensemble of Vietnamese and Western instruments. There are currently around 30 professional *cai luong* troupes nationwide.

BALLROOM DANCING

One of the few Western art forms to take off in Vietnam is ballroom dancing. Major towns, especially Hanoi, have halls dedicated to couples who want to waltz or tango their way through the night. Waiters sometimes double as dance partners, as there tend to be more women present than men.

PUPPETRY IN MOTION

A visit to one of Vietnam's unique water puppet shows is an entertaining way to get closer to the country's culture and heritage.

During the 11th-century Ly dynasty, before a series of dykes was built, the Red River would swell each year, bursting its banks and flooding much of the region. This annual flooding of the lowlands inspired a form of entertainment that is found only in Vietnam, namely water puppetry (mua roi nuoc).

The flooded paddies were the perfect platform to conceal both the puppeteer and the long bamboo poles used to control the puppet. Gradually, these theatrical events transferred to the small ponds and lakes beside the communal houses (dinh) found in a typical 11th-century Vietnamese village.

Today, the puppeteers still perform in a chest-deep pool of water but behind a curtain on stage. The water is kept deliberately murky so as to obscure the poles and mechanics used to control the puppets, which are protected from the elements by a layer of lacquer. The puppets usually range from 30 to 100cm (12 to 39ins) in height and weigh from 1 to 5kg (2 to 11lbs). Larger puppets can weigh up to 20kg (44lbs) and need four people to manipulate them.

As its origins and themes hark back to farming communities in feudal times, water puppetry is not merely enjoyable theatre, but also portrays part of Vietnamese culture. A performance will consist of 12 to 18 acts, each telling a mythological story about Vietnam and its history, while a small ensemble of traditional musicians and cheo singers provides background music. One story, for example, tells of how a tortoise living in Hanoi's Hoan Kiem Lake supposedly emerged from the depths to provide King Ly Thai To with the sword he needed to fight off Chinese invaders.

WATER PUPPETRY STORIES

Characters can be heroic, legendary or mythical, but most are ordinary peasants with plot lines that tend to be action-oriented as the puppets are unable to convey emotional conflicts. The water's surface also reflects what is taking place: calm and serene when fairies sing and dance, but a heaving tempest when a battle breaks out with fire-spitting dragons.

In an attempt to win over modern-day audiences, some scriptwriters have adjusted traditional plots. The Hong Phong puppet troupe from Hai Duong province, for example, has adapted a story called The Frog Sues Heaven, in which a thief sneaks into a Buddhist pagoda under the cover of a dark and stormy night

Water puppet performance.

and steals antique statues, aiming to sell them to overseas buyers. The thief is caught, and after a quick trial under Article 272 of the Criminal Code he is dispatched to jail for three years.

Water puppetry dropped off the radar during the Vietnam War but was revived in the 1980s. While it took time to redevelop the art form due to a lack of numbers and poor facilities, thanks to Vietnam's booming tourism industry, water puppetry has found its way back onto the stage. In fact, some of the best troupes, such as Thang Long (Hanoi) Water Puppet Theatre, have even become famous outside Vietnam, travelling extensively abroad to stage their amazing shows in dozens of countries including Japan, US, France, Australia and Spain.

ART, CRAFTS AND LITERATURE

The Vietnamese are among the world's most literate and poetic people, and their contemporary crafts and art are popular with collectors around the world.

After decades of obscurity and isolation, Vietnamese artists have started to make inroads into the international arena. Sold in galleries and exhibited in museums worldwide, Vietnamese paintings are routinely featured in auctions of Southeast Asian art at Christie's and Sotheby's.

Much of the work making waves in the international art scene shares a gentle, lyrical quality – rarely is any self-indulgent anger expressed – with styles ranging from figurative to abstract and surrealist, at other times expressionist or realist. The abundance of this impressionist and figurative art is testament to the tenacious influence of Western culture within Vietnam.

PAINTING TRADITIONS

While China, Japan and Korea share long painting histories, Vietnam's artistic tradition emerged during 19th-century French colonial rule. Prior to this time, local artistic achievements had been restricted to decorative arts for religious and communal purposes, with only a limited output of paintings, coloured embossments and silk portraits.

In spite of the largely destructive arrival of the French, new opportunities for creative achievement arose during the colonial period, with painting becoming the most developed artistic expression. Through this Western influx, a unique French–Vietnamese amalgamation of cultures emerged. In 1925, under the initiative of the French painter Victor Tardieu, the École des Beaux-Arts de l'Indochine (EBAI) was founded in Hanoi. Scores of painters and sculptors were schooled in the European tradition during its 20-year existence.

Modern Vietnamese art.

The establishment was responsible for creating the "first generation" of Vietnamese masters, most notable of whom were Nguyen Gia Tri, Nguyen Phan Chanh, To Ngoc Van, Bui Xuan Phai, Nguyen Sang and Nguyen Tu Nghiem.

While the influence of these first graduates was felt in the 1930s, the artistic importance of the last group of notable graduates – Bui Xuan Phai, Nguyen Sang and Nguyen Tu Nghiem – was not apparent until the 1960s and 1970s. While not all of these artists shared the same vision or even style, each shared a desire to champion European modernism while remaining true to their Vietnamese spirit and heritage. Through their innovative use of traditional materials and their depiction of domestic themes in warm colours, all these artists can be accredited with freeing Vietnamese painting from its colonial academism.

These philosophies were then passed on to their students at the Hanoi College of Fine Arts – the EBAI's successor – and the College of Applied Arts in Hanoi. The result is that most Vietnamese painters have their roots, in some way, in the traditional European school of painting.

Apricot Gallery, Hanoi.

⊘ GUARDED AESTHETICS

With Vietnamese art now in the international art market, authorities are ever careful to oversee foreigners' perceptions of the country, and paintings with political overtones opposing the government's ideals are potential firecrackers. Truong Tan is a controversial artist who depicts his own individual sexuality by confronting traditional family values and hierarchy, and some of his work has been confiscated by the government. After rejecting the conservative art scene of the 1990s, he moved to Paris and is now one of Vietnam's most established artists. His paintings from the Dynasty series were included in the Asian exposition at New York's Guggenheim Museum in 2013.

A NEW BEGINNING

After decades of war, isolation and censorship, however, the artistic community was torn apart. Nearly everything, from nudes to abstraction, even impressionism, was banned. It was not until the late 1980s, with increasing openness in economic and cultural intercourse and the overall freeing up of Vietnamese society as a whole, that artistic enterprise began to flourish once again.

Nowhere was this rebirth better captured than in the 1991 exhibition Uncorked Soul, organised by Plum Blossoms Gallery in Hong Kong, the first full-scale post-war show of Vietnamese contemporary art outside of Vietnam. Since then, the art scene has not looked back.

Today, a new generation of artists is emerging, who enjoy more freedom and international recognition than ever before. Artists are also working in more diversified media. You can find experimental performance art, video and installations as well as neo-traditionalists who paint nudes, calligraphy and Chinese-style scrolls.

GALLERIES

Both Hanoi and Ho Chi Minh City are awash with highly commercialised art. With fine Vietnamese art selling for six-figure sums or more in international art circles compared to the US$200 or so it used to fetch two decades ago, it's not surprising that a rash of mediocre Vietnamese artists is trying to cash in on its popularity. The sheer number of art shops can be overwhelming for first-time visitors.

In Hanoi, a number of galleries, such as Art Vietnam (www.artvietnamgallery.com), L'Espace (www.institutfrancais-vietnam.com) and Mai Gallery, regularly showcase the country's finest talents while nurturing some of the most promising emerging artists (check www.hanoigrapevine.com for a list of exhibitions). The art scene in Ho Chi Minh City, traditionally less dynamic than in Hanoi, is now improving, with galleries such as Apricot Gallery (www.apricotgallery.com.vn), Galerie Quynh (www.galeriequynh.com) and Thanh Mai Gallery leading the charge.

CRAFT VILLAGES

In the past, entire Vietnamese villages would have specialised in making certain crafts, such as lacquerware, pottery, parasols, conical hats or fishing nets. In time, the village would become associated with the handicraft it produced. Today, certain villages near Hanoi are synonymous with specific products, for instance Van Phuc for silk, Bat Trang for pottery and Dong Ky for furniture (see page 133).

Vietnamese folk art and crafts declined with the onset of French colonisation at the end of the 19th century. By the end of the 20th century, however, village handicrafts were thriving once again. The emergence of several

Woodcarver in the Old Quarter, Hanoi.

fair trade organisations and business ventures including Craft Link (www.craftlink.com.vn), Au Lac Designs (www.aulacdesigns.com) and Reaching Out (www.reachingoutvietnam.com) has contributed to the revival, preservation and promotion of the Vietnamese crafts. Today, the government recognises 1,500 genuine handicraft villages scattered all over Vietnam. This has helped preserve the villages' cultural heritage and also helped alleviate poverty in rural areas.

POTTERY

One expert summed up the freedom and individualism of the Vietnamese ceramic tradition when he said: "Chinese pottery is good for the eye; Vietnamese pottery is good for the heart." The combination of skilled potting, fine finishing and glazing, as well as free and calligraphic embellishing, are all features typical of the Vietnamese ceramic tradition. While the Chinese potter aims for perfect technique and the Japanese tradition strives for accidentally achieved beauty, the aesthetic appeal of Vietnamese ceramics, which combine informality with great technical skill, lies somewhere between these two.

The most famous and longest-standing pottery village in Vietnam is Bat Trang, which is found just outside Hanoi. Nguyen Trai, a great politician, strategist, diplomat and poet, recorded in the 15th century that Bat Trang had provided 70 sets of bowls and plates as tribute paid to China, proof of the villagers' sophisticated craftwork.

WOODCUT

The best examples of woodcuts are known as Dong Ho paintings, an art form which existed as early as the 11th century during the Ly dynasty. At first the prints were limited to black and white, but after the 15th century colour was introduced. The village craftsmen make their own paper and natural colours, and prepare the blocks in variations of classic motifs depicting good luck, historical figures and battles, spirits, as well as popular allegories and social commentary.

Good fortune is symbolised by a corpulent pig decorated with garlands, often accompanied by a litter of suckling piglets. A hen surrounded by chicks symbolises prosperity. The cockerel, herald of the dawn, is the symbol of peace and courage. Social criticism is expressed by caricatures of mandarins, represented by croaking frogs and rats marching with drums and trumpets.

LACQUERWARE

Lacquered wood objects have been found in tombs dating from the 3rd century AD. Today, lacquerware *(son mai)* – including paintings, screens, boxes, vases and trays – has become a relatively lucrative export item. Its quality is a result of the meticulous attention given to the preparation of the lacquer and to the designs of a 1,000-year-old tradition. However, most of the lacquerware sold in the tourist centres is mass-produced and not very durable.

Lacquer is prepared from the resin of the *cay son*, or lacquer tree, which is collected in the same way as latex (from the rubber tree). The resin is then diluted with water and the dark-brown surface layer known as *oil lac* is skimmed off. Two types of lacquer are used. Varnish lacquer is obtained by mixing lacquer resin with *mu* oil, while pumice lacquer, a higher-quality and more durable form, is produced by mixing lacquer resin with pine resin. Unlike varnish lacquer, it is rubbed and smoothed in water after painting to bring out a high gloss finish. With the addition of various ingredients and dyes, including mother of pearl, bone and eggshell

> *The works of Vietnam's artists are becoming less homogeneous and more complex and experimental, ensuring their future in Asia's vibrant art scene.*

Lacquer trays make interesting souvenirs for the home.

⊘ FASHION FORWARD

Vietnam's rich source of materials, textiles and skilled workers provides the raw materials for the country's growing fashion and design scene. Young local designers fuse Vietnamese heritage with Western influences to come up with unique designs. French-Vietnamese designer Linda Mai Phung travels to the most remote parts of Vietnam looking for inspiration and materials. Her award winning handmade, eco-friendly collections promote local Vietnamese textiles and artisanship, blending it with cutting-edge design. Foreign designers, too, are muscling in. Hong Kong-born Christina Yu, founder of Ipa-Nima, is one of the most successful foreign designers to have relocated to Vietnam.

fragments, this is used for the upper layer of lacquer paintings.

HOME ACCESSORIES

A community of Vietnamese and locally based foreign designers has created a vibrant scene in this area. Homeowners will be spoilt for choice with the range of home accessories that combine Asian accents and local materials like wood, silk, lacquer and bamboo with modern design.

Boutique stores in Ho Chi Minh City, Hanoi and Hoi An sell contemporary products – luxurious cushion covers, silk lamps, vases, candle stands and the like – that mesh seemingly disparate colours, materials and styles.

THE LITERARY SCENE

From the *Tale of Kieu* – practically Vietnam's national text – to more recent and controversial works, Vietnamese literature has a rich tradition.

Classical Vietnamese literature has been fed by the country's seemingly endless wealth of oral storytelling traditions – comprising myths, songs, legends, folk and fairy tales. These stories, passed from one generation to the other, are imaginative and captivating, funny and sometimes tragic.

Nearly every Vietnamese reads and remembers the *Tale of Kieu*, a 3,254-verse story published over 200 years ago. During the 19th century it would have been circulated orally in the villages. Today, pupils begin studying it in the sixth grade. *Kieu* was written by one of Vietnam's most respected writers, Nguyen Du (1765–1820). What makes the book as relevant today as it was two centuries ago is Nguyen Du's ability to lay bare the whole spectrum of society. Vices and virtues, ugliness and beauty, nobility and trickery – all are entangled in a seemingly hopeless tragic comedy reflecting the face of Vietnam.

By the time *Tale of Kieu* had become entrenched in the psyche of the Vietnamese people, the French had already colonised their country. During the early half of the 20th century, the Romanised Vietnamese script called *quoc ngu* grew popular. As the literary traditions of France and the rest of Europe became more accessible, Vietnamese literature was enriched with new ideas of Western thought and culture.

One of the finest Vietnamese novels of this era is *Dumb Luck*, a sharp satire on modernisation in Vietnam during the late colonial era. Written by Vu Trong Phung and first published in 1936, it follows the absurd and unexpected rise within colonial society of a street-smart vagabond named Red-Haired Xuan.

During the Vietnam War, writers mostly restricted themselves to penning stories that were meant to unify and inspire people. After the war ended in 1975, Communist Party cadres controlled publishing; even today, government censors must approve writings before publication. In the 1980s authors and poets often used analogy and parody to evade censorship and publish stories that would send ripples of amusement and scandal through the reading public.

Some authors did not skirt around the issue. Duong Thu Huong's anti-establishment novels were banned in Vietnam and she was even placed under house arrest. In 2006, the writer moved to France where she published her most recent novel, *The Zenith* (2012). Dubbed the *Dr Zhivago* of Vietnam, it imagines the final days of Ho Chi Minh and deconstructs his myth. Nguyen Huy Thiep's 1987 short story, *The General Retires*, about the emptiness of Vietnamese society, generated much criticism, with some heatedly denouncing its author on moral grounds. In the early

Vietnamese author Duong Thu Huong.

1990s, *The Sorrow of War*, written by a Vietnamese War veteran under the pseudonym of Bao Ninh, was the first war novel to confront the gruesome realities of armed conflict and the psychological effects upon soldiers. *Ruy* – an autobiographical novel by Montreal-based Kim Thuy – was translated into 15 languages and became a worldwide bestseller in 2012. It is a moving account of the author's flight from war-torn Vietnam to Canada, and brims with emotions, metaphors and deep reflections on war and life.

Despite interest in Vietnamese literature, the lack of English-language translations limits readership. Wayne Karlin, a Vietnam veteran and author, has translated numerous modern works. Together with Ho Anh Thai he edited the *Love after War*.

Hue "royal" cuisine.

VIETNAMESE CUISINE

Piquant rather than fiery, uncommonly healthy Vietnamese food practically dances on your palate with its distinctive mix of sweet and sour, zesty and herbal accents.

Vietnam's cuisine reflects not only its geographical position but also the country's contacts with other cultures over the centuries. From China in the north came the use of chopsticks, the art of stir-frying in a hot wok and the widespread consumption of noodles. From the streets of Paris came freshly baked baguettes (banh mi) and pâté as well as the art of sautéing and the use of meats such as beef.

Despite these influences, Vietnamese cuisine has retained its distinctive character. Thanks to an abundance of fresh local ingredients, it has formed its own flavours and nuances with wonderfully contrasting textures and colours. The national dish may be *pho* noodles, but the seafood found along the coastline is just as tempting and the coconut-influenced dishes of the south have a distinctive edge.

CULINARY DIVIDES

The Mekong Delta and Red River Delta have been described by Vietnamese as the great rice baskets on either end of a bamboo pole. The Red River Delta provides rice and vegetables for north Vietnam, while the fertile Mekong Delta produces rice and an amazing variety of fruits and vegetables for the southern and central regions.

To add flavour to the abundance of fresh food available, Vietnamese cooks use a riot of fresh herbs such as lemongrass, basil, coriander, mint and parsley – as well as garlic, lime, star anise and ginger. In general, as Vietnamese chefs use spices sparingly, its food is milder than that of Thailand and Cambodia.

Vietnamese cuisine varies greatly from one region to the other. Northern food tends to be blander, and uses fewer spices and herbs. In central Vietnam, the food can be a bit spicier.

Fried spring rolls, cha gio, are popular appetisers.

Ⓞ HERBS AND VEGETABLES

Vietnam is blessed with a bounty of fresh veg and herbs that are often served with *pho* noodles, spring rolls and other dishes. Collectively referred to as *rau thom* ("leafy fragrant"), mint, marjoram, bean sprouts, coriander, purple perilla, sawtooth herb and dill are likely to be found, as well as good old-fashioned lettuce and other temperate vegetables grown in the cooler highlands. Tourists are understandably nervous about eating raw greens in Vietnam, so pick a restaurant that looks clean and is well patronised. *Rau thom* adds an explosion of flavours when mixed into your food.

Southern cooking, familiar to Westerners who have eaten in Vietnamese restaurants overseas, tends to be more flavourful and robust.

Many northerners complain they cannot eat southern food, claiming that southern cooks

> There is a local expression that goes "Eating alone hurts". Meal times are very much a communal affair in Vietnam.

Banh xeo, a savoury pancake made from rice flour, corn flour and egg.

dump sugar into everything. This is not entirely true: sugar is used in southern cooking, in dishes such as *pho*, but not in great amounts, and coconut milk is often used to round out the flavours.

Equally, southerners will moan about northern food. The south has one essential advantage: better access to fresh fruit and vegetables. There is a wider variety of food grown in the south and the growing seasons are longer.

SIGNATURE DISHES

Northerners and southerners can also argue endlessly over who has the best *pho*, Vietnam's signature noodle dish. A Hanoian will complain

that the *pho* of Ho Chi Minh City is too sweet, while someone from Ho Chi Minh City will complain that Hanoi's broth is too bland. Nonetheless, with a large Vietnamese diaspora scattered throughout Asia, Europe, Australia and the USA, the clear but subtle flavours of this simple and intoxicatingly delicious dish are known throughout the world.

Pronounced *fuh*, this noodle soup can be eaten for breakfast or as a late-night snack. Steaming hot broth is poured over a bowl of rice noodles topped with chicken or beef, fresh herbs and onion. Sometimes, a raw egg yolk is added, and Vietnamese might also add lime juice, hot peppers, chilli sauce or vinegar to liven up the dish. It is usually served with *quay* – a deep-fried piece of flour dough and a side dish of *rau thom* (see page 87).

Based on literary accounts, *pho* surfaced sometime after the French occupation of Hanoi in the mid-1880s. While its roots remain the subject of debate, there is compelling evidence that it sprang from an unlikely marriage of Chinese and French culinary influences. It is said the French popularised the use of bones and lesser cuts of beef to make the broth, which forms the base of the soup. Some say that *pho* was devised by Vietnamese who learned to make *pot-au-feu* for their French employers. The theory goes that the name actually comes from the French *feu*.

The other great Vietnamese staple is *nuoc mam* (fish sauce), which is used as an ingredient as well as a dipping sauce for dishes such

⊘ DOG MEAT

Dog, snake and turtle occasionally end up on Vietnamese menus, but as these places are often situated on the outskirts of town or in the countryside, tourists hardly notice them. None of these meats are everyday fare and, typically, friends will choose to eat at such an establishment to celebrate a special occasion.

Dog-meat *(thit cho)* consumption is generally more widespread during wintertime in the north, but you can find it throughout Vietnam. It is believed to aid sexual potency: older men eat dog meat in the belief that it will boost virility while young men like to gather at a dog-meat restaurant before a night on the town.

as spring rolls or *banh xeo* pancakes. *Nuoc mam* has a pungent aroma and biting saltiness that is an acquired taste, but it's the perfect complement to the subtle flavours of the

> Drinking alcohol is still a predominantly male pursuit in Vietnam. Boisterous locals raise a toast by saying "Tram phan tram" (100 percent), which means "Drink it in one!"

most popular dishes is *ca kho to* – catfish fillet with slices of coconut served in a clay pot and glazed with a rich, caramelised sauce.

Restaurant menus tend to be dominated by meat, fish and seafood. However, there are plenty of delicious options for vegetarians, too, such as stir-fried spinach with garlic, crunchy green (unripe) papaya salad, or tofu served in a variety of styles. Fried rice may be cooked with pork or squid, so it's best for non-meat-eaters to declare *"toi an chay"* (I'm a vegetarian) when ordering.

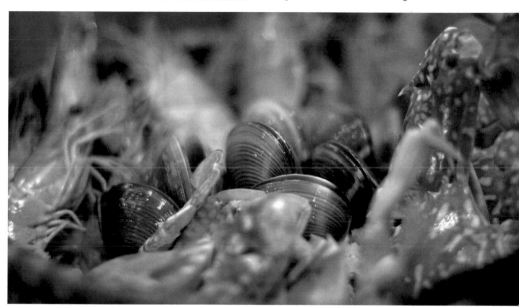

Seafood platter.

food. Produced in coastal cities such as Phan Thiet and Phu Quoc, fish sauce is made by fermenting anchovies and salt in large wooden barrels for about six months. For more, see page 310.

SEAFOOD GALORE

Vietnam's 3,000km (1,800-mile) coastline and numerous rivers and waterways provide an ample supply of fresh fish and seafood all year round. Crabs, prawns, lobsters and squid are often simply boiled or steamed and served with a dip of salt, lemon and chilli. Fresh- and saltwater fish are usually steamed in a hotpot or boiled in a broth in which the flavours mingle with the vegetables and herbs. One of the

⊘ CHANGING TIMES

With so many fresh vegetables, a wealth of fresh herbs, minimal use of oil, and the use of meat as a condiment rather than a main course, Vietnamese food is healthy. Inevitably, however, as elsewhere in the world, the younger generation has a taste for mass-produced Western hamburgers and pizzas. Fast-food chains are everywhere in Hanoi and Ho Chi Minh City. Offering free Wi-Fi and air conditioning, they are seen by young Vietnamese as hip places to hang out. A taste for burgers is also seen as an urbane trait in a country where older generations are notoriously reluctant to try foreign food.

FAMILY AFFAIR

Rice, or *com*, is the mainstay of a Vietnamese meal. A typical lunch or dinner for a Vietnamese family will almost always feature steaming bowls of rice accompanied by a few side dishes. It is so much part of the cuisine that people refer to both lunch and dinner simply as *com*.

Wherever you are in Vietnam, a standard meal will consist of rice plus a meat or fish dish, stir-fried vegetables and a bowl of soup (*canh*). The soup, usually a light, sour broth with vegetables and sometimes seafood, is used to wash down the rice. Also on the table will be various dipping sauces, including soy sauce, salt moistened with lime juice and the ubiquitous fish sauce. Each dish will have its own particular dipping sauce. For example, duck will be dipped in soy sauce, chicken in salt with lime, and pork in fish sauce.

While you can find Vietnamese desserts such as *che*, a sweet bean dessert served in cafés and restaurants, there is no real post-dinner dessert culture in Vietnam. It is most likely your meal

Tucking into pho with all the trimmings.

⊘ VIETNAMESE RESTAURANTS

There's a wide choice of places to eat in Vietnamese cities. Whether you opt for budget meals or high-class dining, the quality will generally be high. Starting with the simplest variety, you can join locals as they pull up a plastic stool at roadside stalls that offer quintessential *pho* (noodle soup). Each of the small tables will have a mix of chillies, bean sprouts, mint and basil that diners add according to their own tastes.

Food markets are ideal places to find cheap and tasty snacks. Each usually has a collection of small restaurants selling everything from freshly baked baguettes to pickled vegetables. As well as roadside stalls, there are hundreds of basic restaurants with bare floors and grey concrete walls that specialise in noodles, and more sophisticated restaurants that focus on local cuisine and cater for wealthy locals and tourists. Street food can be bought from 7am to 10pm in most towns, while restaurants tend to open from 7am to 9pm. For more on street food see page 92.

More upmarket restaurants in the main cities offer ambient settings and a mix of styles, from local to Indian, Thai and French. Service in such places is often far friendlier than in the cheaper, roadside spots. Most restaurants will not have English menus but many have photos of the food, and fellow diners are usually happy to recommend a dish to visitors.

will finish off with a platter of fresh fruit, such as watermelon or dragon fruit.

A great way to enjoy a shared dining experience is a hotpot (*lau*) or steamboat meal. This

---

If you are invited to a wedding, funeral or festival, there will usually be two main courses, one salty and the other sweet. A typical feast will include meatballs, local sausages, chicken stew and a salad.

DIY feast includes plates of assorted meats or seafood, and fresh vegetables and noodles, which are added to a communal pot of boiling broth at the diner's discretion. Vietnamese can sit over a hotpot for hours, adding more stock and ingredients, while chatting and clinking glasses throughout the evening.

MUST-EAT DISHES

Apart from pho and other staples mentioned earlier in the chapter, here are some Vietnamese specialities visitors are likely to encounter.

Banh cuon: rice-flour crêpes stuffed with pork, mushrooms, onion and coriander, and topped with fried onions, alongside fresh herbs and fish sauce.

Banh flan: a delicious dessert with a strong French influence, it is sometimes known as banh caramel. It strongly resembles crème caramel, though the Vietnamese version occasionally substitutes the caramel with black coffee.

Banh khoai: a rice- and corn-flour and egg pancake filled with pork or shrimp, onions, bean sprouts and mushrooms. A Hue speciality.

Banh mi thit/pate/trung: baguette served with either *thit* (meat), pâté or eggs, along with sliced carrots, coriander and other fresh herbs.

Banh xeo: a rice-flour pancake studded with shrimp and crunchy bean sprouts.

Bit tet: Vietnamese beefsteak served in thick gravy with a fresh baguette, French fries and salad.

Bo luc lac: stir-fried beef cubes and onions served over greens and tomatoes. Usually eaten with rice.

Bun bo: a Hue speciality of fried beef, served over noodles with coriander, onion, garlic, cucumber, chillies and tomato paste.

Bun cha: charcoal-grilled minced pork patties or strips of lean pork, served in a bowl of *nuoc cham* with cold rice noodles. While ubiquitous in the north, *bun cha* is rarely found in the south.

Cha gio (often called *nem Saigon* in the north): small rolls of minced pork, prawn, crab meat, mushrooms and vegetables wrapped in thin rice paper and deep-fried until crisp. *Cha gio*

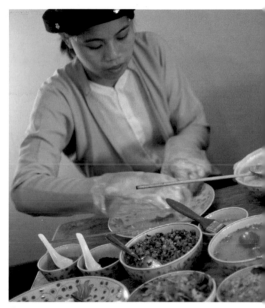
Preparing banh cuon.

is rolled in a lettuce leaf with fresh herbs and dipped in *nuoc cham*.

Che: a popular dessert, made with sticky rice and beans. Often sold in plastic containers, it comes in several varieties, depending on the type of bean that is used.

Ga or **muc xao sa ot:** sautéed chicken or squid with lemongrass, fish sauce, garlic, onion and chillies.

Goi cuon: a cold spring roll of vermicelli, prawns, pork and herbs wrapped in rice paper. It sometimes appears on English menus as "summer rolls".

Mi quang: a complex noodle dish that features strong, opposing flavours mixed with vegetables, rice and herbs.

📷 STREET FOOD

To experience satisfying Vietnamese cuisine as the locals do, head to an inexpensive street market stall.

Hanoi and Ho Chi Minh City have numerous upmarket restaurants with flickering candles and soft music, but the tastiest food is often found outside at the street stalls. It may look basic, with little more than plastic stools and knee-high tables, but Vietnamese street food nearly always delivers. Vendors normally operate from early morning to late evening.

Roadside shacks are found in almost every town and offer quick and simple dishes – a bowl of steaming noodles or a beef stew filled with vegetables. Also ubiquitous are sliced and diced pineapples, mangos and guavas. For those who just want a drink, Vietnam's café culture extends to the street: pull up a stool and wait for the thick, rich coffee to come. For those who want something more filling, the list of options is immense.

Most vendors have the names of their wares printed on their carts. Among the most popular options are bite-size snacks that are deep-fried or grilled. The nation's favourite noodles, *pho*, or snacks such as *ca vien* (fish balls on a stick) are packed with flavour.

Each region has its own culinary quirk. In the north, dishes such as *bun cha*, sliced pork with vermicelli, are famous. In the central provinces, the best-known snack is *banh bao*, a soft, dumpling-like creation. Down south, the use of coconut milk and lime juice is more in evidence. Hu tieu mi, a mass of noodles and vegetables, is a classic southern dish, as is *banh bot chien* (nothing to do with dogs!), a fried rice-flour cake.

Street food is generally safe to eat, but the normal rules apply: go for ice cubes, not the crushed variety, and remember that fruits you can peel have been less exposed to germs than those that have been laid out in the open for hours.

Ca vien, prawn balls, along with assorted street food.

Street food seller in Hanoi.

Banh mi, xuo xich, warmed baguette stuffed with sausage, sliced cucumber and covered in fish sauce.

Crowded roadside tables in the Old City, Hanoi.

Table manners

Chopsticks are commonly used throughout Vietnam. Correct eating etiquette involves holding the bottom of the bowl with your left hand so it is near your face, then using the chopsticks in the right hand to shovel in the noodles or rice. Any other method may result in bemused stares from locals. Other dishes require a fork and spoon, with the spoon held in the right hand.

As with most Asian cultures, avoid sticking your chopsticks upright into a bowl of rice as this is thought to resemble incense sticks at a funeral and so has connotations of death. If you are a guest, be sure to leave some food on your plate. And lastly, you don't need a litre of water at the ready when eating Vietnamese food, as it is far less spicy than other Asian cuisines.

...anh cuon nhan thit, soft spring rolls filled with pork with ...sweet chilli sauce.

...o, the classic Vietnamese noodle dish.

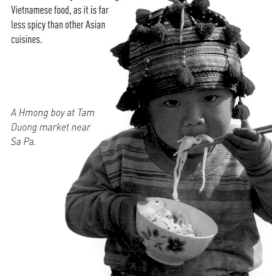

A Hmong boy at Tam Duong market near Sa Pa.

ARCHITECTURE

Vietnamese urban architecture is a wonderful blend of Chinese, colonial and socialist influences. There are also Buddhist pagodas and Khmer temples plus vestiges of the fallen Cham civilisation.

According to the architect William S. Logan, Vietnamese cultural and national survival came about through "bending with the wind". Throughout its history Vietnam has assimilated the cultures of invading countries while preserving its own traditions. As a result, architecture in Vietnam is "characteristically multi-layered" – each layer is an example of the external powers' cultural and political influence.

The Chinese, the ancient Chams and Khmers, the French and the Russians have all made an indelible impression on Vietnam with their distinctive architectural styles. Today, Western architecture makes its presence felt in the urban centres of Hanoi and Ho Chi Minh City, where luxury high-rise offices and apartments are sprouting.

THE CHINESE STAMP

There is no escaping the Chinese influence on Vietnamese architecture: the string of Vietnamese dynasties that ruled from the 10th to the 19th centuries all incorporated Chinese influences into their buildings. Some of the best examples of Chinese architecture are found in Hanoi, founded in 1010 by King Ly Thai To, who constructed a new citadel according to Chinese principles. In 2009, the foundations of several royal palace buildings, a drainage system, wells and thousands of artefacts were discovered when construction work on a new National Assembly House began.

Perhaps the most significant Chinese-style building of this period is the Temple of Literature (Van Mieu), established in Hanoi in 1070 in honour of Confucius. The original structure was demolished in the 19th century to make way for a royal temple, which in turn was razed in 1946

Nine Dynastic Urns at the restored Pavilion of Splendour at the Imperial City in Hue.

during fighting with the French, and rebuilt later in the 20th century according to the original specifications.

The old imperial capital of Hue is another treasure trove of Chinese architecture. When Nguyen Anh took the throne as Emperor Gia Long in 1802 he transferred the royal seat of government to Hue. In 1805 he set about constructing the new royal citadel on the north bank of the Huong (Perfume) River. Stylistically, the Imperial City is a reasonably faithful copy of Beijing's Forbidden City. By 1975 only 20 of the original 148 palaces and buildings were left standing. What remained was still sufficiently magnificent for the Imperial City to be recognised as a Unesco World Heritage Site in 1993. Since 1996, significant progress has been made in restoring the surviving monuments. The largest restoration project, worth over $57 million, was started in 2014 and is planned to last for 8 years.

Another repository of Chinese architecture is found at Hoi An, another Unesco World Heritage Site in central Vietnam. Settled by a Chinese community in the 15th century, the historic town was a thriving port that was regularly visited by ships from all over Europe and Asia. The town features Chinese temples, assembly halls and traditional houses. Japanese traders also constructed wooden temples and homes in the town. While most of these have now disappeared, a Japanese-style bridge acts as a reminder of Hoi An's past. A handful of the merchant houses display an interesting blend of Chinese, Japanese and Vietnamese styles, and many of the town's pagodas also have similar influences.

CHAM RUINS AND KHMER PAGODAS

The Champa kingdom was established in central Vietnam in the 2nd century, and for about 1,000 years, from the 5th to the 15th centuries, Cham rulers presided over an extraordinary renaissance of Hindu art and architecture. What is left of the Champa kingdom is mainly in the form of brick temples and towers scattered over the coastal lowlands and some inland areas. There are several outstanding Cham sites, but the most famous is My Son in Quang Nam province. My Son, which served as the spiritual and intellectual capital of the Champa kingdom, is considered to be the Cham equivalent to the grand cities of Southeast Asia's other Indian-influenced civilisations, like Angkor in Cambodia, Pagan in Myanmar and Ayuthaya in Thailand. In 2015 India allotted $2.5m for My Son restoration. The works are scheduled to last until 2020.

At one time, the mighty Khmer empire stretched across modern Cambodia, Thailand, Laos and Vietnam. Ancient Khmer architecture has survived unscathed in parts of southern Vietnam, and the sparkling golden roofs of elaborate Khmer pagodas can be found across the Mekong Delta, especially in the former Khmer stronghold of Soc Trang province. Its 18th-century Kh'leng Pagoda is especially striking.

FRENCH URBAN PLANNING

The origins of Vietnam's contemporary architecture can be traced to the arrival of the French colonialists. Before the 19th century, the main building material used in Vietnamese architecture was wood. The French brought modern materials and technology as well as ambitious plans for urban redevelopment in Saigon and Hanoi as part of its *mission civilisatrice* (civilising mission).

Towards the end of 19th century, the French began developing both cities' commerce and infrastructure by reclaiming land and

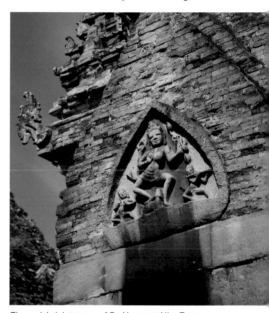

The red-brick towers of Po Nagar at Nha Trang.

⊘ A SENSE OF BALANCE

When it comes to architecture, Vietnamese people strongly believe in the principles of *feng shui*, or *phong thuy* as it's known in Vietnamese. New construction (the first dig of a building) must commence on an auspicious date on the lunar calendar that is decided after consultation with a *feng shui* master. Entire villages have been developed according to these principles.

Another Chinese-style belief relates to numbers: modern Vietnamese office or apartment blocks frequently omit the number four when naming floors as tu (four) sounds like the Sino-Vietnamese word for death.

constructing roads and waterways. This transplanted European urban model came with the attendant neoclassical public buildings, a grand opera house, tree-lined boulevards, parks and generous squares. Today, a stroll down Trang Tien Street in Hanoi or Dong Khoi Street in Ho Chi Minh City will give you a sense of the French architectural vision.

Another legacy from the French was the numerous churches and cathedrals that were built to spread the Catholic faith. The Notre Dame Cathedral in Ho Chi Minh City, built

roof canopies, verandas, patios and ventilation holes, helping to keep the essentially Western-style buildings warm in winter, cool in summer, and to provide protection from the heavy rainfalls and tropical sunshine, while allowing sufficient air circulation.

Vildieu built the Presidential Palace of Vietnam, located beside the Ho Chi Minh Mausoleum, between 1900 and 1906 to house the French governor-general of Indochina. From the outside, the palace is pointedly European; the only visual cues that you are still in Vietnam

A curious amalgam of styles at the Phat Diem Cathedral.

between 1877 and 1883, is a superb example of classical French colonial architecture. Remarkably, every single stone used in its creation was shipped from France. Many of these places of worship are pink in colour, including the distinctive Danang Cathedral, or Con Ga, and Tan Dinh Church in Ho Chi Minh City, known locally as the Pink Church.

EAST MEETS WEST

Auguste-Henri Vildieu, the official French architect for Vietnam at the start of the 20th century, imposed traditional oriental architectural features on Western structures. He adapted European design to the climatic conditions of Hanoi, incorporating long lobbies, thick walls,

are the mango trees growing on the grounds. When Vietnam achieved independence in 1954, Ho Chi Minh refused to live in this grand structure. Instead, a traditional Vietnamese stilt house overlooking a carp pond was built on the grounds to accommodate the president.

Ernest Hébrard, who was appointed head of the Indochina Architecture and Town Planning Service in 1923, later continued developing this "Indochinese" style of architecture. By the 1940s, this style would be apparent in the designs of residential housing.

Another striking edifice fusing cross-cultural design is the late 19th-century Phat Diem Cathedral in Ninh Binh province near Hanoi. This is an extraordinary example of an eclectic architectural style. Designed by a Vietnamese priest, Father Sau, who rallied the local population to build the cathedral, the roof is in the style of a pagoda while the walls are those of a Western church. The interior walls are filled with Catholic iconography but also, curiously enough, Eastern religious symbols such as dragons, unicorns, tortoises and phoenixes.

In Vietnam's larger cities, shopfronts often alternative between old Chinese-style wooden shutters and smart, modern, glass-fronted units that are further proof of how varied Vietnamese architecture has become. On the downside, modern Vietnamese architects seem to favour bland blocks of concrete.

SOVIET INFLUENCES

One of the most important pre-Reunification architectural projects in Hanoi was the Ho Chi Minh Mausoleum, designed by Nguyen Ngoc Chan. Constructed between 1969 and 1975, it successfully combines Soviet-style realism with the simplicity of ethnic minority architecture.

In the wake of Reunification, all efforts were focused on the need to re-establish the national infrastructure. Many new public buildings were constructed in monumental Soviet style during the 1970s and 1980s, their design intended to reflect the power of the state and its ideology. The Ho Chi Minh Museum in Hanoi and the Hoa Binh Theatre in Ho Chi Minh City are among the most significant buildings dating from this period.

MODERN TIMES

Since the turn of the 21st century, the Vietnamese economy has by and large been buoyant. In major urban centres like Hanoi, Ho Chi Minh City, Danang and Haiphong, a rash of high-end shopping malls, office and apartment complexes has been built to accommodate Vietnam's business community and the newly minted rich. Modern villas built to house Vietnam's growing middle class have mushroomed, sometimes resulting in a garish clash of Vietnamese and Western architectural styles.

To meet the demand for premium office and retail space, several large building projects including Keangnam Hanoi complex, Lotte Hanoi Centre and Bitexco Tower (in Ho Chi Minh City) have been realised. High taxes on the frontages of townhouses have had an unexpected

side-effect – the creation of unusual, long, thin properties that became known as "tube houses". Examples of these are particularly common in Hanoi and Hoi An. Their French-style balconies

> In congested Vietnamese urban areas and towns, families will utilise the rooftop as a garden, which offers some respite from the din of the traffic below.

Ho Chi Minh Mausoleum.

would look rather appealing, were it not for the giant iron security gates that tend to be attached to such homes to prevent break-ins.

Real-estate prices in Vietnam's urban centres reached ridiculous levels by 2007, with some commercial areas in Ho Chi Minh City costing around US$180,000 per square metre – more than their equivalent in Hollywood. Spiralling inflation and high interest rates brought prices back down to a more realistic level, but since 2014 the property market has once again livened up, boosted by a package of government incentives including a game-changing law (effective since July 2015) allowing foreigners with a valid visa to buy houses and apartments in Vietnam as well as sub-lease, trade or inherit them.

Spectacular Halong Bay.

Ban Gioc Waterfall spans the Vietnam-China border.

Picturesque Hue and the Perfume River.

Phu Quoc Island.

INTRODUCTION

A detailed guide to the entire country, with principal sights cross-referenced by number to the accompanying maps.

Cu Chi tunnels.

Given the decades of war and destruction, you may be forgiven for imagining that Vietnam's infrastructure is not going to be set up for travellers. However, although the delays and red tape can be tiring, the rewards are immense.

In today's Vietnam the remnants of war have become tourist attractions rather than eyesores. The scars and memorials are a now a part of the country's tourism pull, whether you're burrowing into the depths of the Cu Chi tunnels near Ho Chi Minh City (formerly Saigon) or viewing the rusting heaps of war-time hardware at Hanoi's Military History Museum. The vestiges of a more remote past, from Champa ruins and Hue's imperial city to the elegant colonial streets of Hanoi, are a major lure, as are the glorious natural attractions – from a coastline of powder-soft beaches to the impressive forested mountains.

On the river at Tam Coc.

Northern Vietnam's signature city is Hanoi, an appealing place full of the old villas and facades of the French colonial era which give it a unique ambience. Farther on, the pancake-flat Red River Delta is bordered on the east by the Gulf of Tonkin, where the fabled limestone islands of Halong Bay sit. Beyond the delta's plains, cooler mountain regions, populated by hill tribes, ascend towards the west and Laos and northwards towards China.

Heading south, the country narrows through a chain of increasingly tropical provinces washed by the warm waters of the South China Sea. In the old Imperial City of Hue, a sense of the past pervades, carried over into the nearby town of Hoi An. In the lands of the ancient Champa kingdom further south are decaying temples that testify to the conquest by the Viet people from the north. And all along the serpentine coast are stretches of largely undeveloped white-sand beaches lapped by aquamarine waters.

Beyond the resort of Dalat in the picturesque southern highlands is Ho Chi Minh City, Vietnam's vibrant commercial centre. The far south is dominated by the Mekong Delta, an extensive area of farms and orchards and numerous waterways best explored by boat. Offshore are the newly touristed islands of Phu Quoc and, further east, the Con Dao archipelago.

Vietnam

Lanterns of all colours.

NORTHERN VIETNAM

Home to many of Vietnam's foremost attractions, the north offers jagged mountain ranges and a picturesque coast, as well as the historic capital city of Hanoi.

Ceremonial headgear of the Dao minority.

For those hankering to experience dramatic scenery and colourful ethnic groups, northern Vietnam ticks all the boxes. While parts of the region rush headlong towards modernisation, with many communities becoming increasingly aware of tourist lucre, the north remains a traditionalist stronghold.

Encapsulating the bewildering blend of modernity and traditionalism, Hanoi – the country's political and administrative centre – is the ideal place to start any journey. Always evolving, the 1,000-year-old city's fortunes are reflected in the architecture of its many temples and pagodas, in the lingering presence of a French colonial past, and in the whir of construction as luxury high-rise buildings emerge in old neighbourhoods.

Beyond Hanoi lie timelessly sedate and picturesque provincial regions, where the waters of the Red River (Song Hong) feed brilliant-green rice paddies and fruit orchards. In small, far-flung villages, groves of trees and bamboo enclose modest communities where life revolves around the local communal house and pagoda, and where traditions continue as they have for centuries. In other areas, factories and large-scale assembly plants have sprouted like weeds, providing livelihoods for workers but polluting the local environment and appropriating farmlands.

Mai Chau farm.

On the eastern coast, in the Gulf of Tonkin, is the busy port of Haiphong, gateway to the breathtaking scenery of Halong Bay. The city is recognised as a Unesco World Heritage Site and is famous for its dramatic, mist-shrouded seascape of limestone cliffs and caves. Farther east is the Tonkin Coast, which is speckled with national parks, ancient sites and more beaches.

The highlands of the northern interior are home to several ethnic minority peoples, many of whom live high in the mountains and farm on stunning terraced fields. In Lao Cai province, the picturesque hill retreat of Sa Pa has become famous as a high-altitude getaway with treks into minority villages and homestays in stilt houses, though here more than anywhere the presence of tourists is starting to influence traditional ways of life.

Hanoi Opera House.

HANOI

Brimming with a complex history yet full of modern energy and potential, Hanoi is an attractive and enjoyable city, and a great place to get the measure of 21st-century Vietnam.

For decades the bastion of Vietnamese ideology and conservatism, Hanoi is fast becoming a modern, thriving city: luxury shopping malls and apartments now sit alongside 200-year-old temples, while trendy coffee shops line busy streets. A master plan for the development of Hanoi adopted by the government hopes to turn the Vietnamese capital into a cosmopolitan city on par with London, New York, Moscow or Tokyo by 2050. The results of the hectic growth are already visible with buildings such as the National Assembly House, the new terminal (T2) and further upgrade of terminal 1 at the international airport, the cable-stayed Nhat Tan (Friendship) Bridge and the Keangnam and Lotte Hanoi Centre skyscrapers swiftly becoming new landmarks in the capital.

Despite the changes, Hanoians are passionate about protecting their age-old traditions and culture, and a number of works have been announced to preserve important historic sites. The French-influenced architecture and an abundance of trees and lakes give Hanoi a romantic air. Hanoi may be the Vietnamese capital, but it is far smaller than its southern counterpart Ho Chi Minh City, and thus far easier to navigate. From the charismatic French Quarter to the various parks and open spaces, Hanoi's appeal is instant.

Traffic near Hoan Kiem Lake.

Its long history also means that several major historical attractions are based here, including the Ho Chi Minh Mausoleum and several war museums.

Hanoi is a relatively small capital, with an urban population of over 3.4 million. However, in August 2008, the government announced that the city boundaries had been expanded to swallow up the entire province of Ha Tay and Me Linh District in Vinh Phuc province, as well as four communes within Hoa Binh province's Luong Son District. In one fell swoop, a whopping

⊙ Main Attractions
Old Quarter
Thang Long Water Puppet Theatre
Opera House
National Museum of Vietnamese History
St Joseph's Cathedral
Temple of Literature
Ho Chi Minh Mausoleum
West Lake
Vietnam Museum of Ethnology

Map on page 114

Local women gather by Hoan Kiem Lake for a daily dose of exercise.

Early morning activity at Reunification Park.

3,300 sq km (1,274 sq miles) have been added, now encompassing a population of around 7.6 million.

At the heart of the city is Hoan Kiem District, which comprises the Old Quarter just north of Hoan Kiem Lake and the French Quarter, just east and south of the lake. Most of the action takes place in the Old Quarter, also known as the 36 Streets. In the early 13th century, a collection of small-scale artisan villages evolved into craft guilds, and the streets were named after the products they made, the service they rendered or their location. Today, some road names still reflect the trade that takes place there, but they now share space with backpacker hotels, cafés, shops and restaurants.

Ba Dinh District, to the west of the Old Quarter, is the political and administrative heart of Hanoi, and hosts several sites of historic interest, including the mausoleum of Ho Chi Minh.

North of Ba Dinh and Hoan Kiem districts is West Lake District (Tay Ho District). In this burgeoning area are huge five-star hotels, expensive shops and restaurants, and the extravagant villas of Hanoi's newly minted rich.

Visitors tend to stick to the main urban areas of Hoan Kiem, Ba Dinh and Tay Ho.

In Vietnamese, Hanoi is written as two words: Ha meaning river, in reference to the Red River, or Song Hong, and noi, meaning inside. The city's rich and complex history dates back to the Neolithic era, when the ancient Viet people settled in Bach Hac and Viet Tri regions (present-day Vinh Phuc province), at the confluence of the Red and Lo rivers.

THE ORIGINS OF HANOI

Northern Vietnam once formed the Van Lang and Au Lac kingdoms of antiquity (see page 29). From around the 3rd century BC, the influence of China grew, and by the first century BC much of the region (Nam Viet) had been absorbed into a Han Chinese colony named Giao Chi (Jiaozhi).

After a long period of Chinese domination and periodic local struggles for independence, the Chinese were expelled in the 10th century.

Ly Thai To, founder of the Ly dynasty, is thought to have arrived in Dai La – an ancient city along the Red River – in the early 11th century. Legend says he saw an enormous golden dragon emerge from a lake and soar into the sky above the site. Based on this omen, he moved the capital from Hoa Lu to Dai La, which he renamed Thang Long (Ascending Dragon), present-day Hanoi.

The area between West Lake and the citadel became the administrative city (Kinh Thanh) and at the heart of this was the Royal City (Hoang Thanh). In 1010, the Royal City contained eight palaces and three pavilions, with eight more palaces built during the 11th century. The Temple of Literature, the One Pillar Pagoda and the Tran Quoc Pagoda were all built during this time.

Following the fall of the Tran dynasty (which had succeeded the Ly in 1225), the capital was moved to Thanh Hoa in 1400. Seven years later the armies of the Chinese Ming dynasty invaded, maintaining control of the region until Le Loi defeated the Chinese and moved the capital back to Thang Long (Hanoi) in 1428, renaming it as Dong Kinh (later corrupted by the French as Tonkin). Le Loi took on the name Le Thai To and founded the Le dynasty.

EUROPEAN INFLUENCES

Dutch, Portuguese and French traders arrived during the 17th century, quickly followed by Christian missionaries. With the rise of the Nguyen dynasty in 1802, the centre of power shifted to Hue in central Vietnam and Dong Kinh was renamed Ha Noi. When Hanoi fell into the hands of France in 1883, the city underwent a dramatic transformation.

Hanoi and the north finally defeated the French in 1954, but followed this with a new conflict, as it tried to impose communist rule on southern Vietnam. During the Vietnam War, nearly a quarter of Hanoi was bombed flat by American warplanes. After North and South Vietnam were reunified in 1976, Hanoi was declared the capital of the new Socialist Republic but social and economic problems hampered reconstruction efforts.

Today, Hanoi is a rapidly developing city with striking European embellishments. For a city full of fiercely independent people, it's somewhat ironic that it possesses a decidedly European air. Hanoians may brag about their beautiful city while eating baguette sandwiches and sipping café au lait, but few like to concede that much of this is down to the French.

HOAN KIEM DISTRICT

HOAN KIEM LAKE

Picturesque **Hoan Kiem Lake ❶** (Ho Hoan Kiem) is hugely popular with locals as a recreational site. Set in the heart of the **Old Quarter**, the lake – known to Hanoians as Ho Guom (Green Lake) – comes alive at dawn as t'ai chi, badminton and jogging take place around its shore.

Every evening the lake has a convivial vibe as traders sell all manner of food and toys, the air is filled with

The Old East Gate entrance to the Old Quarter.

Hanoi

0   500 m
0   500 yds

N

Old Quarter

0   200 m
0   200 yds

N

6 Cho Dong Xuan
(Dong Xuan Market)

Quan Chuong ★
(Old East Gate)

Hang Chieu   Nhat Duat

Thanh Ha

Ngo Gach   Nguyen Sieu

5 Den Bach Ma
(Bach Ma Temple)

Hang Buom

N. Dao
Duy Tu

Hang
Chinh

3 Nha Hat Kim Dong
(Hanoi Ancient House)

8 Nha Hat
Chuong Vang
(Golden Bell Theatre)

Lg Ngoc Quyen

PHO PHUONG
(OLD QUARTER)

Hang Bac   Cho Hang Be
(Hang Be Market)

Trung Yen

Hang Quat   Gia Ngu

Cau Go

4 Nha Hat Mua
Roi Thang Long
(Thang Long
Water Puppet Theatre)

Dinh Tien Hoang

2 Den Ngoc Son
(Temple of the
Jade Mound)

Huc
(Rising Sun
Bridge)

1

14 Chua Ba Da
(Ba Da
Pagoda)

Ho
Hoan Kiem
(Hoan Kiem
Lake)

Thap Rua
(Turtle Tower)

7 Nha Hat
Kim Dong

LY THAI TO
(LY THAI TO PARK)

Le Thach

Buu Dien Ha Noi
(Hanoi General Post Office)

Government
Guesthouse

TAY HO

34 Chua Phu Tay Ho
(WestLake Pagoda)

Sheraton
Hanoi Hotel

33 Chua Kim Lien
(Kim Lien Pagoda)

KIM LIEN

Intercontinental
Westlake Hotel

Ho Tay

30

(West Lake)

Sofitel Plaza

31 Chua Tran Quoc
(Tran Quoc Pagoda)

Chua Ngu Xa
(Ngu Xa Pagoda)

Ho Truc
Bach
(White
Silk Lake)

Bao Tang Dan Toc Viet Nam
(Vietnam Museum of Ethnology),
Ciputra International City

32 Den Quan Thanh
(Quan Thanh Temple)

Chua Noe Nhai

Cua Bac
(Catholic Church)

Hoang Hoa Tham

28 CONG VIEN
BACH THAO
(BOTANICAL
GARDENS)

Nha San Bac Ho
(Ho Chi Minh House)

Phu Chu Tich
(Presidential Palace)

**BA
DINH**

Lang Chu Tich Ho Chi Minh
(Ho Chi Minh Mausoleum)

27 Chua Mot Cot
(One Pillar Pagoda)

29 B-52
Ho Huu Tiep

**Ba
Dinh
Square**

**OLD
CITY**

Hoang Thanh Thang Long
(The Imperial Citadel
of Thang Long)

23

**CITADEL
Military Area
(Restricted Access)**

Ga Long Bien
(Station)

see above

PHO PHUONG
(OLD QUARTER)

HOAN KIEM

26 Bao Tang Ho Chi Minh
(Ho Chi Minh Museum)

25 Cot Co
(Flag Tower)

22

24 Bao Tang Lich
Su Quan Su
(Military History
Museum)

Lenin

20 Bao Tang My Thuat
(Fine Arts Museum)

Den Ngoc Son
(Temple of the
Jade Mound)

Ho
Hoan Kiem

21 Van Mieu
(Temple of Literature)

13 Nha Tho Lon
(St Joseph's
Cathedral)

former
Bank of
Indochina

12 Bao Tang Cach Mang
Viet Nam (Museum of
Vietnamese Revolution)

Hang Bot

Ga Ha Noi
(Station)

Hanoi
Towers

15 Ba Tang Nha Bao Hoa Lo
(Hoa Lo Prison/Hanoi Hilton)

11 Bao Tang Lich Su
(National Museum of
Vietnamese History)

Chua Quan Su
(Ambassadors'
Pagoda)

16

Sofitel Legend
Metropole Hotel

**FRENCH
QUARTER**

8

9 Nha Hat Lon
(Municipal Theatre/
Opera House)

17 Vietnamese
Women's
Museum

Hilton Hanoi
Opera Hotel

Cung Van Hoa
Huu Nghi
(Cultural Palace)

10 Dai Hoc Tong
Hop Ha Noi
(University)

**DONG
DA**

Nha Hat Rap Xiec
(Circus Theatre)

18 CONG VIEN
THONG NHAT
(REUNIFICATION
PARK)

Nha Hat
Cheo
(Cheo Theatre)

Nha Hat
Dai Nam

Nha Hat
Tuoi Tre

19 Den Hai Ba Trung (Hai Ba Trung Temple)

music and locals sip coffee or enjoy ice cream in one of several lakeside cafés.

Known as the Lake of the Restored Sword, it is also the stuff of legend. Folklore says that King Le Thai To of the 15th-century Le dynasty received a magical sword from an ancient tortoise. He used the weapon during his 10-year resistance against the Chinese in the early 1400s. After liberating the country, the king took a boat to the centre of the lake to return the sword to the divine tortoise. The tortoise is said to have snatched the sword from his hand and disappeared into the lake. In 2011 a clean-up operation was carried out to improve the polluted lake and succeeded in saving a giant freshwater turtle that had been spotted there.

NGOC SON TEMPLE

Look towards the middle of the lake to see a small 18th-century structure called the **Tortoise Tower** (Thap Rua). Perched on a tiny islet at the north end of the lake is **Ngoc Son Temple**, also known as the **Temple of the Jade Mound ❷** (Den Ngoc Son; daily 8am–5pm). The temple is reached from the shore via an arched bridge, painted bright red and known as The Huc, or the **Rising Sun Bridge**. On the small hillock at the end of the bridge stands a stone column in the form of a brush next to an ink well. Inscribed on the column are three Chinese characters: *ta tien qing*, or "written on the blue sky". Ngoc Son Temple is dedicated to, among others, the famous General Tran Hung Dao (see page 32) and La To, the patron saint of doctors. Inside is a huge 250kg (550lb) stuffed tortoise caught in Hoan Kiem Lake in the 1960s.

THE OLD QUARTER

THE "36 STREETS"

North of Hoan Kiem Lake is an area known as the **36 Streets**, or the **Old Quarter** (Pho Phuong), one of the oldest parts of Hanoi. Formerly a centre for resistance against the French, this part of town evolved in the 13th century when artisan guilds were concentrated along each of the original 36 lanes. The guilds developed independently,

The 18th-century Tortoise Tower on Hoan Kiem Lake.

Rising Sun Bridge (The Huc), leading to Ngoc Son Temple.

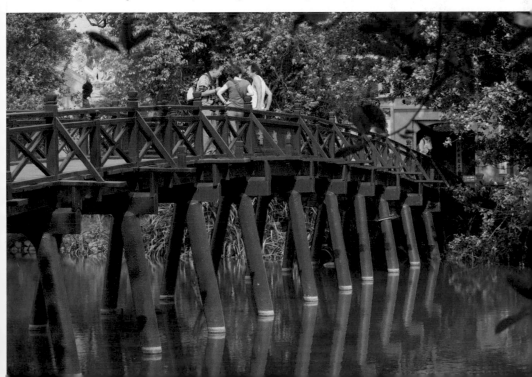

⊘ Drink

Quite possibly the cheapest beer on the planet, Bia Hoi costs from VND3,000 to VND7,000 per glass. Made fresh every day, it contains no preservatives so has to be drunk quickly. That is never a problem in the Old Quarter, where drinkers sit on flimsy plastic stools to enjoy a glass. The beer is light – partly because rice is used in the brewing process – and the alcohol content is only 3 or 4 percent.

A water puppet theatre performance.

separated from each other by walls and gates that were locked each night. Tinsmiths were found on Hang Thiec (Tin Street), bamboo basket makers on Hang Bo (Bamboo Basket Street), and so on. The present-day commercial frenzy that the Old Quarter has become (along with its intense motorbike and bicycle traffic) is all the more amazing considering that, with few exceptions, the communists prohibited private trade until as recently as 1986.

The new tradespeople still cluster along each street by speciality, but the trade doesn't necessarily match the street name any longer. Silver jewellery, as well as gravestones, can still be found on **Hang Bac** (Silver Street), but also here now are travel agencies and tourist cafés. The street called **Hang Gai** (Hemp) specialises in silk, clothing and embroidered articles, while **Hang Dau** (Cooking Oil) is full of shoe shops. However, **Hang Chieu** (Mats) is still the place to find mats, **Hang Ma** (Paper Votive Objects) has mainly stationery shops, and Thuoc Bac does a steady trade in herbal medicines.

Each of the 36 craft guilds once had its own *dinh* (communal house). However, like most of the quarter's pagodas and temples, they were shut down during the communist takeover and transformed into schools or public housing. Similarly, the narrow storefronts, some less than 3 metres (10ft) wide, once contained single-family dwellings. These *nha ong*, or tube houses, extend far to the back and are punctuated by tiny courtyards. Today, in most cases, they have been re-apportioned among several families. You can take a look inside a typical Chinese merchant's well-preserved *nha ong* at the **Hanoi Ancient House ❸** (Nha Hat Kim Dong; 87 Ma May Street; daily 9am–noon and 1–5pm) or at the headquarters of the Management Unit of this quarter (38 Hang Dao) where you can get more information on ancient streets and traditional construction techniques. If you look along Tran Quang Khai you can see the dikes that once kept floodwaters at bay. Also note the narrow fronts to many houses – this was done to avoid taxes, which were once based on a property's width. The best way to experience this area is simply to wander and browse among the endless range of artwork, silk and traditional clothing.

Sweet-toothed tourists head to Hang Buom Street for its astonishing selection of sweets. The street's name means "shop of sails" and derives from the Chinese vessels that used to drop off goods here. They have long gone but today this lively part of the Old Quarter is still very busy. In 2014 it was converted to a pedestrianised cuisine street with stalls serving Hanoi traditional confectionary, beverages and dishes on Fri–Sun evenings.

WATER PUPPET THEATRE

Vietnam's most famous show is a fascinating display of traditional water puppetry. Dating back at least 1,000 years, the performance is a collection of short scenes that depict everything from everyday life through to mythical stories. You can book tickets in advance at the **Thang Long Water Puppet Theatre ❹** (Nha Hat Mua Roi Thang Long; tel: 04-3824 9494; http://

thanglongwaterpuppet.org; shows daily 3pm, 4.10pm, 5.20pm, 6.30pm, and 8pm). The theatre is on the northeast corner of Hoan Kiem Lake along Dinh Tien Hoang Street. An integral part of the nightly performances is the live music, all played with traditional instruments (see page 79).

BACH MA TEMPLE

From Hang Buom Street, you should be able to hear the chanting or smell the incense coming from **Bach Ma Temple ❺** (Den Bach Ma; Tue–Sun 8–11am, 2–5pm), at 78 Hang Buom Street (Sail Street). This is the Old Quarter's most revered temple and honours the white horse that appeared to King Ly Thai To in a dream and led him to build the walls of the old city. A statue of the giant wooden horse is inside, along with a lacquered palanquin adorned with carvings of phoenixes, cranes and tortoises. Originally built in the 9th century, the temple was reconstructed in the 18th and 19th centuries. In regular use, it remains in a good state of repair.

> **⊙ Fact**
>
> Feudal laws taxed shops according to their width, which is why the so-called "tube houses" in the Old Quarter are so narrow and long. In addition, the houses were also built squat and short as they could not be higher than a passing royal palanquin, in deference to the emperor.

Fabrics galore at Dong Xuan Market.

Hanoi's General Post Office (Buu Dien Ha Noi) sits by the calm Hoan Kiem Lake.

Dining out in the French Quarter.

DONG XUAN MARKET

The area around **Dong Xuan Market** (Cho Dong Xuan; daily 5am–7pm) in the northern part of the Old Quarter rewards exploration. The original colonial-era market was rebuilt following a huge fire in 1994 and resembles its original state. This site is the wholesale source for many dry goods and is the largest undercover market in Hanoi. The counterfeit D&G bags and other low-quality apparel seem intended for Vietnamese customers, but it's a good place to shop for home wares or cheap souvenirs. In the surrounding streets, farmers squat on the pavement selling their produce, while florists add a welcome splash of colour with their fragrant blooms. Look out for performances of Ca Tru, a traditional music form sung by women. On **Lang Ong Street**, traditional medicine shops sell all manner of exotic cures, including snake wine and lizards preserved in alcohol.

Nearby, at the end of Hang Chieu and close to Tran Nhat Duat Street, is the crumbling brick gate of **Quan Chuong**,

the last remnant of the wall that once encircled the Old Quarter.

SOUTHEAST OF HOAN KIEM LAKE

On the southeast side of the lake at 75 Dinh Tien Hoang Street is the city's **General Post Office** (Buu Dien), designed by French architects in 1942. One block north is a small patch of greenery known as **Ly Thai To Park** (formerly Indira Gandhi Park). The park is a good place to watch local life go by, from skateboarding youngsters and budding footballers, to friends and couples out for a stroll. A large statue of King Ly Thai To, the founder of the Ly dynasty, dominates the park.

To the east of the park on Ly Thai To Street is the striking Art Deco-style **former Bank of Indochina** (now the State Bank of Vietnam). Across from the park's southeastern corner is the arresting **Government Guesthouse** (no entry) at 12 Ngo Quyen Street. Yellow with green trim and protected by a wrought-iron fence, the building was inaugurated in 1918 as the palace of the French governor of Tonkin.

SOFITEL LEGEND METROPOLE

Southwards, straddling Ly Thai To and Ngo Quyen streets, is the stunning **Sofitel Legend Metropole Hotel** (www.sofitel-legend-metropole-hanoi.com). This gem of a hotel was the only international-standard hotel – called the Grand Hotel Metropole Palace then – in French colonial days and was the epicentre for colonial society people.

Former guests include writers Noël Coward and Somerset Maugham and actors such as Charlie Chaplin (who spent his honeymoon here after his secret wedding to Paulette Goddard) and anti-Vietnam War activist Jane Fonda (who famously took cover at the hotel during American air raids). Writer Graham Greene wrote a few chapters of his classic novel *The Quiet American* at the hotel in the 1950s. During the Vietnam War years, the hotel was used as a base by diplomats and journalists. In the 1980s its condition had severely deteriorated, but a French management team restored the hotel to its former glories and relaunched it in 1992. Its historical value, elegance and high-quality French, Vietnamese and Italian restaurants make it more than just a hotel.

OPERA HOUSE

From here it's only a short walk south on Ly Thai To Street to the grand columned **Municipal Theatre**, often referred to as the **Opera House** ❾ (Nha Hat Lon, http://hanoioperahouse. org.vn). This performing arts centre was built at the turn of the 20th century to keep the French entertained. After years of renovation, this renewed beauty reopened in 1997 and hosts regular performances. Its basement boasts a gourmet restaurant called **Nineteen11**.

Days after the Japanese surrender in World War II cadres rushed in to Hanoi, and on 19 August 1945 they declared the establishment of an independent democratic republic – from the theatre's balcony. Tens of thousands of peasants armed with machetes and bamboo spears were joined by equal numbers of city residents. Only a few days before, few of the latter had ever heard of the Viet Minh, but they were soon caught up in patriotic euphoria and obeyed orders to seize important buildings from the Japanese and their Vietnamese collaborators.

The Opera House is stunning, its interior embellished with a sweeping marble staircase, crystal chandelier, and red and gold-leaf decor. To be able to see around you will need to buy a ticket for a show (www.ticketvn.com), as there are no guided tours. Today, performances include everything from Flamenco and Tchaikovsky to more traditional Vietnamese music. Adjacent is the luxury **Hilton Hanoi Opera** ❾ (www3.hilton.com), with a facade that replicates the style of the Opera House; the interior, however, is contemporary in style. Interestingly, the more obvious title of The Hanoi Hilton was not

The Hanoi Opera House is a visual treat.

A bronze figurine by the facade of St Joseph's Cathedral.

A life-size statue of Ho Chi Minh at the Museum of Vietnamese Revolution.

considered, as this was the ironic nickname given to a prison used to torture US troops during the Vietnam War.

TRANG TIEN STREET

Heading back west and skirting the southern tip of the lake, **Trang Tien Street**, which ends in front of the **Opera House**, was once the main shopping street of the French Quarter. When the communists closed private enterprises, Trang Tien Street was one of the few areas that retained any commerce; today it houses upmarket art galleries, bookshops, and – in the once drab old government department store – the former **Hanoi Securities Trading Centre**, renamed the Hanoi Stock Exchange in 2009. While the street is predominantly known for its range of books, it is also popular as a place to try local ice cream – one delicious option comes with sticky green rice. Look out for the blocks to the south and west, on sedate tree-lined streets, as this is where the colonialists' elegant former villas now house embassies, diplomatic residences and

the headquarters of non-governmental organisations.

VIETNAM NATIONAL UNIVERSITY

The road southeast of the Opera House, Le Thanh Tong Street, runs by **Vietnam National University** ⑩ (Dai Hoc Tong Hop Ha Noi, http://vnu.edu.vn/eng) and its Frenchera buildings. Walk into the main courtyard, to view the fusion of colonial and Vietnamese architecture. Founded in 1906 as the University of Indochina, schools of law, medicine, science and arts were added in the 1930s. The Indochinese students who studied here, including the future General Vo Nguyen Giap, were part of Vietnam's intellectual (and probably financial) elite. The French commitment to education and literacy was somewhat half-baked: in 1937, the student body here numbered only 631.

NATIONAL MUSEUM OF VIETNAMESE HISTORY

Behind the Opera House, with a cupola resembling a pagoda, is the **National Museum of Vietnamese History** ⑪

(Bao Tang Lich Su Viet Nam; tel: 04-3825 2853; http://baotanglichsu.vn; daily 8am–noon and 1.30–5pm, closed every first Mon of the month). The museum occupies the old archaeological research institution of the French School of the Far East, which opened in 1910 and was substantially renovated in the 1920s. High on content and low on propaganda, this may be the best museum in town. The excellent archaeological collection includes relics from the Hung era and Neolithic graves, Bronze Age implements, axe heads, Cham relics, and an eerie sculpture of the Goddess of Mercy, Quan Am, with 1,000 eyes and arms. An ornate throne, clothing and artefacts belonging to the 13 Nguyen-dynasty emperors are also on display. The museum is worth visiting for its stunning architecture alone as it blends French and Chinese features to great effect.

MUSEUM OF VIETNAMESE REVOLUTION

Nearby, the second building of the National Museum of Vietnamese History, widely known as the **Museum of Vietnamese Revolution** ⑫ (Bao Tang Cach Mang; tel: 04-3825 4151; daily 8am–noon and 1.30–5pm), at 216 Tran Quang Khai Street, offers a carefully scripted version of the struggles of the Vietnamese people from 1858 up to the present day. Among the thousands of items on display are wooden fetters used in Buon Ma Thuot to chain prisoners, and the guillotine the French used in Hoa Lo prison.

WEST OF HOAN KIEM LAKE

ST JOSEPH'S CATHEDRAL

Resembling a miniature version of Paris's Notre-Dame, **St Joseph's Cathedral** ⑬ (Nha Tho Lon; the Vietnamese simply call it the "big church") sits just west of Hoan Kiem Lake, where Pho Nha Chung joins Ly Quoc Su Street. Neo-Gothic in style, with distinctive square towers, the cathedral was consecrated on Christmas night in 1886. St Joseph's was built on the site of the Bao Thien Pagoda, which was razed by the French to build the cathedral. Celebration of Mass resumed here

In St Joseph's Cathedral.

Elements of torture and abuse are depicted at the Hoa Lo Prison Museum.

only in 1990 after more than 30 years of repression. On Sundays, the Masses are packed. Inside are beautiful stained-glass windows and an ornate altar decorated with gold leaf.

For a completely different environment, simply walk across the road to **Pho Nha Tho Street** (Church Street), as this and adjoining thoroughfares form a trendy shopping area that specialises in high-end tailors, handicrafts and home decor shops, local designer boutiques and jewellers. It's now a popular place for Hanoi's young people to hang out. There are lots of restaurants and charming cafés where you can take a breather.

BA DA PAGODA

A narrow passageway on 5 Pho Nha Tho Street leads to **Ba Da Pagoda** ⑭ (Chua Ba Da; daily 8am–5pm), tucked between St Joseph's Cathedral and Hoan Kiem Lake. This lovely pagoda was built in the 15th century – though the site itself dates back to the 11th century – after the discovery of a stone statue of a woman (hence its name, Stone Lady Pagoda) during the construction

The Ambassadors' Pagoda, a long-standing Buddhist institution.

of the Thang Long citadel to the west. The statue, which was thought to have magical powers, disappeared and has since been replaced by a replica. The pagoda's modest exterior belies its exquisite interior. An impressive line-up of gilt Buddha statues forms the central altar. Today it houses the Hanoi Buddhist Sangha headquarters, so a sizeable number of resident monks and nuns live on site. This was once one of three pagodas in the area, but one was knocked down by the French to make way for St Joseph's Cathedral. The other, Ly Quoc Su, still exists.

HOA LO PRISON

Better known by its more ironic name, The Hanoi Hilton, this prison site is about three blocks south of Hoan Kiem Lake. **Hoa Lo Prison Museum** ⑮ (tel: 04-3824 6358; http://hoalo.vn; daily 8–5pm) once held the likes of US Republican senator (and failed presidential candidate) John McCain and Pete Peterson, the US ambassador to Vietnam in the late 1990s. The prison is of significance to Vietnamese, too, as the French imprisoned, tortured and guillotined countless revolutionaries within the walled compound, which until recently occupied an entire block.

In 1994, the prison was almost entirely demolished to make way for an enormous foreign-financed steel and glass office and shopping complex called **Hanoi Towers**. The small section that remained was turned into the Hoa Lo Prison Museum. Topped with barbed and electric wire, Hoa Lo's yellow concrete main gate (which reads "Maison Centrale") and a few cells have been preserved along with exhibits of instruments of torture and a guillotine. The images of American and Vietnamese who were kept here are particularly poignant.

AMBASSADORS' PAGODA

One block southwest, the **Ambassadors' Pagoda** ⑯ (Chua Quan Su; daily

7.30–11.30am and 1.30–5.30pm), located at 73 Pho Quan Su Street, is perhaps the busiest pagoda in town. On the first and 15th days of each lunar month, crowds gather to make offerings of incense, foodstuffs and paper goods. In the 17th century, the site was a guesthouse for envoys from other Buddhist countries, hence its name. The long, low buildings surrounding the temples are school-rooms for novice monks and contain a small library of parchment and texts in Vietnamese and Chinese. A handful of monks and nuns still live here.

VIETNAMESE WOMEN'S MUSEUM

To the east, at 36 Ly Thuong Kiet Street, the **Vietnamese Women's Museum ⑰** (Bao Tang Phu; www.baotangphunu.org.vn; daily 8am–5pm) reopened in 2010 with a modern and well-organised exhibition, becoming one of the most popular attractions in Hanoi. The exhibit offers a good insight into the role of women in Vietnamese society and its evolution around three main themes: family, history and fashion. Don't miss an interesting video about street vendors.

On the top floor, the MAM-ART Projects hosts contemporary art exhibitions.

HAI BA TRUNG DISTRICT

REUNIFICATION PARK

About 500 metres/yds south of the Ambassadors' Pagoda is the small but lovely **Thien Quang Lake** (Ho Thien Quang), where visitors can rent pad-dle boats. To the south, just across the street, is an entrance to **Reunification Park ⑱** (Cong Vien Thong Nhat; daily daylight hours). This pleasant and shady area, still known locally by its old name of Lenin Park, is said to have been built by volunteer workers on marshy land once used as a dumping ground. The park is designed around the large **Bay Mau Lake** (Ho Bay Mau) with swan boats and operates a number of children's rides at the weekend. At other times locals come out to jog or couples head out for a stroll in the scenic grounds.

HAI BA TRUNG TEMPLE

Southeast of Reunification Park is the **Hai Ba Trung Temple ⑲** (Den Hai Ba

The entrance to Hoa Lo Prison.

Classical Chinese architecture at the Temple of Literature.

The Vietnam Fine Arts Museum is a veritable treasure trove of Vietnamese art history.

Reliving the days of war at the Military History Museum.

Trung), also known as the Dong Nhan Temple after the village that surrounded the site back when it was built in 1142. The temple is dedicated to two famous Trung sisters who organised an uprising against the Chinese Han invaders in AD 39 and who later committed suicide together by jumping into the river. Two unusually formed stone statues recovered from the Red River, said to represent the two sisters, are kept in a small room inside the temple. Each February the statues are brought out for a grand procession, where they are dressed in new clothes and displayed in reverence. In 2014, huge celebrations of the 2,000th anniversary of the sisters' birthday honoured them as symbols of the heroism and patriotic tradition of Vietnamese women.

BA DINH DISTRICT AND WESTERN HANOI

VIETNAM FINE ARTS MUSEUM

To the far west of Ho Hoan Kiem Lake is the excellent **Vietnam Fine Arts Museum** ⑳ (Bao Tang My Thuat; www.

vnfam.vn; tel: 04-3733 2131; Tue–Sun 8–11.30am and 1.30–4.30pm) at 66 Nguyen Thai Hoc Street. Built in the 1930s as a boarding school for children of Indochinese officials, today the exhibits include displays on minority folk art and history, Dong Son bronze drums, Dong Noi stone carvings, Cham statues and carvings, ceramics, 16th-century communal house decorations and 18th-century wooden Buddha statues in some surprisingly undignified poses. Particularly impressive are the displays tracing the development of Vietnamese paintings from the 20th century to the present. Note the rare examples of lacquer painting on paper. Guided tours in English are available.

TEMPLE OF LITERATURE

One of Hanoi's must-see attractions is the **Temple of Literature** ㉑ (Van Mieu; tel: 04-3845 2917; http://vanmieu.gov.vn; daily 7.30am–6pm, winter from 8am). This historically rich museum is south of the Fine Arts Museum at Pho Quoc Tu Giam Street. Built in 1070 under the reign of King Ly Thanh Tong, the temple

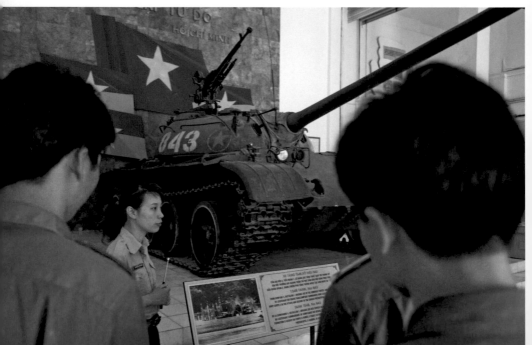

is dedicated to Confucius. When it was first built, the Quoc Tu Giam, or School of the Elite of the Nation – Vietnam's first university – adjoined the temple's grounds. Under the Tran dynasty, the school was renamed the Quoc Hoc Vien, or the National College, in 1235.

After passing exams at the local levels, scholars aspiring to become senior mandarins came here to study for rigorous examinations. Subjects included literature, philosophy and Vietnamese history. Van Mieu became known as the Temple of Literature when the capital was transferred to Hue at the beginning of the 19th century. Above the main gate is an inscription requesting that visitors dismount from horses before entering.

Each of the five walled courtyards inside the temple hosts its own unique story. After passing through the main **Van Mieu Gate** (Van Mieu Mon) and the first two courtyards past this gate, one arrives at the **Pleiade Constellation Pavilion** (Gac Khue Van), where the men of letters recited their poems. Through the **Great Wall Gate** (Dai Thanh Mon), an open courtyard surrounds a large, central pool known as the **Well of Heavenly Clarity** (Thien Quang Tinh). Now regrouped and sheltered under a roof, the **82 stone stelae**, survivors of an original 117, rest on the backs of stone tortoises. Students come to rub the heads of the tortoises as it is believed this will bring them good fortune – and good grades. Before they were restored a several years ago, the stone stelae under the trees on either side of the courtyard were exposed to the elements. The stelae are inscribed with the names, works and academic records of some 1,306 scholars who succeeded in the 82 examinations held between 1442 and 1779 (as well as some less academic modern-day graffiti). The French halted examinations here in 1915 (and in Hue in 1918). By then, the importation of Chineselanguage materials had been prohibited for seven years. The stelae were included in Unesco's 2010 list of world documentary heritage.

Facing the temple is the **House of Ceremonies** (Bai Duong), where

Ho Chi Minh, c. 1962.

☉ UNCLE HO

Ho Chi Minh, or Uncle Ho as he is known locally, was a Marxist revolutionary who helped secure Vietnam's independence. Today much of his ideology has been forgotten, but his image remains as cherished as ever: his face is on every banknote, the nation's capital is named after him and nearly every town has a statue of him. Unravelling the man behind the myth is difficult: Ho Chi Minh was only one of several pseudonyms he used and he rarely gave interviews; even his birthday is disputed.

Ho Chi Minh lived in the USA and the UK before heading to France, where he studied communism and began calling for the French to leave his homeland. After studying further in the Soviet Union and China, he returned to Vietnam in 1941 to fight the French. As president of North Vietnam, he inspired the fight against the US-backed administration in the south.

He did not live to see the North's victory. News of his death, on 2 September 1969, was carefully managed – an announcement was made 48 hours afterwards to prevent it from coinciding with the anniversary of the founding of the Democratic Republic of Vietnam. Today, his legacy and image are fiercely guarded by the government, which regularly censors anything that does not match with the official version of Ho's life.

The One Pillar Pagoda is a familiar Hanoi city landmark.

The body of the revered Uncle Ho lies within the Ho Chi Minh Mausoleum.

sacrifices were offered in honour of Confucius. Today, musicians perform traditional music and charge a fee to those who care to sit and listen. Nearby are the Eastern Gate and the Great Success Sanctuary.

In the final courtyard was once the National Academy, destroyed by French aerial bombing in 1947. These were the academy buildings where the final examinations were held. A two-storey building contains a small museum and shrines to great scholars.

IMPERIAL CITADEL OF THANG LONG AND MILITARY HISTORY MUSEUM

Virtually all that remains of the former Hanoi citadel can be found several blocks north on Dien Bien Phu Street. **Flag Tower** ㉒ (Cot Co; daily 8.30am–4.30pm) was built in 1812 by the Nguyen dynasty as part of the citadel. The main structure was ravaged by fire at the end of the 19th century and now this hexagonal, 33-metre (108ft) -high tower, all that remains, is an important national symbol and a flagpole. A

branch of the upscale domestic café chain **Highlands Coffee** (http://highlandscoffee.com.vn) has an outdoor outlet at the base of the tower.

During the construction of the new National Assembly House near the Ba Dinh Square in 2009, the vestiges of an ancient citadel dating from the 11th century and the Ly Dynasty period were discovered atop the remains of an earlier Chinese fortress. The site was added to Unesco's World Heritage List in 2010. Used as a military base until recently, it is now open to the public. You can stroll in the peaceful gardens of the **Imperial Citadel of Thang Long** ㉓ (entrance at 19C Hoang Dieu Street; www.hoangthanhthanglong.vn; Tue–Sun 8am–5pm), or visit well preserved military bunkers and an archaeological site.

Next door to the Flag Tower is the **Military History Museum** ㉔ (Bao Tang Lich Su Quan Su; tel: 04-733 6453; www.btlsqsvn.org.vn; Tue–Sat 8–11.30am and 1–4.30pm), which details Vietnam's battles for independence and unification against the French and

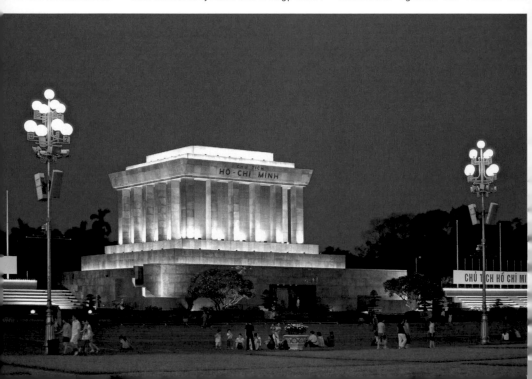

American patrons of South Vietnam. The uniforms of captured US pilots and images of Vietnam's war heroes are interesting, but the real draw here is the wreckage of a decrepit B-52 bomber that sits in the outside courtyard. Military buffs can also visit other branches of the museum – **the Museum of Military Zone Thu Do** (also known as the **B52 Victory Museum**) at 57, Doi Can Street and the **Air-Defence and Air Force Museum** at 171 and 179 Truong Chinh Street – to see more military equipment.

ONE PILLAR PAGODA

Continuing northwest up Dien Bien Phu Street, a small road called Chua Mot Cot leads to the **One Pillar Pagoda** ㉕ (Chua Mot Cot; daily 8am–5pm; free) and the Ho Chi Minh complex. Originally built in 1049 by King Ly Thai Thong, this unique wooden pagoda rests on a single concrete pillar rising out of a murky green pool – it is supposed to symbolise the sacred lotus sprouting from the waters of suffering. It is said the king saw a goddess

who, while seated on a lotus flower, handed him a male heir. The king later married a peasant girl who gave him a son, and the pagoda was built in gratitude for the premonition. The pillar is a late 1950s replacement after French soldiers cynically blew up the original structure in 1954. Prime Minister Nehru of India planted the banyan tree behind the pagoda in 1958 during an official visit to the then fledgling Vietnamese republic.

HO CHI MINH MUSEUM

Behind the park with the pagoda is the eclectic **Ho Chi Minh Museum** ㉖ (Bao Tang Ho Chi Minh; tel: 04-3845 5435; http://www.baotanghochiminh.vn; Tue–Thu and Sat–Sun 8–11am and 1.30–4.30pm). The museum, arranged into chronological sections and opened on 19 May 1990 (the 100th anniversary of Ho's birth), chronicles the great man's revolutionary life and the pivotal role he played in Vietnam's history and international development. Part of the museum focuses on the past, with a collection of photos, documents

Escape the bustle of Hanoi at the serene Botanical Gardens.

Ho Chi Minh's humble abode.

The area around West Lake has seen recent development, mainly in the form of expensive housing.

The area around White Silk Lake is a wining and dining hotspot.

and personal effects, such as the actual disguise he used to flee to Hong Kong. The modern section is far more obscure and symbolic, from the gigantic lopsided table scene to the car that seems to be crashing through a wall. Jingoistic explanations accompany most displays, though the meaning of the battered mortars that lie in front of ornate plates seems to have eluded even the caption writers.

HO CHI MINH MAUSOLEUM

Immediately north looms the imposing marble-and-granite-clad **Ho Chi Minh Mausoleum** ㉗ (Lang Chu Tich Ho Chi Minh; www.bqllang.gov.vn; Tue–Thu, Sat–Sun 8–11am), built on the spot in **Ba Dinh Square** where Ho Chi Minh delivered Vietnam's declaration of independence in 1945. The embalmed corpse of Uncle Ho lies in a glass casket within this monumental tomb, despite his wish to be cremated and have his ashes scattered in the north, centre and south of the country. In late autumn/early winter it is advisable to check beforehand whether his

body is in residence. Rumour has it he is packed off to Russia for embalming three months out of every year. Dressed in his trademark khaki suit, the heavily guarded body lies displayed on an elevated platform in a dark and chilly room.

Upon entering the mausoleum, visitors are ushered quickly past either side of the body. No cameras or handbags may be taken inside so these have to be checked in at the entrance. The white-uniformed guards who control the flow of traffic will not hesitate to eject anyone not displaying the proper decorum – so talking or laughing is out, and hats are off. Part of the fascination is watching the Vietnamese reverence for Ho, which is unfailing. The changing of the guards outside is worth waiting around for as it is a rather grand event. Ho Chi Minh died in 1969, on the same date as his declaration of independence.

HO CHI MINH HOUSE

The wooded grounds of the Presidential Palace are right by the mausoleum, and although it is closed to the public there are two buildings within the grounds that are worth exploring. Built in 1906, the palace was formerly the residence of the French governor-general. Today, it has been turned into a government guesthouse for foreign dignitaries. Ho led a simple life, and it's not surprising that he preferred not to stay in the palace, using it only for government council meetings and receiving guests.

Instead, Ho lived in two unassuming houses on the same grounds: the first (said to be the electrician's house) was his home from 1954 to 1958, before he moved to a specially constructed but still austere house built on stilts. The **Ho Chi Minh House** (Nha San Bac Ho; http://ditichhochiminhphuchutich.gov. vn; Tue–Sun 8–11am, 1.30–4pm, Mon 8–11am, in the summer open from 7.30am), with its immaculately varnished wooden exterior, overlooks a carp pond in a quiet and leafy section of the park. The modest living quarters consist of two small rooms with an open-air meeting room below. Ho lived here from May 1958 to August 1969. Vietnam is clearly intent on preserving not just Ho's body, but also his personal items, as everything from his furniture to his pens are here. There is even a garage housing his Peugeot 404.

BOTANICAL GARDENS

Behind the Presidential Palace, but best reached from Hoang Hoa Tham Street, are the **Botanical Gardens** ㉘ (Cong Vien Bach Thao; daily daylight hours), with rolling hills, peaceful lakes and numerous trees for shade. The park was designed by French landscape engineers in 1890 on the site of a former zoo; a few monkeys and peacocks are still kept here today. A handful of sculptures add character to this park, which is a fantastic spot for a picnic. This is one of the few genuinely quiet places in Hanoi, and so it makes for an ideal picnic lunch location.

B-52 LAKE

Wander a kilometre from the Ho Chi Minh Mausoleum on Hoang Hoa Tham Street and duck down a winding alley and you'll be greeted by a **B-52** ㉙ sticking out of a small, brackish pond. This is the remains of the *Rose 1*, an American B-52 bomber that was shot down on 19 December 1972. Of its crew of six, four survived the attack and were taken prisoner and two were killed. Sadly, the "lake" is often used as a garbage dump by local residents.

WEST LAKE (HO TAY) DISTRICT

WEST LAKE AND SURROUNDINGS

North of the main city centre lies the vast **West Lake** ㉚ (Ho Tay), formerly known as the Lake of Mists, an area popular with wealthy expats. This lake, the largest in Hanoi, lies on an ancient bed of the Red River (Song Hong). The palaces of emperors and generals once graced its banks, all of which have been destroyed in feudal battles. One legend says the lake was formed when a

The Quan Thanh Temple is steeped in rich history.

The Vietnam Museum of Ethnology gives an insight into the culture and lifestyles of Vietnam's 54 ethnic groups.

⊘ Eat

The idea of eating dog may provoke howls of protest in the West, but in Hanoi canine snacks are the norm. Vietnamese believe consuming dog will bring them good fortune or even, for men, a stronger libido. The main restaurants are just north of Hanoi in Pho Nghi Tam. Each restaurant displays its wares on tables, while inside diners can order a variety of dog-based dishes. Dog is eaten on particular dates, according to lunar laws, so at times the restaurants may be closed for a week or more.

Displays at the Vietnam Museum of Ethnology.

golden buffalo calf mistook the sound of a giant bell for that of its mother's call, and trampled the land, thus creating the lake. Another myth says a dragon king formed the lake after slaying a nine-tailed fox. Since the 1990s, the area surrounding the lake has seen considerable building activity – particularly along its northeast bank.

TRAN QUOC PAGODA

During an uprising against the occupying Chinese in 545, national hero Ly Bon built the National Foundation Pagoda (Chua Khai Quoc) beside the Red River. In the 17th century, the pagoda was transferred to its present site on a tiny peninsula off West Lake and renamed the **Tran Quoc Pagoda**, or the National Defence Pagoda ㉛ (Chua Tran Quoc; daily 8am–5pm). Tran Quoc is perhaps Vietnam's oldest pagoda; the stela, dating from the year 1639, recounts its long history.

WHITE SILK LAKE AND QUAN THANH TEMPLE

Separated from the lake by Thanh Nien Road is **White Silk Lake** (Ho Truc

Bach). This was the ancient site of Lord Trinh's summer palace, which later became a harem where he detained his wayward concubines. The lake derives its name from the beautiful white silk these concubines were forced to weave for the princesses.

Nearby, the ornate **Quan Thanh Temple** ㉜ (Den Quan Thanh; daily 6am–6pm) beside the lake was originally built during the Ly dynasty (1010–1225). This temple has a huge bronze bell and a 4-tonne bronze statue of Tran Vu, guardian deity of the north, to whom the temple is dedicated. The street that runs along the perimeter of White Silk Lake is famous for its street stalls that serve *pho cuon*, tender slices of beef wrapped in rice noodles with herbs, and is a popular nightspot among Vietnamese teenagers.

KIM LIEN PAGODA AND FLOWER VILLAGE

Further up the northern bank of West Lake, tucked away in a small neighbourhood beside the plush Intercontinental Hotel, are **Kim Lien Pagoda** ㉝, also known as Golden Lotus Pagoda (Chua Kim Lien; daily 8am–5pm), and the **Kim Lien Flower Village**. In the three small lanes that wind their way towards the lake from the pagoda, courtyards spill over with tropical flowers of unimaginable variety, in particular many exotic varieties of orchid. The Kim Lien Pagoda, built in its present form in 1711 and renovated in 1983, is dedicated to the Buddha and to Princess Tu Hoa, the daughter of King Ly Than Tong who is said to have taught local villagers how to cultivate mulberries, raise silkworms and weave silk.

WEST LAKE PAGODA

Even further north, at the tip of a small peninsula at the end of Dang Thai Mai Street, is **West Lake Pagoda** ㉞ (Chua Phu Tay Ho; daily 8am–5pm; free), a popular destination for pilgrims and unmarried Vietnamese, particularly on the 15th day of each lunar month. The lane just before the pagoda is lined with lakeside restaurants specialising in *banh tom* (shrimp cakes). Inside the pagoda, the hall to the right is especially garish, its altars crammed with statuettes of strange beasts, grottoes and miniature sailing ships. Worshippers bring heaps of fruit and packets of biscuits, among other things, and pile them in front of the altars as offerings to the deities.

From West Lake Pagoda, visitors can take a pleasant walk north, passing large villas on the right and serene lotus ponds on the left. Restaurants near here are renowned for their *bun oc*, or snail soup.

NORTHERN HANOI

VIETNAM MUSEUM OF ETHNOLOGY

The **Vietnam Museum of Ethnology** (Bao Tang Dan Toc Hoc Viet Nam; tel: 04-3756 2193; www.vme.org.vn; Tue–Sun 8.30am–5.30pm) on Nguyen Van Huyen Street is Hanoi's most modern museum. Located about 20 minutes by taxi from the city centre, the museum brilliantly details the lives and history of the country's 54 ethnic minorities. Many special events – like artisan demonstrations, traditional games, films and lectures – are held here, especially at weekends and during the holidays.

The open-plan two-storey museum was designed by a member of the Tay ethnic group in the form of an ancient Dong Son drum. There are displays of handicrafts, garments, weapons, musical instruments and various artefacts as well as audio and video recordings and full-scale models of village communal houses. The displays are labelled in English and French and, for a small extra fee, a guide is available. The museum is also wheelchair-friendly.

WESTERN HANOI

The fast developing district of Tu Liem in western Hanoi boasts several recent landmarks such as the **Keangnam Landmark 72,** the tallest building in Vietnam and indeed, all of Indochina. This big business and residential complex contains a 5-star Intercontinental Hotel; a cinema; shopping, fitness and spa centres; restaurants; and the **Sky72 observatory deck** (http://www.landmark72.com; Pham Hung boulevard; daily Mon–Fri 10am–10pm, Sat–Sun 9am–10pm).

On the same street, the **Hanoi Museum** (Tue–Sun 8.30–11.30am, 1.30–4.30pm) boasts a spectacular building in the form of an inverted pyramid, built to celebrate the city's millennium anniversary in 2010. It stands in a park with many water features and a reconstructed traditional Vietnamese village. Sadly, the exhibition telling the story of Vietnamese people is not as interesting as the museum's interior, which includes a large spiral ramp; its design gives the sensation of floating above the landscape.

> **⊙ Fact**
>
> Legend has it that in a dream King Ly Thai To saw the goddess Quan Am seated on a lotus leaf offering him a male child in her outstretched arms. Shortly after his dream, the king married a young peasant girl who bore him the male heir of whom he had dreamt. As a sign of his gratitude, he is said to have built Hanoi's One Pillar Pagoda (see page 127).

Displays at the Vietnam Museum of Ethnology.

Steps leading up to Tay Phuong Pagoda.

AROUND HANOI

The urban and rural areas that surround Hanoi are rich in history and natural beauty. Many of the sacred pagodas, ancient citadels, traditional craft villages and national parks can easily be visited on a day trip from the capital.

Excursions to the scattering of pagodas, parks and villages around **Hanoi** ❶ are worth the effort. Most day trips can be booked with tour agencies in the city, while others may require the use of slow and uncomfortable local buses or hired cars (the more adventurous can jump on a motorbike or even bicycle). The land surrounding the capital is agriculturally rich, nurtured by the Red River (Song Hong) which spreads its alluvial deposits over much of northern Vietnam. Beyond the rice paddies and occasional rocky outcrops, several ancient pagodas are just a few hours' drive away, as are a number of highland escapes. Boat trips pass by limestone cliffs bedecked with spectacular pagodas, the national parks are full of wildlife and treks through thick tropical forests end up at tumbling waterfalls. Closer to Hanoi are traditional craft villages which produce fine silks, pottery and woodcarvings. Several old French hill stations give a glimpse of how life used to be.

SOUTH OF HANOI

BAT TRANG VILLAGE

Some 10km (6 miles) southeast of Hanoi, potters carry on a 500-year-old tradition in the village of **Bat Trang** ❷. Rather incongruously, large showrooms with wide glass windows dominate the main street, while the oldest part of town, near the river, is threaded with walled alleyways. What appear to be cowpats stuck on the brick walls are really blobs of coal drying out for use as fuel. A ceramics market has been built for tour groups, but the most interesting areas are hidden in the alleys behind the modern shop fronts. Inside these tiny workspaces are brick kilns and great vats of white liquid clay fed by a network of troughs. Bat Trang artisans used to make bricks, but now

Map on page 134

Main Attractions

Bat Trang
Dau Pagoda
Van Phuc
Perfume Pagoda
Thay Pagoda
Tay Phuong Pagoda
Ba Vi National Park
Hung kings' Temples
Tam Dao

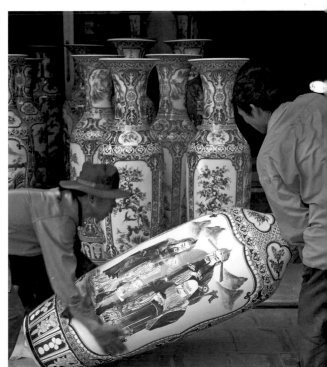

Ceramic urns at Bat Trang.

Eat

If you fancy snacking on snake in Le Mat, then there are plenty of places to choose from. It is not for the squeamish though, as the creatures are slain in front of diners, their hearts are removed and then used as part of a drink. Grass snakes are the most popular variety, but cobras are available – and much more expensive.

they concentrate solely on glazed ceramics, which include teapots, dinnerware and 3-metre (12ft) -tall blue-and-white urns destined for temples and pagodas.

Along the riverside is the village **communal house**, dedicated to Bach Ma (White Horse), King Le Thanh Tong's guardian spirit, as well as five village heroes, including Hua Chi Cao, who introduced ceramics to the area. A wall plaque, villagers say, was a gift from Emperor Gia Long and honours Bat Trang for making the bricks used to construct the imperial city of Hue in the early 19th century.

LE MAT SNAKE VILLAGE

The return from Bat Trang to Hanoi can include a snake dinner at **Le Mat**, only 7km (4 miles) outside the city. Le Mat locals are experts in hunting snakes, raising snakes, serving snake cuisine and creating snake-based medicinal tonics. Restaurants in the touristy village offer cobra and buffalo snake in soups, entrées and appetisers. Traditionally the domain of men, these days

women are also welcome to partake of snake meat. Guests are welcome to watch the snake being seized from its cage, gutted, and then to witness its blood squeezed into a glass of rice alcohol. Bottles of this snake "elixir" with a small cobra suspended inside are sold everywhere, and are said to act as a natural form of Viagra. Be sure to check prices before ordering, as certain snakes are far more expensive than others. On the 23rd day of the 3rd lunar month a special festival is held, featuring ritualistic performances that celebrate the slaying of a giant mythical snake.

EAST OF HANOI

DONG KY VILLAGE

The once infamous craft village of **Dong Ky**, about 15km (9 miles) northeast of Hanoi, was the country's firecracker factory until 1995, when firecrackers were banned throughout Vietnam. At one time the highlight of the year was the January firecracker festival, when competitors armed

A Dong Ky craftsman applies a coat of varnish on hardwood furniture.

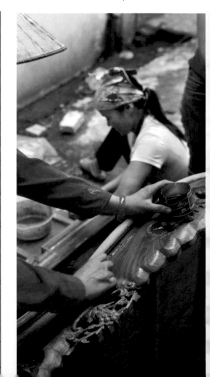

with pillar-sized creations vied to produce the loudest bang. The festival probably evolved from ancient religious rites that invoked thunder, lightning and rain. With the demise of their explosives business, Dong Ky villagers have taken on a more serene occupation – the crafting of intricately carved hardwood furniture, sold locally and in numerous shops in Hanoi.

DAU PAGODA

Dau Pagoda ❸ (Chua Dau; daily 8am–5pm), 30km (20 miles) east of Hanoi in Bac Ninh province, dates from the 13th century. The pagoda is off the beaten track, but the trip is rewarding as the route passes through picturesque countryside and gives glimpses of traditional village life.

Officially called Thanh Dao Tu or Phap Vu Tu, the pagoda is dedicated to the Buddha as well as the Goddess of Rain. Its most interesting attributes are the two lacquered statues that contain the **mummified remains** of two monks – Vu Khac Minh and Vu Khach Truong

– who lived here centuries ago. The story goes that when Vu Khac Minh was approaching death in 1639, he and his nephew locked themselves in the pagoda and asked their disciples to leave them alone for 100 days so they could meditate in peace. When the disciples eventually entered the building, they found the monks motionless but perfectly preserved. The disciples concluded that the monks had attained nirvana and decided to preserve their bodies by covering them in lacquer. The two statues of the pagoda were restored and they are now back in place. The detailed architecture around the pagoda is noteworthy as it reflects all kinds of folklore.

Thrill-seekers can witness a deadly cobra being slaughtered before having it for dinner at Le Mat snake village.

NORTH OF HANOI

CO LOA CITADEL

North of Hanoi, 16km (10 miles) away in Dong Anh District, is Vietnam's first fortified citadel, **Co Loa ❹** (Co Loa Thanh; daily 8am–5pm), built in the third century BC by King An Duong. The citadel briefly contained

The annual festival at Co Loa.

❂ CO LOA FESTIVAL

The annual Co Loa festival held in the first lunar month honours King An Duong Vuong. It takes place over several days and is a great way to see numerous traditional celebrations and activities. A procession of a dozen sedan chairs arrives at the village gate, followed by an incense-offering ceremony, with village elders resplendent in their ceremonial silk gowns. On the main day, the sixth of the first lunar month, another procession takes place featuring a small statue of the king and another, headless, statue of his daughter. The decapitated figure symbolises her punishment for revealing a magic crossbow to her Chinese husband. Festivities involve ear-splittingly loud firecrackers, traditional games, cock fighting, archery, human chess, wrestling and dance.

Buddha figurines in a temple at the Co Loa Citadel.

Entrance to the temple dedicated to King An Duong at Co Loa.

the national capital (AD 939–44), and was constructed within walls in three concentric circles that formed an 8km (5-mile) battlement, parts of which still survive today. In 2014, archaeologists discovered another citadel underneath, belonging to the Dong Son Civilisation (1,000 BC–100 AD) as well as Dong Son potteries, iron products and traces of stoves.

Inside the ramparts is a temple dedicated to King An Duong (257–208 BC) and his daughter Princess My Chau, which has been rebuilt in the last 50 years. According to legend, King An Duong was given a magic crossbow by a golden tortoise that made him invincible in battle. His daughter, married to the son of a Chinese general, showed her husband the crossbow and he in turn stole it and gave it to his father. As a result, the Chinese were able to invade and defeat King An Duong and claim large tracts of his land. Realising he was doomed, the king killed the princess and then himself. A pond also houses a statue of King An Duong shooting the legendary crossbow.

One of the pagodas is dedicated to the princess My Chau, while another, **Am Mi Chau**, contains an array of archaeological finds that are of limited interest. A festival held at the start of the first lunar month remembers the unfortunate king and his crossbow.

THANH CHUONG VIET PALACE

Thanh Chuong Viet Palace ❺ (http:// vietphuthanhchuong.com; Tue–Sun 9am–5pm) in Hien Ninh commune (Soc Son district) is a two-hour drive north of Hanoi (there is no public transport, so a taxi, rented car or a bicycle are the only ways to get there). Designed and built by painter Thanh Chuong in 2003, this 10,000 sq m complex features historic-looking buildings, including traditional two-tiered stilt houses and a thatched cottage with earthen walls, said to be the replica of the artist's childhood home. The interiors are decorated with antiques (or at least good replicas) and Thanh Chuong's Picasso-like paintings. There is even a small water puppet theatre by the pond, where shows for up to 80 visitors are held. Wonderfully located on the slopes of mount Day Dieu, the palace is a traditional Vietnamese living space where, as the artist says, 'the sky, earth, animals and trees exist in perfect harmony'. A 100-year-old upgraded building in the middle of the magnificent garden houses a nice restaurant. There is also a tea house and a gift shop catering to tourists.

WEST OF HANOI: HA TAY PROVINCE

The area west of Hanoi and the provinces to the southeast and southwest are the most interesting and diverse destinations within touching distance of the capital. Technically, Ha Tay is still a part of the capital, as Hanoi extended its administrative boundaries in 2008 to include all of this province.

Leave Hanoi by the southwest on Highway 6. It can take up to an hour to negotiate the sprawl of vehicles and construction around the city, but the traffic will eventually thin out, and the two-lane road is flat and in good condition. The first point of interest is **Van Phuc ❻**. This is a traditional silk-weaving village within the town of **Ha Dong**, which is sometimes a stop on day tours to the Perfume Pagoda.

Families in Van Phuc have been producing silk for centuries, but it was only during the late 1990s that the numerous retail shops lining the main street sprang up. Many of the shop owners here also own silk shops along Hanoi's Hang Gai Street, but prices are, not surprisingly, lower here. As well as purchasing silk fabrics by the metre and ordering made-to-measure clothes, you can also see old-fashioned electric looms introduced by the French still being used in the workshops.

A short distance further on, the **National Museum of Ho Chi Minh Trail** (Bao Tang Duong Ho Chi Minh; www.btlsqsvn.org.vn; Tue–Sat 7.30–11am and 1.30–4.30pm) lies 13km (8 miles)

southwest of Hanoi. Heavy on propaganda, the three floors of exhibits focus on the efforts of the thousands of people who struggled to create and maintain the vital arms supply route through Vietnam, Laos and Cambodia. War buffs will appreciate the incredible displays of weaponry.

PERFUME PAGODA

When it comes to visiting the **Perfume Pagoda ❼** (Chua Huong; http://chuahuong.vn; daily 7.30am–6pm), the journey is just as important as the destination. Around 60km (38 miles) southwest of Hanoi, this sacred pilgrimage site is best approached by rowing boat on the dramatic and swiftly flowing Yen River (Song Yen). Looming over the quiet countryside are the jagged karsts of the Hoang Son mountains.

The dreamy landscape has been compared to Guilin in China. An oarswoman, rowing in a particularly strenuous fashion, will propel the flat-bottomed boat that will take you to the Perfume Pagoda. If a Vietnamese

⊙ Tip

Day trips to the Perfume Pagoda booked in Hanoi should include transport, entrance fees, boat fees and lunch. With just about every tour agent offering the trip, prices can vary anywhere from US$20–60 per person, with the cheaper trips likely to involve large groups. Be prepared for persistent souvenir peddlers.

Visitors arrive by rowing boat at the Perfume Pagoda, set amid beautiful limestone hills.

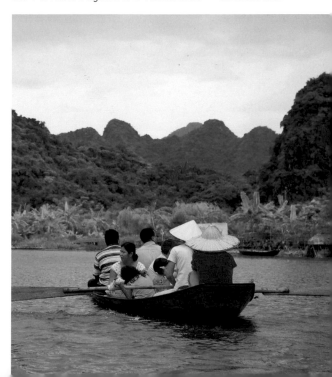

interpreter accompanies you on the ride, the oarswoman can point out peaks with such quaint names as the Crouching Elephant, Nun and Rice Tray – otherwise you will just have to make out the shapes for yourself.

After a winding 4km (2.5-mile) river journey that takes about 90 minutes, the boat will pull up to a cluster of pavilions and market stalls. A short walk up the bottom slopes of **Huong Tich Mountain** (Mountain of the Fragrant Traces) leads visitors to a path that ascends 4km (2.5 miles) to the pagoda complex. The hike is arduous and slippery and can take 1–1.5 hours. To improve access, a **chairlift** (daily 7am–6pm) takes pilgrims up and down in a few minutes – the views are stunning.

The collection of pagodas and Buddhist shrines at the top of the mountain is built into the limestone cliffs and caves. Among the sites are **Pagoda to Heaven** (Chua Thien Chu), **Pagoda of Purgatory** (Giai Oan Chu) and the main attraction itself, the **Pagoda of the Perfumed**

Stairway down into the Pagoda of the Perfumed Vestige (Huong Tich Chu).

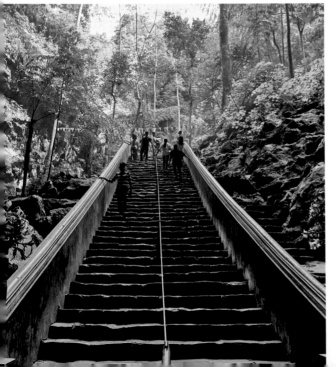

Vestige (Huong Tich Chu). The latter is located inside the **Huong Tich Grotto**, which lies just below the summit of the mountain. Some 120 stone steps bedecked with Buddhist flags lead down to the "dragon's mouth" entrance, where worshippers jostle to rub banknotes on a large, wet stalactite said to bestow wealth. In the darkness of the 50-metre (160ft) -high cave, surrounded by stalactites and stalagmites, are numerous gilded Buddhist statues with altar offerings of fruit and incense. Centre stage is an image of Quan Am – Goddess of Mercy and the female personification of Buddha.

Visiting during the pagoda's annual seven-week festival, from March to April, is not advised, as the grounds are thronged with thousands of worshippers and it can be a struggle to get around. At any time of year overly aggressive vendors can be a problem.

THAY PAGODA

One of Vietnam's oldest pagodas, **Thay Pagoda** ❽ (Chua Thay; daily 8am–5pm), also known as the Pagoda of the Master, is nestled against the hillside in **Sai Son Village**, about 37km (23 miles) west of Hanoi. It shares its compound with the smaller **Ca Pagoda** (Chua Ca).

Founded in 1132 by King Ly Thai To, Thay Pagoda has been renovated a number of times. It is dedicated to three individuals: Ly Than Tong, king of the Ly dynasty from 1127 to 1138; Sakyamuni, the historical Buddha and his 18 *arhat*, or disciples; and the venerable monk Dao Hanh. All are represented by elaborate lacquer statues, some dating back to the 12th and 13th centuries. The pagoda complex itself is divided into three sections: the outer section is for ceremonies, the middle section is a Buddhist shrine, while the inner temple is dedicated to Dao Hanh. Known as The Master, Dao Hanh was a great herbalist who is said to have created the water puppet theatre. Dao Hanh is commemorated by a large sandalwood statue within the main pagoda.

On the fifth, sixth and seventh days of the third lunar month, the district's premier puppet troupes stage elaborate shows on the pond in front of the pagoda. Folk plays, chess games, a recital of Dao Hanh's feats and a procession of tablets also take place. The two arched, covered bridges – **Moon Bridge** and **Sun Bridge** – date from 1602.

A climb up the hillside leads to two more small shrines and a superb view of the pagoda complex and surrounding countryside. Several limestone grottoes in the vicinity are worth exploring, notably **Hang Cac Co**. As the pagoda grounds are vast, it is worthwhile hiring a local guide.

TAY PHUONG PAGODA

About 6km (4 miles) from the Thay Pagoda complex – and usually visited in conjunction with day trips from Hanoi – is **Tay Phuong Pagoda** ❾ or the Pagoda of the West (Chua Tay Phuong; daily 8am–5pm), in the picturesque village of **Thac Xa**. It is perched atop the 50-metre (164ft) Tay Phuong hill, which is said to resemble a buffalo. The pagoda dates from the 8th century, though the present structure was rebuilt in 1794. It is famous for its 74 statues of *arhats* (Buddhist saints) carved from jackfruit wood, which illustrate stories from the Buddhist scriptures and all aspects of the human condition.

The pagoda is reached by climbing 238 laterite steps, closely pursued by incense and souvenir vendors. Built of ironwood with bare brick walls, the pagoda comprises the **Prostration Hall** (Bai Duong), the **Central Hall** (Chinh Dien) and the **Back Hall** (Hau Cung). The overlapping roofing of the halls is decorated with ornate carvings and lacquer figures of dragons

and animals. Day tours to the Thay and Tay Phuong pagodas sometimes stop at nearby **So village**, which specialises in the age-old trade of making noodles from the flour of yams and manioc.

BA VI NATIONAL PARK

Some 48km (30 miles) west of Hanoi and still within Ha Tay province is the scenic **Ba Vi Mountain** (Nui Ba Vi) and **Ba Vi National Park** ❿ (Vuon Quoc Gia Ba Vi; http://vuonquocgiabavi.com.vn; daily daylight hours). The park's protected forest boasts a number of rare and endangered plants and animals, including several varieties of flying squirrel, though tourist activity in the area means your chances of seeing them are limited. Regardless, the park's large orchid garden and many hiking paths make it a favourite destination for many city-weary Hanoians looking to commune with nature.

At the summit of the 1,276-metre (4,861ft) Ba Vi Mountain is a temple dedicated to Ho Chi Minh. The walk is gruelling but rewards from the summit

The statues of Buddhist saints at the Tay Phuong Pagoda are carved from jackfruit wood.

Ornate dragon motifs on the roofs of the Tay Phuong Pagoda.

Image of a 3rd-century BC guardian warrior, protector of the Hung kings.

Ba Vi National Park is a green getaway for city-dwellers.

are astounding views of the surrounding countryside and even Hanoi on clear days. At the base of the mountain is Vietnam's oldest golf course, **BRG Kings' Island Golf Resort** (tel: 04-3368 6555; http://brgkingsislandgolf.vn).

PHU THO PROVINCE

To the northwest of Hanoi is the province of Phu Tho, which is considered to be the cradle of the pre-Vietnamese Hung Lac people and the ancestral home of the Viet, who settled in the area before moving into the Red River Delta. Ancient bronze relics up to 4,000 years old have been discovered in the region, including the famous Dong Son drums, and the area still bears the marks of its early settlers, evidenced by the remains of the Hung kings' temples.

HUNG KINGS' TEMPLES

The original Hung temples date back to the 3rd century BC, when a line of 18 Hung kings graced the throne of Vang Lang, as the kingdom was then known. In the third month of the lunar calendar, a major festival is held at **Thuong Temple** (Den Thuong; daily 8am–5pm; free) in Phu Tho province to celebrate the lives of the Hung kings. The event is a major event and draws thousands of devotees from Hanoi.

Altogether there are three **Hung kings' temples** (open daily) on the slopes of **Nghia Linh Mountain** (Nui Nghia Linh), some 90km (56 miles) northwest of Hanoi. The **Lowest Temple** (Den Ha) is reached by climbing up 225 steps and is dedicated to Au Co, the legendary mother of the Viet people. At the back of this temple is an incredible statue of a Buddha with 1,000 arms and eyes. Below the temple, at the foot of the hill, is an arched portal flanked by two huge stone columns engraved with two parallel sentences glorifying the origins of the Vietnamese people.

A further 168 steps lead up to the **Middle Temple** (Den Hung), where the seventh Hung king was crowned and where the rulers would gather to discuss state affairs. Only another 102 steps remain to reach the **Superior Temple** (Den Thuong). This temple is dedicated to the deities of heaven, earth and rice, as well as to Than Giong, the infant hero who in the 3rd century BC is said to have chased out the Chinese Han invaders, assisted by a genie that took the form of an iron horse. The temple, rebuilt in the 15th century, is adorned with dragon and guardian warriors. The well at the foot of the mountain is said to be where the 18th Hung king's daughter brushed her hair and watched her reflection in its clear water.

VINH PHUC PROVINCE

BINH SON TOWER AND VINH SON SNAKE FARM

Northeast of Phu To province is Vinh Phuc province, where **Binh Son Tower**, part of the **Vinh Khanh Pagoda** (Chua Vinh Khanh; daily 8am–5pm),

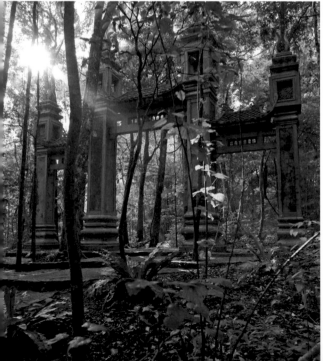

rises some 16 metres (52ft) into the sky in Lap Thach District. Built in the 13th century during the Tran dynasty, the impressive 11-tiered baked-clay tower of the pagoda is adorned with many intricate carvings.

Nearby, in Vinh Lac District, is the **Vinh Son Snake Farm** (daily 8am–5pm; free). Established in the 1990s, the farm breeds indigenous snakes and produces snake wine and an ointment containing snake venom that is used by Vietnamese to relieve muscle and joint inflammation.

TAM DAO

Tam Dao ⑬ is a popular place to escape the capital's summer heat and humidity. Established as a hill station by the French in the early 1900s, Tam Dao sits at an altitude of 880 metres (2,886ft) on a large plateau some 70km (43 miles) north of Hanoi in the Tam Dao mountain range. These mountains stretch 80km (50 miles) from northwest to southeast, separating Vinh Phuc province from Thai Nguyen province in the north.

Tam Dao means "three islands", the name deriving from three mountains – **Thien Thi**, **Thach Ban** and **Phu Nghia** – which rise to about 1,400 metres (4,592ft) and dominate the landscape. From a distance they resemble three islands jutting above a sea of clouds.

Tam Dao hill station is part of the **Tam Dao National Park** (Vuon Quoc Gia Tam Dao; daily daylight hours; www.tamdaonp.com.vn). Rare trees and plants cover the mountain slopes, while the forests teem with more than 200 bird species and dozens of kinds of mammal, but you will need a local guide to see anything other than the butterflies and birds. It can be chilly and damp throughout the year, but it's a refreshing escape from Hanoi during the enervating summer heat. Facilities and accommodation are rather run-down. The town's restaurants and shops sadly do booming business in illegal game meat and animal parts. During the high season from May to August, bus-loads of Vietnamese arrive to dine at the game meat restaurants, then drink and sing at karaoke bars. As far as hiking options go, a 20-minute walk from Tam Dao leads to the popular 45-metre (148ft) -high **Silver Waterfall** (Thac Ba). To reach the more remote forested areas is a full day's walk.

For the Vietnamese, Tam Dao also has melancholy revolutionary significance. After the disastrous Thai Nguyen mutiny and uprising in August 1917, nearly 100 survivors fled here to make a doomed three-month last stand against the French army. Close to the end, one legendary leader, Sgt Trinh Van Can, committed suicide. The French made every effort to track down and kill every last rebel soldier and political prisoner who escaped; in the end, the French claimed that only five eluded them.

The Tam Dao Golf Course (www.tamdaogolf.com) opened in 2007 and is a notable addition to the area's facilities.

⊘ Tip

In some areas surrounding Hanoi it's not uncommon to find all manner of wildlife on restaurant menus. Despite legislation, leopards, bears, gibbons, macaques, pangolins, lizards, turtles, cobras, pythons and tigers are illegally hunted for food and medicine. Visitors should avoid buying these wildlife products.

Tam Dao.

Northern Vietnam

Vinh Bac Bo

(Gulf of Tonkin)

N

0   50 km
0   50 miles

Terraced farms near Sa Pa.

NORTHWEST VIETNAM

The far northwest is a wild, untamed land that demands exploration. Those who dare to brave the perilous roads and rough terrain are treated to magnificent scenery and remote minority villages.

To the west and northwest of Hanoi, the flat-as-a-pancake, rice-growing delta of the Red River (Song Hong) soon gives way to deep green valleys and craggy mountain ranges inhabited by a number of ethnic minority groups. These days, the people farm in the shadow of modern hydroelectric dams supplying power to much of the rest of the country. Bounded on the north by lengthy borders with Laos and China, this is a stunningly wild and picturesque region, but those who venture this far on the "northwest loop" can expect poor roads, treacherous passes and few modern tourist amenities. Travellers who do make the journey are rewarded for their efforts with serene valleys and some of the most spectacular mountain vistas anywhere in Southeast Asia. These include the Son La and Moc Chau highlands and the enormous Hoang Lien Son mountain range in the extreme northwest.

Heading southwest from Hanoi, Hoa Binh province's scenic Mai Chau Valley offers a chance to explore the lush landscape and stay overnight in an authentic White Tai minority village. Further northwest, French colonial rule met its end in a mountainous valley known as Dien Bien Phu. From here, a trip north takes visitors to the hill retreat of Sa Pa, the most popular destination in the northwest. Sa Pa is a lively mountain town filled with colourful ethnic minority markets, serious trekking opportunities and access to the highest peak in Vietnam: Fansipan Mountain. Development has been rapid, with hotels and more souvenir sellers, while ethnic groups, notably the Hmong, have embraced the town's new-found fame and many work as guides. Reaching the northwest is easy as trains connect Hanoi to Lao Cai, near Sa Pa, followed by a short minibus ride. Getting around the region can be more time-consuming,

◎ Main Attractions

Mai Chau Valley
Dien Bien Phu City
Sa Pa
Mount Fansipan
Bac Ha

Map on page 142

Flower Hmong ethnic minority girls.

though here it really is as much about the journey through the mountains as it is the final destination.

HOA BINH PROVINCE

HOA BINH CITY

Those who arrive in **Hoa Binh City** may wonder what its appeal is. While it may appear rather industrial and plain, the city is a great base from which to visit ethnic groups and natural sites. Among those who make their home near here are Muong, Hmong, Tai, Tay and Dao (pronounced "Zao") ethnic groups.

Hoa Binh, about 75km (47 miles) west of Hanoi, was the site of much bloodshed during the early 1950s when the French and Viet Minh forces battled for control of the area. Some of the bloodiest battles were waged on the Black River (Song Da) around the so-called Notre Dame Rock. In the end, the French forces retreated, but for the Viet Minh, Hoa Binh was a dress rehearsal for a later, decisive showdown at Dien Bien Phu (see page 148).

Today, **Hoa Binh City**, the provincial capital, is a sprawling industrial area. Just outside of the urban area is the **Hoa Binh Dam** and hydroelectric power station, which supplies energy to towns as far away as the Mekong Delta. Built in 1979 with technical assistance and money from the former Soviet Union, construction of the dam took 15 years and displaced approximately 50,000 people from the Black River Valley, which is now submerged. It's worth taking a look at the dam; there are tours available and tickets may be purchased at the entrance (daily 8–11am, 2–5pm).

While few ethnic minority people wear their traditional clothing, it is possible to visit more rural areas and stay overnight in nearby villages where their presence and culture are obvious. Hoa Binh's markets and shops are good sources of tribal souvenirs, in particular brocade garments and weaving. Local dishes include rice cooked in bamboo. On the whole, though, foreign tourists generally give Hoa Binh a miss, stopping only briefly

The Hoa Binh Dam is an important source of energy for the country.

before heading for the pleasantly rural ambience of nearby Mai Chau Valley, a picturesque Thai ethnic minority area.

MAI CHAU

Located 135km (84 miles), or 3.5 hours' driving time, from Hanoi on Highway 6 is the serene **Mai Chau Valley** . If you've stopped at Hoa Binh City, Mai Chau is only 60km (40 miles) further along the road. The valley makes for an excellent weekend outing and is an ideal base for treks to nearby highland villages, with none of the hassling hawkers that plague other areas. Famous for its *ruou can* (a rice wine drunk through long bamboo straws), Mai Chau is a collection of small villages, farms and individual stilt houses spread out over a vast, verdant valley. Peaceful and charming, it is also the closest place from Hanoi where countryside trekking can be done, along with overnight stays in an authentic ethnic minority village.

While most tour agencies drop off guests at **Lac Village** (Ban Lac), a commercial White Tai village popular with Vietnamese tourist groups, it's better not to linger here. Stop for a meal after the drive from Hanoi and then set off with a guide to one of the farther-flung and more authentic White Tai villages deeper in the valley.

White Tai women are renowned master weavers. Beneath their stilt houses is usually a loom or two where they create their fine textiles. At the village centre are shops with displays of beautiful shawls and scarves. White Tai womenfolk wear tight blouses held together in front by a row of silver clasps. Their sarong-style skirts are usually dark-coloured with thin plain or warp *ikat* horizontal stripes and embroidered hems. The Sunday market is the highlight of the week for most, and sees women from nearby ethnic groups come to sell fruit. Traditional dances are also an integral part of the market.

SON LA PROVINCE

Continuing northwest, **Moc Chau** in neighbouring Son La province is a stunningly beautiful highland valley

Farmland amid rolling hills and expansive valleys at Mai Chau.

Ethnic music and dance performance at Mai Chau.

Vendor selling barbecued corn at a Son La Market.

Former prison cell at the restored Son La Provincial Museum.

surrounded by low mountains. Sprinkled with prosperous villages of Muong and White Tai and Black Tai people, it is laced with a vast irrigation network that feeds the fields of wet rice as well as the stilt-house villages. Traditionally fishermen, each Tai household has its own fish pond and prominently displayed nets.

MOC CHAU

Moc Chau owes much of its current fame to the Dutch. Cows from the Netherlands were imported to the area, and a dairy industry was born: you'll know when you are approaching Moc Chau when you see the black-and-white dairy cows wandering across the road. Much of the area is devoted to dairy farming (many farmers relocated here following the building of the new Son La hydropower plant), so be sure to try out some of the famously rich yoghurt, ice cream or Moc Chau-branded chocolate bars. Visitors can even get closer to nature by milking the cows themselves. During the coldest months, January and February, the

temperature can fall to –3°C (27°F). With central heating nearly impossible to find, visitors need to pack appropriate clothing.

Highway 6 from Moc Chau climbs west past hills cultivated with tea, coffee, cotton, and fruit trees, including mulberry, whose leaves feed silkworms. The road winds through the mountainous landscapes of Son La province close to the border with Laos. The region is home to many ethnic minorities, including Hmong, Mnong, Muong, Mun, Kho Mu, Dao, Tay, White Tai and Black Tai, Xinh Mun and Hoa peoples.

Further northwest along Highway 6, the road passes through idyllic Muong and Black Tai villages with their long, precarious suspension bridges and miniature hydroelectric generators. While the forest edging the road here seems thick, locals have long plundered it for firewood and house-building materials. From here on, one will often see Black Tai and Muong people walking along the roadside. Black Tai women can be identified by the

⊙ THE END OF FRENCH RULE

French colonial forces tried, and ultimately failed, to tame the wild northwest for 40 years. In 1953, as part of Vietnamese efforts to eject the French, General Vo Nguyen Giap and his Viet Minh soldiers launched excursions into northern Laos, reaching the outskirts of the royal city of Luang Prabang. The French, believing Dien Bien Phu was key to preventing a communist takeover of Laos – a French protectorate – easily recaptured it in late 1953. At that time, Dien Bien Phu was an old and ramshackle trading village at the intersection of three major drug routes.

General Vo and his Viet Minh forces launched decisive attacks starting on 13 March 1954, and 56 days later the Viet Minh had managed to rout the French troops, led by General Christian de Castries, and planted their flag on the main command bunker. The Battle of Dien Bien Phu is hugely significant as it finally booted the French out of Vietnam and its other colonies in Indochina. But the victory was bittersweet: the Geneva Agreement, signed months after the war in August 1954, resulted in Vietnam being divided at the 17th parallel – a communist north and a capitalist south, with tragic consequences in the following years.

elaborately embroidered folded cloths that they balance precariously on their heads. Muong women usually wear white rectangular scarves, long skirts and short vests open at the front. Their skirts are usually adorned with a large silk belt embroidered with all kinds of fantastic creatures.

Dai Yem Fall is about 4km (2.5 miles) from Moc Chau. Two streams join together here and fall from a height of 100 metres (330ft) into a clear lake, surrounded by scenic forest.

SON LA CITY

The capital of Son La province, **Son La City** ❸ is 100km (60 miles) northwest from Moc Chau. The minuscule "city" runs for just over a kilometre on the southwestern bank of the **Nam La River** (Song Nam La). Despite increased development and a scattering of shiny new government buildings, it is still the familiar, faceless Vietnamese provincial town of dusty roads and tall, narrow houses. In the early mornings, many traditionally dressed Hmong, Muong, Xinh Mun, and Black and White Tai minority people gather to trade in the market.

The city's main **To Hieu Street** is named after a political prisoner jailed for sedition in the 1940s. He died in prison from malaria, and is best known for planting the prison compound's single, symbolic peach tree. A number of local landmarks bear his name.

Above To Hieu Street, on a wooded promontory, the brick ruins of the former French prison have been converted into the **Son La Provincial Museum** (Bao Tang Tinh Son La; tel: 02-285 2022; daily 7.30–11am and 1–5.30pm). Originally built in 1908, the prison was once the residence of thousands of political prisoners. Visitors can view the prison's original cells, complete with their food slots and leg shackles. Partially rebuilt for tourists, most of the compound was blasted away during the war with the French. The site also sustained heavy damage when it was used as a dumping ground for unused ammunition by US bombers returning from missions to Hanoi and Haiphong. As

Figurines of coal miners in the tunnel at A1 Hill.

A strong military presence remains in Dien Bien Phu City.

The significance of Dien Bien Phu's past is easily lost on the younger generation. Pictured here is A1 Hill, which was the scene of much bloodshed.

Artefacts from the battle of Dien Bien Phu – such as the charred remains of military jeeps – are on display at the Museum of the Dien Bien Phu Victory.

well as being a historically important site, it also has an interesting display of objects belonging to the dozen ethnic groups that live in the area.

AROUND SON LA

After the drabness of the city, Son La's environs are refreshingly verdant and lush, offering rice fields, fruit orchards and attractive ethnic minority villages. **Ban Mong**, a Black Tai village outside of Son La, about 6km (4 miles) south of the prison, has some scummy-looking public hot springs that are best avoided. The **Tham Coong Cave**, northwest of town, isn't worth the admission price, but there are nice walks in the countryside. Ask at your hotel for directions. Tham Tet Tong is a series of caves just over 1km (0.5 miles) from Son La and is worth checking out.

The Vietnamese government has big plans in store for Son La as it is expected to become part of a planned trade corridor that extends into northern Lao. However, this development comes at the expense of the

170km (106-mile) stretch of Highway 6 between Son La and Dien Bien Phu, which will be torn up, re-cut and re-laid in the future.

DIEN BIEN PROVINCE

Continuing west from Son La for about 90km (56 miles) brings you to the small town of **Tuan Giao**. The intersecting road to the west is Highway 279, the route to **Dien Bien Phu ❹**, which is a further 80km (50 miles) and at least 3.5 hours' driving time away.

DIEN BIEN PHU CITY

Famed for being the site of a battle that signalled the end of French colonialism in Asia, **Dien Bien Phu City**, the capital of Dien Bien province, lies on the east bank of the **Nam Rom River** (Song Nam Rom) at the northern end of the Muong Thanh valley. Named Muong Thanh by its Tai rice farmers, the heart-shaped, pancake-flat valley extends 20km (12 miles) from north to south and 6km (4 miles) east to west. This valley was the site of a 57-day siege – the famous Battle of Dien Pien Phu– which spelt the ignominious end to French colonialism in Asia. It is encircled by steep, green hills from which tens of thousands of Viet Minh troops launched their assault on the French garrisons in 1954. The road leads on from Dien Bien Phu to the border with Laos, just 35km (22 miles) away, but is not generally open to tourists.

Dien Bien Phu was just another grey, concrete town until 2003, when it was bestowed city status in preparation for its new role as provincial capital. In 2004, the celebration of the 50th anniversary of the French defeat brought about a mini tourism surge and building boom, soon to be followed by an increase in the number of flights from Hanoi. The 2014 60th anniversary celebrations attracted 315,000 tourists, including 48,800 non-Vietnamese. However, generally tourists are something of a rarity and facilities are limited, with only basic accommodation available. For the hardier traveller, the route from Sa Pa has gorgeous views.

BATTLEGROUND SIGHTS

Tourists can visit **A1 Hill**, known as "Eliane 2" to the French, was the scene of fierce fighting and is now a war memorial dedicated to the Viet Minh who died here. There's also a bunker and entrance to a tunnel dug by coal miners. The miners stuffed the tunnel with 1,000kg (2,205lbs) of explosives and detonated it on 6 May to signal the final assault on the French bases.

The state-of-the art **Museum of the Dien Bien Phu Victory** (Nha Trung Bay Thang Lich Su Dien Bien Phu; daily 7–11am and 1.30–5pm) was inaugurated in 2014 to mark the 60th anniversary of the famous battle which dealt a deadly blow to the French colonial empire in Indochina. Built in the shape of a truncated cone – which symbolises the camouflage nets worn on helmets by the Vietnamese soldiers during the battle – the museum covers an area of 22,300 sq metres (240,035 sq ft) and features displays, reconstructions (including General de Castries's main command bunker), photographs and

⊙ **Tip**

Avoid taking photos in areas adjacent to the border and anywhere within sight of a military installation. Travellers who learnt the hard way have had to pay large punitive "fees" and had their cameras confiscated.

Black Hmong people in the hills outside Sa Pa. Although increasingly touristy these days, Sa Pa still retains its idyllic feel.

OPIUM IN THE NORTHWEST

Despite government efforts, the lucrative rewards for growing opium are hard to resist for the poor farmers of northwest Vietnam.

Lan, a 27-year-old Black Hmong woman from Lai Chau province, toils at her family's small patch of rice paddy at least eight hours a day. Each morning well before dawn, she and her husband trek for 9km (6 miles) down a hillside to a piece of land given to them by the government. Lan and her husband Mo were given the land because both their parents are opium addicts, as are a number of their neighbours. Under a programme to provide arable land to ethnic minorities in the rugged northwestern highlands, the government hopes to curb the region's propensity for cultivating – and using – opium.

Though pleased to have a good plot of land, Lan says the government doesn't do enough to lift

Harvesting the opium poppy for heroin is lucrative but illegal.

Hmong like her out of poverty, leaving many to feel they have no choice but to grow and trade the illicit drug. Struggling with poverty and a lack of alternatives, Lai Chau and other provinces in northwestern Vietnam have a long history of opium cultivation and use. A valuable cash crop, ethnic minorities have used opium not only medicinally but also as a means of alleviating hunger.

GOVERNMENT PROGRAMMES

The central government tried hard to eradicate opium cultivation after independence in 1945, but demand for heroin – processed from the opium poppy – became so great in the 1960s as a result of the US military presence in the south that its production in places like Lai Chau boomed. After the US Army departed in 1975, demand for opium dropped back down to pre-1945 levels.

Since then, the government has done much to destroy poppy fields, though little to provide economic alternatives. According to estimates, poppy cultivation in Lai Chau fell from 12,200 hectares (30,144 acres) in 1992 to just 32 hectares (80 acres) in June 2004, the last time the Vietnamese government released official figures. However, the scale of the problem remains vast: in 2014 the number of opiate users in Southeast Asia was estimated at 3.4 million.

The region's proximity to Laos and China and its porous borders have long made northwest Vietnam a major transit point. Also driving production is the fact that drug abuse has surged sharply in Vietnam's big cities in the past decade.

Today, those selected for the government-run crop diversification programme from Lan's village grow rice, cotton, fruit, tea and spices at the bottom of a remote valley. But due to the long, backbreaking work that brings in less than half the worth of a season's poppy crop, Lan is tempted to return to the old ways.

The consequences of buying, possessing or using opium, heroin or any other drugs are extremely harsh in Vietnam. Traffickers are subject to the death penalty, and charges of simple possession can land a foreigner up to five years in jail. Purchasing opium from ethnic minority people reinforces an unhealthy practice, and some sellers are known to work for the police.

plenty of weapons used during the conflict, which lasted from 1945 to 1954. Across the street is a **Viet Minh Cemetery** where some of the Viet Minh soldiers are buried.

Towering over town from its vantage position at D1 Hill is the Dien Bien Phu Victory Monument, a huge bronze statue measuring 12.6 metres (41ft) and weighing 220 tonnes. It depicts three soldiers standing atop the French garrison, one holding a flag, another holding a gun, and the third carrying a child with flowers. On the flag is written *"Quyet chien, quyet thang"* (determined to fight, determined to win).

LAI CHAU PROVINCE

Wedged in between China to the north and Laos to the west, Lai Chau province is covered in thick forests. It was once known for its wildlife, including tigers, bears, bison and pheasants, but sadly this is now hugely diminished due to rampant deforestation, slash-and-burn farming and increased trade in illegal animal products.

MUONG LAY

Running due north of Dien Bien Phu, Highway 12 connects with the historic Thai town formerly known as Lai Chau, some 104km (65 miles) away. Today known as **Muong Lay ❺**, this small town is a good place to stop for lunch or an overnight stay on the way to Sa Pa. Here, the surroundings are striking in their contrast: jagged, unforgiving peaks are set against dense tiers of thick forest. The road into town is in good condition but during the rainy season between May and August, landslides can cause serious delays.

BLACK RIVER DAM

There is much discussion about the damming and inundation of the **Black River** (Song Da) into the Muong Lay Valley for the **Son La hydroelectric power plant**, which is the biggest in Southeast Asia. The first turbines were connected to the national grid in 2010 and the project was completed in 2013. It is estimated that 20,000 households, mainly from ethnic groups, were relocated. The US$2 billion project has a

Red Dao woman doing embroidery work.

⊘ HILL TRIBE ETIQUETTE

While it is essential to be patient when photographing ethnic minority people, it is even more important to be respectful. It is tempting for the beautiful surroundings, striking beauty of the people and their costumes to make photographers forget basic etiquette. Taking a picture without the subject's permission may be interpreted as offensive. Once permission is given, children and adults alike will clamber over travellers to get a glimpse of themselves on the camera's screen. In Sa Pa, industrious Hmong have become used to being photographed (though they often insist that you buy something from them in return). Other ethnic minority groups, including some Red Dao, believe that having their picture taken is bad for their health. Always ask first.

capacity of 2,400 megawatts. Earlier plans for an even grander dam were scaled down owing to environmental and safety concerns.

LAI CHAU TOWN

The new capital of Lai Chau province was moved 150km (93 miles) northeast to the (new) **Lai Chau ⑥** town, which was formerly known as **Tam Duong**. New shops and hotels are a sign of how bustling this town has become. Much of the appeal comes from the White Hmong and Flower Hmong, White Tai and Black Tai, Dao Khau and Giay hill tribes. Visits to ethnic minority villages are popular, but most are only accessible by motorbike. The immediate surroundings here are dirty and dusty, as the nearby hills have been dug out to create more flat land for construction.

LAO CAI PROVINCE

TOWARDS SA PA

Black Hmong farmhands.

The 90km (56-mile) stretch of road from **Lai Chau** to the hill-town retreat of **Sa Pa** – Highway 4D – runs southeast along the dramatic Hoang Lien mountain range. Here, the mountains become higher and craggier and are more thickly forested. The road winds through **Tram Ton Pass**, the highest mountain pass in the country. The sealed road carved into the steep mountainsides was once unstable and subject to landslides because the dirt, laterite and gravel road was repaired by manual labour. Nowadays, this work is performed by heavy machinery and the road is in good condition. During the winter, thick fog and mists can make for a terrifying but eerily beautiful ride.

SA PA TOWN

The picturesque town of **Sa Pa ⑦** is rightly renowned as the jewel in the northwest's crown. At around 1,600 metres (5,500ft) above sea level, its cool climate and rich mix of ethnic groups makes it an unmissable part of any northwest itinerary. It is a relatively small town though, and its sudden rise in popularity has also resulted in an increasingly determined group of locals keen to exploit Sa Pa's new-found fame.

Travellers will know they are approaching once they reach the village of **Binh Lu**. The ethnic minority people who live around here are neither shy nor indifferent to tourists or their cameras. On the contrary, they often take off their metal jewellery and headpieces and proffer them for sale. Primarily villages of Dao people, the women traditionally have close-cropped hair, usually hidden under a black turban, which holds the headpiece, a kind of metal cap with a small box-like crown.

Originally a Black Hmong settlement, Sa Pa was used by the French as a hill-station retreat during the summer months. The temperate climate at an elevation of 1,650 metres (5,413ft) was a welcome respite from the stifling humidity at the lower levels, and reminded the French of home. While the French made it a favourite spot in the 1940s, Sa Pa's current incarnation as a bustling tourist town only took place in the mid-1990s, with the arrival of large numbers of backpackers.

Dramatically perched on the edge of a high plateau, it is surrounded on all sides by theatrical dark-blue peaks enveloped by shifting mist and cloud. All along the lower hillsides of the valleys are terraced rice fields interspersed with minority hill-tribe villages. It is all unbelievably scenic, and best of all, it doesn't take more than 10 minutes to stroll beyond this small frontier town to the breathtaking countryside.

WHEN TO VISIT

Sa Pa can be uncomfortably cold in the winter, especially in January and February when temperatures frequently drop below freezing. It's at times like these that the French open fires are particularly welcome. The busiest tourist season is summer, when the Vietnamese arrive to escape the heat – although this period also coincides with the rainy season. The optimum times for a visit are September to November and March to May, when the skies are bright and the weather is nippy at night.

Any time of year, Sa Pa experiences a tourist surge from Fridays to Sundays. Just about every travel agency in Hanoi offers a weekend getaway to the hill retreat, with many hyping the so-called weekend "love market". No doubt local ethnic minority youth do come to town in the hope of meeting the opposite sex from other villages, but they are wise enough to avoid the gawking tourists and their cameras. What foreigners will see is the weekly rendezvous when villagers come to town to buy, sell and socialise at the bustling marketplace.

ETHNIC MINORITIES

With one of the largest populations of ethnic groups in Vietnam, Sa Pa is the ideal place to interact and learn about the hill tribes. Ethnic Vietnamese make up 15 percent of Sa Pa's population of

Always ask permission before photographing local people.

⊙ Fact

Overnight buses make the 440km (273 mile) trip from Lao Cai to Kunming in China. They stop in Hekou on the Chinese side of the border, from where a taxi takes visitors to Lao Cai. To travel from Vietnam to Uang Khua in Laos, go by bus to the border at Tay Trang, though the onward journey is arduous and time-consuming. Some agencies offer a 4x4 to reach the border, and while it may cost a few extra dollars, it is a wise choice.

Sa Pa Catholic Church.

less than 10,000, with more than half belonging to the Hmong group. Both Black Hmong men and women in this area wear dark-blue, almost black, clothing. It's been dyed with indigo, and there are always indigo fields near Hmong villages. The women and girls wear indigo turbans, skirts, vests and leggings, accessorised with big silver hoop earrings. Their hands are often stained a mixture of blue and green from working with the dye. Men wear baggy shirts and trousers and a long vest, as well as silver and bronze necklaces. Although their embroidered decorations are minimal, the motifs are very similar to those used by the Hmong in Thailand and Laos. Hmong babies here also wear colourful little tasselled caps.

The clothing of the Red Dao people, like their culture and architecture, varies considerably throughout Vietnam. In Sa Pa, the Dao men's attire is similar to the Hmong, but the little patches of embroidered decoration instantly identify them. Like that of their counterparts in Laos and Thailand, Dao embroidery is incredibly dense and colourful and often incorporates dozens of coins and silver beads. Dao women wear loose trousers that stop below the knee. However, Dao women here wear a jacket with a very long back panel, and a cushion-like red turban.

SA PA MARKET

All manner of hill-tribe clothing, jewellery and handicrafts, some quite old, are sold – after fierce bargaining – in the main **Sa Pa Market**. The ethnic minority attire on sale has been adroitly altered for foreign body shapes. Vendors gather at the market every day, but the best time to visit is early on Saturday and Sunday mornings. Throughout the week, Black Hmong and Red Dao women wander about town aggressively touting their clothing and jewellery. Long accustomed to dealing with foreign tourists, these women – some barely in their teens – can usually string together a few words in a number of languages, and English and French quite well.

They can be decidedly tenacious, so don't even glance at their goods unless you're really interested in buying something. While this market is notoriously geared towards tourists these days, markets outside of town are far better places to see how locals live and trade.

SA PA CHURCH

Replaced in the last decade with all manner of mini-hotels and karaoke bars, only a few original buildings – with balconies and cupolas – linger from Sa Pa's days as a French hill station. One of the most noteworthy is **Sa Pa Catholic Church**. Built in 1930, it was shelled in 1952 by the French and again in 1979 by the Chinese. Repaired in 1994, a priest comes in from Lao Cai twice a week to preach to a packed congregation able to recite mass from memory. In the courtyard is the tomb of Father Trinh, a priest who was brutally decapitated on the church grounds in 1952 after confronting a young monk who was having a romantic affair with a village girl.

SA PA TREKS

Trekking is one of the main activities in Sa Pa and the town has several companies that can arrange trips. Most treks follow a similar pattern, heading out from the town for a few hours' trekking, then sleeping over in a remote village – where facilities are understandably basic – before awaking for another morning along makeshift paths. Such tours usually ensure trekkers get to visit the villages of various ethnic groups so a variety of cultures can be seen. Physically, some of the trekking is tough, so those taking part need to be in good physical health, although softer trekking options head for outlying villages like Ta Van, Sin Chai and Ta Phin.

One of the most popular destinations is just 3km (2 miles) outside of Sa Pa: the well-trodden Black Hmong village of **Cat Cat**. The Black Hmong children here squat bare-bottomed in the dirt and pose for tourists' cameras (naturally, in return for money). Dozens of visitors tramp through this small stilt-house village daily on their

Red Dao women at the Sa Pa Market.

way to the nearby **Silver Falls** (Thac Bac), about 12km (7 miles) out of town. Also near the falls is a long, wooden suspension bridge called **Cloud Bridge** (Cau May). Another place of interest is **Can Cau**, up near the border with China. Its Saturday market draws ethnic groups from all around, including some from across the border. Several outlying villages like Ta Vin, Sin Chai and Ta Phin make for pleasant and relatively easy treks.

Hotels and travel agencies in Sa Pa will have more details on all trekking options. Another ideal way to see Sa Pa is by bicycle. Companies around the town have similar packages on offer: most involve overnight stays in a village and some challenging routes through the countryside. Cycling around Sa Pa is increasingly popular and allows visitors to see several different villages within a relatively short space of time.

Flower Hmong women at Bac Ha sell their ebulliently coloured ethnic clothing to tourists to make a living.

MOUNT FANSIPAN

For the truly adventurous (or foolhardy), there is **Mount Fansipan** ⑧ (Nui Phan Si Pan) to conquer. At 3,143 metres (10,310ft) and directly west of Sa Pa, this is Vietnam's highest peak. A guide is mandatory, although there is a trail blazed by previous trekkers. Most visitors book a tour with a travel agency, such as Sapa Sisters Private Trekking Adventures (http://sapasisters. com) or Trekking Sapa (www.trekkingsapa. com). Located in **Hoang Lien Nature Reserve**, the scenery is magnificent, notable for its rhododendron-rich forests and exceptional birdlife. Don't count on seeing any animals though – most of them have either been poached or are extinct.

While there is some rather threadbare camping equipment available for rent in Sa Pa, most climbers choose to outfit themselves for the trek in Hanoi, where it's easy to find good fleece jackets and sturdy shoes. While not technically demanding, the excursion to Mount Fansipan takes at least three days, often longer in rain or misty conditions. Closer to the top, the ascent involves negotiating a number of steep, rocky patches and can be treacherous if the ground is wet. March is perhaps the best time to visit as this is the peak of the dry season. If you decide to make the trip, be sure to book with an experienced local operator.

LAO CAI TOWN

There's little reason to linger in the town of **Lao Cai** ⑨ on the Chinese border. The 40km (25-mile) descent from Sa Pa, however, has spectacular views and the road is in excellent condition. Most travellers who skip the northwest loop and travel directly from Hanoi to Sa Pa take the overnight train for the 320km (199-mile) journey to Lao Cai's terminus first, from where they get off and transfer by bus or car for the road trip to Sa Pa.

In the French days, the colonial elite were carried up and down this route on sedan chairs. Unless tensions crank up again between China and Vietnam, it's perfectly legal to enter and exit China by walking across the **Lao Cai international border** gate bridge during daylight hours. Beyond is the Chinese town of Hekou, where you can take the train to Kunming. Travellers must have a Chinese visa in hand, issued in either Hanoi or Beijing, if they wish to go across the border.

Lao Cai is an ugly, sterile town, partly because it was flattened when China invaded in 1979. It was not the first time it had been occupied by the Chinese. Ironically, the Vietnamese rebuilt it to resemble just another communist Chinese city, with lots of grim cement boxes, wide streets and very little greenery. But the Chinese aren't solely to blame. In early 1951, while testing out his new heavy artillery and the ins and outs of offensive warfare, General Giap set his sights on Lao Cai. With Viet Minh troops outnumbering French five to one, he took the town within a few days. Now there is little here except a casino that plays host to bus loads of Chinese tourists and a bustling market filled with crates of cheap electronics and other goods destined for Hanoi or Beijing.

BAC HA MARKET

About 63km (39 miles) northeast of Lao Cai, little **Bac Ha ⑩** is best known for its colourful and lively **Sunday market**. The town itself is smaller, usually warmer, and has more of a frontier feel than Sa Pa. The market's appeal stems from the sheer variety of hill-tribe minorities represented. Most people in this area belong to one of the Hmong groups, including the colourfully dressed Flower Hmong people, but there are also Dao, Giay, Laichi, Lolo, Nhang, Nung, Phulao, Tai, Thulao and Hoa as well as Vietnamese. Each Sunday, the women gather to socialise and trade, while their husbands drink themselves under the table on rice wine.

Some 2km (1.2 miles) from Bac Ha, through cornfields, is a Flower Hmong village called **Ban Pho**, famous for its maize alcohol. Further afield, the **Can Cau Market**, in a village 18km (11 miles) north of Bac Ha, runs on Saturday and was originally a livestock market.

View of Mount Fansipan, Vietnam's highest peak.

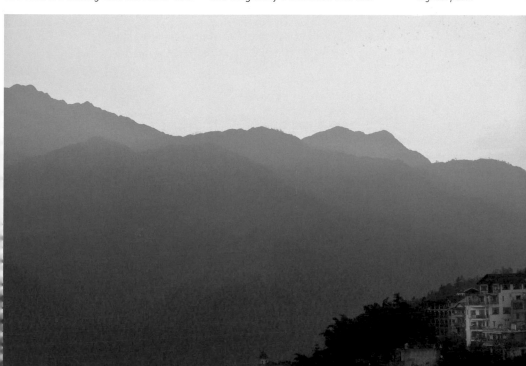

📷 ETHNIC MINORITY CULTURE AND CLOTHING

Vietnam's ethnic minorities live mostly in isolated highland areas, but their traditional culture is under threat from an influx of curious tourists.

The ethnic minorities of Vietnam can be divided into the northern group and the south/central group. Each has its own distinct origins, cultural practices and reactions to change.

In the northern highlands, populations of Tai, Dao, Hmong, Tay and Nung people have migrated from southern China over the past 500 years. They live in stilt houses, wear homespun costumes and sustain some of the best-preserved traditional highland cultures in Southeast Asia.

The central highlands are inhabited by the indigenous Bahnar, Ra De (Ede), Jarai and Sedang people. The rolling hills are suitable for coffee cultivation, and have recently been settled by large numbers of Vietnamese.

The ever-growing number of visitors to Vietnam has given the country's ethnic groups a dilemma: how can they generate an income from tourism but not destroy their culture in the process. In some towns, the push for tourist dollars means certain groups are in danger of becoming caricatures of themselves as their true heritage fades away.

Many minorities have adapted to modern life, building houses on the ground and abandoning their loincloth for clothes. In some areas, notably around Sa Pa, the tourist trade provides a good living. Others, wishing to maintain their traditional lifestyle, move deep into the remaining forest to live in isolation and sustain themselves through slash-and-burn agriculture. They can be seen in urban centres on market days trading their produce.

Women of the Red Dao minority at the market.

Flower Hmong women in their trademark colourful garb. They gather at Bac Ha Market near Sa Pa every Sunday sell handicrafts and silver jewellery.

Hmong girl in traditional indigo-coloured clothing.

Elaborate embroidered detailing on a Red Dao costume.

Hill-tribe textiles

All the hill tribes of the northern highlands have retained their own textile industries, and these are currently enjoying a revival as the number of overseas tourists and Vietnamese visitors increases.

White Tai people in Mai Chau Valley use hand looms to weave long cotton scarves, which are then dyed in brightly coloured stripes using traditional vegetable dyes and tied at the ends into elaborate tassels. In the Sa Pa region, Hmong women carry their embroidery with them to the terraced rice fields and work on their bags and hats during rest periods.

Large numbers of imitation embroidered items are now sold at the market. Visitors are urged to make their purchases with caution if they want the genuine article.

Intricate silver jewellery figures prominently in the cultures of the hill-tribe minorities.

...e red belt on this Red Dao women's costume is a bridal ...coration, only worn on the wearer's wedding day.

...broidery is a thriving trade as hill-tribe minorities find ...eady market among visitors in the northern and central ...hlands.

This Ede woman's clothes look traditional, but are in fact a modern innovation.

Chinese-style junk on Halong Bay.

NORTHEAST VIETNAM

The northeast is characterised by dramatic karst scenery and the beautiful coastline around Halong Bay. Bordering China, the region has been a frequent battleground over the centuries.

Between the Red River Delta and the sea, northeast Vietnam is an area rich in agriculture and history, as well as a regional engine of growth for industry and tourism. Scenic Halong Bay and Cat Ba Island draw crowds who sail peacefully through a dreamy seascape of rocky limestone outcrops, while the bustle of Haiphong makes it clear that this area is a vital artery in the country's industry and trade.

Few visitors venture much beyond Halong Bay, but farther north the landscape is filled with dramatic mountain passes, towering waterfalls, lush national parks and ancient royal citadels. Ethnic hill-tribe minority villages, tucked away at the foot of mountains, offer trekking opportunities, while lakeside retreats are an escape from the stifling summer heat. Cao Bang province has some of the country's most beautiful scenery, with sweeping verdant hills and waterfalls. At Mong Cai, the easternmost border gate with China, goods (and people) pass in and out between the two countries, and beach resorts and colourful markets abound. China invaded, occupied and generally interfered with Vietnam for centuries, with the northeast being their principal gateway. Chinese forces last invaded in 1979 as retaliation for the Vietnamese occupation of

Cambodia, and the resulting war devastated parts of the region. These days, border trade is buoyant in some parts of the northeast, but the Vietnamese remain guarded about how much China and its now vast economic power may influence life here.

THAI NGUYEN PROVINCE

MUSEUM OF THE CULTURES OF VIETNAM'S ETHNIC GROUPS

Some 80km (50 miles) north from Hanoi on Highway 3, **Thai Nguyen** ⓫

Ⓞ Main Attractions

Museum of the Cultures of
   Vietnam's Ethnic Groups
Ba Be National Park
Ban Gioc Waterfall
Haiphong City
Halong Bay
Cat Ba Island

**Maps on pages
142, 164**

Display at the Museum of the Cultures of Vietnam's Ethnic Groups.

Life-size figurines of ethnic warriors at the Museum of the Cultures of Vietnam's Ethnic Groups.

is a grimy industrial city and home of Southeast Asia's first steel mill, built with Chinese aid in the 1950s. The sole reason to stop here is to visit the city's excellent **Museum of the Cultures of Vietnam's Ethnic Groups** (Bao Tang Van Hoa Cac Don Thoc Viet Nam; summer Tue–Sun 8–11am and 2–4.30pm; http://mcve.org.vn). The museum has a number of displays featuring the culture and artefacts of the country's 54 ethnic groups. Of particular interest are the clothes used by some ethnic groups that are said to be able to identify magical sounds, along with hunting tools and examples of handicraft. Although they can't be recognised by their everyday attire, many of the city's factory workers come from the Muong, Nung, Tay and Tai minority communities.

A Communist Party stronghold, Thai Nguyen claims a landmark in revolutionary history. In 1917, Luong Ngoc Quyen, a nationalist student, was imprisoned and tortured by the French authorities here. This spurred the local garrison to mutiny and to seize the town. Peasants and miners, under the banner of the League for the Restoration of Vietnam, supported the soldiers. French troops from Hanoi suppressed the rebellion within a few days and Luong was killed. Surviving members of the group who fled westwards were ultimately slaughtered in Tam Dao in 1918. During the First Indochina War, Thai Nguyen had considerable strategic importance as a key Viet Minh base for supplies from China in the fight against the French.

BAC KAN PROVINCE

BA BE NATIONAL PARK

North of Thai Nguyen is Bac Kan province, where the top attraction is **Ba Be National Park** ⑫ (Cong Vien Quoc Gia Ba Be; www.vietnamnationalparks. org; daily daylight hours). The national park covers more than 7,000 hectares (17,300 acres) and is home to high mountains and deep valleys, as well as waterfalls, lakes and caves. More than 300 animal species live here, including

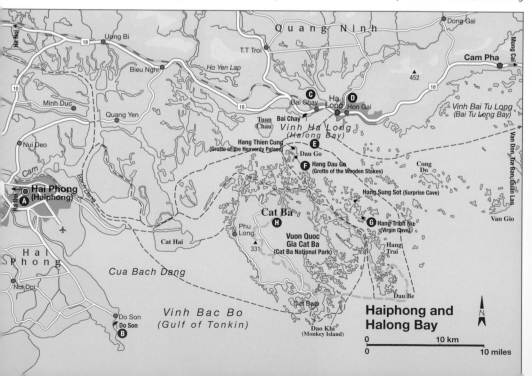

bears, macaques, pheasants and, supposedly, tigers. A few small colonies of the indigenous Tonkin snub-nosed monkey, recently thought to be extinct, have also been found here. One reason for the park's fabulous flora is a government initiative that pays villagers not to lop down trees. Such schemes are often little more than an uneasy truce between villagers and nature though, so visit Ba Be while it's still looking good.

BA BE LAKE

In the southwest of the national park, **Ba Be Lake** (Ho Ba Be), or Three Seas Lake, is the largest natural body of water in the country. Comprising three linked lakes stretching 9km (6 miles) long and over 1km (0.6 miles) in width, it reaches a depth of over 30 metres (98ft) and is surrounded by limestone cliffs and lush forests. The lake's major attractions are boat trips to nearby caves, waterfalls and minority villages where visitors can stay overnight. In July and August, the height of the tourist season for Vietnamese, the normally peaceful lake is crowded with tour boats for hire.

Highlights in the area include **Dau Dang Waterfall** (Thac Dau Dang), which can only be reached by boat, and **Puong Cave** (Hang Puong), which runs completely through a mountain and is traversed by a river, meaning it can be explored by boat. Regular trips go into the cave and guides are available.

For visitors wishing to spend the night, there are two options. The Tay minority who live in the park and surrounding areas have cottages and rooms for rent inside the park boundaries. Outside the park, slightly more expensive lodgings in the form of guesthouses and air-conditioned villas are available.

CAO BANG PROVINCE

NATIONAL HIGHWAY 4

Wildly beautiful Cao Bang province to the northeast has only opened its borders to foreigners in the past 15 years. **National Highway 4** runs down to the coast through ravines and mountain

Tranquil Ba Be Lake.

passes parallel to the Chinese border. This highway was the site of numerous clashes in the late 1940s between French colonial troops and the Viet Minh guerrillas. Protected by a thin string of French forts that were constantly under attack, French-speaking soldiers dubbed the then-Highway 4 "the Street without Joy".

CAO BANG CITY

The provincial capital is also called **Cao Bang** 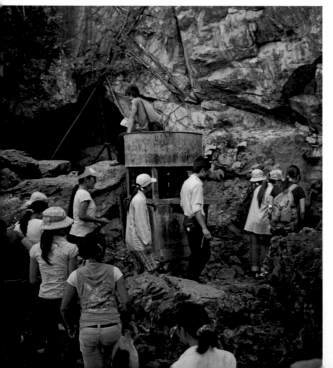. Shelled by the Chinese in 1979, the town itself has limited tourist appeal, but it does serve as a launching pad for visits to the nearby mountains and the Chinese border. In the past few years, the town has undergone significant development, with new government buildings, hotels and shops popping up all over. Its market is said to be the biggest in the country, selling all manner of fruit and vegetables and some household items. When it comes to eating, try breakfast favourite *bahn mi*, a satisfying baguette that is toasted and filled with meat, salads and a spicy

Pac Bo Cave.

sauce. To walk off your food, climb the hill that leads to a war memorial and enjoy the spectacular views at the summit. Cao Bang's relatively high altitude gives it a pleasant climate.

Throngs of hill tribes, including Tay, Hmong, Nung, Dao and Lolo, gather at the morning markets in the surrounding villages. Enquire at your hotel about these markets, and be prepared to make an early start.

AROUND CAO BANG

Cao Bang province shares a long border with China. Forests make up the majority of the province and the climate is quite cool, with chilly winters. The culturally diverse province has a population of about 520,000 people, and it covers an area of 6,707 sq km (2,589 sq miles) of high, rocky terrain. Due to the lack of available farmland, Cao Bang's economic value lies in its rivers, which have been harnessed by hydroelectric stations to generate power, as well as its recently upgraded roads that link Vietnam's inland provinces with China.

⊘ NUNG HILL TRIBES

Along with Lang Son and Bac Kan provinces, Cao Bang province is home to almost all of Vietnam's more than 1 million-strong Nung community. They farm at both valley floors and high altitudes like the 1,000-metre (3,300ft) -high Dong May Plateau. The Nung are excellent weavers and makers of bamboo furniture and baskets, and are known for their musical traditions. The women wear long indigo dresses and headscarves. Linguistically and culturally, the Nung share much with their neighbours, the Tay, who number over 1.5 million. Their shared language is clearly Thai, but because both the Nung and Tay have lived in Vietnam for over 2,000 years their cultural practices are closer to the Vietnamese and Chinese. Their practice of ancestral worship, for instance, includes Confucian and Buddhist elements.

PAC BO CAVE

A two-hour drive north of Cao Bang City, along potholed roads, is **Pac Bo Cave** (Hang Pac Bo), yet another stop on the Ho Chi Minh pilgrimage trail. As well as being a fantastically scenic spot, just a kilometre (0.6 miles) from the Chinese border, it also has great historical importance. Here, in 1941, a man then known as Nguyen Ai Quoc crossed into his homeland for the first time in almost 30 years. Later, after taking the name Ho Chi Minh, he lived in the cave near the Nung village of Pac Bo – the proximity of the Chinese border providing a quick escape route if French soldiers discovered his hiding spot. Ho returned to China in 1942 for two years, spending some of that time in prison before heading back south.

In Pac Bo there is a small **museum** (Tue–Sun 7.30–11.30am and 1.30–4.30pm) with information on the surrounding area as well as arte-facts that belong to Ho, his jungle hut, a replica of his simple bed and, of course, tourist trinkets. In true communist style, Ho named the stream flowing in front of the cave as **Lenin Creek** and christened a nearby mountain **Karl Marx Peak**.

BAN GIOC WATERFALL

Vietnam's largest waterfall is Ban Gioc, sometimes known as Ban Doc. Close to the Chinese border and about 80km (50 miles) northeast from Cao Bang, the falls are hugely popular with Vietnamese and Chinese tourists. The 300-metre (984ft) width of the falls stretches from Vietnam and across the border into China and is at its most spectacular during the rainy season from May to September. Ask your hotel to arrange a visit, as the land around Ban Gioc is a military area and access can be restricted. Boat trips can be arranged to within fairly close range of the falls.

NGUOM NGAO CAVE AND THANG HEN LAKE

Some 2km (1.2 miles) away from the waterfall is **Nguom Ngao Cave** (daily daylight hours). The 3km (2-mile) -long

Lakeside lodge at Ba Be Lake.

Numerous fierce battles have been fought through the ages at Chi Lang Pass between the Vietnamese and Chinese.

Nguom Ngao Cave.

cave network is so extensive that you will need a guide. There are two sections to the cave; the smaller cave is beautifully lit, therefore simple to navigate, but to explore the second, larger cave you need a torch and a guide. The latter cave apparently has a secret entrance near Ban Gioc Waterfall. In the low season, visitors are scarce so tourists that do visit often have the caves to themselves.

Limestone mountains and lush forests surround another of the province's beauty spots, **Thang Hen Lake**. This is one of seven scenic lakes in the area, but access to it can be difficult and tourism infrastructure is scant. Wild orchids grow in profusion throughout the region. It is best visited during the rainy season, when rafts can be taken out onto the lake.

LANG SON PROVINCE

South of Cao Bang is Lang Son province, which shares a border with China's Guangxi province. High mountains and thick forests cover around 75 percent of the land area and

shelter wildlife including leopards, pangolins and monitor lizards as well as a variety of primates and various species of deer.

Tay, Nung, Hmong, Dao, Nghia and Hoa are among the ethnic minorities living in this part of Vietnam. The **Ky Cung River** that flows through the province is unique in that it flows northwards to China – the other rivers in the region all flow south.

CHI LANG PASS

The narrow gorge at **Chi Lang**, a series of passes connected by tortuous tracks forged between high mountains south of the Chinese-Vietnamese border, is a battleground where the Vietnamese have fought many major battles against Chinese invaders throughout history. In 1076, the Vietnamese defeated 300,000 Chinese Song-dynasty troops here, and in 1427 nearly 100,000 Ming-dynasty troops received the same treatment. The gorge's northern entrance is known as the **Barbarian Invaders Gate** (Quy Quan Mon) and the southern exit is called the **Swearing Path** (Ngo The).

LANG SON CITY

National Highway 1A, which originates here and travels the length of the country, intersects with Highway 4 in the provincial capital of **Lang Son** ⑭, 150km (94 miles) northeast of Hanoi. Today, unsightly bombed-out buildings are being replaced by equally unsightly new ones. When 85,000 Chinese troops invaded Vietnam in February 1979, Lang Son was a prime target. Sixteen days later, 80 percent of the buildings were rubble, with both sides counting the costs. After the Chinese troops withdrew, the town was rebuilt and entrepreneurs on both sides of the border re-established trade. Today all manner of commerce – both legal and illegal – flourishes here.

The city is situated on the banks of the Ky Sung River, which is also

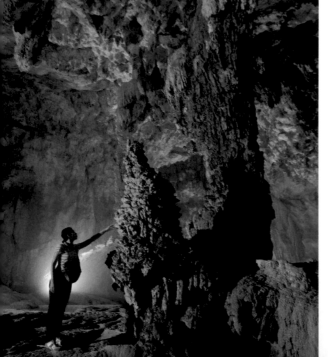

home to the Ky Lua market. While walking across the bridge to the market, look for a mountain summit that resembles a mother holding a child. Known as Vong Phu Mountain (Waiting for Her Husband), folklore says a woman waited at the spot so long for her husband to return from war that she and her child were turned to stone.

TAM THANH/NHI THANH CAVES

Several kilometres west of the city is an area riddled with numerous caves and grottoes, many of which are used for the worship of spirits. The two main examples, **Tam Thanh Cave** and **Nhi Thanh Cave** (both daily daylight hours), are illuminated and contain Buddhist altars. Tam Thanh is 2.5km (1.5 miles) from Lang Son, and Nhi Thanh is about 500 metres/yds beyond Tam Thanh. A short walk from Tam Thanh Cave, up a flight of stone stairs, are the ruins of an ancient city wall that belonged to the 16th-century **Mac Dynasty Citadel**. Within the winding passages is a mass of graffiti and carvings left behind by some of the cave's erstwhile visitors. Some of these scribes were poets who came here to write their works. The grotto at Nhi Thanh has more than a dozen carvings, which provide valuable insights into the history of the area. Inside is an engraved statue of Ngo Thi Si, the leader who found the caves, probably in the 1770s.

BAC SON VALLEY

In the mountains just west of Lang Son is a highland valley called **Bac Son** and a market town inhabited by Tay (Tho) and Nung people. Briefly allied with the newly arrived Japanese, in 1940 Tay guerrilla bands attacked isolated French military posts. While the Japanese soon reconciled with the French, the guerrilla insurgency had significant momentum, and in 1940 it staged a general uprising in Bac Son and eight southern provinces – collectively known as the **Bac Son Uprisings**. The French stamped out the rebellion and executed 100 cadres. The repercussions were especially

Buddhist altar, Tam Thanh Cave.

The steps up to Mac Dynasty Citadel near Lang Son.

devastating for the Communist Party in the south. However, it meant that Bac Son and the far north became the base from which the communists would rebuild from virtually nothing.

MUSEUM OF BAC SON

An unmarked white building perched on stilts, the **Museum of Bac Son** (Bao Tang Bac Son; tel: 02-581 2631, mobile tel: 091-337 6661; open on request; free) contains a small collection of artefacts from the Bac Son period (5000–3000 BC), as well as exhibits and displays related to the Bac Son Uprising of 1940, including documents penned by Ho Chi Minh. Unfortunately, no English translation is available.

DONG DANG

In 1979 **Dong Dang** ⑮ was flattened during a Chinese invasion. Today the town, about 18km (11 miles) northwest of Lang Son City, has made a comeback thanks to cross-border trade. The crossing here is known as the **Friendship Gate** (Huu Nghi Quan), a somewhat ironic moniker given the

sporadic exchanges of gunfire between Vietnam and China that happened until as recently as 1992.

For foreigners, this is probably the most popular exit to China from Vietnam, and it is possible to board a train here for the 45-hour (direct) journey to Beijing. Visas, however, must be issued either in Hanoi or Beijing. Once called Porte de Chine, it was through here that Japanese troops entered Vietnam in 1940 before attacking Lang Son.

QUANG NINH PROVINCE

MONG CAI

About 180km (112 miles) southeast from Lang Son is **Mong Cai** ⑯, a bustling coastal city on the border with China. The town was destroyed by retreating Chinese troops in 1979 and reconstruction began only when the border was reopened in 1991. This is one of three land-border gates to China open to foreigners, though visas must be issued in either Hanoi or Beijing. Business here is brisk as Vietnamese come here to buy cheap Chinese goods; Chinese flock here to gamble in its two casinos. Despite its dreary appearance, this is one of the wealthiest places in Vietnam, with a significant proportion of households enjoying incomes of up to US$20,000 per year.

TRA CO BEACH

Tra Co is a relatively undeveloped beach resort in the far northeast which hosts a growing number of Chinese and Vietnamese tourists. Located at the starting point of Vietnam's famous "S" shape, the beach stretches for 17km (11 miles). The sand is coarse and uninviting and there is litter but that doesn't deter the thousands of visitors who flock here. Unless you don't mind large crowds, avoid visiting the area from May to August, as this is when both Chinese and Vietnamese tourists

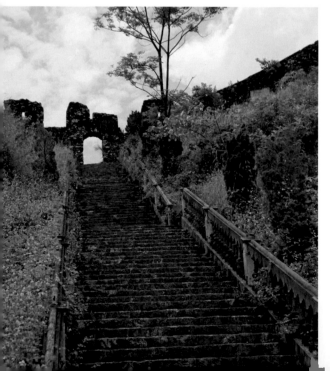

arrive in droves. The resort's seafood restaurants serve up seriously fresh food at reasonable prices. A few kilometres offshore is the Con Mang sandbank, the perfect place to see the sunset. About 1km (0.6 miles) north of the beach is the large and impressive **Tra Co Church**, built in 1880 and restored by the French in 1914.

At the southern end of the beach, **Mui Ngoc** is where you can catch a hydrofoil to **Van Don Island** (Dao Cai Bauwq), which is part of Halong Bay. From here, it is 240km (150 miles) southwest to Haiphong.

HAIPHONG

Further along the coast, northern Vietnam's most important port, **Haiphong**, gladly yields to what lies beyond: Halong Bay (Vinh Ha Long), a wondrous cove that was created when an ancient dragon swished its immense tail – or so the story goes.

GETTING TO HAIPHONG CITY

From Dan Tien Port in Mong Cai, it is possible to take a Russian-made hydrofoil for the 4.5 -hour ride – departing daily at 2.30pm – southwest along the coast to **Haiphong City** . A hydrofoil also travels twice daily from Dan Tien Port direct to Halong Bay's Bai Chay area at 9am and 2pm. Just show up at the port ahead of time and tell the person in charge where you want to go.

From Hanoi, the two-hour drive on the upgraded 100km (62-mile) road to Haiphong heads deep into the densely populated Red River Valley. In the late 1940s and early 1950s at the height of the guerrilla campaign against the French, this road, **Highway 5**, was lined with garrisons, walchtowers and massive forts surrounded by barbed-wire fences, trenches, bunkers and minefields. Vehicles ventured along this road only in convoys and during daylight hours. At night, the road was officially closed – though not to elusive Viet Minh guerrillas.

Today, trucks, cars, bicycles and motorbikes on their way to and from Haiphong's busy port constantly trammel the well-maintained road.

During the 1970s and '80s, Haiphong was a significant port of departure for many Vietnamese refugees.

Busy street in Haiphong City.

*The distinctively hued
Haiphong Museum.*

*Haiphong's neocolonial
Grand Theatre.*

Many of Haiphong's outer industrial areas sprang up after the French left; approaching the city you will see numerous large, ugly industrial plants and factories.

HAIPHONG'S HISTORY

Haiphong, Vietnam's third most populous city and the North's most important port, is located in the northeast of the **Bac Bo Delta**. A small port town at the time of the French conquest in 1873, it quickly grew as the Europeans set about draining swamps and constructing monumental buildings. As 16 rivers cross the city, setting the foundations in the soggy ground was no simple task.

The most famous of Haiphong's waterways is the **Bach Dang River**. The first of the French warships arrived in Haiphong in 1872 seeking access, via the Red River, to China's Yunnan region. Coincidentally, the last of the French expeditionary forces exited the same way in 1955.

More was to come: during the war with the US, Haiphong was sporadically bombed from air and sea between 1965 and 1972. In 1972, US president Richard Nixon ordered the mining of the harbour to stem the influx of Soviet military supplies. However, less than a year later, the US led efforts to remove the mines under the terms of the Paris ceasefire agreement.

Haiphong's troubles didn't end after the Americans left in 1975. For more than a decade, the harbour was the most popular departure point for the "boat people" fleeing economic and political hardship. Persecuted during the 1979 war with China, most members of the city's large ethnic Chinese community joined the exodus, if they hadn't already fled by then.

DOWNTOWN HAIPHONG

Haiphong doesn't attract many tourists, which means those that do arrive can enjoy its laid-back feel without being hassled by touts. Inside the boundaries of the Old City, wide shady streets, well-tended spots of greenery and a surprising number of colonial-era buildings are still in excellent condition.

The city centre curves around the **Tam Bac River** (Song Tam Bac). In this area are several impressive hotels, administrative buildings and the raspberry-coloured **Haiphong Museum** (Bao Tang Haiphong; Tue–Sun 8–11am, Wed and Sun 7.30–9.30pm).

At 56 Dinh Tien Hoang is a square overlooked by the yellow, neo-colonial **Grand Theatre**, which dates back to 1912. During the first days of the 1946 French attack, actors with antique muskets held off French troops here. In 2003, the government spent US$6.3 million to renovate the interior.

Another sight worth seeing is the **Haiphong Cathedral** (daily; free), on Hoang Van Thu Street. Built in the late 1800s, the church has an unusual statue of the Virgin Mary.

Haiphong has far more of a café culture than a pumping nightlife, but after dark there are some interesting places to hang out, the best of which is Maxim's Café, with live music nightly (http://maximshotel.vn).

TEMPLES AND PAGODAS

The **Du Hang Pagoda** (Chua Du Hang; daily 8am–5pm) in the south of the city was built in 1672 by a wealthy mandarin-turned-monk. Since then it has been restored many times. It is dedicated to Le Chan, a female warrior who aided the Trung sisters in the uprising against the Chinese in AD 39. The long, low wooden building with its magnificent carvings and swooping roof is reached by passing through a triple-tiered bell tower and an open courtyard. Behind the carved offering table is a baby Buddha protected by nine dragons.

It is easy to confuse – as do many locals and even some *xe om* drivers – Du Hang Pagoda with the nearby **Hang Kenh Communal House** (Dinh Hang Kenh; daily 8am–5pm). The communal house, built in 1856, is just off Nguyen Cong Tru Street and is fronted by a lotus pond. Beyond the spacious courtyard is a similar wooden building to that of the Du Hang structure, with a curling, tiled roof. Within the dim interior, 32

A gilded statue of Buddha at the Du Hang Pagoda.

Bai Chay's beachfront hotels.

ironwood pillars support the roof, and there is an enormous palanquin decorated with carvings of dragons. The beams of the ceiling are adorned with 308 carved dragons.

DO SON BEACH

About 20km (12.5 miles) southeast of Haiphong, at the tip of a peninsula, is **Do Son Beach** Ⓑ, home of one of a few legal casinos and an area famous for gory buffalo fights. These take place on the ninth day of the eighth lunar month and are very popular with Vietnamese tourists. Aside from this, there is little worth seeing. The hotels and guesthouses are shabby and the beach disappears completely during high tide. While the sand here is better than in Tra Co, the sea has an unappealing rust colour, a result of silt deposited by the Red River.

HALONG CITY

BAI CHAY

Sunset at Halong Bay.

Formally established in 1994, **Halong City** – about 165km (102 miles) from Hanoi and about 3.5 hours by car – comprises two smaller towns, **Bai Chay** and **Hon Gai**, as well as their surrounding districts.

Most hotels, tour agencies and restaurants can be found in **Bai Chay** Ⓒ. Shops specialise in kitschy souvenirs fashioned from pearl, coral and limestone rock. There are dozens of expensive hotels and even more tacky mini-hotels with karaoke bars. On summer weekends, the latter are filled with Vietnamese tourists and their overseas relatives. During the winter months, Bai Chay is nearly deserted.

Bai Chay's saving grace is its fresh and well-prepared seafood. Most popular are the open-air restaurants lining the main avenue, which runs along the waterfront. A short walk along this avenue reveals two swimming beaches that are packed in the summer. Hundreds of tonnes of clean white sand have been dumped on the original muddy beach to make it more picturesque, and, although crowded and noisy, the view over the bay at sunset is spectacular.

HON GAI

Across the bay, **Hon Gai** has a much more bustling feel. The ferry from Bai Chay to Hon Gai only takes a few minutes, but it is also possible to take the 903-metre (2,691ft) **Bai Chay Bridge** which connects both points. Hon Gai, which means "coal mine" in Vietnamese, is known for its open-pit mining in the surrounding hills, as well as its coal warehouses. When the French launched their final successful campaign in the north, they seized Hon Gai in 1883 to safeguard the coal mines. Despite its association with the coal industry, Hong Gai has turned into a busy spot with new shops, hotels and houses.

Near the Hon Gai ferry dock is the 106-metre (348ft) -high **Poem Mountain** (Nui Bao Tho), named after King Le Thanh Tong who etched a poem about its beauty into the rock in 1486. At the foot of the mountain, the gaudy **Long Tien Pagoda** (Chua Long Tien; daily 8am–5pm; free), guarded by statues of fierce armoured soldiers, was built in 1941 and is dedicated to the popular General Tran Hung Dao of the Tran dynasty. A bomb-damaged colonial church is just north of Hon Gai and has some of the best views of the area.

HALONG BAY

Halong Bay's exquisite limestone islands and numerous outcrops are amongst the most outstanding sights in Southeast Asia. Any trip to northern Vietnam must include a visit to **Halong Bay** (Vinh Ha Long).

The bay's tranquil beauty encompasses some 1,500 sq km (579 sq miles) of indigo sea and is dotted with more than 3,000 limestone islands and rocky outcrops, or karsts, most of them uninhabited. Weirdly shaped rock sculptures jut dramatically from the sea, and numerous grottoes create an enchanted, timeless and almost mystical world. The soaring sails of Chinese-style junk boats and sampans gliding on the bay add to the beauty of the scene. Not surprisingly, the bay has been declared a Unesco World Heritage Site – twice, in fact: in 1994 for its natural scenic beauty, and then again in 2000 for its biological

Explore Halong's caves, created by the gradual erosion of limestone formations.

Touring Halong Bay.

⊙ Fact

The cave discovered at Halong Bay in 2009 is being touted as one of the best in the area. Named Golden Fruit Cave and in Cat Hai district, it is 30 metres (98ft) wide and 100 metres (328ft) deep and is divided into two parts, both filled with stalactites and stalagmites.

diversity. Between March and April, visibility can be poor.

LEGEND OF THE DRAGON

Halong means "dragon descending", and its name is steeped in local legend. The story goes that a heavenly celestial dragon and her offspring were ordered by the Jade Emperor to halt an invasion from the sea. To combat this, the dragons spewed out bits of jade and jewels that turned into wondrous islands and karst formations on contact with the water, thereby scuppering enemy ships.

Other versions of the legend claim the bay was created when the dragon flung herself into the water. In the process, her swishing tail gorged deep valleys and crevices in the mainland, which were subsequently filled by the sea. The dragon was so pleased with her creations that she settled among them and is said to now live under the bay. Some people claim to have seen this Vietnamese equivalent of the Loch Ness Monster, a black creature resembling a snake about 30 metres (98ft)

in length. Called a *Tarasque* by former French residents of the area, enterprising boat owners have made a career out of taking tourists in search of the beast.

The more practical explanation for the karst outcrops says that they were formed by a giant limestone sea bed that eroded over the centuries until only their pinnacles were left behind. Many of these limestone piles have strange and otherworldly shapes, some of which are known to local fishermen by fanciful nicknames such as the Dog, Turtle and Toad, derived from the rocks' uncanny resemblance to the shape of certain animals. Over time, rain and the elements created caves within some of these limestone rocks, several of which can be visited.

EXPLORING THE BAY

A rushed one-day tour from Hanoi is a far from ideal way to experience this wonderful place; by the time you get to Halong Bay and board your boat, almost half the day is gone. Those with time and specific sites in mind could spend a few days cruising around the bay. Tickets for the many tour boats are available at the pier in Bai Chay, though a better option is to book a package from a Hanoi-based tour operator. As some of the caves are wet (and dark), a sturdy pair of shoes and a flashlight are handy items to have.

Another alternative is to use Cat Ba Island, the bay's largest island and a national park, as a base from which to explore. Not only is it cleaner and less crowded than some other parts of the bay, it is also closer to many of the most dramatic grottoes.

HALONG'S CAVES

The most spectacular cave at Halong Bay is on the island closest to Bai Chay, the vast **Grotto of the Wooden Stakes** ❻ (Hang Dau Go). There are three chambers filled with an assortment of stalactites and stalagmites that resemble beasts, birds and human forms. It was here that General Tran Hung Dao

Cruise in style on scenic Halong Bay from the comfort of a Chinese-style junk.

stored hundreds of wooden stakes that were used to destroy the ships of Kublai Khan's invading Mongol hordes in 1288. It was christened the Grotte des Merveilles (Cave of Wonders) by the first French tourists to visit in the late 19th century. Unfortunately, modern-day tourists have left their mark in the form of graffiti and piles of litter.

Also worth seeing on the same island is the **Grotto of the Heavenly Palace** (Hang Thien Cung), which is adorned with stalagmites, stalactites and limestone growths that look like cauliflower heads.

On another nearby island, folklore claims that the **Virgin Cave** (Hang Trinh Nu) was named after a young girl whose parents were poor and could not afford a boat. They had to rent one from a rich man, but when they could not pay what they owed him, the rich man demanded their beautiful daughter in lieu of the debt, and so forced her to marry him. The poor girl refused all his advances. He had her beaten but she still refused to submit to him. He finally exiled her to a grotto, where she starved to death and was subsequently immortalised in stone by a rock that resembled her figure, which magically emerged from her burial site.

Tunnel Cave (Hang Hanh) extends underground for 2km (1.2 miles) and features some amazing stalactites. Getting there is tricky, however, as you need to arrive at half tide. **Surprise Cave** (Hang Sung Sot) is also very popular, with three large chambers filled with strange rock formations, including one that resembles a giant phallus.

Several other caves are open to the public. Boats usually visit a number of caves en route, admission to which is covered by the flat entrance fee included in the price of your boat tour. The caves that boats visit depend on the weather, tide levels and the number of other vessels out on the water on that day.

Some boats stop off at **Tuan Chau Island** (Dau Tuan Chau), 5km (3 miles) west of Bai Chay. The island once served as an exclusive retreat for the colonials. Today, its decaying villas have been replaced with resorts catering to wealthy Vietnamese. Ho Chi

> **⊙ Tip**
>
> Biking is a great way to see Cat Ba Island, and the majority of hotels and guesthouses rent out cheap Chinese-made bicycles. For those hoping to make more strenuous trips, good-quality mountain bikes can be rented at the Flightless Bird Café (south end of Nui Ngoc St; tel: 031-388 8517).

Surprise Cave.

A vista of Halong Bay from a cave on Cat Ba Island.

Minh used to spend his summers here and his house, of course, has been preserved as a memorial.

CAT BA ISLAND

The **Cat Ba Archipelago** consists of 366 islets and islands that cover 200 sq km (77 sq miles) of sea and are peppered with beautiful beaches and grottoes. Just 20km (12 miles) from Haiphong, with the Gulf of Tonkin to the west and Halong Bay to the east, the main **Cat Ba Island** ❶ covers about 354 sq km (137 sq miles), with a stunning landscape of lush forested hills, coastal mangroves and freshwater swamps, as well as lakes, waterfalls and reefs.

These days the island's permanent population is just over 17,000, less than half the number some 20 years ago. With its remote harbours, Cat Ba's fishing fleet was ideally situated to serve the needs of fleeing "boat people" in the late 1970s. When Vietnam began persecuting its Chinese minority shortly before its war with China in 1979, Cat Ba islanders, most of whom were ethnic Chinese, joined the exodus to safer lands. As a consequence, many of those left behind today have relatives in the US, Canada and Australia.

Gifts and loans from overseas relatives helped to build the narrow mini-hotels, shops and restaurants in the clunky cement village of **Cat Ba**. Overlooking the Gulf of Tonkin, it is the island's main settlement and port. Scattered along the coast are a number of floating fishing villages, though these are best visited by boat. Each one tends to have a small number of families who increasingly are starting to welcome tourists to help boost their meagre income.

CAT BA NATIONAL PARK

Half of the island and 52 sq km (20 sq miles) of the surrounding inland waters are part of the **Cat Ba National Park** (Vuon Quoc Gia Cat Ba; tel: 031-368 8981; daily; www.vuonquocgiacatba.com.vn). The thickly forested island has a rich diversity of flora and fauna, including 78 species of bird – including the hornbill – numerous reptiles and 32 species of mammals, such as wild cats, boar, porcupines, various monkeys and deer. However, you are unlikely to see anything other than birds and insects – and possibly primates – whilst hiking the park's many paths. Poaching is still a problem on Cat Ba, despite educational programmes, increased surveillance by park rangers and greater affluence brought about by tourism. The golden-headed langur, for example, is unique to Cat Ba Island and is in danger of extinction as there are only around 65 left. Human remains and stone tools from the Neolithic era have been discovered in some of the island's caves.

Despite its considerable size, the park boasts only a handful of good beaches, and all of these are within easy access of Cat Ba village; they are inventively named Cat Co 1, 2 and 3. Rocky cliffs line most of the island, with a few sandy beaches tucked in between the coves. Cat Ba can be easily explored by motorbike along its limited network

◉ HALONG BAY SAILING OPERATIONS

Almost all Hanoi tour operators arrange boat trips to Halong Bay lasting one to four days. These include transportation, meals and accommodation. Valiant efforts have been made by the Halong authorities to regulate the local boats and the haphazard ticketing system, but it's still best to book with a well-known, reputable agent. For those with limited time, one-day tours from Hanoi are available, but these are usually rushed affairs; Halong should be savoured at a more languid pace. Trips that last several days allow travellers to explore the lagoons, virgin beaches and caves dotted around this spectacular area in greater detail. Hopping in a kayak to paddle out to some spots is the preferred form of transport here.

Most tour operators use standard engine-powered wooden boats with dormitory-style cabins. Luxury junks, with top-notch dining, large sundecks and en-suite cabins, are also available. **Handspan** (tel: 04-3926 2828; www.handspan.com) operates the most economical trips aboard its 18-cabin *Aloha Junk*. **Buffalo Tours** (tel: 04-3828 0702; www.buffalotours.com) operates the mid-priced *Jewel of the Bay* luxury junk with five cabins, and a three-day trip to Bai Tu Long Bay on one-, two- or four-cabin junks. **Emeraude Classic Cruises** (tel: 02 03384 2218; www.emeraude-cruises.com) runs the most expensive cruises on its 36-cabin luxury replica paddle steamer.

of roads. There are several trails that lead deep into the forest; the easiest hike extends just 2.5km (1.5 miles). As long as it's not rainy (and muddy) the walk isn't difficult, but it's a good idea to buy a trail map from the park office. The forest path is clearly marked with numbered signs, and these correspond to the informative descriptions on the map. Alternatively, hire a local guide at the park office who will be more adept at spotting forest life. Trekking trips can also be arranged with Cat Ba's hotels. Camping is allowed in the park (check with the park office), but you'll need to bring or rent your own gear. Rock climbing is perhaps the ultimate activity here, given the views from their peaks. Several companies, such as Asia Outdoors (www.asiaoutdoors.com.vn), offer day trips that include a range of routes up, offering various degrees of difficulty. Top-rope systems are generally used to make things as safe as possible.

Improved infrastructure, including a bridge, due for completion in 2017, could mean that things will get a lot busier here.

BAI TU LONG

While nearly all visitors to this area stick to Halong Bay, Bai Tu Long is every bit as jaw-droppingly gorgeous. To some, this national park may hold even more appeal as it has all the beauty but far fewer visitors than Halong Bay; the downside of this is that there are fewer tourist facilities. Bai Tu Long, which sits northeast of Halong Bay, was created when a limestone plateau sank, revealing its numerous islands. Van Don island, the largest and busiest of these, has the greatest number of amenities, which isn't saying much. A bridge connects the island to the mainland. Boats leave from Van Don for another substantial isle, Tra Ban, which has dense jungle and incredible views. Or there is Quan Lan, an island with a small community, a handful of guesthouses and plenty of unexplored land. To reach Bai Tu Long it's possible to take a five-hour boat ride from Halong Bay or hop on a hydrofoil, which makes the same trip in an hour. Another option is to go by land to Cai Rong and catch a boat from there.

> ### ⊘ Fact
>
> Do Son Resort Hotel in Haiphong is Vietnam's first casino. It is aimed primarily at the Chinese tourists, not Westerners. Vietnamese are now allowed to enter under certain conditions. This was recently changed with the Decree on Casino Businesses being approved.

Kayaking at Cat Ba Island.

Flooded rice fields framed against limestone hills in Ninh Binh province.

THE TONKIN COAST

One of the poorest parts of Vietnam's north central region, the Tonkin Coast has several priceless natural wonders and some good beaches.

Heading south out of Hanoi, **National Highway 1A** passes through varied landscapes as it enters an area known to the French as the Tonkin Coast. Comprising several provinces that contain just about every terrain imaginable, the vistas include mountains, limestone hills, low-lying plains, inland waterways, rice paddies and long stretches of sand. Rich in culture and revolutionary history, the area is home to ancient citadels and temples and was the birthplace of Ho Chi Minh himself. One of the poorest parts of the country, the people here are among the friendliest anywhere in Vietnam. The Tonkin Coast's Sam Son Beach, popular among Vietnamese tourists, is rarely visited by foreigners.

National Highway 1A stretches for 2,300km (1,430 miles) along the length of the entire country, from the Huu Nghi Quan border gate to China in Lang Son province all the way to Nam Cam township in southern Ca Mau province. Recent development projects have drastically improved the condition of the roads – previously in poor repair – and the **Ho Chi Minh Highway** (Duong Ho Chi Min) has helped take the pressure off the coastal road.

On the arterial roads, however, traffic still moves at snail's pace as buffalo and bicycles vie for space. It doesn't help that farm produce is often placed

A rural scene near Ninh Binh.

to dry on the dusty edges of the road – everything from straw, rice and corn to chilli peppers, peanuts and tea.

NAM DINH PROVINCE

NAM DINH CITY

The city of **Nam Dinh** ⑰, on Highway 21 about 90km (56 miles) south of Hanoi, is the capital of Nam Dinh province. Nam Dinh City and the surrounding areas are a Catholic stronghold, although many former residents were among the 500,000 Vietnamese who

⦿ Main Attractions
Golden City Ruins
Keo Pagoda
Hoa Lu
Trang An
Cuc Phuong National Park
Phat Diem Cathedral

⦿ Map on page 142

The old ways of life continue on the water.

A trader sells her wares on a rowing boat in Thai Binh.

fled south after the communist takeover in 1954. Portuguese, Spanish and French missionaries converted their ancestors to Catholicism in the 16th and 17th centuries, long before the French colonial conquest.

Nam Dinh is a large industrial city that lies on the bank of the **Nam Dinh River** (Song Nam Dinh) and is famous for its textiles. In 1899, the French built the **Nam Dinh Textile Mill**, which still operates today. In the early 19th century, a large citadel surrounded Nam Dinh. The French dismantled it after occupying the area in 1882, but a single lookout tower survives. Head to the old riverside, where artisans and merchants still congregate in an area similar to Hanoi's Old Quarter.

TRAN-DYNASTY RUINS

Just 3km (2 miles) north of Nam Dinh is the village of **Tuc Mac** and the ancient Tran-dynasty ruins of the **Golden City** (Thang Vang). These ruins are all that remain of the palaces built by the Tran kings who defeated the Mongol Yuan-dynasty invaders from China three times in the 13th century. Among the ruins are the **Thien Truong Temple** (Den Thien Truong; daily 8am–5pm), built in 1238 and dedicated to the 14 Tran kings, and the beautiful **Pho Minh Pagoda** (Chua Pho Minh; daily 8am–5pm), built in 1305. The pagoda contains an impressive 13-storey tower and an amazing statue of King Tran Nhan Tong lying on his side, about to enter nirvana. The complex of temples is at the centre of the festival that begins on the 12th day of the first lunar month to celebrate the glorious dynasty and its feats.

THAI BINH PROVINCE

To the east of Nam Dinh, the tiny Thai Binh province has one of the highest population densities in the country, with over 1,200 people per square kilometre. Salt flats cover extensive areas on the coastal shores. Under the French, all salt had to be produced under the aegis of the government's salt monopoly. With a monopoly also on opium sales, the government reaped great revenues, but at tremendous cost to peasants

⊘ SONS OF THAI BINH

Thai Binh province, known best for its salt flats and tropical storms, is also the birthplace of several influential people, including the first Vietnamese man to travel into space (in 1980), Pham Tuan. Also from Thai Binh was Ta Quoc Luat, the soldier who captured French commander Christian de Castries and who planted the victory flag in the battle of Dien Bien Phu. Some Thai Binh natives are among the richest in Vietnam, including Vu Quang Hoi, owner of the Bitexco Financial Tower in Ho Chi Minh City, and Vu Van Tien, founder of AB Bank. Quach Tuan Ngoc, as a professor of computer science at the Hanoi University of Technology, authored the first successfully commercial domestic software for processing and translating Vietnamese text, the *Bach Khoa Editor*.

and fishermen who were crippled (and sometimes inspired to revolt) by prices that continued to rise regardless of demand. Private production of salt during this time was severely punished.

KEO PAGODA

East of Nam Dinh on the road to Haiphong is the site of 11th-century **Keo Pagoda** ⑱ (Chua Keo; daily 8am–5pm). Destroyed by a flood in 1611, the pagoda has undergone significant reconstruction but still retains the spirit of the original design. Considered one of the finer examples of traditional Vietnamese architecture, it is dedicated to the Buddha, his disciples, and an 11th-century monk named Minh Khong who is said to have cured King Ly Thanh Ton of leprosy. Look out for the many traditional rituals and diverse forms of entertainment that are performed at the pagoda – some of them centuries old – particularly during the Tet holidays.

NINH BINH PROVINCE

NINH BINH CITY

At the intersection of National Highway 1A and Highway 10, about 30km (20 miles) from Nam Dinh and 91km (57 miles) south of Hanoi, the dusty city of **Ninh Binh** ⑲ in the eponymous province has few redeeming features. However, as it's only two hours from Hanoi, the city is a good base for explorations of the far more interesting ancient capital of **Hoa Lu**, the scenic beauty of **Tam Coc** and several other interesting sights.

Ninh Binh City is dusty mainly because of a nearby rock quarry. Most of the city's inhabitants are employed by the quarry, either carting around large rocks and transporting them by truck or working in the tourism industry. With an increasing number of people visiting the city on their way to nearby tourist sites, new mini-hotels and restaurant stalls are appearing all over town. Under the government's

development plan, Ninh Binh is to become a national tourist hub by 2030 and expand to a metropolis of about 4 million inhabitants.

Across the river rises a large, bare crag. In the French colonial days, a fort was perched on top. In 1951 the Viet Minh temporarily overran the French positions in and around Ninh Binh. Eighty French soldiers holed up in the local Catholic Church, of whom only 19 survived. In the eastern part of town, in front of the train station, stands the Catholic Ninh Binh Cathedral with its decidedly Asian spire; the eave and window treatments echo the curved lines of a temple.

HOA LU

Only 13km (8 miles) northwest of Ninh Binh is **Hoa Lu** ⑳, site of the 10th-century capital of the Vietnamese kingdom known as Dai Co Viet, or Great Viet Land. This was a rather small feudal kingdom, covering an area of 300 hectares (741 acres), and was ruled by the Dinh and then the Le dynasty from AD 968–1010. A citadel that bordered the

Buddha statue at Keo Pagoda.

No nails were used in the 11th-century construction of Keo Pagoda.

Hoang Long River (Song Hoan Long) and stretched along the Yen Ngua limestone hills originally enclosed the kingdom. The enemy at the time were the Chinese, who had been expelled in 939.

Though much of the capital has long since been destroyed, there remain vestiges of the earthen citadels, palaces, shrines and temples, albeit in a state only archaeologists could appreciate. What has survived are two 17th-century temples modelled on 11th-century originals, which were built after the capital was transferred from Hoa Lu to Thang Long (now Hanoi) in 1010.

DINH TIEN HOANG TEMPLE

The **Dinh Tien Hoang Temple** (Den Dinh Tien Hoang; daily 8am–5pm) was originally built in the 11th century and was reconstructed in 1696. Dedicated to the founder of the Dinh dynasty, Dinh Tien Hoang, who reigned in the late 10th century, the temple now faces east, although the original faced north. It is entered by passing through two brick arches, the so-called **Outer Triumphant**

Picturesque mountain ranges and valleys frame Dinh Tien Hoang Temple in Ho Loa.

Arch and the **Inner Triumphant Arch**. The 17th-century **Dragon Bed**, in an area once used for sacrifices, lies in the centre of the courtyard in front of the main building. It was carved out of a single rock. Lightly carved on the surface is a strange-looking dragon floating in a mass of clouds: it has a long beard, the head and ears of a buffalo, paws resembling human hands, and fish-like scaly skin. Surrounding it are carvings of a carp, shrimp and mice. Gifts and food offerings are placed on the slab during festivals.

Crude statues of mythical animals – part-dog, part-lion – guard the doorway of the small temple. A huge drum in the forecourt was used by peasants to get the attention of mandarins. Inside the temple, King Dinh Tien Hoang, also known as Dinh Bo Linh, is worshipped at a central altar. On one of the temple pillars is written "Dai Co Viet", the name Dinh Tien Hoang gave Vietnam. Behind the altar, past some heavy carved beams, is a windowless back room with a 19th-century wooden statue of a paunchy Dinh Tien Hoang, framed by statues of his three sons. While Dinh Quoc Lien was the eldest, he was not chosen as heir apparent, and as a result, he masterminded the assassination of the anointed heir, his infant brother Dinh Hang Lan, in 979. The next year, a palace official assassinated both the king and Dinh Quoc Lien. The six-year-old youngest son (whose statue does not appear childlike at all), Dinh Toan, became king but only ruled for six months. Le Hoan, seizing the opportunity, eliminated him and founded the 29-year-long Le, or "Earlier Le", dynasty and went on to repel invasions by the Chinese.

LE HOAN TEMPLE

The second temple, called **Le Hoan** (Den Le Hoan; daily 8am–5pm), is a miniature of the Dinh Tien Hoang temple and is dedicated to Le Hoan (who later assumed the title King Le Dai Hanh). In addition to fending off the Chinese, Le Hoan is known for launching a military expedition against the Champa kingdom in 982, sacking the citadel in present-day Quang Nam province. The 17th-century carvings around the entrance door and on the roof beams portray dragons holding a pearl in their mouths, surrounded by clouds. The temple has a series of three chambers: the **Hall of Worship**, **Hall of Heavenly Fragrance** and **Inner Shrine**. In this last, dimly lit back room are statues of Le Hoan, his queen Duong Van Nga (supposedly the widow of Dinh Tien Hoang) and his two sons.

NHAT TRU PAGODA

Not far from Dinh Tien Hoang Temple is **Nhat Tru Pagoda** (Chua Nhat Tru; daily 8am–5pm; free), a lively and active place of worship. In front of the entrance stands a stone column engraved with Buddhist sutras dating from 988.

Adjacent to Dinh Tien Hoang Temple is the steep **Ma Yen Hill** (Nui Ma Yen). Those who are willing to climb

the 260-plus stone steps (and ignore aggressive hawkers flogging souvenirs) will be rewarded with a panoramic view of the ancient kingdom as well as the site of **Dinh Tien Hoang's tomb**.

TAM COC

The enchanting scenery of **Tam Coc** (Three Caves) is known as "Halong Bay on Rice Paddies" owing to the jagged limestone outcrops that jut out dramatically from the flooded rice paddies. Usually combined with a visit to Hoa Lu on day trips from Hanoi, Tam Coc can also be accessed from the Van Lam Wharf, 9km (6 miles) southwest of Ninh Binh City. If not travelling with a tour group, this is where travellers can hire a small, flat-bottomed boat manned by two people (a rower and poler, both usually women) for the stunning journey – which was immortalised in the 1992 film *Indochine* – along the atmospheric **Ngo Dong River** (Song Ngo Dong).

In the initial segment of the two- to three-hour journey, the narrow and lazy river blends into the adjacent flooded rice fields. In the dry season,

Devotees burn joss sticks and present offerings in remembrance of Dinh Tien Hoang atop Ma Yen Hill.

Dinh Tien Hoang Temple.

☉ Tip

Use plenty of sunscreen and wear a hat on the boat trip up the scenic Ngo Dong River in Tam Coc. The open boats offer no protection from the fierce sun.

the river meanders alongside the rice fields, but during the height of the rainy season the river can sometimes merge with the adjacent paddy fields. Soon, the waterway meanders through three large tunnel caves (*tam coc*) that have bored through the limestone hills over the centuries. The last cave is so low passengers need to duck down. The largest cave has stalactites and stalagmites. In between are shallow, glass-smooth lagoons encircled by verdant limestone cliffs. Birdwatchers might catch sight of herons and kingfishers. Note how the oarsmen and women row the boat with their feet.

After numerous complaints of aggressive vendors and pushy boat operators, the tourist police have issued strict rules that have minimised such hassle. The vendors will still push you to buy embroidery, drinks and snacks, but at least they wait until the boat has turned around and is on the way back to the wharf.

Past the wharf and the stalls of T-shirt sellers is **Van Lam**, a village where shirts and table linen are embroidered. This is where most of the similar items sold in Hanoi's Old Quarter originate. At least one member of every family is engaged in the art of embroidery, and tourists are welcome to browse. Prices here are cheaper than in Hanoi.

BICH DONG PAGODA

About 2km (1.2 miles) southwest of the boat wharf is the Jade Grotto, better known as **Bich Dong Pagoda** (Chua Bich Dong; daily 8am–5pm). At the pagoda entrance, stone steps hewn into a limestone rock dotted with shrines lead up to a cave entrance where three Buddhas sit atop lotus thrones. Walk through here and climb up the steps cut into the cliff face, where there are more Buddhist shrines and a terrace with stunning valley views. The complex dates back to the early 15th century, when King Le Thai To was in power. Beware of locals trying to sell fake entrance tickets.

TRANG AN GROTTO COMPLEX

Located 4km (2.5 miles) southwest of Hoa Lu, the **Trang An Grotto Eco-Tourism Complex** (daily 8am–6pm) comprises a series of caves with lyrical names such as Three Drops (Ba Giot), Holy Land (Dia Linh) and Cloud (May), beautiful limestone mountains and a vast network of underground rivers. There is also the 200-metre (650ft) **Bai Dinh Pagoda Mountain**, which is being advertised as a pilgrimage site to rival the Perfume Pagoda near Hanoi. Its main attractions include a 36-tonne "great bell" unsurprisingly located in Bell Tower, as well as the magnificent Avalokitesvara Bodhisattva statue. All in all there are some 47 historical ruins to see, 50 caves and numerous trekking trails to explore in the complex. Locals here boast that the area is 10 times more beautiful than Tam Coc. The unique beauty of Trang An landscape and its rich cultural heritage

Picturesque boat ride along the Ngo Dong River, Tam Coc.

was acknowledged in 2014 by Unesco, which inscribed it on its world heritage list.

KENH GA FISHING VILLAGE

Just 21km (13 miles) northwest from Ninh Binh, **Kenh Ga** was once a charming little fishing village, with most of its residents living on houseboats and earning a living from fishing. In the past five years, however, many of the wealthier villagers have built concrete homes on the land, and only the poorest remain on the water. Kenh Ga, or Chicken Canal, supposedly got its name from the wild chickens that used to live in the area, and can be reached by boat and motorbike.

Kenh Ga residents' pride and joy is their rustic **Catholic Church**, with its ancient wooden shutters on the outside, and heavy wooden beams and pillars with interesting carvings within.

A 15-minute boat ride from the Dong Chua Port in Kenh Ga are the **Kenh Ga Hot Springs** (daily 8am–6pm), a large tourist development geared towards wealthy Vietnamese. Chaotic and noisy, the mammoth complex includes a 20-room hotel, a stilt house, a 150-seater restaurant and a series of hot spring and whirlpool tubs.

CUC PHUONG NATIONAL PARK

Continuing west 24km (15 miles) along on the same road that runs by the Kenh Ga pier, you will arrive at the entrance to the 25,000-hectare (61,000-acre) **Cuc Phuong National Park** ㉑ (Cong Vien Quoc Gia Cuc Phuong; tel: 03-084 8018; www.cucphuongtourism.com; daily daylight hours). If visitors can only visit one national park in northern Vietnam, this should be the one.

Declared open by Ho Chi Minh himself in 1962, the biodiversity here is compelling. The park was established to shelter 250 bird and 64 mammal species, including tigers, leopards, bats, boars, civet cats and flying squirrels, as well as the endangered Delacour langur. However, given the propensity for poaching and Vietnam's lax environment protection laws, there is little likelihood of most visitors coming across any animal (and least of all

Kenh Ga is a sleepy backwater village.

The Bich Dong Pagoda is set in limestone caves.

The critically endangered grey-shanked Douc langur species can only be found at Cuc Phuong's Endangered Primate Rescue Center.

Educational tour at Cuc Phong's Endangered Primate Rescue Center.

a dangerous one). Unlike staff at other parks in Vietnam, however, the park wardens at Cuc Phuong seem to have a genuine interest in wildlife and environmental protection.

Even without glimpsing the larger wildlife, visitors can get a sense of the great diversity of insects and flora within the park. Some of the trees *(Parashorea stellata* and *Terminalia myriocarpa)* reach over 50 metres (165ft) in height, and are estimated to be over 1,000 years old, and close to 500 medicinal plants and herbs, of both native and foreign origin, have been discovered in the park. Some of Cuc Phuong's many caves and grottoes are also easily accessible within two mountain ranges that enclose a valley with a microclimate quite different from that of the surrounding region. Three tombs, excavated in one of the grottoes in 1966, contained shells, animal teeth, rudimentary stone tools and prehistoric human remains.

As Cuc Phuong is only 45km (30 miles) from Ninh Binh (and 140km/87 miles from Hanoi), it can be easily visited on a day trip. It will be a rushed day trip, however, and visitors will not have time to explore the various hiking trails, including the popular 7km (4-mile) trail that starts at the park centre. Visitors can go on longer hikes in the national reserve but guides are mandatory. You can stay either at the bungalows run by the park authorities or at one of the Muong villages within the park.

ENDANGERED PRIMATE RESCUE CENTER

A highlight of any visit to Cuc Phuong is the **Endangered Primate Rescue Center** (tel: 03-084 8002; www.eprc. asia; daily 9–11.30am and 1.30–4pm; charge), located 500 metres/yds in front of the park reception office. Run by a team of German and Vietnamese biologists, the goal of the centre is to protect, study and breed the park's rare primates.

Founded in 1993, the centre is home to more than 180 primates, including six langur species found nowhere else in the world – the endangered

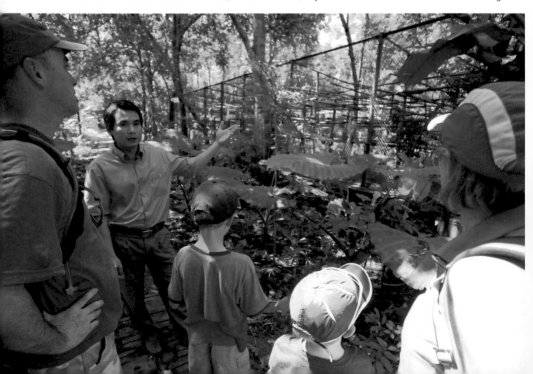

grey-shanked Douc langur, the Dela-cour langur, the Cat Ba langur, the Hatinh langur, the black langur and the Laos langur. The work of the centre is funded primarily by donors, so visitors can help out by buying postcards and souvenirs, or by participating in their "Adopt-a-Monkey" programme.

PHAT DIEM CATHEDRAL

The towering stone edifice called **Phat Diem Cathedral** (http://phatdiem.org; Mass held Mon–Sat 5am and 5pm, Sun 6am, 10am and 4pm) is an architec-tural wonder that is little known out-side of Vietnam. It is located in the town of **Phat Diem** (also known as **Kim Son**), about 25km (16 miles) southeast of Ninh Binh. While the road is a bit bumpy, traffic is thin, making it well suited for motorbikes or bicycles. It is best to visit the church during Mass times as the main buildings are locked for most of the day – although if this is the case, ask the staff at the tour kiosk just outside the main entrance to open up the buildings for you; Phat Diem is a popular tourist site for Vietnamese and the staff will usually oblige.

Built in 1891, the Sino-Vietnamese-style cathedral with elements of Euro-pean Gothic has sturdy stone walls and is fringed with boxy cupolas with upturned tiled roofs. It was designed by a Vietnamese priest, Father Tran Luc (more popularly known as Father Six), who insisted that the stone used to construct the church be towed from hundreds of kilometres away. Father Six's tomb is in the square in front of the cathedral. Not counting the bish-op's quarters behind a rear wall, there are half a dozen other structures in the complex, including a tomb-like stone chapel and a magnificent bell tower.

The **main cathedral** has a nave that extends for 74 metres (240ft) and is supported by 52 iron-wood pillars, 16 of which are 11 metres (36ft) high. The front sanctuary area above the single-slab altar is decorated with orthodox-style

lacquered and gilded carved woodwork. Note the angels with Vietnamese faces near the vaulted ceiling.

The two-tonne bronze bell in the **bell tower** was hauled up there on a ramp of earth. Climb to the top for sweeping views of the town.

Phat Diem and its surroundings are Catholic country (about 6 million of Vietnam's 86 million-strong population are staunchly Roman Catholic). There are also at least 10 well-maintained churches in the vicinity.

On the road back to Ninh Binh, look out for the quaint 19th-century covered **Phat Diem Bridge**, made of wood and arching across the **Day River** (Song Day).

THANH HOA PROVINCE

Leaving behind Ninh Binh province, one enters Annam, the traditional central region of Vietnam, and the beautiful but impoverished Thanh Hoa province. This is the first of a succession of seven coastal provinces hemmed between the South China Sea – known to the Vietnamese as the "East Sea" – and the Truong Son mountain range.

Container for holy water at the Phat Diem Cathedral.

Sunday-morning Mass at Phat Diem Cathedral.

From Thanh Hoa down to the former Demilitarised Zone (DMZ) – that is, through Thanh Hoa, Nghe An, Ha Tinh and Quanh Binh provinces – National Highway 1A is crowded with trucks, cars, motorbikes, bicycles, buffalo carts and pedestrians. Given the sporadic road construction along the way, the train is an attractive option. Provincial governments are charged with road maintenance, so the state of the road reflects a province's poverty, and Thanh Hoa is among the poorest in the country. The sandy soil has never made for good harvests and is only able to grow one rice crop a year, with peasant families scraping by on manioc and peanuts. However, since the 1980s, with seed money from Britain, many farmers in Thanh Hoa have become successful apiarists and honey producers.

HAM RONG BRIDGE

There is little to see in the provincial capital, **Thanh Hoa City**, although just 3km (2 miles) to the northeast of the city limits, the historic 160-metre (525ft) -long **Ham Rong Bridge** (Cau Han Rong) crosses the Ma River (Song Ma) to link the central and northern sections of Vietnam. A crucial transport link for the Vietcong during the Vietnam War, the bridge was continuously targeted by the US Air Force from 1965. It was only in 1972, however, that the Americans finally managed to destroy the bridge with laser-guided bombs, but the enterprising Vietnamese quickly built a replacement pontoon. All in all, the US is said to have lost 70 planes in missions to destroy Ham Rong, more than against any other wartime target. Than Hoa saw a rapid expansion in recent years, its population swelling to about 436,000. Tho Xuan airport, located 45 km to the east of the city, was upgraded in 2013 to also receive civilian planes – it was previously only used by the military.

DONG SON CULTURE

Thanh Hoa is well known as the cradle of **Dong Son culture**. The province harbours a number of ancient historical sites and is also an important settlement area for the Muong minority. At the beginning of the 20th century, archaeologists discovered many relics of the Dong Son civilisation (which lasted for approximately the entire millennium from 1000 BC) dispersed along the length of the **Ma River** (Song Ma) **Valley**: bronze drums, musical instruments, statues, jewellery, various tools and domestic objects. Some of these are now displayed at the Fine Arts Museum in Hanoi. The Muong still adhere to their ancient language, similar to Vietnamese, and use the bronze drums in their unique culture and festivals. Although there has been much intermarriage and cultural melding over the centuries, the Muong probably predated the Viets in Vietnam.

LAM SON VILLAGE

Thanh Hoa's highlands are relatively untouched and support an array of wildlife and various hill tribes. The

The wooden Phat Diem Bridge over the Day River.

Muong village of **Lam Son** ㉓, in the Thanh Hoa highlands, about 50km (30 miles) west of Thanh Hoa City, was the birthplace of Vietnam's national hero, Le Loi, who became King Le Thai To. It was from here that Le Loi launched a decade-long uprising against the Chinese Ming-dynasty occupiers of Vietnam in the 15th century. The struggle, waged from 1418 to 1428 in this mountainous region, finally ended in victory for Le Loi and his troops.

In the village is the **Le Loi Temple** (Den Le Loi; daily 8am–5pm; free), dedicated to Le Loi. It contains a bronze bust of his likeness cast in 1532. Nguyen Trai, Le Loi's adviser, penned the epitaph on the large stone stela, dedicated to the life and works of Le Loi.

SAM SON BEACH

Some 16km (10 miles) southeast from the city of Thanh Hoa, the white sands of **Sam Son Beach** ㉔ stretch for 3km (2 miles) along the coast of the South China Sea. There are actually two beaches here, separated by rocks. Both are busy, but more businesses are located on the northern beach. Superb scenery surrounds Sam Son, named after the coastal mountains. A popular spot for domestic tourists, rapid development has unfortunately left the area buzzing with seedy karaoke bars, sex workers and aggressive beachside vendors. Accommodation is of the mini-hotel variety, though prices will spike during the summer. The resort is packed in the summer months but mostly deserted the rest of the year.

GOD FISH STREAM AND BEN EN NATIONAL PARK

Other attractions in Than Hoa province include the **God Fish Stream** in Cam Luong, Cam Thuy and **Ben En National Park**. Located north east of Thanh Hoa City at the base of Truong Sinh Mountain, the God Fish Stream is known for

a particular type of fish deemed magical by the local population. The legend has it, the fish brings bad luck and therefore can't be caught or eaten. The stream is set in amazing scenery dominated by rugged mountains, long rivers and covered with dense forest.

Ben En National Park (http://benennp.com.vn/web/), situated 36 km south of Thanh Hoa City, is an amazing labyrinth of lakes, caves, mountains peaks and forests that make for a perfect ecotourism and hiking area. But first and foremost, the park is a breeding ground for many rare species, while its thick forest abounds with valuable trees such as green ironwood and mahogany.

NGHE AN PROVINCE

South of Thanh Hoa is Nghe An province. With a long history of peasant uprisings, this is the birthplace of several revolutionaries, including Phan Boi Chau and Nguyen Ai Quoc (more famously known as Ho Chi Minh). It was also the birthplace of national poet Nguyen Du (1765–1820), author of the *Tale of Kieu*, Vietnam's famous poetic

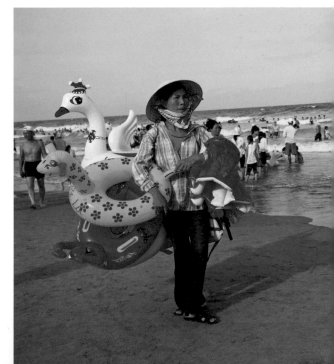

Vendors at Sam Son Beach inflate prices during the summer months, when the beach is often crowded.

epic (see page 85). The city of **Vinh** is the capital of Nghe An province but it isn't very exciting. A modern industrial base, it was bombed by the US Air Force and then completely rebuilt in a drab, grey Soviet style. Most travellers use Vinh as a rest stop, or use the city as a transit point en route to the Laos border.

In Nghe An province and its neighbour to the south, Ha Tinh, the mountains give way to wide plains along a 230km (143-mile) coastline, and forests cover more than half of the land. The climate is harsh – the area is frequently hit with severe typhoons and flooding. There are more than 100 rivers and streams, the longest of which is the **Lam Dong River** (Song Lam Dong) that feeds the two provinces.

HOANG TRU AND KIM LIEN VILLAGES

In 1959, the inhabitants of **Hoang Tru village** ㉕, 14km (7 miles) northwest of the nondescript provincial capital, **Vinh**, re-created the humble three-room house, with bamboo walls and a

palm-leaf roof, where Ho Chi Minh was born as Nguyen Sinh Cung in 1890. Ho's family moved from here to Hue when he was five.

Ho's father, a mandarin and minor official in the Hue court, became disillusioned with the French rulers and was eventually dismissed. He returned to this area in 1901 and settled close to Hoang Tru, in nearby **Kim Lien village**, where he and Ho Chi Minh's grandfather taught. Young Ho Chi Minh spent a few years here before he and his father returned to Hue.

Kim Lien villagers constructed a replica of the second house, also in 1959, and turned it into yet another Ho Chi Minh shrine. It is very similar to the one in Hoang Tru. Nearby is a dusty three-room museum displaying memorabilia, old photographs, Ho's poems and some actual shirts he wore. All the sites can be visited daily from 7.30–11.30am and 1.30–5pm, and depending on who is working, visitors may be asked to pay a small fee, or alternatively to buy flowers to leave at the shrines.

Fishing boats along Sam Son Beach.

It's easy to confuse these two Ho Chi Minh houses since there is little English-language information at either. It is not obvious that these are replicas of the original homes or that Ho spent little of his life in either place. During his 30-year odyssey, Ho rarely contacted his family, and he returned to his childhood homes just once in his life, in 1961.

CUA LO BEACH

About 20km (12 miles) north of Vinh is **Cua Lo Beach**, which, like Sam Son Beach, attracts mostly local Vietnamese. The waters are clean and the stretch of sand is inviting, but the karaoke bars, massage parlours and general tackiness may deter many.

QUANG BINH PROVINCE

Quang Binh province was one of the earliest battlegrounds between the Viets and the Champa, in their struggle to control Vietnam. Although now a quiet backwater, it was the home of several well-known historical figures in Vietnam, including the poet Han Mac Tu, former president Ngo Dinh Diem, and one of the most respected Communist war veterans in the country, Vo Nguyen Giap.

The Unesco World Heritage Site **Phong Nha-Ke Bang National Park** ㉖ was created to protect some of the world's most extensive karst landscapes. The park is best known for its caves, including **Phong Nga**, which is home to the world's longest underground river, and the world's largest cave passage, Son Doong, discovered by British explorers in 2009. It is possible to explore both the huge cave and river with guided tours. A boat tour of the cave is the highlight of any visit to this region.

DONG HOI

About 55km (34 miles) from Phong Nga, quaint **Dong Hoi** ㉗ makes a good base for day trips to the caves and exploring the DMZ. There was once an ancient citadel here but little remains other than moats and vestiges. The local beach, Nha Le, is a lovely and very quiet place to get away – there's little there in the way of service and accommodation, apart from Sun Spa Resort.

Ⓘ Tip

It is possible to travel from the Tonkin Coast to Laos. Around 100km (60 miles) west of Vinh is Cau Treo, and a bus runs from Hanoi to Vientiane, passing here on the way, though it can be a gruelling 24-hour journey. Laos visas may be obtained at this point, but tourists entering Vietnam here will need to arrange visas in advance.

The house in Kim Lien village, where Ho Chi Minh once lived.

Bucolic setting at Thanh Toan Bridge, near Hue.

Buddha image among the Cham
ruins at My Son.

CENTRAL VIETNAM

The central stretch of Vietnam offers some of the country's most alluring attractions, including a trio of Unesco World Heritage sites – Hue, Hoi An and My Son.

Fishermen at Lang Co, near Danang.

The central region of Vietnam is a showpiece of the country's rich history, from the ancient Sa Huynh culture centred in Quang Ngai province to the devastation of war in the former DMZ, or Demilitarized Zone. At the heart of Vietnam is Hue, the imperial capital of the Nguyen kings. A few hours south, the charming old town of Hoi An makes for an exquisitely relaxing break.

The Nguyen dynasty ruled from Hue for 143 years, leaving behind a substantial imperial city as well as a revered collection of tombs which dot the countryside along the fabled Perfume River. In contrast to the brief reign of the Nguyens, the Champa kingdom ruled most of central Vietnam from the 7th to 15th centuries. Its most celebrated ancient red-brick temple-towers are found at My Son, but there are several other Champa sites scattered across the entire central coast. These ancient structures stand as silent testimony to the kingdom that flourished here before its absorption by the Vietnamese descending from the north.

To Mieu Temple, Hue.

Outside Hue, the narrow, central coastal provinces of Quang Tri and Dong Ha, positioned directly south of the DMZ, suffered immeasurably during the Vietnam War. The cities of Danang, Quang Ngai and Qui Nhon all had a strong American presence throughout the war, but each now offers a chance to soak up the quiet local ambience of Vietnamese life. All three cities are close to spectacular white-sand beaches backed by tall, jagged mountains. Danang is the central commercial hub of the country and boasts all of the modern conveniences of Ho Chi Minh City and Hanoi in addition to a fine museum on the Cham civilisation.

The 15th-century town of Hoi An was once the biggest seaport and most important centre of trade in the country, when it was known to Europeans as Faifo. Its beautifully preserved assembly halls, merchant shops and family homes reflect the influence of the Chinese, Japanese and Westerners who settled in the region. Today, numerous tailor shops, cafés and restaurants jostle for space with an assortment of older buildings.

The extravagant tomb
of Khai Dinh.

HUE

The former imperial capital is a sleepy, romantic city, badly damaged during the Vietnam War. Nearby, along the Perfume River, are the ancient tombs of the Nguyen emperors.

An imperial citadel still stands proudly in Hue, despite violent bombardment during the Vietnam War (1954–75) by the Viet Cong and the Americans. Ask Vietnamese about Hue and they'll often remark that it's a sad and sleepy city. This may have something to do with the old architecture and crumbling ruins (many of Hue's residents have built a livelihood based around the city's past). Hue is also prone to exceptionally rainy weather compared to the rest of Vietnam, particularly in the second half of the year.

Once the capital of Vietnam and the seat of the Nguyen dynasty (1802–1945), **Hue ❶** is located 12km (7.5 miles) from the coast on a narrow stretch of land in Thua Thien-Hue province, which borders Laos in the west. It is roughly midway between Hanoi to the north and Ho Chi Minh City to the south. Today, the city is one of Vietnam's more noteworthy attractions, thanks to its eventful history as well as its cultural and intellectual connections, made all the more inviting by its scenic location along the banks of **Song Huong** – the Vietnamese name for the Perfume River.

Hue is a pretty city, crisscrossed by dozens of bridges, lakes, moats and canals. On the river's north bank is the ancient imperial citadel and residential areas, while the new commercial

A pavilion within the Imperial City grounds.

area, the old French quarter and the hotel district are all on the south bank. Further south are several tombs that belong to the emperors of the Nguyen dynasty.

HUE'S HISTORY

Hue's modern history goes back to 1601, when Nguyen Hoang, of the powerful Nguyen Lords faction (see page 34), arrived. The Nguyen Lords administered the whole region with the agreement of the – often rival – Trinh lords. This arrangement

⦿ Main Attractions
Imperial City
Royal Antiquities Museum
Thien Mu Pagoda
Tu Duc's Tomb
Minh Mang's Tomb
Khai Dinh's Tomb
The DMZ

⦿ Maps on pages
200, 202, 209

Central Vietnam

0   25 km

0   25 miles

operated smoothly at first, but hostilities soon flared as the territory extended southwards. Bloody battles broke out between the two warring families, but eventually the Nguyen Lords gained the upper hand. The Nguyens also managed to crush the remnant of Champa in the south along the way, gradually dissolving their autonomy. Nguyen feudal lords ruled over the area until 1802. That year, after quelling the Tay Son uprising, the 10th Nguyen Lord proclaimed himself Emperor Gia Long and founded the Nguyen dynasty, which would last for 143 years, until 1945.

Just 33 years into the dynasty's reign, the French invaded Hue. They retained the Nguyen as something of a puppet regime, with nominal governance over central Vietnam (Annam) and northern Vietnam (Tonkin). Thanks to French manipulation, a quick succession of emperors occupied the throne. The anti-French demonstrations and strikes of the colonial era were followed by the Japanese occupation in World War II and the abdication of Bao Dai, the last of the Nguyen emperors, at the end of the war.

The relative peace that reigned after 1954, when Hue became part of South Vietnam following the country's division into two by the UN, was short-lived. During the Tet Offensive of 1968, Hue's imperial city suffered extensive damage when the Viet Cong held out in the fortified ancient citadel against American attack for nearly two months. Many priceless historical monuments and relics were destroyed in the battle. In the ensuing years, typhoons and flooding caused further damage, and what remained was generally neglected until Hue began to develop as a tourist destination in the 1990s.

THE IMPERIAL CITY

On the northern side of the Perfume River, Hue's **Citadel** (Kinh

Thanh) covers some 520 hectares (1,285 acres) and is enclosed by a wall made of stone, brick and earth and measuring 8 metres (26ft) high and 20 metres (65ft) thick. The wall – all 10km (6 miles) of it – is punctuated by 10 large fortified gates, each topped with watchtowers, and surrounded by a moat. On the southern side of the wall, facing the river, is the large Flag Tower (Cot Co), visible from all over the city.

A second, 6-metre (20ft) -high defensive wall within the Citadel guards a far smaller area, the **Imperial Enclosure** (Hoang Thanh; daily 6.30am–5pm), with its palaces, temples and flower gardens. Most of what visitors come to see today is found within this inner zone, which was fashioned after Beijing's Imperial City and built during the reign of Emperor Gia Long. Four richly decorated gates provided access: Hoa Binh (northern gate), Hien Nhon (eastern gate), Chuong Duc (western gate) and the **Ngo Mon Gate** (southern gate, or noon gate), first built of granite

in 1834 during the reign of Emperor Minh Mang. The main entrance point into the Imperial Enclosure, this gate is topped by the **Five Phoenix Watchtower** (Lau Ngu Phung), with its roofs brightly tiled in yellow over the middle section and green on either side. From here, the emperor used to preside over formal ceremonies and rites. It is perhaps the most recognisable structure in the entire city.

Outside of the gate – between it and the outer wall (and the Flag Tower) – are the **Nine Deities' Cannons** (Sung Than Cong). The five cannons on the western side represent the five elements – metal, water, wood, fire and earth – while the four to the east represent the four seasons. Each cannon weighs about 10 tonnes.

THAI HOA PALACE

Pass through Ngo Mon Gate and walk across the **Golden Water Bridge** (Trung Dao), which at one time was reserved for the emperor. It leads to **Thai Hoa Palace** (Dien Thai Hoa), or Palace of Supreme Harmony, the

Cyclos passing in front of the Ngo Mon Gate.

⊙ Tip

You may exit the Imperial Enclosure and re-enter later in the day to attend a performance at the royal theatre. Just check with the ticket booth at the front gate when you exit.

most important administrative structure in the Imperial City. Here the emperor would hold bimonthly audiences with the court, including male members of the royal family; civil mandarins on the left, and military mandarins on the right.

FORBIDDEN PURPLE CITY

Beyond Thai Hoa lies the third and final enclosure, the **Forbidden Purple City** (Tu Cam Thanh). This city within a city was reserved solely for the emperor and the royal family, who resided here behind a brick wall. The Forbidden Purple City was almost completely destroyed during the Tet Offensive of 1968 when the Viet Cong used it as a bunker. Today, the structures within are undergoing reconstruction work.

To the left and right are the **Halls of the Mandarins**, which are annexes to the demolished Can Chanh Palace. In the **Left Hall** (Ta Vu), visitors can be photographed in period costumes, while the **Right Hall** (Huu Vu) houses an extension of the **Royal Antiquities Museum**, with small but representative exhibits of silver, bronze and wood belonging to the Nguyen royalty.

The **Royal Theatre** Ⓓ (Duyet Thi Duong) behind and to the right (east), stages 30-minute shows (http://www.nhanhac.com.vn/index.php; daily 10.00am and 3pm) that feature dancers in elaborate costumes backed by a traditional orchestra.

The emperor's **Reading Pavilion** (Thai Binh Lau) sits behind the theatre, ornately decorated with ceramic tiles. This is one of the few structures to have survived the Tet Offensive, although it is in a poor state of repair and looks like it could collapse at any time.

Beyond, a number of **covered walking corridors** (truong lan) are still under construction, imitating the Nguyen-dynasty style. In the empty expanse behind to the left and right is a pair of octagonal **Music Pavilions** (Nhac Lau).

DIEN THO PALACE

To the west, between the walls of the Forbidden City and the Imperial

Enclosure, is **Dien Tho Palace** Ⓔ, the traditional residence of the various queen mothers. There are some 20 structures at this site, most notably the **Phuoc Tho Pagoda**, the **residence of Emperor Bao Dai** and the lovely **Truong Du Pavilion**, which is nestled over a small lotus pond. The beauty of this complex rivals that of Thai Hoa Palace.

Just behind Dien Tho Palace is **Truong Sanh Residence**, which served as a sort of social area for the queen mothers. Constructed during the time of Emperor Minh Manh, the building has undergone renovation works worth some US$1.8 million.

THE TEMPLES

The temples within the Imperial Enclosure are dedicated to various lords and royal family members: in the southeast corner, the temple of **Trieu To Mieu** (now used as a plant nursery) was built to honour Nguyen Kim, while the adjacent **Thai Mieu** was dedicated to Nguyen Hoang and his successors.

The **To Mieu** complex in the southwest corner houses numerous shrines of significance as well. The **Hung Mieu** is devoted to Nguyen Phuc Luan, Gia Long's father. To its left is the well-preserved **The Mieu**, dedicated to the sovereigns of the Nguyen dynasty. A restoration project of three marvellous royal altars and Trieu To's facade was completed in 2015.

In front of The Mieu temple and completely restored is the magnificent **Pavilion of Splendour** Ⓕ (Hien Lam Cac), with the **Nine Dynastic Urns** (Cuu Dinh) lined up before it. The urns are decorated with motifs of the sun, moon, clouds, birds, animals, dragons, mountains, rivers, historic events and scenes from everyday life. Each urn represents an emperor of the Nguyen dynasty and weighs up to 2,500kg (5,600lbs).

BEYOND THE IMPERIAL CITY

Another world lies beyond the walls of the Imperial City, which is flanked to the south and east by Hue's

The Ngo Mon Gate, entrance to the Imperial Enclosure.

The impressive Pavilion of Splendour and the Nine Dynastic Urns.

commercial centre. The modern downtown area is south of the river between **Trang Tien Bridge** and **Phu Xuan Bridge**. Trang Tien Bridge is the most recognisable modern structure in the city and is lit up every evening in a multicoloured light show. The hotel, shopping and restaurant district is concentrated within a triangle formed by Ben Nghe and Ha Noi streets; the main nightlife hub is in the northeast corner of that triangle, between Le Loi and Tran Cao Van streets.

There are attractive parks on both sides of the river, abuzz with stalls and cafés in the evening.

HUE HISTORICAL AND REVOLUTIONARY MUSEUM

Near the east gate of the Imperial City, the **Hue Historical and Revolutionary Museum** (Bao Tang Tong Hop; Tue–Sun 8–11am, 2–5pm) is easily recognised by the tanks and artillery sitting out front. The central building, built in the style of a traditional *dinh* (communal house),

Dien Tho Palace interior.

contains a humble collection of archaeological discoveries (mainly pottery and Cham relics) from the area. To the left, in a separate pavilion, is an uninspiring presentation of the First Indochina War (against the French) with plenty of photos but few artefacts. The pavilion on the right is dedicated to the Second Indochina War (against the Americans) in similar fashion.

ROYAL ANTIQUITIES MUSEUM

Near the citadel is the **Royal Antiquities Museum** Ⓖ (Tue–Sun summer 6.30am–5.30pm, winter 7am–5pm) at 3 Le Truc Street, which occupies a nicely renovated former Nguyen palace called Long An Palace. Despite the museum's name, the exhibits are not antiques per se, as the collection dates from years 1802–1945 and includes pieces of porcelain, silver objects, coins, weapons, jewellery and items from the royal wardrobe. All in all, there are about 10,000 exhibits on display. Some items were given as gifts to the Nguyen

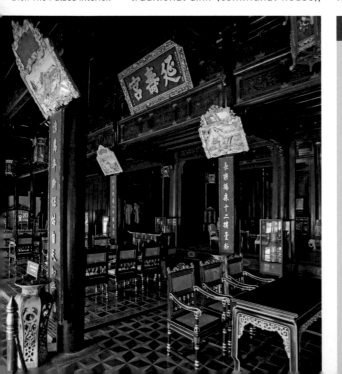

Ⓞ NHA NHAC

Nha Nhac, or music of the royal court, is the highest form of traditional Vietnamese music. Instruments commonly included in a traditional orchestra of the former royal court are the *dan ty ba* (a pear-shaped lute with four strings), *dan nguyet* (a moon-shaped two-string lute), *dan tam* (a fretless lute with three strings and a snakeskin-covered body), *dan nhi* (a two-stringed vertical fiddle), *ken bau* (a conical oboe), *sao truc* (a bamboo transverse flute), *trong* (a large drum played with sticks), and occasionally gongs, bells and other percussion. Around Hue, performances can be seen at the Royal Theatre in the imperial city, Tu Duc's tomb, and various tourist restaurants in the new city. For more on the Royal Theatre, see page 202.

emperors by dignitaries, while others represent the high level of craftsmanship during the Nguyen dynasty. The downside is that there is sometimes a lack of satisfactory description and detailed information.

PHU CAT

The neighbourhood of **Phu Cat** is home to the Hoa people (Vietnamese-Chinese), who arrived as "boat people" from China in the early 1800s. The lively **Cho Dong Ba** Ⓗ is the city's main market and offers a great variety of local products and food delights. Buy one of the famous "poem hats" which, when held up to a light source, reveals the shadow of a scene or a poem.

THUAN AN BEACH

Thuan An Beach is located about 30km (19 miles) east from Hue. Ancient Cham relics and ruins found scattered in the nearby coastal dunes long pre-date the nearby imperial city. Seldom visited by tourists, Thuan An is undeveloped and lined with

seafood shacks and drink stands. Reclining chairs occupied by Vietnamese families sit under tattered umbrellas. The beach itself isn't as nice as the stretch from Danang to Hoi An, but it is a pleasant escape from town for visitors with ample free time. The Ana Mandara (http://anamandarahue-resort.com) is arguably the best resort on the beach.

THIEN MU PAGODA

Some 3km (2 miles) to the west of the Imperial City, situated on a hill overlooking the Perfume River, is **Thien Mu Pagoda** Ⓘ (Celestial Lady Pagoda; daily 8am–5pm). Built by Nguyen Hoang in 1601, the seven tiers of the temple's octagonal tower – **Phuoc Duyen** – each represent a different reincarnation of the Buddha. Six images of deities guard the pagoda, which contains a gilt statue of the laughing Buddha and three other glass-enclosed statues. Many generations have heard the tolling of the pagoda's enormous 2,000kg (4,410lb), 2-metre (6ft) bell since it was cast

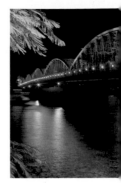

The resplendent Trang Tien Bridge across the Perfume River.

Dien Tho Palace.

⏱ Tip

It is a good idea to carry a small pocket-umbrella and poncho when visiting the imperial city or tombs. Hue can be very rainy virtually any time of the year. Street vendors sell disposable ponchos but they come in only one size and the quality is very poor at best. Most don't last more than a single wear.

in 1701. It makes such a resounding racket that it can be heard up to 16km (10 miles) away.

In 1963, Thich Quang Duc, a monk from this temple, travelled to Saigon and burnt himself to death in protest at President Ngo Dinh Diem's repressive regime in South Vietnam. The Austin car which he drove to Saigon, as well as the famous photo of the monk alight in flames that captured headlines all over the world, are on display behind the pagoda.

THE NGUYEN TOMBS

The Nguyen imperial tombs lie scattered on the hillsides on either side of the Perfume River, to the west and south of Hue. Although the dynasty had 13 sovereigns, only seven of them reigned until their deaths, and only these are laid to rest in this valley: Gia Long, Minh Mang, Thieu Tri, Tu Duc, Kien Phuc, Dong Khanh and Kai Dinh. Three generations of emperors forcibly removed from power are buried at Duc Duc's Tomb: Duc Duc himself (and his wife), their

The evocatively named Perfume River.

son Thanh Thai and their grandson Duy Tan.

The tombs of the Nguyen emperors are well spread out and could easily take up two full days if you visited all of them. However, many people choose to skip the tombs of Gia Long and Kien Phuc because they are further afield.

The poor state of the roads leading to the tombs is surprising given that this is one of Vietnam's most important cultural sites. The road from Khai Dinh's tomb to the Perfume River, for instance, is little more than a pavement. It's also very easy to get lost as there are many turn-offs (beware of locals sending you along forest trails that lead nowhere). Roads are poorly and infrequently signposted, and often in Vietnamese only.

There is no one efficient way of touring the tombs, so if you choose to see the majority, it may require some backtracking.

GENERAL TOMB LAYOUTS

Each tomb has a large brick-paved courtyard, called *bia dinh*, that contains several stone figures of elephants, saddled horses, soldiers, and civil and military mandarins. In front of this stands the stelae pavilion, containing the tall marble or stone stela engraved with the biography of the deceased king, usually written by his successor. Beyond this is the temple, or *tam dien*, where the deceased king and queen are worshipped by their families and their royal belongings are displayed. The king's widows would keep incense and aloe wood perpetually burning before the altar until their own deaths. Behind and on either side of the temple are the houses built for the king's concubines, servants and the soldiers who guarded the royal tomb. The emperor's body would be laid in a concealed place, or *bao thanh*, enclosed by high walls behind well-locked metal doors.

NAM GIAO DAN

To reach the tombs from Hue, head south on Dien Bien Phu Street, first passing **Nam Giao Dan** ❶ (Terrace of Heavenly Sacrifice; daily 8am–5pm; free) on your left, an esplanade surrounded by a park of pine trees around 2km (1.2 miles) from Hue's commercial centre. Built by Gia Long in 1802, in its day it was considered a most sacred and solemn place. Composed of three terraces – two square and one circular, the esplanade represents the sky and the earth.

During the Nguyen dynasty, the Nam Giao (Festival of Sacrifice) took place at the centre of the circular esplanade once every three years. Here, the emperor would have a buffalo sacrificed to the Vietnamese God of the Sky, who is believed to govern the destiny of the entire world.

TU DUC'S TOMB

The **tomb of Tu Duc** ❻ (daily 7–11.30am and 1.30–5.30m) is less than 3km (2 miles) west of Nam Giao Dan via Xuan Thuong 4 Street, and is surrounded by a clutch of incense and souvenir shops. The mausoleum construction began in 1864 and took three years to complete. The result resembles a royal palace in

⊙ **Fact**

The pronunciation of "Hue" is somewhere between "hey" and "h-way". The vowel combination forms an odd sound to English-speakers due to the "high rising" tone on the final "e".

The octagonal Phuoc Duyen tower at Thien Mu Pagoda.

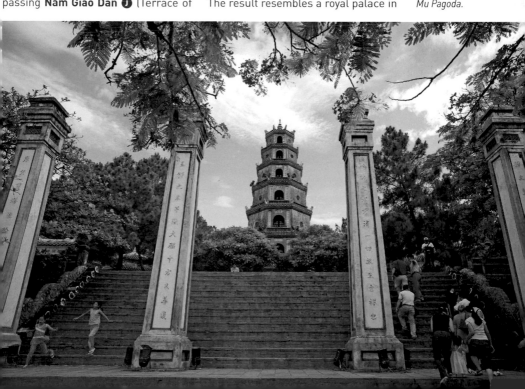

Tip

Local maps tend to oversimplify the route to Minh Mang's tomb. At the Perfume River, loop east on to the highway and cross the river via Tuan Bridge. Then take the next three left forks to reach the tomb.

miniature and harmonises beautifully with the natural surroundings. It is perhaps the loveliest of all the Nguyen tombs and certainly the most visited. Live traditional music is periodically performed within the tomb grounds.

Tu Duc, the son of Thieu Tri and the Nguyen dynasty's fourth king, reigned for 36 years, the longest reign of any of the Nguyen kings. He spent his leisure hours in the two pavilions beside the lake, Luu Khiem. The more popular of the two lakeside pagodas is **Xung Khiem Pavilion**. A staircase leads to the Luong Khiem mausoleum, which contains a collection of furniture, vases and jewellery boxes. Further on is the terrace leading to the tomb, with its stone elephants, horses and mandarins. The actual crypt, which is inaccessible, is covered by dense pine forest. The tombs of Tu Duc's adopted son, Kien Phu, and Queen Le Thien An, lie beside the lake.

The **tomb of Dong Khanh**, the nephew and adopted son of Tu Duc who ruled for just four years from 1885, lies just outside the complex.

The restoration of the smallest of the Nguyen tombs is currently underway.

THIEU TRI'S TOMB

The **tomb of Thieu Tri** ❶ (daily 7–11.30am and 1.30–5.30pm) is located a few kilometres to the south. Thieu Tri, Minh Mang's son, was the third Nguyen emperor and reigned from 1841 to 1847. His tomb was built in the same elegant architectural style as his father's but on a much smaller scale. Now crumbling, the mausoleum sprawls across several lakes and is largely open, and, unlike most other tombs, is not enclosed by walls.

HON CHEN TEMPLE

On the western bank of the Perfume River is **Hon Chen Temple** ❿, where the goddess Po Nagar, protector of the Champa kingdom, is worshipped. Po Nagar, greatly venerated by the Cham people, is also to a lesser extent worshipped today by some local Vietnamese as Tien Y Ana. A festival takes place here on the 15th day of the seventh

Khai Dinh's tomb.

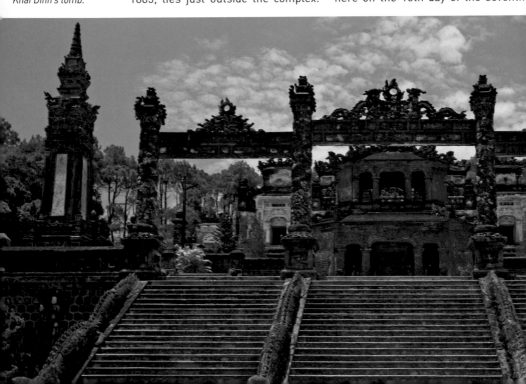

lunar month every year, when worshippers march in a long procession accompanied by ceremonial music and a heavy cloud of incense.

MINH MANG'S TOMB

The **tomb of Minh Mang** (daily 8am–5pm) is located about 5km (3 miles) south, where the Ta Trach and Huu Trach tributaries of the Perfume River meet. Minh Mang was Gia Long's fourth son and the Nguyen dynasty's second king. He was responsible for the building of the Imperial City and was highly respected for his Confucian outlook and opposition to the French presence in Vietnam. The construction of the tomb was begun a year before his death, in 1840, and was finished by his successor Thieu Tri in 1843. The setting blends the beauty of nature with majestic architecture and superb stone sculpture.

KHAI DINH'S TOMB

About 4km (2.5 miles) south of Nam Giao Dan, on Minh Mang Street, the tomb of **Khai Dinh** (daily 7–11.30am and 1.30–5.30pm) somewhat resembles a European castle, its architecture a blend of the oriental and the occidental. Made of reinforced concrete, it took 11 years to complete and was only finished in 1931. Khai Dinh, Bao Dai's adopted father, ruled for nine years during the colonial era. A grandiose dragon staircase leads up to the first courtyard, from where further stairs lead to a courtyard lined with stone statues of elephants, horses, and civil and military mandarins. In the centre of the courtyard stands the stela inscribed with Chinese characters composed by Bao Dai in memory of his father.

Once inside, however, the contrast is striking and more identifiable with the ostentatious character of the emperor. Coloured tiles pave the floor, and a huge "dragon in the clouds" mural, painted by artists using their feet, adorns the ceiling of the middle chamber. Jade green antechambers lead off to the left and right. Bright frescoes composed of

Hue: The Nguyen Tombs

⊙ Tip

A tour of the DMZ will often take all day, but this is mainly due to the long driving distances. Many agencies in Hue conduct tours of the DMZ. Note: remnant mines and other unexploded ordnance are another problem, so even if you get off the bus, be sure to stay on the paths.

many thousands of inlaid ceramic and glass fragments depict various themes. Animals, trees and flowers provide a visual feast after the morbid, blackened exterior of the mausoleum. The back room contains a small museum of the emperor's possessions, including photos, clothing, ceramics, crystal, furniture and a clock. A life-size bronze statue of Khai Dinh, made in France in 1922, rests on a dais on top of the tomb.

GIA LONG'S TOMB

The rarely visited tomb of **Gia Long ⓟ** (daily 7–11.30am and 1.30–5.30pm), located 16km (10 miles) south from Hue and on a hillside, is somewhat inaccessible by road; a more pleasant way to reach it is by boat on the river. The tomb, begun in 1814, was completed a year after Gia Long's death in 1820. Gia Long was the founder of the Nguyen dynasty, and his tomb perhaps served as a model for the later tombs. Unfortunately, the site was located right in the middle of a particularly active battleground

The understated beauty of Minh Mang's tomb.

during the Vietnam War and bombs damaged the tombs which are now being painstakingly restored. The wild beauty of the site itself, with its mountainous backdrop, makes the effort to get there worthwhile.

THE DMZ

The **Demilitarized Zone**, or DMZ, is where some of the bloodiest fighting of the Vietnam War took place. The DMZ stretched for 8km (5 miles) on either side of the **Ben Hai River**, 100km (60 miles) north of Hue. It was the line of demarcation between North Vietnam and South Vietnam, established at the Geneva Conference in 1954 after the end of the war against the French. Following the 17th parallel, the border was supposed to be temporary, until elections could be held in 1956. The elections never took place and Vietnam remained divided along this line until the two countries were officially reunified in 1976, following the collapse of South Vietnam.

Today, there are still desolate stretches of scorched earth. Just

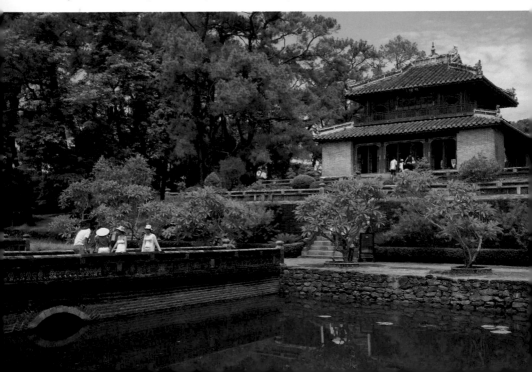

south of the Ben Hai, Highway 9 passes sites of famous Vietnam War battles and old US military bases like **Con Thien** and **Khe Sanh**. It is believed that 10,000 North Vietnamese, around 500 US soldiers and countless civilians were killed at the 1968 battle of **Khe Sanh** ❷ (daily 7am–5pm). After being nearly obliterated by more than 100,000 tonnes of bombs and assorted chemical weapons, vegetation has only recently begun to regrow here.

North of the DMZ, in **Vinh Moc** ❸ (daily 7am–5pm), a series of tunnels that are similar but more developed than those of Cu Chi (see page 303) is located where an entire village camped out for several years to escape the constant bombings. Most of the people evacuated to other parts of the country after the bombings began, but some stayed put. For five years, from 1966 to 1971, some 300 people lived in the 2,000-metre (6,500ft) long network of tunnels. Seventeen babies were said to have been born in this subterranean home. Unlike Cu Chi to the south, the tunnels here are easy to walk through, and so tend to be popular with visitors.

Another important DMZ site is the **Truong Son National Cemetery** ❹. Located 17km (11 miles) off Highway 1A and 13km (8 miles) north of Dong Ha, this large memorial is dedicated to the North Vietnamese soldiers who died along the Ho Chi Minh Trail in the Truong Son Mountains during the war. It is a sobering testament to the cost of war, with more than 10,000 tombstones dotting the hillsides. Each bears the Vietnamese words *Liet Si*, which means "martyr". It should be noted that there are no memorials, here or anywhere else in the country, for soldiers who fought for the South and were killed during the war.

Most visitors see sights in the DMZ as part of a shared all-day bus or shuttle tour with a large group. While this may be an easier and cheaper route, it means spending many boring hours in transit and waiting for the group. For a more enjoyable time, rent a motorbike and explore independently, or a private car and guide.

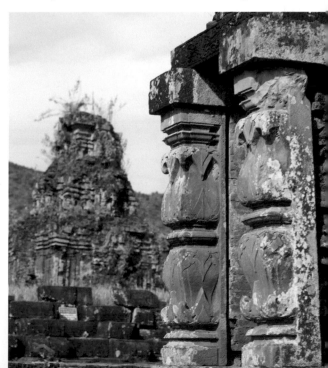

Preserving the national heritage.

☉ RUSH TO PRESERVE

For a country with a long and rich history, Vietnam boasts relatively few ancient architectural landmarks. Those that have managed to survive the centuries of war, typhoons and the effects of the tropical climate have subsequently suffered from neglect. In the last decade, however, Vietnam has shown an active interest in saving its historical sites. In part, this movement to preserve is part of the government's emphasis on nationalism. Restoring architectural ruins is one way to develop national pride. But more significantly, it is now perceived as commercially viable. All government officials needed to do was notice tourists flocking to Cambodia's Angkor Wat to figure out that there is money in a pile of old ruins. If the ruins are well maintained and easily accessed, that is.

Linh Ung Pagoda,
Marble Mountains.

DANANG AND HOI AN

Anchoring the centre of the country is busy Danang, one of Vietnam's largest cities. Nearby – but worlds apart – is Hoi An, a delightful old port town. All along the coast are sandy beaches interspersed with ancient Cham sites.

Danang, the business and commercial centre of central Vietnam, is an overlooked treasure trove of natural beauty and local culture. Fronted by the renowned "China Beach", the broad stretch of pristine sandy coastline changes name several times on its way past the Marble Mountains. These limestone outcrops were once host to ancient Cham temple sites, burrowed in their damp caves.

Nearby is the once-important port of Hoi An, preserved today as a Unesco World Heritage Site. It still retains its lovely old-town atmosphere and architecture, but also has the dubious honour of being central Vietnam's top shopping destination – there are more bespoke tailors per square metre here than anywhere else in the country. Hoi An was once the commercial hub for an extensive trade route spanning much of central Vietnam and far into the mountains. Cham, and then later the Chinese, Portuguese, French, Japanese and Vietnamese came here to trade cinnamon, ceramics, textiles and other goods, most of which went to China. Hidden away in the green folds of nearby foothills, the ancient temple city of My Son was the holy land of the Champa kingdom, and is today another Unesco World Heritage Site.

HAI VAN PASS TO DANANG

The 110km (68-mile) route from Hue to **Danang** via the 1,200-metre (4,000ft) **Hai Van Pass** is one of the most dramatic in Vietnam. The 3.5-hour drive over Highway 1A follows a vertiginous route up, down and around mountains that hug the coast.

Along the way is the peninsula of **Lang Co** ⑤, which rates as one of the most superb beaches in the country. To one side lies a stunning blue-green lagoon, and, on the other, kilometres of white sandy beach. Lang Co was once

◎ Main Attractions

Lang Co
Museum of Cham
  Sculpture
China Beach
Marble Mountains
Bach Ma National Park
Hoi An Old Town
Cua Dai Beach
Cu Lao Cham Marine Park
My Son

**◉ Maps on pages
200, 214, 225**

Fishermen, Lang Co Beach.

the resort playground of the Nguyen Kings; the ruins of their villas are still visible. Lang Co Beach Resort is the primary accommodation at the beach. Nearby excursions include visits to nearby streams, waterfalls, lagoons, villages and activities like snorkelling, fishing and camping. Despite the beach's fame, most tour buses today speed past without stopping. The climate becomes noticeably warmer and more humid after you pass the summit of Hai Van Pass and descend into the scenic coastal region. Taking the 6km (4-mile) -long **Hai Van Tunnel** shaves 30 minutes off the ride from Hue to Danang (Lang Co is itself 30 minutes from Danang) but you do miss out on some nice scenery. If you wish to take the Hai Van Pass route you'll need your own transport, as buses take the tunnel.

Danang ❻ lies at the midpoint of the country, about 800km (500 miles) from both Hanoi and Ho Chi Minh City. It broke away from Quang Nam province in 1996 to become an independent municipality, and is now Vietnam's fourth-largest city. Danang straddles the east and west bank of the Han River, between Nam O Beach to the north and China Beach to the south. While it's not as hectic as Hanoi or Ho Chi Minh City, this is central Vietnam's main economic centre and host to the country's third-busiest port. With its international airport, Danang is also a jump-off point for tourists, and resorts and numerous golf course developments are sprouting up all along the nearby coast.

Danang is as good a place as any to gauge the flavour of modern Vietnam, and has prospered in the economic boom of recent years. There are glitzy new shopping centres and high-rise buildings, and all the conveniences and entertainment of Ho Chi Minh City, generally without the attendant traffic and crowds.

HISTORY

Known as Tourane to the French, Danang is perhaps best remembered for the role it played at the beginning and end of the Vietnam War. Because of

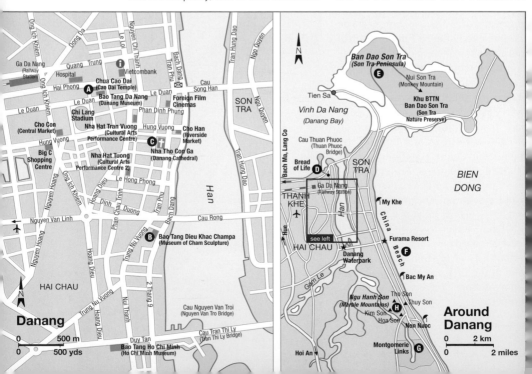

its location in the centre of the country, it found itself a city divided during the war. Many people in the area supported the South Vietnamese government, while others quietly worked for the Viet Cong.

It was at Danang that the first 3,500 US Marines came ashore on Vietnamese soil in 1965. Ten years later, communist troops rolled into town, facing little resistance as South Vietnamese soldiers shed their uniforms along the side of the road and fled. Two American 727 jets evacuated refugees, most of them soldiers, in a scene of panic broadcast around the world. So many people tried to climb onto the planes that, as one of them took off, people clinging to the wheels fell into the sea.

Other foreigners came to this part of Vietnam long before the Americans, however. In the 17th and 18th centuries, the first Spanish and French landings were made here. In the course of the 19th century, Danang superseded Faifo (present-day Hoi An) as the most important port and commercial centre in the central region.

CAO DAI TEMPLE

Danang's **Cao Dai Temple** (63 Haiphong Street) dates back to 1956, and locals claim it is the second-largest temple for the religion outside its base in Tay Ninh (see page 305). In reality, the fact is overstated as Cao Dai temples of approximate size can be found in numerous cities throughout Vietnam. An archbishop and 15 priests serve Danang's congregation of about 20,000 people. Like other Cao Dai temples, daily services are held every six hours: 6am, noon, 6pm and midnight. Visitors are not allowed into the temple, but are welcome to observe from the periphery.

A ceremony at Danang's Cao Dai Temple. It is estimated that there are 6 million Cao Dai followers in Vietnam.

MUSEUM OF CHAM SCULPTURE

For an insight into Vietnam's ancient Cham civilisation, visit the **Museum of Cham Sculpture** (Bao Tang Dieu Khac Champa; www.chammuseum.danang.vn, daily 7am–5pm) at the corner of Trung Nu Vuong and Bach Dang streets in the southern part of the town. Danang's most noteworthy attraction was established in 1915 by the Ecole

Museum of Cham Sculpture.

Danang Cathedral.

Cham figurines on display at Danang's Museum of Cham Sculpture.

Française d'Extrême-Orient as an open-plan colonial structure embellished with Cham-inspired motifs. The museum contains the largest display of Cham artefacts in the world, with each room dedicated to a different Cham era and city of origin: My Son, Tra Kieu, Dong Duong and Thap Mam. In total, the rooms cover over 1,000 years of Cham history.

Finely crafted figures from the pantheon of Hindu deities, notably Vishnu, Shiva, Uma, Ganesh and Nandi, are a recurrent theme, as indeed is the female breast, an important icon of Cham religious art. Perhaps the most famous of all the carvings is the exquisite dancing *apsara* of Tra Kieu (late 10th century) on display in the northwest corner of Gallery Three. The top floor has displays of traditional instruments and costumes.

Guides are available at the museum for a small fee. You can also buy a copy of the booklet called *Museum of Cham Culture: Danang*, written by the museum curator, Tran Ky Phuong, on sale at the entrance (US$10). Don't expect a guide to the museum collection, however; the book covers the general art history of the Cham civilisation.

DANANG CATHEDRAL

Pastel-pink **Danang Cathedral** Ⓒ, at 156 Tran Phu Street (English Mass Sun 10am), was built in 1923 and is one of the most recognisable landmarks in the city. Locals refer to the church as Nha Tho Con Ga (Rooster Church) because of the weathercock above the steeple.

The church runs the **Thanh Tam School** at 47 Yen Bay Street (tel: 0511-395 8545; http://thanhtamschool.com) for deaf and disabled children. Visitors are welcomed, so be sure to stop by their gift shop, internet café and fruit-shake stand outside the gate on Yen Bay Street (directly behind the cathedral). Deaf students not only make all the crafts but also run all three shops.

BREAD OF LIFE

Bread of Life Ⓓ (tel: 0511-356 5185; http://breadoflifedanang.com; Mon–Sat 8am–10pm), at the riverside

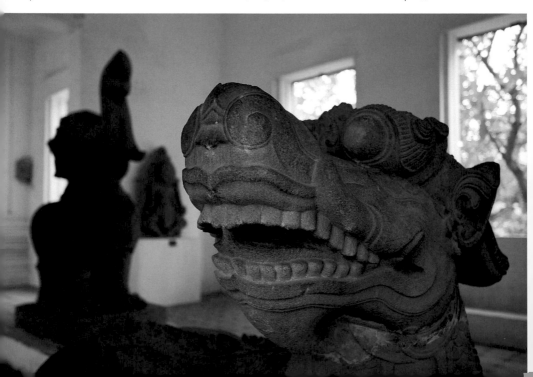

roundabout on the intersection of Bach Dang and Dong Da streets, is more than an outstanding bakery, Wi-Fi café and restaurant which happens to be run by deaf staff. It is an organisation that has brought heart and hope to the deaf community of Danang and Quang Nam province and beyond. The deaf in Vietnam are generally viewed as a burden, incapable of learning basic life skills. Most have never been taught to read or write, nor do they know anything about sign language. Bread of Life teaches young people a Vietnamese version of sign language as well as training them in vocational skills so that young deaf people can build a future for themselves. Committed foreign volunteers are welcomed.

AROUND DANANG

Danang's countryside is more famous for its natural beauty than for any historical landmarks. Surrounded by three nature reserves, jagged mountains and many kilometres of wide sandy beaches, this area invites leisurely exploration.

SON TRA PENINSULA

The **Son Tra Peninsula E**, also known as Monkey Mountain to US servicemen during the Vietnam War, is a beautiful nature reserve just northwest of Danang. The mountain is best explored by motorbike or bicycle, taking the new road winding around steep cliffs and dense rainforest. Macaques and civet cats are among the wildlife sometimes spotted. There is a lighthouse at the far eastern end of the peninsula, but unfortunately, visitors are not welcome. Likewise, a number of beautiful beaches line the coves below, but most of them have been taken over by new resort hotels.

A military base previously occupied the mountain, but now you can wander freely to the abandoned observatory or the highest pinnacle for views (weather permitting) of the coast, city and surrounding mountains.

CHINA BEACH

Several bridges connect Danang over the Han River with the beach, but the most striking is **Song Han Bridge**. The

> **⊘ Fact**
>
> Danang was the first landing point for Christian missionaries in Vietnam, and has retained a thriving Protestant population. Altogether there are a total of nine authorised churches, as well as an international church for foreigners only. There are also several Catholic churches dotted around the city.

The French villas at the 1920s Ba Na Hill Station were recently given a new lease of life.

swing suspension bridge is lit up at night and has become one of the city's modern symbols. Two smaller bridges lead to the beach further south. To the north, at the river's mouth, is the huge **Thuan Phuoc Bridge**, currently under construction.

China Beach is the name given by American servicemen during the Vietnam War to the 30km (19-mile) stretch of white-sand beach extending from Son Tra Peninsula past Danang all the way east to Cua Dai Beach near Hoi An. The Vietnamese refer to specific stretches of China Beach by different names, like **My Khe**, **Bac My An**, **Non Nuoc** (just adjacent to the Marble Mountains), **An Bang** and finally **Cua Dai** (see page 227) just east of Hoi An.

The section of China Beach closest to Danang, called My Khe, was the R&R hangout of American soldiers seeking reprieve from the rigours of the Vietnam War. For nearly three decades following the war, much of the beach remained deserted. But not anymore. Investors who've realised the tourism potential of this famous stretch of sand

have bought up tracts of prime beach-front. Several upmarket hotels, such as the Furama Resort, are already up and running, and more are on the way.

Danang has a burgeoning golf scene. Both the **Montgomerie Links** (www.montgomerielinks.com), designed by Scottish golfer Colin Montgomerie, and the **Danang Golf Club** (www.dananggolfclub.com), designed by Australian Greg Norman, are 18-hole courses located across from China Beach.

MARBLE MOUNTAINS

About 11km (7 miles) south of Danang, not far from Non Nuoc Beach, stand five large hills known as the **Marble Mountains** (Ngu Hanh Son). Each hill is named after one of the five Taoist elements: **Kim Son** (metal), **Thuy Son** (water), **Moc Son** (wood), **Hoa Son** (fire) and **Tho Son** (earth). These mountains were once a group of five offshore islets, but due to silting over the years they eventually became part of the mainland. The caves within were once used by Cham people and now shelter altars

Painted deities sit on altars in caves at the Marble Mountains.

dedicated to the Buddha, and various *bodhisattvas* and local deities worshipped by the area's inhabitants.

The most famous peak, which is riddled with caves, temples and paths, is **Thuy Son** (daily 8am–5pm). Nearly all tour buses stop at the large cave at the base. The paths weaving through the mountain are well marked and easy to navigate. The highest cave, **Huyen Khong**, has a small tunnel that leads to the very top of the hill, where there is a lookout with views of the sea and the countryside. During the Vietnam War, the Marble Mountains became a hideout for the Viet Cong because of the view over the surrounding area.

The mountains were once a valuable source of red, white and blue-green marble. At the foot of Thuy Son and the other mountains, skilful marble carvers chisel out a great variety of objects, ranging from small souvenirs to giant statuary. Some will proudly tell you that they worked on the construction of Ho Chi Minh's mausoleum, but most will pester you incessantly until you visit their shop.

BA NA HILL STATION/SUOI MO

Just west of Danang, at an elevation of 1,136 metres (3,727ft), is the **Ba Na Hill Station ➐** (daily daylight hours), built by the French on **Chua Mountain** (Pagoda Mountain) in the 1920s to escape the summer heat. The hill station, where temperatures are typically around 10°C (18°F) lower than at the coast, was later abandoned and reclaimed by the jungle and the ravages of war. In recent years the government and private enterprise have sought to revive the old villas by turning the hill station into an ecotourism destination. In Vietnamese fashion, however, some of this has translated into loud karaoke, monkeys in small cages and restaurants serving exotic animal meat. Still, a great variety of flora and fauna can be seen along walking trails at **Ba Na-Nui Chua Nature Reserve**, including lively monkeys and birdlife, colourful butterflies, bizarre insects and delicate orchids – many of which cannot be found in the valleys below.

Construction of the new Ba Na Hills Resort has been completed, and

The Marble Mountains near Danang.

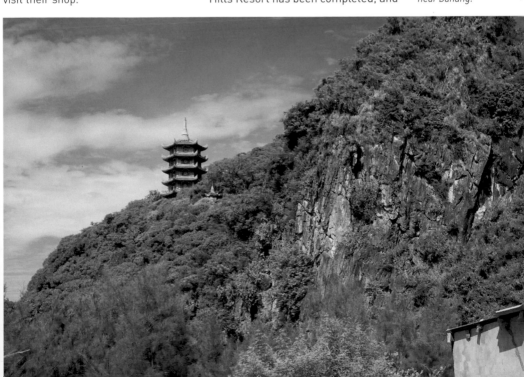

⊙ Tip

Don't wait for the tour buses at Ba Na Hill Station to show you around the mountain – their job is to direct you to the restaurants. Agree on the time you'll finally leave and hike the rest on your own.

the mega-tourism complex dominates the top of the mountain. **Linh Ung Pagoda** sits nearby on a cliff, where a giant 24-metre (79ft) high-seated Buddha gazes over the valleys below. Near the pagoda is a **gondola** service (charge), which is one of the highlights of a visit to the hill station, and now runs regularly.

Some, however, may find that **Suoi Mo** (Dream Spring; daily daylight hours; charge) is actually more enjoyable than Ba Na, even though it's only a side-trip on the way. Just 2km (1.2 miles) from the Ba Na turn-off, this pristine mountain river offers swimming and several waterfalls. The water is so clear that the bottom can be seen at virtually any depth. Bring a picnic lunch and watch the swarms of butterflies and the colourful birdlife.

BACH MA NATIONAL PARK

Towering 1,450 metres (4,757ft) northwest of Danang is **Bach Ma Mountain**, which, like Ba Na, served as a hill-station resort for the French in the 1930s. Even before the French discovered it,

the area had caught the attention of conservationists seeking to protect the resident population of rare Edward's pheasants. In the 1940s, the species was thought to be extinct, but more than 50 years later it was rediscovered at Bach Ma. The hill station was abandoned when the French left Vietnam, and over the course of time, the 139 villas that once hosted the French were reduced to rubble.

Today, **Bach Ma National Park** ❽ (tel: 054- 387 1330; http://bachma park.com.vn; daily daylight hours) is a 22,031-hectare (8,916-acre) treasure trove of flora and fauna, with numerous species unique to Vietnam. At the last count some 2,147 plant species, 132 mammals, 358 birds, more than 50 reptiles and amphibians, 57 fish and 894 species of insects (identified thus far) have been documented. Nine species of primate have been recorded in Bach Ma, including various macaques, langurs, loris and gibbons. The rare saola (*Pseudoryx nghetinhensis*), a type of antelope, was discovered in Vietnam only in

Fine sand and clear waters at China Beach.

1992 and is also present in the park. Tigers and leopards may still lurk in remote areas.

Bach Ma has a unique climate thanks to its high altitude. It is considered the wettest place in Vietnam, with approximately 8 metres/yds of rainfall each year, much of which falls in a series of deluges between September and December. The summit of Bach Ma Mountain is several degrees cooler than the surrounding lowlands as well. Warm clothing and rain gear are necessary during the rainy and winter seasons.

Several drinking fountains have been built along the summit road at the head of each trail, allowing hikers to fill their water bottles while exploring the park's numerous trails. The **Rhododendron Trail** descends 689 steps to a cliffside waterfall that plunges 300 metres (990ft) and eventually feeds the Perfume River in Hue. The park is famous for the red rhododendrons, which bloom from February to March. The **Five Lakes Cascade Trail** follows a series of waterfalls and pristine swimming areas. Several waterfalls can also be visited near the **Visitor Centre**, including **Thuy Dien** and **Da Dung**. The **Summit Trail** is one of Vietnam's most spectacular spots for watching the sunrise and sunset. Some 5km (3 miles) from the park gate, the **Pheasant Trail** leads you through rainforest to a waterfall and swimming hole of the same name. As the name suggests, several species of pheasant can be spotted along the trail.

Bach Ma is located 60km (37 miles) northwest of Danang. Just after the Hai Van Pass and past Lang Co Beach (see page 213), drive another 15km (9 miles) to the turn-off for **Suoi Voi** (Elephant Springs; daily daylight hours), a mountain stream with numerous crystal-clear swimming holes. Continuing west on Highway 1A, the entrance to Bach Ma is 3km (2 miles) from the turn-off at the town of Cau Hai. Visitors are required to park at the entrance and take a shuttle bus to the top.

HOI AN

Located some 25km (15 miles) southeast of Danang is the ancient town of **Hoi An** ❾. One of the key attractions of central Vietnam, it occupies a scenic location along the banks of the **Thu Bon River**, just a few kilometres inland from the coast and the charms of lovely Cua Dai Beach (see page 227).

BACKGROUND AND HISTORY

Hoi An traces its roots back to the ancient Champa kingdom, when it was a seaport known as Dai Chien. In the 13th and 14th centuries, it developed under the control of the Tran dynasty (1225–1400). At the beginning of the 16th century, the first Portuguese arrived to explore the coastline of central Vietnam, to be followed by expeditions led by the Chinese, Japanese, Dutch, British and French. The Europeans brought the first Catholic missionaries (and later

⊙ Where

To get to Ba Na from Danang, head west on Hung Vuong Street. Turn left on Road No. 601 and pass the commercial zone outside Danang. The turn-off for Ba Na to the left and Suoi Mo to the right is about 28km (17 miles) from town. Stop at the reception desk at the foot of the mountain to pay the admission charge. As it's a steep uphill climb from here, you have to take the shuttle bus for the final 20km (12 miles) to the top of the mountain.

Ba Na Hill Station.

A trip to Danang is incomplete without a visit to the picture-perfect beach of Lang Co.

Traditional ao dai dresses.

the Protestants), making Hoi An one of the earliest places to be exposed to Christianity. Among them was the Jesuit priest Alexandre de Rhodes, who devised the Romanised form of the Vietnamese language.

Hoi An appeared in Western travelogues in the 17th and 18th centuries as Faifo or Hai Po. For several centuries, it was one of the most important trading ports in all of Southeast Asia and an important centre of cultural exchange between Europe and the Orient. By the beginning of the 19th century, however, its fortunes were in free fall. The conflict between the Trinh and Nguyen Lords and the Tay Son faction caused considerable damage, while the mouth of the Thu Bon River silted up and prevented the flow of sea traffic. Another port was built at the mouth of the Song Han River, and Danang replaced Hoi An as the centre of trade.

In the early 1980s, Unesco took the initiative and funded a restoration programme to safeguard Hoi An's Old Quarter and historic monuments, leading to it achieving the status of World Heritage Site in 1999. Unfortunately many of Hoi An's monuments are threatened by annual floods (mainly between October and November) when the water spills over the river banks and submerges streets in up to 3 metres (10ft) of water, causing serious damage.

These days, Hoi An is a relaxed town of about 120,000 people, 10 percent of whom live in the Old Quarter, which has been turned into a historical showpiece for tourists. Many of the older homes, with their wooden beams, carved doors and airy, open rooms, have been turned into souvenir shops masquerading as museums. While it's certainly the old architecture that draws the tourist buses, there's no denying that shopping is the new heart and soul of Hoi An. Bespoke tailor shops are found everywhere, and it's not uncommon to see tourists lugging entire suitcases filled with newly tailored suits and dresses. In fact, some worry that the very thing that makes Hoi An attractive – its quiet charm and peaceful atmosphere – is

⊙ ALLURE OF THE AO DAI

The national dress of Vietnamese women is the *ao dai,* alluring, beautiful, and provocative yet discreet. In 1744, the Nguyen dynasty, ruling central and southern Vietnam, dictated a change in dress towards the lines of the Chinese style. Buttoned coats and trousers replaced skirts and split coats tied in front. Emperor Minh Mang imposed the wearing of trousers for all women. In the 1930s, an artist from a liberal reform group attempted to modernise the Vietnamese woman's dress through diversity in colour and design. His new creation of a longer coat used different materials and could even be bare-shouldered. His innovations evolved to become today's *ao dai.*

being ruined. Nearly all the buildings in the Old Town have been turned into shops or restaurants, and about 80 percent of the residents now derive their income directly from tourism.

An admission ticket (sold at numerous ticket booths around the perimeter of the Old Town for about US$6) gains you entry to the Old Town and up to five (out of 21) places of interest including museums, old houses, assembly halls, the Japanese Bridge or the Quan Cong Temple. Most sites are open daily from 7–11am and 3–5.30pm.

OLD TOWN WALKING TOUR: WEST SIDE AND JAPANESE QUARTER

The oldest part of town is in the southern section bordering the Thu Bon River. Running perpendicular to the river, Le Loi was the first street to be built in the middle of the 16th century. The Japanese quarter, with its covered bridge and Japanese-style shops and houses, followed half a century later on the west side of town. Next came the Cantonese quarter 50 years later.

Hoi An's past is superbly preserved in its architecture. The Old Quarter is a fascinating blend of temples, pagodas, community houses, shrines, clan houses, shophouses and homes. Twenty clan houses stand in the centre of the Old Town. Most of these were built by the Chinese migrant community between 1845 and 1885. It is the dense concentration of heritage structures in such a small area that gives Hoi An its unique ambience.

Le Loi Street is centrally located and a good place to start your exploration. Heading south towards the river, buy your ticket at the **ticket office** on your right as you enter the Old Quarter. Turn right on Tran Phu Street and head to the **Cantonese Assembly Hall Ⓐ** at No. 176, founded in 1786. It's a pleasant spot with a fountain in the middle of the courtyard, with statues of a twisted dragon trying to devour a carp, and a turtle spying from behind. Large red coils of incense hang from the ceilings, hung by worshippers as offerings.

Just opposite, the **Museum of Sa Huynh Culture Ⓑ** (daily 7am–5.30pm)

Tourists flock to Hoi An to have suits and dresses tailor-made.

Fresh produce at Hoi An's Central Market.

Tan Ky House.

Restaurants by Hoi An's Thu Bon River.

at 149 Tran Phu Street has a collection of pottery and jewellery from excavations of the Sa Huynh cultural site (see page 236). The upstairs used to house a fairly typical communist **Museum of the Revolution** which has been relocated to a new building on Le Loi Street .

Continue down Tran Phu Street to one of the most remarkable architectural highlights in town, the **Japanese Covered Bridge** Ⓒ. Built by the Japanese community in the late 16th century and renovated several times since, it links the Chinese and Japanese quarters, and Tran Phu Street with Nguyen Thi Minh Khai Street. The bridge's curved shape and undulating green-and-yellow tiled roof give the impression of moving water. According to legend, a monster with his head in India, his tail in Japan and his heart in Hoi An was causing mayhem by causing earthquakes and disasters to occur. The bridge was subsequently erected in Hoi An (the heart) to kill this monster. Apparently, work on the bridge was started in the year of the

monkey and finished in the year of the dog. Thus, a pair of stone replicas of each animal now stands at either end of the bridge as guardians. In the middle of the bridge is a shrine, **Chua Cau**, dedicated to Tran Vo Bac De, Emperor of the North. There is nothing really to see at the shrine other than a modest altar with a small idol and a pair of phoenixes.

Further up on the right at 4R Nguyen Thi Minh Khai Street is **Phung Hung House** Ⓓ (daily 8.30am–6pm), which has both Japanese and Chinese architectural influences and is still family-owned after nearly 230 years. The family conducts guided tours and operates an embroidery shop in the back and a gift shop upstairs.

From here, turn back to the Japanese Bridge and make your way to the right on Nguyen Thai Hoc Street, continuing until you reach **Tan Ky House** Ⓔ at No. 10 (daily 8.30am–6pm). This elongated house extends all the way to Bach Dang Street behind, which faces the river. Typical of the old houses in Hoi An, it is built of wood in a very

Ⓞ HOI AN ARCHITECTURE

Hoi An is an amalgamation of Chinese, Japanese, French and Vietnamese architectural styles. Pristine examples of each culture can be seen in the Japanese Covered Bridge, the colonial villas of the French quarter and the many Chinese assembly halls. Most buildings combine features from the four cultures however, such as the Chinese tile roofs, French balconies and window shutters, Japanese support joists, and Vietnamese tube-house configurations with multiple courtyards. While examples of Chinese temples, French villas and Japanese bridges can actually be found in other parts of the country, such a large collection of architectural styles in a small area, as well as the blending of these traditions, is unique to Hoi An.

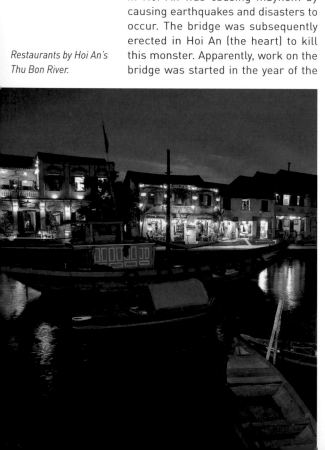

refined, two-storey style. An inner courtyard is open to the sky with a veranda linking several living quarters. Although many of the old Hoi An homes have been restored over the years, they retain their original wooden framework, distinctive crab-shell ceilings, carved doors and windows, and decorative stuccos. Many of the houses also contain rare antiques from China, Japan and France, as well as Vietnam.

OLD TOWN WALKING TOUR: EAST SIDE AND FRENCH QUARTER

Continue down Nguyen Thai Hoc Street, passing **Hoi An's Department of Swallow Nests F** at No. 53. Since the nests are only gathered from Cham Island (see page 227) twice each year, there is only a remote chance of seeing any activity here. The swallows' nests, more precisely the dried saliva the birds produce to bind their nests, are a prized delicacy among the Chinese, forming the main ingredient for bird's nest soup and prized for their reputed energy-enhancing and healing properties.

Further down the same street at No. 33 is the **Museum of Folklore in Hoi An G** (daily 7am–5.30pm), which occupies a large old house with a craft shop on the ground floor, and an excellent museum upstairs with exhibits of artisan tools, ancient crafts and local folklore.

The **Hoi An Artcraft Manufacturing Workshop H** is located in a 200-year-old Chinese merchant shop at 9 Nguyen Thai Hoc Street. Lanterns and other souvenir crafts are made and sold in the back of the shop. While there is a large selection, there's nothing here you won't find in most shops in Hoi An. The main draw is the traditional music and dance show at 10.15am and 3.15pm each day.

Continue east and make your way through the **Central Market** (Cho Hoi An), which is a great place to pick up snacks, fresh fruit and better bargains than at most streetside shops.

Take a left on Hoang Dieu Street, then a right on Nguyen Duy Hieu Street, heading northeast to No. 157, **Chaozhou Chinese Assembly Hall I**

Burning joss sticks at a Hoi An temple.

Tailor shop assistant.

Hoi An

0   200 m
0   200 yds

(daily 8am–5pm), also known as the Trieu Chau Assembly Hall. Dating back to 1776, its altars are considered to be among the finest examples of woodcarvings in Hoi An. The roofs of the structure are decorated with elaborate miniature figures of soldiers, deities, dragons and mythical beasts – all made from colourful ceramic tiles.

Continue along Nguyen Duy Hieu Street, which after the junction becomes Tran Phu Street. The **Hainan Chinese Assembly Hall ❶** (daily 8am–5pm) on the right at No. 10, built in 1851, is a memorial to the 107 Chinese merchants who were murdered by a rogue commanding officer in Emperor Tu Duc's navy. Ton That Thieu looted the ships and massacred those on board, claiming that they were pirates. The crimes were later discovered and the officer and his men were executed.

Further along at 24 Tran Phu Street, across from the market, is **Quan Cong Temple ❻**, also known as Chua Ong. Built in 1653, the temple is dedicated to Quan Cong, a general from the Three

Kingdoms period (AD 221–65) who is deified for his loyalty and sincerity. Inside the temple is a large papier-mâché statue of Quan Cong, flanked by his general Chau Xuong and the mandarin Quan Binh. The temple is really more interesting outside than inside. Behind it, at 7 Nguyen Hue Street, is the **Hoi An Museum of History and Culture ❶** (daily 8am–5pm). It houses a single, underwhelming exhibition room filled with a few artefacts tracing the history of Hoi An.

Continue on Tran Phu Street to the **Fujian Chinese Assembly Hall ❿**. The largest and most elaborate of Hoi An's assembly halls, it dates to 1792 (the triple-arched gateway at the entrance, however, was built in 1975). Inside is a temple dedicated to Thien Hau (Tin Hau) and other minor Chinese deities. Worshippers believe Thien Hau, who sits in the back chamber, rescues sailors from sinking ships. Her assistants, Thuan Phong Nhi (red skinned) and Thien Ly Nhan (green-skinned), stand in glass cases on either side of the room. They

A fusion of Japanese and Chinese cultures at the Phung Hung House.

are said to inform her whenever the calls of sailors in peril are heard.

Pass the **All-Chinese Assembly Hall** at 64 Tran Phu Street on your right. It is unmarked and empty other than a small shrine in the back. Next up is the **Museum of Trading Ceramics** at No. 80, which is set in a lovely old wooden house and contains a modest display of broken ceramics. You would expect to find a ceramics souvenir shop in the back, but oddly enough the shop sells handbags. On the opposite side at No. 77 is **Quan Thang House** Ⓝ, which is more than 300 years old and has been in the current family for more than six generations. It is sparsely decorated with two family altars and a small courtyard. The highlights are the beautiful and well-preserved carvings on the inner walls.

AROUND HOI AN

CUA DAI BEACH

Just 5km (3 miles) from Hoi An is the broad, silvery expanse of **Cua Dai Beach**. This stretch of sand is lined with several good beachside hotels, including one of Vietnam's most expensive resorts, the fabulously indulgent **Nam Hai**. The sprawling low-rise resort sits on 25 hectares (62 acres) of prime beachfront land and many of its elegant villas have their own private pools.

Palm-fringed Cua Dai beach is perfect for those looking to combine the pleasures of sun and surf with the sightseeing and dining options of Hoi An town.

CU LAO CHAM MARINE PARK

Some 20km (12 miles) or 25 minutes by speedboat from Hoi An and Cua Dai Beach is **Cu Lao Cham Marine Park** Ⓟ, which comprises eight islands that make up the **Cham Islands** archipelago. The marine park is one of the finest diving spots in central Vietnam and harbours a large variety of fish and coral. Diving trips – the best months are from June to September – can be organised with Rainbow Divers (tel: 091-340 8146). The main **Cham Island** is known for its rich bounty of swallows' nests (the species in

Entrance to the Fujian Chinese Assembly Hall.

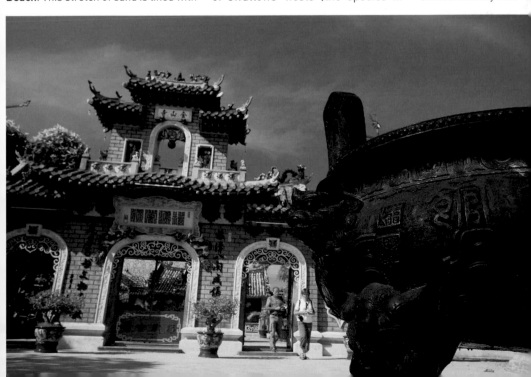

Idyllic Cua Dai Beach.

question is, in fact, Germain's swift-
let), a prized delicacy all over Asia.
Numerous boats take visitors to swim
along the reefs each day, but few tourists venture onto the island.

MY SON

The ancient kingdom of Champa, which
dates back to the 2nd century AD and
flourished from the 5th to 15th centuries, once occupied the central Vietnamese coast all the way to Nha Trang
in the south. The Chams soon became
Hinduised through commercial contacts
with India, and their kingdom functioned
as a loose confederation of five states
named after regions of India – Indrapura
(Quang Tri), Amaravati (Quang Nam),
Vijaya (Binh Dinh), Kauthara (Nha Trang)
and Panduranga (Phan Rang).

At the beginning of the 10th century,
Champa came under severe pressure
from the successive Viet rulers, who
were beginning their long push to the
south. In 1069 Indrapura was lost, and
by 1306 Champa's northern frontier
had been pushed back as far as the
Hai Van Pass with the subsequent loss

of Amaravati. The process of Vietnam-
ese expansion proved inexorable, with
Vijaya falling in 1471 and Champa –
now reduced to the rump kingdoms of
Kauthara and Panduranga – effectively
a broken power. The final absorption by
Vietnam was delayed until the reign of
Minh Mang in 1832, by which time the
Vietnamese were already engaged in
the occupation of the lower Cambodian
regions of Prey Nokor (later renamed
Saigon) and the Mekong Delta.

Thus Champa disappeared – but not
the Cham people. As their kingdom
was swallowed piecemeal by the invading Viet, increasing numbers of Cham
fled to neighbouring Cambodia, though
others chose to remain under Viet tute-
lage in their former homelands. Today,
there are approximately 100,000 Cham
people left in southern Vietnam.

My Son ⓫ (daily 8am–5pm), nestled under the green slopes of Cat's
Tooth Mountain (Nui Rang Meo) some
50km (31 miles) from Hoi An, is the
site of Vietnam's most important
Cham monuments and was declared a
Unesco World Heritage Site in 1999. It

is one of the most atmospheric locations anywhere in the country, with the crumbling ruins set in a verdant jungle. Chosen as a religious sanctuary by King Bhadravarman I in the 4th century, many temples and towers (kalan) were built in this area. Most were dedicated to kings and Brahman divinities, especially the god Shiva, who was considered the creator and defender of the ancient Champa kingdom.

According to legend, the Cham towers were ingeniously constructed from raw bricks and fired in a giant "bonfire". Recent research has shown that the bricks were actually bonded using a vegetable resin (dau rai), allowing them to withstand the onslaught of time and the elements, but not, however, the Vietnam War. In 1969, American B-52s bombed the temples, where the Viet Cong had established a base and mined the valley. Many of the ancient buildings were badly damaged or completely destroyed. In 2015, the Indian government said it would provide US$2.5m for a five-year renovation project at My Son.

There are 11 designated temple groups in My Son, and there are likely to be other groups of ruins that are either unpublicised or undiscovered. Of the listed groups, H, G and L are off-limits. The first cluster of temples at B, C and D are the most intact. Two *mandapa* (meditation halls) in D have been turned into small galleries with modest sculpture displays, although the best pieces have been carted off to other museums. Stone symbols abound throughout the temples, in the form of the male phallic *linga* and female spout-like *yoni*. As you walk among these ancient structures, imagine them humming with monks' incantations. At the height of the Champa kingdom, only a handful of attendants would have resided here, leaving the area a place of quiet mysticism for the gods to live in.

Note: the route to My Son is not clearly signposted, so it's better to book a tour in Hoi An or Danang. Seeing all the temples requires a significant amount of walking, so be sure to wear comfortable shoes and a hat.

⊙ **Fact**

Regional products include cinnamon from Tra, pepper from Tien Phuoc, tobacco from Cam Le, silk from Hoa Vang, saffron from Tam Ky, carvings in rosewood, ironwood and ebony, and sea swallow nests from the Cham Islands.

My Son's Group B cluster of temples.

Cham towers.

SOUTH TO QUY NHON

Lofty mountains, empty beaches and isolated vestiges of the Cham civilisation mark the stretch of coast south to Quy Nhon. The poignant and chilling My Lai memorial is in stark contrast.

The road south from Hoi An to Quy Nhon is one of the least touristy stretches of coastline in Vietnam, following scores of pristine, uncrowded beaches, hot springs, waterfalls and rocky mountains spanning the provinces of Quang Nam, Quang Ngai and Binh Dinh. The natural beauty is matched only by the rich cultural history surrounding the region, from the Long Wall of Quang Ngai – a Nguyen Dynasty barrier between the Vietnamese and indigenous people – to the ancient Champa capital at Quy Nhon. This is also the site of the My Lai massacre, one of the worst atrocities of the Vietnam War. The scenic stretch remains relatively unexplored by tourists, thanks in part to authorities that have only recently warmed up to the idea of tourism.

AROUND TAM KY

About 50km (31 miles) south of Hoi An, Highway 1A passes through **Tam Ky**, the provincial capital of Quang Nam province. Some 5km (3 miles) before Tam Ky, three Cham towers dating from the 11th century rise from a walled enclosure at **Thap Chien Dang** ⑫ (daily 8–11.30am and 1–5pm). A small museum here has fine sculptures of creatures from Hindu mythology as well as more everyday images of dancers, musicians and elephants.

Cham sculpture.

A short distance south of Tam Ky is **Thap Khuong My** ⑬ (daily 8am–5pm), another important Cham site. The temple complex here dates from the 10th century and is renowned for the richness of its decorated pillars, pilasters and arches. Both sites provide a sneak preview of Cham monuments yet to come further south in Binh Dinh province.

QUANG NGAI PROVINCE

Quang Ngai is a name shared by both the Quang Ngai province and its

 Main Attractions

Thap Chien Dang
Thap Khuong My
Quang Ngai Provincial Museum
Thien An Pagoda
Son My Memorial Museum
Quy Nhon
Quang Trung Museum
Thap Banh It

 Map on page 200

Tableau, Son My Memorial Museum.

capital. **Quang Ngai City** 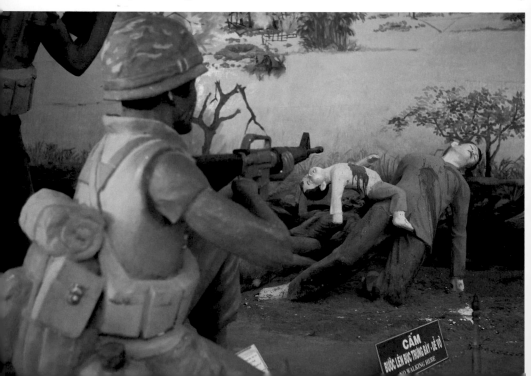 is located on the southern bank of the **Tra Khuc River**, about 15km (9 miles) from the coast. Locals gather along the riverfront at sunset, when the area is transformed nightly into a long succession of stalls offering fruit shakes and fresh seafood.

Few tourists venture to these parts, other than to visit the memorial museum at neighbouring **My Lai**. Visitors who choose to stay, however, will be rewarded with cultural treasures and scenic vistas of rainforest-clad mountains, pristine lakes, rivers, beaches, ancient relics of the Sa Huynh civilisation, and also ethnic minority villages of the Koor, H're and C'dong peoples. At least 35 ruins of Cham origin, dating to as early as the 8th century, are scattered throughout the province, although most are undocumented and difficult to reach.

Quang Ngai is not as progressive as its neighbouring provinces. The Communist Party fervour of the local provincial government is evident in the many red banners, slogans and party symbols that are hung up all over town. Indeed, there are a number of infamous hamlets in the province, including Ba To and Van Tuong, which have been highly honoured in the past for their unflagging support of the Viet Cong during the Vietnam War. Numerous *nghia trang liet si* ("martyrs' cemeteries") for Viet Cong who fought against the Americans dot the hillside, clustered around large communist monuments. Big Brother keeps himself busy here – everything requires a few more papers signed and questions answered.

Still, the fact that Quang Ngai is not a major stop on the tourist track has many advantages. Prices are much cheaper – there is often little need to haggle in the markets – and people are friendlier and more hospitable than in other areas of Vietnam. Scenic areas are much less developed and pollution is minimal. In many ways Quang Ngai is the Vietnam of the early 1990s.

Change is on the horizon, however, with further extension of the **Dung**

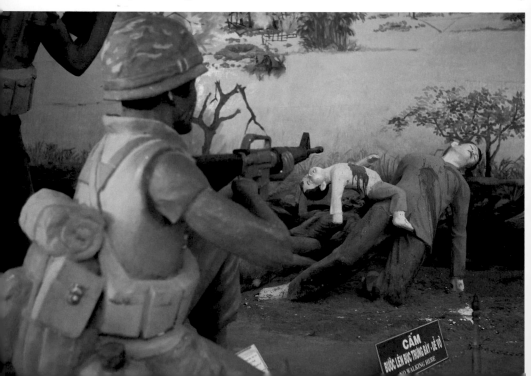

Quat Deep Sea Port and Oil Refinery to be completed by 2021. Quang Ngai is poised to become an industrial powerhouse over the next decade. New hospitals, schools, housing complexes and high-rise hotels have already been constructed to support the anticipated growth.

There are few notable landmarks within the city. The **Quang Ngai Water Tower**, built in the 1930s to collect and store water, is the city's most recognisable piece of architecture, with little "horns" decorating the rim of its roof. The tower, which is found at the edge of the city square, is no longer in use today.

QUANG NGAI MUSEUM

The **Quang Ngai Provincial Museum** (Tue–Sun 7.00–11am and 1–5pm), at 99 Le Trung Dinh/Hung Vuong streets, is definitely worth a visit. The ground floor has an impressive exhibit of ancient Sa Huynh artefacts, including pottery, jewellery, weapons, burial displays and a giant bronze kettle. An adjoining section has displays of ancient Champa relics. Most of the floor, however, is devoted to cultural displays and artefacts from the Koor, Hre and C'dong minority hill tribes, as well as 16th-century antique clothing displays from the dominant Kinh people.

The upper floor is a typical museum tracing the communist revolution. Outside the museum, amid cannons, artillery and broken Cham statues, is a replica of a hill-tribe bamboo communal longhouse.

THACH NHAM LAKE

Road 626, heading west out of Quang Ngai City, passes by the old **Quang Phu Airstrip**, which was used by the Americans during the war. It is still in remarkably good condition and actually forms part of the road. The road continues for some 25km (16 miles) through rice paddies and minority villages before climbing into the mountains to meet the Tra Khuc River once again, at **Thach Nham Lake and Dam**. This is a superb place to swim or have a picnic, surrounded by lush green mountain slopes.

Quang Ngai Water Tower.

⊘ THE MY LAI MASSACRE

US intelligence had suggested that Son My (My Lai) was a Viet Cong stronghold, yet not a single shot was fired against the American soldiers during the massacre. It is believed that the killings were motivated by revenge after heavy US casualties were inflicted by the 48th Local Forces Battalion of the North Vietnamese Army (NVA), who led the Tet Offensive against Quang Ngai in the previous month. In the course of a few hours, not only were the residents murdered, but all of the homes were burnt, the livestock killed, wells poisoned, and several women and children were raped.

Of the 25 men sentenced, only Lieutenant William Calley was convicted, but even then, his punishment was a travesty: Calley served only three days of his life sentence of hard labour before it was commuted to house arrest by President Nixon. He was paroled three years later. In 1998, three US veterans were awarded medals by the US government, including Warrant Officer Hugh Thompson, Jr, for protecting some of the villagers during the carnage.

Four Hours in My Lai, by Michael Bilton and Kevin Sim, is perhaps the most exhaustive account of the events of the My Lai massacre and its aftermath.

A jade-green Buddha statue stands atop a lotus throne at the Long Khanh Pagoda, Quy Nhon City.

THIEN AN PAGODA

Sitting on the northeastern banks of the Tra Khuc River, **Thien An Mountain** offers fabulous views of Quang Ngai and the surrounding valleys. Built in 1627, **Thien An Pagoda** (daily 8am–5pm; free) is perched on the highest point. The temple was founded by a Chinese monk who is buried underneath an enormous nine-tiered tower. A bronze bell, more than 350 years old, sits inside the temple, while a much newer replica hangs out front. Don't be confused by the Disney-style cement animals outside the entrance. This is the oldest and most famous pagoda in the province, with an active monastery.

To reach Thien An Mountain, first head north out of Quang Ngai City on the Tra Khuc Bridge. Turn right on the other side of the river in Son Tinh village, heading towards My Khe Beach. A large sign of the pagoda hangs at the base of the mountain, just outside Son Tinh.

SON MY (MY LAI)

Binh Hai Beach with seaweed piled on its shores.

On 16 March 1968, Lieutenant William Calley led Charlie Company from the First Battalion of the American forces in the most infamous atrocity of the entire Vietnam War. Shortly after 7am the soldiers attacked the My Lai and My Khe hamlets of **Son My** ⑮, killing perhaps 500 of its residents (the actual number is still in question today), half of whom were children, the elderly and pregnant women. Although the American military tried to cover up the massacre, the truth was eventually uncovered by journalist Seymore Hersh, working for *Newsweek* magazine, with the assistance of former GI Ronald Ridenhour and photographer Ron Haeberle.

The **Son My Memorial Museum** (tel:08 8524 5856; daily 7am–5pm), 12km (8 miles) east after crossing the Tra Khuc Bridge, is a stark reminder of the horrors that took place here. The grounds contain a re-creation of the village in cement, as it would have been just after the massacre, with a few mass graves off to the side. Inside, the museum retells the gruesome story through

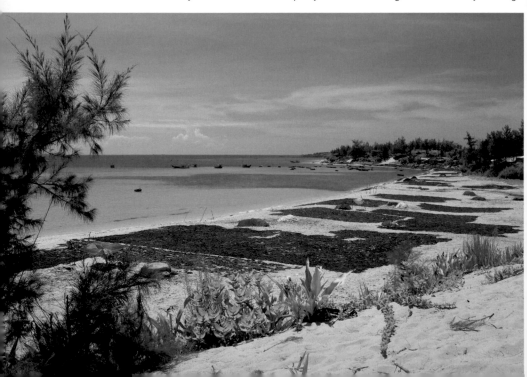

photographs, dioramas, mannequins and mementoes of the victims.

Just a few minutes further down the road from the Son My Memorial is a pleasant stretch of white sand – a good spot for a rest after the museum but not particularly remarkable. There isn't much development along the shore, accommodation is scant, but a few cafés offer parking, beach chairs and drinks.

BINH HAI BEACH

About 30km (19 miles) northeast of Quang Ngai via the turn-off for Dung Quat Bay is **Binh Hai Beach**, nestled against high coastal bluffs on the Batangan Peninsula. The beach is a long crescent of powdery white sand, and encroaching upon it is an ancient fossilised reef that extends from the shore to the sea like a flat concrete pavement. Formed by shell deposits over millions of years, it forms a living reef that attracts schools of vividly coloured tropical fish. With the Dung Quat Oil Refinery looming over the horizon, however, the future of this natural phenomenon is uncertain.

THE LONG WALL OF QUANG NGAI

In 2005 Dr Andrew Hardy, head of the Hanoi branch of École Française d'Extrême-Orient (EFEO; the same organisation that founded the Museum of Cham Sculpture in Danang and which is responsible for cataloguing and preserving many of the ancient monuments in Vietnam), discovered a Nguyen-dynasty document referring to a previously undocumented "Long Wall of Quang Ngai" (Truong luy Quang Ngai). After years of research and exploration, he and a team of archaeologists announced the discovery in late 2010.

The wall, which spans 127.4km (79.2 miles) from northern Quang Ngai to the province of Binh Dinh, was built in 1819 as a protective barrier separating the ethnic Vietnamese from the Hre people. The Hre – once part of the Champa Kingdom – did not always get along well with their new neighbours, who

Bustling fish market along the coast of Quy Nhon.

vanquished Champa in 1471. Besides security, the wall also helped to regulate commerce along an adjacent, much older trade route connecting Hoi An, Quang Ngai, Binh Dinh and the Central Highlands. While still largely undeveloped for tourism, the wall – along with the associated 50 or more military forts, surrounding minority villages, hot springs, rugged mountains and beautiful countryside dotted with waterfalls – presents a fascinating opportunity for exploration. A few sites are signposted but exploring with a guide is recommended.

SA HUYNH

Highway 1A continues south towards **Sa Huynh** ⓰, where the coastal estuaries have been turned into shrimp farms and salt-evaporation ponds. The pungent aroma of the Sa Huynh Fish Sauce Factory on the edge of town wafts across the highway. Sa Huynh, which means "golden sands", is a small town 60km (37 miles) south of Quang Ngai with nearby pristine,

Blue-green waters of Quy Hoa Beach.

yellow-sand beaches interspersed by boulder-strewn capes.

The town is most famous for its archaeological discoveries of the Sa Huynh culture, beginning in 1909. A contemporary of the Dong Son culture in the north and Oc Eo of the Funan empire in the south, the Sa Huynh (1000 BC–AD 200) are believed to be the predecessors of the Champa people. The Sa Huynh cremated their dead and buried them in large clay jars, some of which are on display at museums in Quang Ngai City and Hoi An. The Sa Huynh women wore ear ornaments that featured two-headed animals, usually made of jade or glass. Virtually all of these artefacts were removed from the excavation sites in the area, and locals were apparently never educated about the important discoveries made here. A sundial and a few unmarked excavation sites remain scattered in the surrounding hills.

QUY NHON

Situated at the southern coastal tip of Binh Dinh province, 115km (72 miles)

south of Sa Huynh, the capital city of Quy Nhon ⑰ (also spelt Qui Nhon) has held a prominent place in Vietnam's political and cultural history for nearly 1,000 years. After Emperor Le Hoan of the Ly dynasty in northern Vietnam sacked the Cham capital of Indrapura in AD 982, the Cham people were forced to move their capital to Cha Ban, just west of Quy Nhon. The new kingdom, which was firmly established by the early 10th century, was named Vijaya (Victory). Despite its name, however, the kingdom suffered frequent wars and conquest by the Dai Viet (the northern Vietnamese empire) and the Khmers to the west. Weakened by constant conflict, the empire suffered a gradual decline until the capital city was captured and destroyed in 1471 by the Dai Viet emperor Le Thanh Ton. As many as 60,000 Cham people were killed in the process, and another 30,000 carried off as slaves.

Nearby Tay Son village was the birthplace of the infamous Tay Son Rebellion, which began in 1771. The area encompassing Quy Nhon was used as a launching point for the armies of Nguyen Hue and his two brothers, who eventually conquered the entire country by overthrowing the Le-dynasty emperor and the two rival feudal houses of Trinh in the north and Nguyen in the south. Nguyen Hue changed his name to Quang Trung and crowned himself emperor of a united Vietnam in 1778.

More recently, during the war with America, Quy Nhon was a strategic military port. Viet Cong, South Vietnamese and American soldiers were all active here during the war. Its Thi Nai Port is still an active commercial port today.

A team of New Zealand surgeons was stationed in Quy Nhon during the war. After the country opened up to foreigners in the 1990s, medical missions from New Zealand returned to assist the community and a small group of Kiwis still live here.

It is amazing that with so much natural beauty and a rich history, Quy Nhon has never figured very much on the

Statue of Emperor Quang Trung at the Quang Trung Museum.

popular tourist trail. Perhaps this adds to its charm. Despite its relatively large size, this inexpensive, sleepy beach town is a great place to escape the crowds of Nha Trang to the south and soak up the ambience of a Vietnamese culture as yet untainted by mass tourism.

PHUONG MAI PENINSULA

Thi Nai Bridge, built in 2006 and the longest sea bridge in Vietnam, crosses the Thi Nai Lagoon and connects Quy Nhon with the **Phuong Mai Peninsula**. The crossing is actually a series of connected bridges (the final one stretching 2,500 metres/yds), passing over mangrove forests and shrimp farms. At the far end of the peninsula, above Phuong Hai fishing village (reachable only by boat), stands the **Tran Hung Dao Statue**, pointing north. The legendary general thwarted two Mongol invasions led by Kublai Khan during the 13th century.

THAP DOI CHAM TOWERS

Located right in the middle of a busy neighbourhood in Quy Nhon city are the pair of Cham towers called **Thap Doi** (886 Tran Hung Dao; daily 8am–5pm). Built in the late 12th century, both towers have pyramidal peaks rather than the characteristic terracing found on most Cham towers. Although the peaks are original, some of the decorative carvings you see on the towers are a recent addition by overzealous restoration workers who have taken creative liberties. A garden surrounding the towers and a small visitor centre were constructed in 2008.

BINH DINH MUSEUM

The only museum in Quy Nhon is the **Binh Dinh Museum** (daily Apr–Sep 7–11am and 2–5pm) at 26 Nguyen Hue Street. It has four wings containing Champa statuary as well as ceramics of Cham and other foreign origin, but most of the exhibits recount Vietnam's more recent war history. In the central atrium is an elaborate wooden loom, typical of the ones used by local minority hill-tribe communities.

The Quang Trung Museum celebrates the three Nguyen brothers who instigated the Tay Son Rebellion.

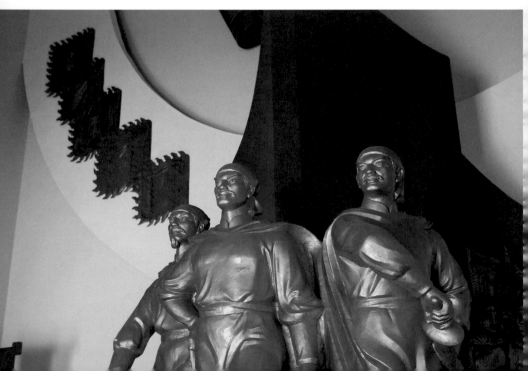

QUY NHON'S BEACHES

The city's main **Central Beach** sprawls before Xuan Dieu Street and is one of the most popular night-time hang-outs in town. Hundreds of homes were torn down in 2008 to make way for a large boulevard and parks along the beachfront. Locals don't usually swim here as the beach fronts an active fishing harbour and the water is not very clean.

At the far southern end of An Duong Vuong Street, **Queen's Beach** (Bai Tam Hoang Hau) is not actually a beach but a scenic coastal drive. Said to have been a favourite holiday spot of Queen Nam Phuong (wife of Emperor Bao Dai), the road climbs Ghenh Rang Mountain, providing scenic views of the bay, the offshore islands and the Quy Nhon cityscape. The grave of the popular romantic poet Han Mac Tu (1912–40) is signposted.

The road then descends to a quiet cove near the **Quy Hoa Leper Hospital**, which is right in front of **Quy Hoa Beach**, easily Quy Nhon's finest.

It is clean and the water is a transparent emerald green. A drink shop, souvenir stand and beach shacks are scattered under a grove of palm and pine trees. A small village sits at the southern end of the beach.

All of the tiny beaches and coves for the next couple of kilometres have been taken over by small local-style resorts and snack and drink shacks.

A few kilometres past **Bai Xep village** – a picturesque little fishing village facing three small islands offshore – is **Bai Bau Beach** (Pregnant Beach). The enormous theme-park-style billboard at the entrance greatly exaggerates Bai Bau's modest facilities. It's a lovely spot for a picnic and a swim.

AROUND QUY NHON

The following sites can be visited on a single day trip by motorbike or car using Qhy Nhon as a base.

QUANG TRUNG MUSEUM

Binh Dinh province's **Quang Trung Museum** ⓲ daily 7–11am and

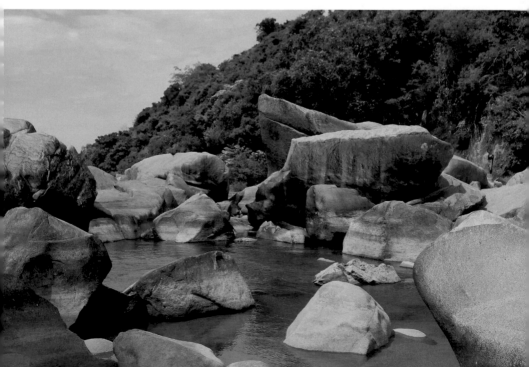

Swimming spot at Ham Ho.

1.30–5pm), also known as Tay Son Palace, is located in the town of Phu Phong, 50km (31 miles) west of Quy Nhon via Highway 19. The museum exhibits highlight the military campaigns of Emperor Quang Trung (Nguyen Hue) and the Tay Son dynasty (1778–1802) that followed after. Other exhibits include clothing, jewellery and weapons used by the local Banar and Ede ethnic minorities; two brass pagoda bells dating from the 18th and 19th centuries; and coins and ceramics from local excavations. The museum is well kept and air-conditioned, a rare luxury in this part of central Vietnam.

To the right of the museum is the **Temple of Tay Son**, which is dedicated to the worship of the generals involved in the Tay Son Rebellion. Built in 1978, the temple represents a common religious practice in Vietnam that is condoned by the communist government: the formal worship of historical military leaders.

A **performance pavilion** on the far left of the museum grounds is reserved for daily performances of Tay Son martial arts, and cultural shows with Ede and Banar performers, although there is no strict performance schedule. In front of the pavilion is the most striking structure at the museum – an enormous **Banar thatched longhouse**. The interior is creatively decorated with weapons, deer antlers, jars, drums, gongs and other traditional instruments.

HAM HO

The mountain river of **Ham Ho** is a beautiful swimming spot about 5km (3 miles) from the Quang Trung Museum. The water here is a little dark-coloured, not caused by pollution but by the natural tannins that seep from the lush jungles that cling to the mountains on either side. Hoa Loc Vung, a restaurant serving traditional Vietnamese cuisine with specialities made from ingredients from the surrounding jungle, is located at the first swimming hole. There are beaches and other choice swimming spots among the giant boulders.

The rustic beauty of the red-brick Thap Banh is often understated.

QUY NHON'S CHAM TOWERS

Several Cham towers are scattered in the vicinity of Quy Nhon. The ancient Cham people could not have picked a lovelier spot for the cluster of four towers called **Thap Banh It** ⑲ (daily 7.30–11am and 2–4pm). It is located some 20km (12 miles) north of Quy Nhon on a hill overlooking a river valley inhabited by a quaint village and surrounded by lush green mountains. One tower sits apart from the others, claimed by a Buddhist temple seeking to benefit from the spiritual energy of the site. A gate and ticket office stands at the entrance, but no fee is collected.

Another 30km (19 miles) north is another important Cham site, **Thap Duong Long** (daily 8am–5pm). The three enormous towers, ravaged by time and weather, have recently undergone renovation.

Other lesser-known Cham towers are difficult to find, largely because they are not part of the usual tourist circuit. About 40km (25 miles) northwest of Quy Nhon on Highway 1A, **Thap Canh Tien** (daily 8am–5pm), the "Fairy Wing Tower", rises above the trees like a giant candelabra behind an expanse of rice paddies. The tower and outer wall foundations are all that remain of the citadel of **Cha Ban**, the former capital of the Champa kingdom of Vijaya.

On the other side of Highway 1A, on a hill above the river, stands the solitary **Thap Phu Loc** (Golden Tower). **Thap Thu Thien** is located just off Highway 19, halfway between Thap Banh It and the Quang Trung Museum. Once a treasure trove of ancient relics, the 11th-century tower has been greatly damaged by pillaging over the years.

Thap Binh Lam, the most difficult Cham tower to reach, is located about 20km (12 miles) north of Quy Nhon near the far end of Thi Nai estuary. It is believed that this tower, built in the late 10th to the early 11th century, marks an ancient port and the transitional capital city for the Champa kingdom of Vijaya, before Cha Ban was constructed.

The Thap Doi Chan Towers stand as a reminder of Quy Nhon's ancient Cham past.

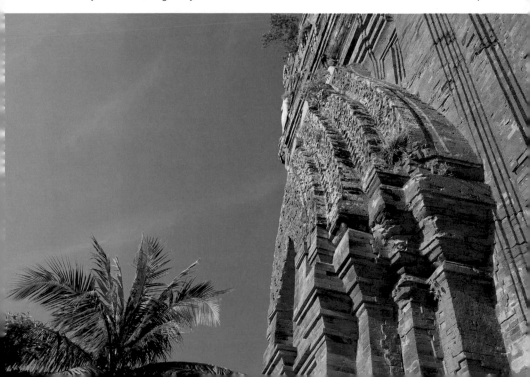

CHAM ART, ARCHITECTURE AND SCULPTURE

The remains of its magnificent temples all over central and southern Vietnam serve as a reminder of the once-powerful Champa kingdom.

The Cham people have always had a thriving artistic culture, of which their ancient temples are most lauded. **My Son**, inland from Hoi An, has the highest concentrations of known temples. Other well-preserved temples worth visiting include **Po Shanu** in Mui Ne, **Po Rome** and **Po Klong Garai** in Phan Rang, and **Po Nagar** in Nha Trang.

Temple buildings contain a single inner chamber with cathedral ceilings, no windows, and only one eastward-facing door. Cham temple complexes usually consist of three or more buildings, all made of red-baked bricks. In the centre of the main building sits a *linga* (male phallus) and/or *yoni* (female counterpart).

The best examples of Cham statuary can be found at the **Museum of Cham Sculpture** in Danang. Common subjects include Hindu gods, particularly Shiva, as well as Vishnu, Brahma, Ganesh, Nandin the bull, Garuda (a bird-like deity), historical kings and uniquely Cham deities such as the goddess Po Nagar.

The Cham have always been known for their brightly coloured and very beautiful textiles, which are still woven on looms in homes. Cham holy men wear bright white robes with orange or red sashes and satchel, and a white turban with red tassels. The village of **My Nghiep** near Phan Rang is most famous for its textile weaving.

Female Cham dancers performing to traditional Cham dances in Nha Trang, Vietnam.

Sandstone carving of the Goddess Uma at the Museum Cham Sculpture, Danang.

A carved phallic symbol – known as a lingam stone – at the My Son temple ruins.

An elderly Cham woman in Tuam Tu village.

Preserving Cham culture

Frenchman M.C. Paris rediscovered the holy city of My Son in 1898. A year later, members of the scholarly society, École française d'Extrême Orient (EFEO), began to study the inscriptions, architecture and art of My Son. In 1900, Frenchman Henri Parmentier began his work rediscovering and cataloguing most known Cham temple sites across the country. EFEO set up the Museum of Cham Sculpture in Danang to protect much of the best artwork retrieved from temples and archaeological sites around Vietnam. EFEO has continued to spearhead preservation work and study at My Son, but many of Champa's other monuments have been left largely unprotected and continue to be destroyed both by local residents and the government, hoping to exploit the resources where the temples are located. A few have indeed been imaginatively "restored" by local workers or foreign organisations using unproven techniques. However, the original technology used by the Cham to create the temples so far cannot be duplicated. Restorations tend to erode within a few years and cause the original structure – often more than 1,000 years old – to disintegrate along with it.

Restoration work at the Duong Long Cham Towers near Qui Nhon.

The Po Klong Garai Cham Towers date back to the 14th century rule of King Jaya Simharvarman III.

Intricate carving at Chien Dan Cham Tower, near Quang Ngai.

A tropical beach idyll at Nha Trang.

A gondola connects Nha Trang to Hon Tre Island.

NHA TRANG AND DALAT

These two popular holiday spots could not be more different. Nha Trang is all sea, sand and sun, while Dalat is an elegant old hill station.

Strawberry farm, Dalat.

The cities of Nha Trang and Dalat are a dynamic contrast. Both are popular vacation spots for locals, but while Nha Trang offers modern tourism infrastructure and sunny beaches, Dalat has a pleasantly cool climate and the rustic elegance of an old-world French colonial mountain retreat. Nha Trang is a transition zone of climate and culture between southern and central Vietnam, while Dalat is the gateway to the central highlands and the minorities that inhabit them. Both cities, but particularly Dalat, have much to explore outside their metro area. Many visitors spend a few days with a motorbike guide driving through the central highlands, north of Dalat.

Nha Trang is larger and livelier than Mui Ne to the south, but has far fewer resorts. The emphasis here is on the beach and the urban nightlife – the latter rivalled only by Ho Chi Minh City and Hanoi. Dozens of bars and restaurants ribbon the beach, including well-known haunts like the Sailing Club and Louisiane. Additionally, the islands off Nha Trang shelter some of the most popular scuba-diving spots in Vietnam. Visitors can earn diving certifications while they explore the beautiful reefs during their stay.

Ana Mandara Resort, Dalat.

Dalat is all about ambience. Old colonial villas and historic hotels perch around lakes, gardens and a golf course. Mist rolls through the pine-forested hillsides each morning and down to the beds of roses, strawberries and bountiful produce grown nowhere else in the country. On the hillsides, the K'ho minority grow coffee and tea amid spectacular waterfalls and forested mountain peaks. K'ho women produce some of Vietnam's most beautiful handwoven silk fabrics, embossed with traditional tribal patterns.

Vietnam's most beloved Frenchman, the extraordinary Dr Alexandre Yersin, made his home in Nha Trang and was the first European to explore the central highlands. As a result of his time in the hills, he encouraged the French to build a hill station in Dalat. Yersin is most famous for discovering the cause of the bubonic plague, and for opening a branch of the Pasteur Institute in Nha Trang (another was built later in Dalat, too) to develop the serum and cure the disease.

NHA TRANG AND SURROUNDINGS

When travel in Vietnam gets too wearying, consider an escape to Nha Trang with its fine beaches, tourist facilities and nightlife. Nearby are the crumbling ruins of the old Champa empire.

Beaches. Nightlife. Diving. These three words encapsulate the experience of **Nha Trang ❶** for most travellers. Vietnam's favourite party town has many hidden charms, however, for those who delve deeper and explore its museums, aquariums and rich ethnic culture. Within striking distance in the hinterland are several important sites where the ancient Cham culture has left its mark. What is more, Nha Trang is serviced by daily flights from Hanoi, Danang and Ho Chi Minh City, making an idyllic beach holiday within easy reach when these big cities start to grate on your nerves.

Nha Trang is the ideal place to break a journey, relax and soak up the sun. With its population of over 400,000, it is the fifth-largest city in Vietnam, and the capital of Khanh Hoa province. The province is relatively unexplored in regard to tourism. The countryside is inhabited by Raglai, Churu and other hill tribes whose villages sit along small mountain and river roads.

NHA TRANG

Nha Trang has a stunning location, bordered by mountains one side and a beautiful stretch of **beach** on the other. There are always visitors basting away in the warm sun, and a cool breeze blowing at popular beach spots fronted by bars and restaurants

such as the **Sailing Club** and **Louisiane Brewhouse**. Upmarket resorts like the plush **Ana Mandara** shield their patrons from the persistent hawkers selling fruit, barbecued seafood and sunglasses.

As a tourism showpiece, Nha Trang's golden sandy beach is kept pretty clean, but the water quality can vary during the year from clear and sparkling blue to murky and speckled with bits of garbage from the Cai River; the latter usually happens after heavy rain causes the river to run off into the bay.

Main Attractions
Po Nagar Cham Towers
Thap Ba Hot Springs
Hon Chong Promontory
Dam Market
Alexandre Yersin Museum
Oceanographic Institute
Hon Tre
Hon Heo Peninsula
Po Klong Garai

Maps on pages
252, 254

Fishing boats at Nha Trang.

Activities abound on the beach: there is an amusement park, diving, jet-skiing, sailing, windsurfing, surfing and parasailing. There are no designated areas for most of these activities, so water-sports enthusiasts constantly launch and land among groups of swimmers – not an ideal situation.

The main tourist area lies mostly on the north-south parallel streets of Tran Phu, Hung Vuong and Nguyen Thien Thuat, in the four blocks between Nguyen Thi Minh Khai and Tran Quang Khai streets. This is where the largest concentration of hotels, bars and restaurants is found. A seedy element has grown in tandem with the tourist industry – prostitutes, pickpockets, and even elements of the Vietnamese mafia, mingle among the tourists at night – so keep an eye on your belongings and be careful about flaunting expensive camera equipment or jewellery.

PO NAGAR CHAM TOWERS

On a hill above the **Cai River**, at the city's northern entrance, stand the majestic towers of the famous Cham sanctuary and temple **Po Nagar** (tel: 058-383 1569; daily 6am–6pm). The 25-metre (82ft) main tower is dedicated to the Cham goddess Po Yan Inu Nagar (worshipped by local Buddhists as the goddess Thien Y Ana), the "Holy Mother" of the Champa kingdom, and considered to be Shiva's female form. Her statue resides in the main temple, but it was decapitated during French rule; the original head now resides in the Guimet Museum in Paris. Only four of the sanctuary's original eight temples, all of which face east, remain standing. These were apparently constructed over an extended period of time between the 7th and 12th centuries. The 22 pillars and steep steps leading up to the main tower hint at the grandeur of the original temple. In the late 1990s the towers were carefully restored, and today they are swamped by tourists – both Vietnamese and foreign – throughout the day.

Personal religious expression is highly restricted by the local

Water sports at Nha Trang.

government in this part of Vietnam. Signs around the temple forbid the burning of incense or what are deemed to be superstitious behaviours. Cham people who try to worship here and place offerings of flowers and incense in front of the phallic *linga* at the main tower are sometimes forcibly removed by the police.

Ethnic Cham performers from Phan Rang present live traditional music and dances daily from 7.30 to 11am and 2.30 to 4.30pm. Shops behind the temples sell a variety of Cham crafts. Some of the textiles sold here are woven using traditional looms on site.

XOM BOM VILLAGE

Opposite the Po Nagar Cham towers, across Xom Bong Bridge at the mouth of the Cai River, is a picturesque fishing village called **Xom Bom**. Although the settlement is being chipped away by new resorts moving in, it occupies a remarkable natural harbour punctuated by small islets and boulders. From either **Xom Bong Bridge** or **Tran Phu Bridge**, you can watch the

blue and red fishing boats returning with their fresh catches; early mornings are best.

THAP BA HOT SPRINGS

Following the Cai River west of Po Nagar are the **Thap Ba Hot Springs** Ⓑ (15 Ngoc Son St; tel: 058-383 5345; www.thapbahotspring.com.vn; daily 7am–7.30pm; charge), famous for their mineral mud baths, although there are also a number of thermal pools with the water simmering at a toasty 40°C (104°F), and a swimming pool with a man-made waterfall. The natural spring water here does not bubble to the surface. It is pumped via a well from a short depth. Apparently much of the mud is also brought from another location, and it's not entirely clear how sanitation is ensured.

This is one of the rare tourist attractions that appeals equally to both local and foreign tourists. If the thought of sharing a bath with strangers does not appeal, book a special "VIP Spa" with private soaking pools,

The Po Nagar Cham towers are among the most famous Cham monuments in Vietnam.

The sheltered bay at Hon Chong is perfect for swimming.

steam bath and massage. A number of good restaurants are located at the park, making Thap Ba a convenient place for families to spend the afternoon. Do avoid the souvenir shops if they are found selling lacquered sea turtles, however.

Little known to visitors (or, for that matter, most Vietnamese), hot springs are a fairly common phenomenon throughout Vietnam. Many other coastal provinces also have them, though not all have been developed for tourists. Unfortunately, their popularity in some places has spawned a few fake "mineral hot springs" and "mineral mud baths" in tourist areas around the country. When visiting water parks, be sure to ask where the hot water and mineral mud actually come from.

HON CHONG PROMONTORY

Rinsing off the mud at Thap Ba Hot Springs.

Just northeast of Xom Bom, the promontory of **Hon Chong** ⓒ juts out into the aquamarine waters of the South China Sea. The spot is a perfect place for swimming as it's a bit more sheltered than the main beach at Nha Trang. The beach here is usually crowded with children at the weekend. An on-duty policeman keeps things in order.

North, across the bay, is **Co Tien Mountain** (Nui Co Tien), or Fairy Mountain. Its three summits are thought to resemble a fairy lying on her back; the first peak on the right resembles her face, the middle one her breasts and the third (and highest) her crossed legs.

DAM MARKET

Some of Nha Trang's most interesting French colonial architecture and crumbling 19th-century Chinese houses can be seen around **Dam Market** ⓓ (Cho Dam), near the Cai River. This former Chinese quarter is truly the most underrated part of town. The busy market sees surprisingly few foreign tourists, and is a welcome contrast to the rest of the modernised city – and a great place to snack on local foods. While souvenirs abound, refrain from purchasing dried sea products, including sharks' fins, sea horses, puffer fish and other reef animals. Buying these goods only encourages further destruction of Nha Trang's already frail coral reefs.

NHA TRANG CATHEDRAL

Just east of the Nha Trang railway station stands the large **Nha Trang Cathedral** Ⓔ (Nha Tho Nui Nha Trang; tel: 058-382 3335; Mass Mon–Sat 5am and 4.30pm, Sun 5am, 7am and 4.30pm) at 31 Thai Nguyen Street. Built in a Gothic style between 1928 and 1934, this Catholic cathedral is one of the city's defining landmarks. Its beautiful stained-glass windows depicting Jesus, Mary and a variety of saints reflect the coloured neon lights that encircle the statues inside.

LONG SON PAGODA

On the top of Trai Thuy Hill and to the west of the city centre a white, 19-metre (62ft) statue of the Sakyamuni Buddha overlooks the city from behind **Long Son Pagoda** Ⓕ (daily 8am–5pm). The original pagoda was built here in 1886 and has been renovated several times since.

The Buddha statue at Long Son Pagoda, which is seated on a lotus blossom throne, was erected in 1963 to commemorate the Buddhist struggle against the repressive South Vietnamese regime of Ngo Dinh Diem, which was overthrown that same year. Images of the Buddhist nuns and monks who killed themselves as a final protest are displayed at the base of the statue. The most famous of them, Thich Quang Duc, made headlines when he immolated himself in the centre of Saigon in 1963.

NHA TRANG EVANGELICAL CHURCH

The large, cathedral-style **Nha Trang Evangelical Church** Ⓖ (Sun service 8am) at 29 Le Thanh Phuong Street is the administrative centre for the large Protestant population of Khanh Hoa province. Several of the pastors here have spent years in and out of prison for openly expressing their faith under the communist system.

Ⓞ Tip

Signs posted at Dam Market entrance are remarkably candid: "Notice for Foreign Visitors... Please deal with the stall owners directly. Do not trust the interpretation and recommendation of the strange guides." Outgoing strangers in markets are often running scams.

Alexandre Yersin and his telescope.

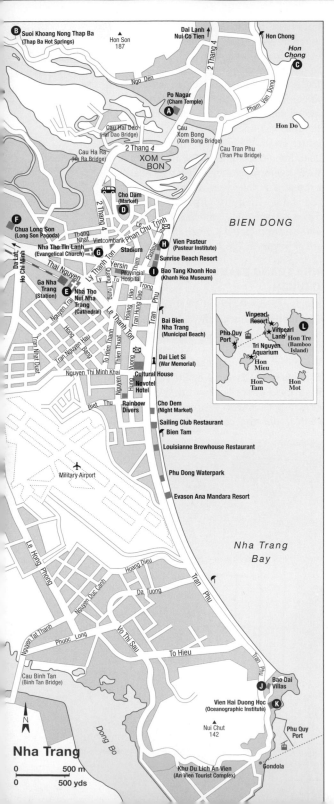

Nha Trang

0   500 m

0   500 yds

The Sunday service is always packed to the rafters.

ALEXANDRE YERSIN MUSEUM

The **Pasteur Institute** Ⓗ, on Nha Trang's seafront at 10D Tran Phu Street, was founded in 1895 by Dr Alexandre Yersin (1863–1943), a French microbiologist, military doctor, explorer and overall Renaissance man who had worked at the Pasteur Institute in Paris, where he helped Emile Roux discover the diphtheria bacterium. He arrived in Vietnam (via Nha Trang) in 1891 and was one of the first Europeans to explore extensively the Mekong Delta area and the central highlands.

Yersin was instrumental in the development of the hill station at Dalat and was also responsible for introducing Brazilian rubber trees and establishing *quinquina* plantations – quinine-producing trees – in the Suoi Dau region southwest of Nha Trang. He is buried here among his rubber trees, with a pagoda built nearby to honour him.

In 1894, Yersin was sent to Hong Kong by the French government and the Pasteur Institute to investigate an outbreak of the bubonic plague. He soon discovered the link between rats, fleas and eventually the bacteria that cause it (later renamed *Yersinia pestis* in his honour). Returning to Nha Trang in 1895, he built a laboratory to manufacture the serum for the disease. Ten years later, in 1905, the lab became an official branch of the Pasteur Institute. Today, Nha Trang's Pasteur Institute still produces vaccines and carries out research, despite being constrained by a very tight budget.

The small **Alexandre Yersin Museum** (tel: 058-382 2355; Tue–Sat 7.30–11am and 2–4.30pm) attached to the institute displays many of the great man's personal effects, furniture, documents and antique laboratory equipment (including an enormous telescope). Many of his old books are still kept in the library.

KHANH HOA PROVINCIAL MUSEUM

A few doors down from the Pasteur Institute is the small **Khanh Hoa Museum** ❶ (tel: 058-382 2277; Mon, Wed, Fri and Sun 8–11am and 2–5pm) at 16D Tran Phu Street. The museum's left wing contains relics from the Xom Con (about 3,000 years old), the Dong Son (c.2000 BC–AD 200) and Cham (which peaked between the 7th and 12th centuries) cultures. The most unusual item is the ancient stone lithograph (a musical instrument similar to a marimba) estimated to be 3,000 years old. The museum's right wing contains photos of modern Khanh Hoa province and a random mix of old ceramics. Notably absent are exhibits on Vietnam's wartime history or about Ho Chi Minh.

BAO DAI'S VILLAS

At the southern end of Nha Trang, near the Cau Da Port, are **Bao Dai Villas** ❿ (Vinh Nguyen; tel: 058-359 0147). The five ageing villas are set on three hills amongst well-manicured trees and shrubs, and date back to the 1920s when they were built for Bao Dai (the last emperor of Vietnam's Nguyen dynasty) and his family. From the mid-1950s until 1975, high-ranking officials of the South Vietnamese government used the villa as a holiday home. After 1975, communist leaders from Hanoi supplanted them. Today, the buildings have been restored and the provincial tourism authorities run the complex as a hotel. The grounds, restaurants and a somewhat scruffy little beach facing the port are all open to the public. The rates are slightly overpriced, but it's a nice spot to take some photos and have a picnic. You can sneak into the tower of the main house for a better view of the bay.

OCEANOGRAPHIC INSTITUTE

Sandwiched between the Bao Dai Villas and Cau Da Port is the **Oceanographic Institute** ⓚ (tel: 058- 359 0037; daily 6am–6pm), founded in 1923

The statue of Buddha at Long Son Pagoda overlooks Nha Trang from the top of Trai Thuy Hill.

Idyllic Whale Island Resort.

⊘ Tip

The best diving in Nha Trang is during the dry season from June to September. The optimum time to take advantage of these conditions is during late August and September when the crowds tend to be at their thinnest.

and housed in a large French-colonial complex. The institute has about a dozen large, open tanks – most notable are the prowling sharks, inquisitive rays and the seemingly oblivious sea turtles. Smaller tanks are filled with bizarre reef fish and sea horses. The main building houses a large collection of preserved specimens. Impressive are the giant humpback whale and dugong skeletons, as well as an entire pickled dugong (which might turn a few stomachs).

NHA TRANG'S ISLANDS

HON TRE (BAMBOO ISLAND)

From Nha Trang Beach, the outline of large **Hon Tre ❶** (Bamboo Island) in the distance is clearly visible. The island is rather dominated these days by the **Vinpearl Land Amusement Park** (tel: 1900 6677 – ext. 1; http://nhatrang.vinpearlland.com/en; daily 8.30am–9pm) and **Vinpearl Resort**. The blindingwhite, Hollywood-style lettering on the mountain proudly announces who is responsible for the

environmental degradation. Thankfully the park looks much better on the inside. A **gondola** (charge) – which incidentally holds the Guinness World Record for the longest ocean-crossing cable car at 3,320 metres (10,892ft) – departs from **Phu Quy Port** and delivers visitors to the centre of the amusement park. If you find the idea of a 10-minute cable-car ride daunting, take the ferry instead (20 minutes) from Phu Quy Port. The park contains a number of rides and a roller-coaster, a games area, water park, a shopping centre and several restaurants.

The crowning feature of the park is the modern **Underwater World**, with more than 20 fresh- and sea-water tanks of varying sizes, including an impressive walk-through wraparound tank featuring sharks, rays, morays and a large variety of reef animals. The aquarium is controversial within Nha Trang's diving community, however; some have accused it of pillaging the local reefs for the marine specimens, including a well-known moray that divers used to seek out.

The park is a fun way to spend a day with children, but the near US$20 basic entry fee for the park and aquarium will keep out most local Vietnamese and budget travellers. Visitors can choose to stay on the island's five-star Vinpearl Resort, an over-the-top beach-front resort with 400 rooms, Vietnam's largest swimming pool and myriad facilities.

OTHER ISLANDS

From Phu Quy Port, visitors can take a 20-minute boat ride to **Hon Mieu**, where the large **Tri Nguyen Aquarium** (tel: 058-359 9689; daily 8am–5pm), designed to look like a tall ship that has been sunken and fossilised, is located. The facility, which has seen better days, is primarily a fish breeding ground. The surrounding tropical gardens are pleasant.

⊙ UNDERWATER NHA TRANG

One of the star attractions of Nha Trang is its beautiful coral reefs – largely encompassed by the Hon Mun Marine Protected Area, which includes nine offshore islands. During marine surveys in the 1990s, some 190 species of coral and 176 species of marine life were documented in its waters.

Sadly, and predictably, Nha Trang's reefs are rapidly deteriorating due to pollution, overfishing and mismanagement by the government. Visibility, which was once 30 metres (98ft), is typically restricted to 10 metres (33ft). Boats supplied to the government by NGOs to monitor the reefs now sit idly by while fishermen in full view drop nets and, even worse, dynamite and cyanide, on marked dive spots. Meanwhile several sewers spew black waste water directly into the sea.

Visitors should support eco-friendly companies that help conserve the reefs. Safety is also paramount, as some companies have had their licences revoked for abandoning divers at sea.

In 2010, *National Geographic Traveller* ranked Nha Trang, together with Mui Ne, among the world's worst beaches, largely on environmental grounds. The sensational listing got the attention of the provincial government. Whether they take positive steps to improve the situation is yet to be seen.

Several other islands are located in the vicinity of Nha Trang, including **Hon Mot** (no popular English translation), **Hon Mun** (Ebony Island), **Hon Yen** (Bird's Nest Island), **Hon Ong** (Whale Island) and **Hon Lao** (Monkey Island). Most of these islands, as well as beaches on Hon Mieu and Hon Tre, are easily visited on a boat tour (which can be booked at any tour office or guesthouse in Nha Trang). Tours include snorkelling at various reef spots. Most require additional marine park fees, not included in the tour price.

A word of caution: **Hon Lao**, though tempting to visit, is best avoided. The large population of macaques running free there is highly aggressive and some of them are bred for scientific research. Due to the genetic experiments and the conditions they live in, it's not only possible but also likely that the monkeys carry dangerous diseases communicable to humans. Many would also consider the circus-style animal shows held here to be inhumane.

Hon Ong is occupied by the French-run **Whale Island Resort** (tel: 0935 466245; www.anislandinvietnam.com) and is a permanent diving station for **Rainbow Divers**. The island's future and its pristine coral reefs, however, are hanging in the balance as the government has proposed dredging the channel and building a steel mill on the island in the near future.

NORTH OF NHA TRANG

BA HO WATERFALLS

About 25km (16 miles) north of Nha Trang, near the village of Phu Huu, are the **Ba Ho Waterfalls** (Sui Ba Ho; daily 6am–6pm). Here, amid lush green forests, are three pools in ascending height, formed by water cascading over large boulders. Enterprising youngsters will follow you the entire 2km (1.2-mile) -long

trek, offering helping hands (and selling drinks), all of which become much appreciated as the climb grows increasingly steep and slippery. When reached, the falls are a splendid spot for a picnic.

DOC LET BEACH

Further north on its own peninsula is the lovely secluded **Doc Let Beach**, which looks out over the South China Sea. This palm-tree-fringed expanse of gently sloping sand has relatively calm waters and is very popular with Vietnamese tourists at weekends. Several small and low-key resorts here offer budget accommodation. Some rubbish from the nearby fishing village tends to mar the beach at times, but thankfully most resorts keep their own respective beaches quite clean.

In the west, **Me Con Mountain** (Nui Me Con) reaches a height of about 2,000 metres (6,600ft). From a distance, its silhouette resembles that of a woman carrying a child, hence its name, Mother and Child Mountain.

Preserved specimens at the Oceanographic Institute.

Many islands, such as Hon Yen (Bird's Nest Island), are home to Germain's swiftlets, whose famous nests – gathered in vast quantities – are a source of nutrition and income.

The exclusive Six Senses Hideaway resort.

HON HEO PENINSULA

North of Nha Trang is the **Hon Heo Peninsula** ❷, an idyllic world of secluded beaches and tall boulder-strewn mountains, inhabited by large populations of one of Indochina's rarest primates – the black-shanked Douc langur *(Pygathix nemaeus nigripes)*. The two beaches on the peninsula have become legendary destinations themselves. The first, **Jungle Beach**, is on the northern side, some 40km (25 miles) from Nha Trang, about an hour's drive away. The beach here is pristine and the water sparkling and clear year-round, with permanent populations of bioluminescent algae that magically light up when swimmers stir the water at night. The rustic **Jungle Beach Resort** occupies the prime position here. On the southern side of the peninsula, reachable only by boat, is an exclusive getaway for people with money to burn. The **Six Senses Ninh Van Bay** offers luxury private villas, each with its own personal butler, swimming pool and private terrace and deck which has a ladder descending into the clear waters below.

SOUTH OF NHA TRANG

Heading 35km (22 miles) south of Nha Trang, the coastal road passes Cam Ranh Airport and then arrives at **Cam Ranh Bay** ❸ (Vinh Cam Ranh), the deep-water bay used as a naval base, first by the Americans, later by the Soviets, and finally by the Vietnamese. After modernisation works by Russian specialists, it is to be reopened as a naval maintenance and logistics facility for foreign warships. South of Cam Ranh, the road enters Ninh Thuan province. The coastal road passes through a rather monotonous, sand-covered landscape.

PHAN RANG AND THAP CHAM

The town of **Phan Rang** ❹ and its sister city of **Thap Cham**, 7km (4 miles) to the west, are co-capitals of Ninh Thuan province, and the modern cultural centre of the Cham people, who are now settled along the **Cai River**.

Local residents often walk about town in traditional dress, the men in white gowns and turbans with red sashes, and women with heads covered in Muslim fashion. The towns are located in an extremely arid landscape dotted with menacinglooking cacti and poinciana trees. This is one of Vietnam's poorest areas, due to the lack of agricultural resources and discriminatory policies of the communist government. Grape-growing has recently taken root, however, and more and more vineyards can be seen in the countryside.

PO KLONG GARAI

Four 13th-century Cham towers known as **Po Klong Garai** ❺ (daily 7am–5pm) stand on an arid hill about 7km (4 miles) west of Phan Rang, toward Dalat on Highway 20. These brick towers were built under the reign of the Cham king Jaya Simhavarman III to worship King Po Klong Garai, who had constructed a much-needed local irrigation system. The entrance to the largest tower is graced with a dancing, six-armed Shiva, and inside a statue of the bull Nandi, recipient of offerings brought by farmers to ensure a good harvest. A *linga* (stone phallus) painted with a human face sits below the main tower.

PO RO ME

About 15km (10 miles) south of Phan Rang is the tower of **Po Ro Me** ❻ (daily 7am–5pm; free), named after the last king of Champa, who ruled from 1629 to 1651 and died a captive of the Vietnamese. Po Ro Me, which dates back to the early 16th century, is one of the last towers built by the Champa kingdom. An image of King Po Ro Me is found at the top of the tower, flanked by reliefs of the bull, Nandi.

Like Po Klong Garai, the tower is a focal point of the annual Kate Festival (Cham New Year), but receives fewer holiday revellers. To reach the tower, head south from Phan Rang on Highway 1A for about 9km (6 miles), and then head west at Hau Sanh for the remaining 6km (4 miles).

Po Klong Garai.

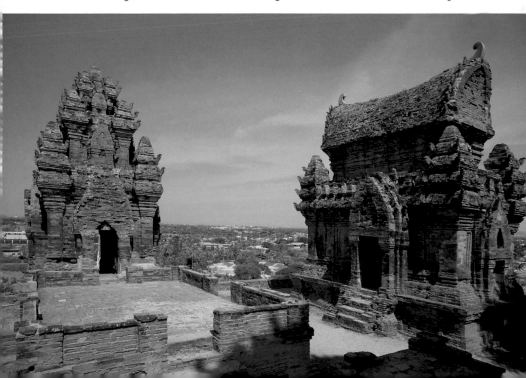

VIETNAMESE FESTIVALS

Festivals in Vietnam are a time of fun. The main festival of Tet is especially vibrant as the whole country joins together in celebration.

Vietnam is a great place for festival-lovers. Colourful festivities, most with a strong Chinese cultural influence, take place throughout the year, although the most interesting ones occur in spring and autumn. Nearly all coincide with the lunar calendar. For a complete list of festivals (including many region-specific events) and precise dates, check www.vietnamtourism.com. Here are a few nationwide highlights.

Jan/Feb, Tet: The first seven days of the Lunar New Year mark the most important holiday in Vietnam (Tet Nguyen Dan), although only the first four days are a national holiday (see page 71 for more details).

Mar/Apr, Thanh Minh: Many people visit the graves of their ancestors to make offerings.

May/June, Buddha's Birthday: Better known as Vesak, this is a big day at temples, with religious processions and ceremonies.

May/June, Tiet Doan Ngo: Summer Solstice Day is observed by making offerings to spirits to ward off summer epidemics. It is often celebrated with dragon-boat races.

Aug, Trang Nguyen: Wandering Souls Day is the second-largest celebration after Tet.

Sept/Oct, Trung Thu: The Mid-Autumn Festival is a time for eating "moon cakes" filled with nuts, seeds and egg yolks. Children are given lanterns in the shape of dragons, carps and stars to play with.

Buddhist monks and nuns, dressed in simple brown tunics, welcome visiting worshippers. Most are happy to sit over a cup of green tea, explaining in detail the history and the imagery of their pagoda or temple. Vesak is the main Buddhist festival.

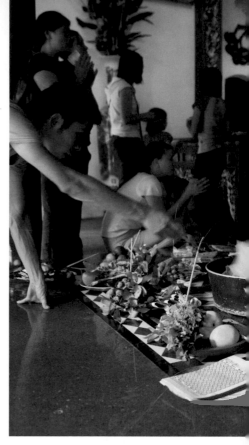

Ancestor worship is widely practised in Vietnam, co-existing with Buddhist, Confucian and Taoist beliefs. The ancestor cult is a homely affair but it is also celebrated publicly with effigies placed on pagoda altars.

On the eve of Tet, and during Wandering Souls Day, families burn paper offerings to their ancestors. They often do so right on the pavement outside their house, so watch your feet!

The colourful rong mua lan, or dancing lion, is a centrepiece of Tet festivals and other major festivals in villages throughout the country. The dance is said to scare away evil spirits and usher in good luck.

Village festivals

The best time to observe village festivals is just after Tet, a word which itself means "festival". During the first two lunar months (February and March), most villages organise a fête of some sort. Families will visit the village pagoda and light incense to local deities and their ancestors. Youngsters play games, swinging on giant bamboo swings or playing "human chess" with people or metre-high models moving between squares marked on a courtyard.

Villages near the Red River (Song Hong) in northern Vietnam send boats to collect ceremonial water to offer to the water god, Ha Ba. The most spectacular of these traditions is when young men put on the elaborate costumes of the dancing lion and dance energetically among the revellers to the sound of beating drums. One of the most popular of these occasions is the quan ho festival at Lim village, near Hanoi. Here, young couples sing love songs to each other in a fertility rite to welcome the spring, a time-honoured tradition that goes back to ancient times.

Beautifully crafted candlelit lanterns are carried by children during the atmospheric Mid-Autumn Festival in either September or October. This is also the time when "moon cakes" are eaten.

...eration Day is celebrated on 30 April. This nationwide ...day marks the surrender of South Vietnam to the North ...namese Army in 1975. A year later Vietnam was officially ...ed under the Communist Party. Other national holidays ...ude the Founding of the Vietnamese Communist Party (3 ...ruary), and National Day (2 September).

DALAT AND SURROUNDINGS

A cool and tranquil retreat from the crowded lowland cities, Dalat is situated among pine-covered mountains and misty forests. A bounty of fresh produce and flowers flourishes here.

The bracing cool mountain climate that **Dalat** ❼ enjoys at an altitude of 1,500 metres (4,920ft), its large open spaces, picturesque waterfalls, colonial architecture and incredibly fresh produce provide respite for those wishing to escape the heat and humidity of Ho Chi Minh City and the lowlands of southern Vietnam. It is easy to see why the French were so enamoured of Dalat during the colonial days and why it was the favourite getaway for Vietnam's last emperor, Bao Dai. For those seeking culture and exotic adventures, Dalat is also the gateway to the central highands area where hill-tribe villages abound.

In 1893 Dr Alexandre Yersin (see page 254) was the first European to survey the area, under the authority of Paul Doumer, the French governor-general of Indochina at the time. He suggested that a hill station and sanatorium be built here to take advantage of the mild climate and beautiful scenery. The area surrounding the Cam Ly River was eventually developed from a small fort in 1899 into a thriving resort town over the next few decades.

Annual temperatures range between a comfortable 16°C (61°F) and 24°C (75°F), making Dalat one of Vietnam's most popular retreats and its top honeymoon destination. The dry-weather months usually run from November to March, while the wet season is from April to October. These latter months are not so good for a visit. Nights can be quite chilly.

Dalat is a well-connected holiday hub, with major highways leading conveniently to Ho Chi Minh City (320km/200 miles; 6–7 hours' drive), Mui Ne (247km/ 153 miles; 5–6 hours), Phan Rang (108km/67 miles; 4–5 hours) and Nha Trang (205km/127 miles; 5–6 hours).

TOURISM IN DALAT

The town receives plenty of domestic tourists. Some of its attractions,

◎ Main Attractions
Dalat Palace Hotel
Central Market
Hang Nga's Crazy House
Bao Dai's Summer Palace
Lam Dong Museum
Tiger Falls
Lang Dinh An Village
Elephant Falls
XQ Historical Village

**Maps on pages
252, 264, 268**

Radish farm in the lush highland countryside.

therefore, are geared towards Vietnamese tastes, and often seem rather kitsch to international visitors. At some of its parks and lakes, men in American cowboy costumes lead tourists on pony rides, while actors in monkey suits twirl spears for photo opportunities. Scores of souvenir sellers jostle for space with giant, brightly painted concrete statues of animals, mushrooms and Disney characters. You may want to avoid the notably kitsch **Valley of Love** (Thung Lung Tinh Yeu), 6km (4 miles) north of town, and the **Lake of Sighs** (Ho Than Tho), 5km (3 miles) northeast.

This does not have to be your Dalat experience, however. The city has been spared the ravages of war suffered by the rest of the country. During the Vietnam war, representatives from both sides came here for rest and recuperation (and probably for a bit of spying on each other). As a result, the beautiful colonial architecture has been preserved like nowhere else in Vietnam. Most of the old villas and government buildings can be found in the French Quarter along the south side of Xuan Huong Lake and Cam Ly River.

Dalat is a wonderful place for walking with its many gardens and lakes, but it is difficult to navigate without a map in hand, as the narrow streets wrap themselves haphazardly around the hills. Elephant rides and horse carriages, once common, have fallen out of favour due to the harsh treatment of the animals. A paddle boat, available for rent at several lakes in and around Dalat, is a pleasant way to spend an afternoon.

TWO HISTORIC HOTELS

The hill resort was originally built around the grand Langbian Palace Hotel in the early years of the 20th century, an historic hotel that was renovated and reopened in 1995 as the **Dalat Palace Heritage Hotel Ⓐ**. Construction of the original Langbian Palace began in 1902 and laboured on for 20 years (at the time travel from the coast took more than a week, making any new construction a slow and difficult task). The Hôtel du Parc, just diagonally opposite, followed in 1932. It has regained its old name after a series of recent re-brandings. Both hotels retain much of their original architectural charm and the Dalat Palace still maintains over 4 hectares (10 acres) of grassy lawn, a rarity in Vietnam.

Just north of the Palace, **Xuan Huong Lake** (Ho Xuan Huong), formerly part of the town's colonial-era golf course before it was flooded, extends through the heart of the town. The surrounding hills, French-style villas and pine forests provide a lovely backdrop, although the water itself is muddy with red clay after the rains.

On the northern banks of the lake, a golf course originally built for the last emperor, Bao Dai, has been supplanted and expanded into the **Dalat Golf Club** (tel: 063-382 3507). The 18-hole championship course is a sister club to the Ocean Dunes Golf Club in Phan Thiet.

CENTRAL MARKET

Dalat's **Central Market** ⓑ (Cho Da Lat; daily 6am–10pm) is one of the largest in the country, and one of the city's principal attractions. Set in a deep hollow of a hillside and surrounded by rows of cafés and shops selling wine and candied fruit, the current market was built in the 1960s. The original market, sitting on the hill above, was built in the 1920s and later converted into a cinema. The series of three central buildings can be confusing to navigate, and it may take several sweeps to find all the floors.

The food is the highlight here. The second floor of the middle building is devoted entirely to food stalls – mostly rice served with local specialities, and bowls of *che*, a dessert made with sweetened beans and candied fruit.

The ground floor of the market offers a peek into the great diversity of produce grown in the region: strawberries, tomatoes, avocados, asparagus and just about any fruit, flower and vegetable found in countries with temperate climates.

Lat ethnic minority girl dressed in traditional costume.

Dalat Palace Golf Club.

On Saturdays and Sundays from 7–10pm, the streets surrounding the market are closed to vehicles and a carnival-like atmosphere ensues with an influx of pedestrians, souvenir and clothing pedlars, and more food vendors.

CHURCHES AND PAGODAS

North of the Central Market is the yellow **Dalat Evangelical Church ⊙** (Nha Tho Tin Lanh) at 72 Nguyen Van Troi Street. Built in 1940, most of the congregation is composed of impoverished hill-tribe minorities. Since 1975, local Protestants have suffered persecution as the communist government associates Protestants with the former American military presence. Even today the government restricts the activities of this church.

To the west, perched on the hilltop at Ngo Quyen Street, is **Domaine de Marie Convent Church ⊙** (daily 5am–4pm). Constructed in 1942, this French convent used to have almost 350 nuns in residence. Today, only 25 or so remain, running an orphanage and selling

Fresh produce and dried goods at the Central Market.

unique handmade crafts, embroidery, knitted sweaters and ginger candy to raise funds for local orphans, the homeless and the disabled.

In the southern part of town is the large, pink-coloured **Dalat Cathedral ⊙** (Nha Tho Con Ga; Mon–Sat Mass at 5.15am and 5.15pm, Sun Mass 5.15am, 7am, 8.30am, 2.30pm and 4pm). Located at the intersection of Tran Phu and Le Dai Hanh streets, the church is more popularly known as the Rooster Church on account of the rooster weathervane on top of the steeple. The cathedral, rarely open outside mass hours, was built in 1942, with stained-glass windows made by Louis Balmet, in Grenoble, France. Sunday Masses see large and enthusiastic crowds turning up. Across from the cathedral, taking the form of a mini Eiffel Tower, is Dalat's telecommunications tower.

Dalat's Buddhist temples were all built in the last century, but most are atmospheric and provide important places of worship for Chinese and ethnic Vietnamese immigrants.

Thien Vuong Pagoda (also known as the Chinese Pagoda) is located 3km (2 miles) southeast of town on Khe Sanh Street. The temple, built in 1958, is fairly unremarkable but for the three giant sandalwood Buddha images that it houses.

The highlight of a visit to Lam Ty Ni Pagoda (2 Thien My Street) is not the architecture or the idols, but rather the solitary monk, Vien Thuc, who lives there. Made famous by an episode of the TV series *Globetrekker*, the "Crazy Monk" draws poems, paints and writes poetry, which he sells to visitors.

Linh Son Pagoda sits on top of a hill at 120 Nguyen Van Troi Street, in the centre of town. The building has an attractive entrance and beautiful carved wooden doors, which lead behind to one of the largest monasteries in the central highlands.

HANG NGA'S CRAZY HOUSE

For anyone travelling with children, or those who have played in tree houses themselves as children, **Hang Nga's Crazy House** (tel: 063-382 2070; www.crazyhouse.vn; daily 8.30am–7pm) at 3 Huynh Thuc Khang Street will surely appeal. This is a whimsical and inspiring piece of architecture that is guaranteed to delight. The never-completed house is continuously being added to, with tunnels, stairways and halls meandering into secret rooms and towers, and reading nooks occupied by statues of giant kangaroos, giraffes, eagles and bears.

The master architect, Dr Dang Viet Nga, daughter of the deceased General Secretary of the Communist Party in Vietnam, began construction of the fantasy house in 1990. Gift shops occupy a couple of rooms, selling unique handmade crafts. The other rooms may be rented as accommodation, but guests may find the constant stream of visitors rather intrusive.

BAO DAI'S SUMMER PALACE

Tucked away under pine trees on a hill about 1km (0.6 miles) from Nga's Crazy House at Trieu Viet Vuong Street is the **Summer Palace of Bao Dai** (Biet Dien Quoc Truong; tel: 063-382 6858; daily 7am–4pm). This Art Deco-influenced abode of Vietnam's last emperor was built between 1933 and 1938. Also referred to as Dinh III, this is actually one of three palaces (the others being Dinh I and Dinh II, neither of which is currently open to the public) belonging to Bao Dai in Dalat. It's said that all three are connected by tunnels so that the emperor could secretly visit his mistresses in each one. Although guides will say that the furnishings and artefacts in the house were used by Bao Dai, it is a well-known fact that many of his belongings were carted away in the early years. Outside the mansion, a carnival-like atmosphere prevails, with souvenir vendors, pony rides and Disney characters. To appreciate the villa better, visit it right after it opens in the morning, or just before lunch.

A peek into the Summer Palace of Emperor Bao Dai reveals his Western tastes.

The unconventional Crazy House.

The Lam Dong Museum has a wide array of exhibits and makes for an interesting afternoon.

LAM DONG MUSEUM

On Hung Vuong Street in the eastern part of town is the **Lam Dong Museum** (Bao Tang Lam Dong; tel: 063-381 2624; www.baotanglamdong.com.vn; daily 7.30–4.30pm), recognised by the United Nations for its extensive collections of musical gongs used by the local K'ho, Ma and Churu minorities. Other exhibits at this former colonial villa include an impressive taxidermy collection of local wildlife; relics from the Champa or Funan empire (this is debatable) excavated at Cat Tien National Park; artefacts found in recent excavations from still unidentified cultures; and full-sized Ma and K'ho tribal longhouses, decorated with musical instruments, weapons and common household items.

Dalat University in the north of the city is one of the top schools in the country, and its many students live in tiny boarding houses that line most of the surrounding alleys. The city owes its abundance of cheap, delicious street food to the presence of so many students. Have a stroll around nearby

The colourful Dalat Train Station.

Dalat Flower Park (2 Phu Dong Thien Vuong St, open 8am–5pm) to find out why Dalat is often called "the city of a thousand flowers". The park is also a venue of the annual four-day Flower Festival, usually held at the end of December/beginning of January when an astonishing abundance of ortensiaes, mimosas, roses, daffodils and lilies are on display.

EAST OF DALAT

Outside of the main town centre are several sights in the surroundings of Dalat that can be easily visited on half- or full-day trips. It is best to hire a car, taxi or motorbike to get to these places.

DALAT TRAIN STATION AND TRAI MAT VILLAGE

The picturesque colonial-style **Dalat Train Station** (Ga Dalat) at Quang Trung Street opened in 1932, and was once the terminus of a train service that ran all the way to Phan Rang, just east of Nha Trang on the coast. The track, however, was damaged during the Vietnam

War and never repaired. The only line that exists today is a short 7km (4-mile) stretch that carries a small diesel-run train transporting tourists to **Trai Mat village** east of the city. There are five daily departures, at 7.45am, 9.50am, 11.55am, 2pm and 4.05pm; a minimum of six passengers is required. The ride takes 30 minutes and passes through some lovely countryside.

There isn't much to see in Trai Mat for the moment, save for the grandiose **Linh Phuoc Pagoda** (Chua Ling Phuoc; daily 8am–5pm; free). Built in 1952, the imposing seven-tiered pagoda is just a few hundred metres from the train station, on the other side of the street.

TIGER FALLS

Tiger Falls (Thac Hang Cop; daily daylight hours) is the grandest waterfall in Dalat's environs, and thankfully the least visited or developed, largely because of the long drive down a poor road and a further walk down a very steep hill. The falls are an ideal outing for nature-lovers who wish to do a bit of adventure trekking, following the stream as it crashes among the boulders in the rainforest canyon below. Tiger Falls is 14km (9 miles) east of Dalat, past Trai Mat village, where there is a signposted turning on the left.

SOUTH OF DALAT

DALAT CABLE CAR

The **Dalat Cable Car** (Cap Treo Dalat; 8–11.30am and 1.30–4.30pm,) is located about 3km (1.8 miles) south of town. The cable-car ride stretches over 2km (1.2 miles) and offers lovely panoramas of villages and mountain forests, all the way to the **Bamboo Forest Meditation Centre** (Thien Vien Truc Lam).

This Zen-style Buddhist monastery was built in 1993 and has about 100 monks and 80 nuns in residence. The temple is famous because of its perfect *feng shui* placement, with **Pin Haat Mountain** (Nui Pin Haat) behind and **Quang Trung Reservoir** (Ho Tuyen Lam) below. Below the monastery is a picnic area with tables and chairs that

The Dalat Cable Car connects to a few attractions worth visiting.

⊘ Fact

The resourceful K'ho and Ma women are excellent weavers and still dye their cloth using natural bark extracts. The impoverished minority women also sell street food in the Dalat Central Market.

overlooks the tranquil reservoir. The artificial lake is now a recreational area with rowing boats and canoes for rent.

DATANLA WATERFALL

The turn-off for **Datanla Waterfall** (Thac Da Tanla; daily daylight hours) is about 5km (3 miles) south of Dalat, or just a few hundred metres past the turn-off for the Bamboo Forest Meditation Centre. There is a 10-minute walk through the rainforest, down to the falls below (allow 20 minutes for the return walk). The waterfall makes for great photos, if you can overlook the kitschy pony rides, girls in fake minority costumes and men in bear suits. The mechanised toboggan run (extra charge) down to the falls and back is the most enjoyable aspect of the commercialism that has taken root here. It is also possible to arrange abseiling tours with Groovy Gecko Adventure Tours.

LANG DINH AN VILLAGE

Once a favourite stop for tourists wishing to see the K'ho ethnic minority,

Lang Dinh An village (more popularly known as Chicken Village), 17km (11 miles) south from highway 20, today resembles most other villages in Dalat's environs, with one exception. Its unique focal point is a giant concrete chicken, which isn't at all as tacky as it sounds. It's actually a rather striking sculpture with an interesting story behind it.

The K'ho were once a nomadic tribe, subsisting on slash-and-burn agriculture. After 1975, the communist government tried to get them to move out of the hills and to one of the villages closer to Dalat, where they could assimilate with the Kinh colonists, and thus be under the watchful eye of the government. The local K'ho chief, however, said that the tribe would only agree if the government built a giant chicken statue, with nine claws, to adorn the centre of the new village.

According to an ancient K'ho legend, a girl had approached the mother of her lover, asking permission to marry her son (as is the custom in the

The mighty Elephant Falls.

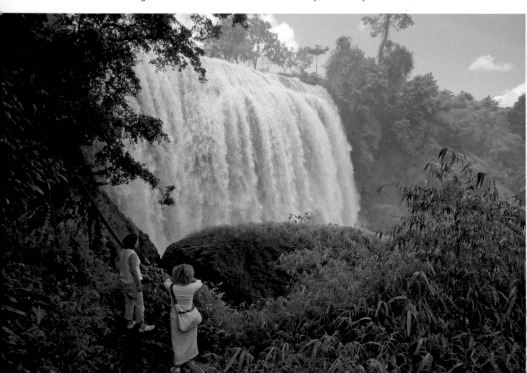

matriarchal K'ho culture). The mother, who disapproved of the pairing, told the girl that she would only consent if she could bring her a chicken with nine claws (knowing this to be impossible). The girl thus began an epic search for the unlikely chicken, but eventually died in her quest.

This rooster statue that the chief requested stands as a symbolic offering to the legendary maiden, putting her finally at peace. The irony, which many have missed altogether, is that much like the mother who sent the maiden on a fool's errand, the chief probably never expected the government to accede to his strange request. As a result of the agreement, however, many K'ho families were forced to move out of the hills, much against their wishes, to this new village.

Shops around the chicken statue sell lovely handwoven blankets, handbags, tablecloths and other items with brightly coloured tribal patterns that prominently feature horses and elephants.

WEST OF DALAT

Elephant Falls (Thac Voi), 30km (19 miles) southwest of Dalat, is a favourite stop on tours of Dalat's countryside led by local guides. The dramatic rock formations are just as arresting as the falls themselves, which look like a movie set from Peter Jackson's *King Kong*. It's a bit of a climb down to the bottom of the falls for the best views, but steps have been skilfully carved into the rocks to make the trek easier. A shop above the falls sells beautiful handwoven K'ho blankets and crafts, all made on-site.

NORTH OF DALAT

LANGBIANG MOUNTAIN

The 12km (7-mile) drive from Dalat to **Langbiang Mountain** (Nui Lang Bian) passes through quaint **Lat Village**, inhabited by K'ho, Lat and Ma minorities. The villagers make a meagre living from the squash, tobacco, coffee, tea and cotton that they grow on the hillsides.

Visitors can explore Langbian Mountain's hiking trails on their own, but hiring a guide offers more options. The mountain is a favourite trekking location of adventure tour companies such as Groovy Gecko and Phat Tire. There are breathtaking vistas of the countryside, and the surrounding pine forests are said to harbour a few surviving bears, deer, leopards and boar.

XQ HISTORICAL VILLAGE

About 6km (4 miles) north of town and across the street from the Valley of Love is the **XQ Historical Village** (tel: 026 3355 2348; http://xqvietnam. com; open daily 8am–8pm). Although run as a commercial enterprise and not really a village, this attraction offers an entertaining and informative experience, engaging all the

---

⊘ Tip

Avoid buying the tiger and bear claws in the market shops (sold with the full knowledge of the police), as it encourages poaching of endangered wildlife around Langbiang Mountain. The animal teeth in the shops tend to be plastic fakes, but the claws are generally the real thing.

⊘ DALAT'S EASY RIDERS

The best way to explore the central highlands is to book a tour with an adventure guide company like Groovy Gecko or Dalat's Easy Riders, rather than go it alone. The Easy Riders is a loose association of motorbike guides, and they are a popular option. Just stand on the street above Dalat's Central Market and one will surely find you. If you do want to book in advance tel: 012 2221 9890 or visit http://dalat-easyrider.com. Usually no particular preparations are needed when you travel with a guide. They tend to take care of all your needs.

Tours of varying lengths, including stays in hill-tribe villages, can be arranged to end in either Nha Trang, Quy Nhon or Hoi An. It is possible to drive yourself but not advised. Driving can be dangerous in Vietnam, more so because of the other people sharing the road, rather than the actual road conditions. Also, while police don't normally enforce the law in the highlands, technically foreign drivers are required to have a Vietnamese licence (Vietnam does not honour its commitment to accept the International Driving Permit) and this is not easy to get. That being said, due to the climate, scenery and absence of traffic, the central highlands are the best place in Vietnam to drive or ride a motorbike.

Langbiang Mountain.

senses in a way that few other tourist attractions in Dalat can. XQ is Vietnam's top brand of embroidered paintings – its works are a favourite gift from the government to visiting dignitaries and celebrities.

XQ's high-quality embroidery is one of Vietnam's success stories. The company has a presence in every major city in Vietnam – but it goes far beyond mere shops. Most include live music shows, serve inexpensive but delicious local cuisine at in-house restaurants, and have extensive art galleries of embroidery works which are not for sale. Its outlet in Dalat includes all of this plus a fine museum on the culture of embroidery as well as local minority handicrafts. A cluster of gift shops and a café (in addition to the restaurant) await customers at the end of the village tour, during which you will get the chance to meet the artists and see them at work. XQ has two much smaller store outlets in Dalat, one on the top floor of the Central Market, and another across the street.

CENTRAL HIGHLANDS

Far north of Dalat, the area known as the central highlands is a tempting lure for the adventurous traveller. The cities of the north do not feature significantly in most travellers' itineraries, however. This is mainly because police do not allow tourists to travel very far from the cities and into the surrounding countryside.

The largely Protestant (and impoverished) hill-tribe communities in these provinces, also known as Montagnards, supported the Americans during the war and have been a source of grief for the communist government ever since. Needless to say, the government's attempts to encourage the Kinh majority from other parts of Vietnam to settle down in the central highlands have not been received favourably by the Montagnards. As such, this is an area of periodic unrest, and the government requires that all foreigners obtain permits (virtually impossible to do without a government recommendation and professional credentials) to travel off the main highways, unless travelling to

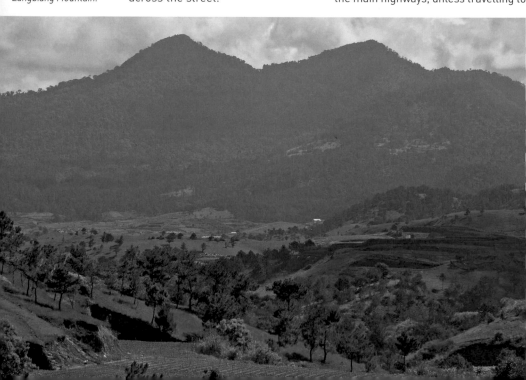

the three provincial capitals, Yuk Don National Park, and a few of the main lakes and waterfalls.

About a day's drive north of Dalat, the shores of **Lak Lake** ⑧ (Ho Lak) are inhabited by displaced members of the M'nong tribe. A number of villages can be visited by boat.

Originating from Cu Yang Sin Mountain, the three waterfalls **of Dray Sap**, **Dray Nur** and **Gia Long** ⑨ (daily 7am–5pm) form a 100m/yds-wide cascade.

Two hours east of the falls, and 200km (124 miles) north of Dalat, is **Buon Ma Thuot** ⑩, the capital of Dak Lak province, as well as the capital of Vietnam's coffee production. Just south of the city centre, on the corner of Le Duan and Y Nong streets, the **Museum of Ethnology** (daily 8am–4pm) has one of the finest collections of central highlands hill-tribe crafts and relics.

Drive another hour west and spend the evening inside **Yok Don National Park** ⑪ (Vuon Quoc Gia Yok Don, Buon Don District; http://yokdonnationalpark.vn; daily during daylight hours). This 115,545-hectare wildlife reserve contains at least 63 species of mammals and 250 species of birds. There are known to be around 50 Asian elephants, 10 tigers, golden jackal, leopard and green peafowl living in the park.

Foreigners are not allowed to venture outside the capital Pleiku (200km/124 miles north of Buon Ma Thuot) or off Highway 14 without signing up for a government bus tour. Just north of town on the east side of the highway is Sea Lake (Ho Bien), a volcanic crater that forms a lake.

Kon Tum ⑫ is the provincial capital of the province by the same name, and the last city of the central highlands. The city is situated 47km (29 miles) north of Pleiku. Communal stilt homes (known as rong) of ethnic Banhar and S'tieng fill the suburbs of Kon Tum, their thatched roofs towering above the villages. There are several points of interest in the city, besides the obvious cultural richness, including the beautiful wooden cathedral, French seminary, and provincial museum.

Dray Sap Waterfall in Buon Ma Thuot.

People's Committee Building, HCMC.

Drying shrimps, Phu Quoc.

SOUTHERN VIETNAM

Defined by the vibrant capital city, the lush Mekong Delta and some superb beaches, Vietnam's deep south is one of the most appealing parts of the country.

Fisherman, Mui Ne.

That southern Vietnam has a character quite different from the north should come as no surprise given their separate histories: rather than a millennium of Chinese rule, the south evolved from centuries of Indian and Khmer civilisations. Where the north is traditionally perceived as authoritarian and disciplined, the south is considered more entrepreneurial.

The southern character is epitomised in Ho Chi Minh City, the nation's largest city and its commercial and industrial hub. Cosmopolitan, urbane and frenetic, the erstwhile Saigon is all about consumerism. In turn, Ho Chi Minh's neighbours prosper; the Mekong Delta is Vietnam's most productive agricultural area. The Southern Economic Zone (Ho Chi Minh and surrounding provinces) is Vietnam's new industrial powerhouse, its investment in various industries accounting for nearly half of the nation's GDP. The south is helped by plenty of natural resources and an inherent southern entrepreneurial spirit, driven mostly by the Overseas Vietnamese (Viet Kieu), many of whom were the original boat people who fled in the 1970s and 1980s.

Ben Thanh Market.

Blessed with a beautiful landscape, from sand dunes to scenic beaches and lush rainforests, as well as an array of cultural attractions and the best windsurfing in Southeast Asia, this region has plenty to offer. Ho Chi Minh City makes an ideal base from which to explore the wetlands of the Mekong Delta or Cat Tien National Park, one of the country's largest areas of lowland tropical rainforest. There is also an abundance of beautiful beaches, islands and coastline at Vung Tau and Mui Ne. Off the coast are Phu Quoc and the Con Dao archipelago, with gorgeous white-sand beaches, jungle-clad mountains and rich marine life.

Ho Chi Minh statue (People's Committee Building).

HO CHI MINH CITY

Big and bold, Vietnam's southern capital is its most vibrant and exciting city. Filled with historic attractions and, increasingly, world-class tourism facilities, it still retains plenty of old Saigonese charm.

Compared to other cities in Vietnam, **Ho Chi Minh City** (HCMC; Thanh Pho Ho Chi Minh) is relatively young, celebrating its 300th anniversary only in 1998. Yet this chaotic and mesmerising city has always been the backdrop to momentous history. Although the pace of development is furious, reminders of the past are inescapable in HCMC. History makes up its very essence, and evokes memories of French, Vietnamese, Chinese, Soviet and US influence.

BACKGROUND AND HISTORY

Situated 40km (25 miles) inland from the South China Sea, northeast of the Mekong Delta and alongside the Saigon River (Song Sai Gon), Ho Chi Minh City sits on top of what was once a Khmer settlement – the name "Sai Gon" comes from the Khmer word "Prei Kor", meaning "Kapok Tree Forest".

Until the 17th century, this was a thinly populated area of forest and swamps. The southern outpost of Saigon was established in 1698 as a territory and governmental base of Gia Dinh Prefecture. Due to its strategic riverside location, it became an important trading centre for foreign merchants. Towards the late 18th century, ethnic Chinese (Hoa) from the southeastern seaboard of China settled in present-day Cholon (see page 295), establishing a thriving trading area.

Advancing south, French forces captured Saigon in 1861, which emerged as capital of the French Protectorate of Cochinchina (South Vietnam). In 1887, it became part of the French Union of Indochina and was transformed into a major port city. As in Hanoi, the colonials modelled the city after their own image and it soon acquired the air of a French provincial town, albeit with an oriental edge (see page 286).

After being defeated in 1954, the French withdrew and the Geneva Convention divided Vietnam into two

Main Attractions
Reunification Palace
Notre Dame Cathedral
Dong Khoi Street Area
Municipal Theatre
People's Committee Building
War Remnants Museum
Ben Thanh Market
Museum of Vietnamese History
Jade Emperor Pagoda

 Map on page 280

Food vendor.

Ho Chi Minh City

1000 m
1000 yds

Sai Gon (Saigon)

Boat Pier

14 Bao Tang Ho Chi Minh (Ho Chi Minh Museum)

QUAN 4

13 Bao Tang Lich Su (Museum of Vietnamese History)

16 Thao Cam Vien (Saigon Zoo and Botanical Gardens)

15 Bao Tang Chien Dich Ho Chi Minh (HCMC Campaign Museum)

Trung Tam Thuong Mai Sai Gon (Saigon Trade Centre)

4 Nha Hat Thanh Pho (Opera House)

6 Majestic Hotel

Sherico Financial Tower (Saigon Skydeck)

17 Chua Ngoc Hoang (Jade Emperor Pagoda)

former US Embassy

Buu Dien Saigon (General Post Office)

3 People's Committee Building (UBND Thanh Pho)

5 Rex Hotel

2 Nha Tho Duc Ba (Notre Dame)

7 Bao Tang Thanh Pho Ho Chi Minh (HCMC Museum)

12 Le Cong Kieu (Antique Street)

An Duong Vuong

13 Cho Dan Sinh (Dan Sinh Market)

Den Tho Tran Hung Dao

Nha Tho Tan Dinh (Catholic Church)

1 Hoi Truong Thong Nhat (Reunification Palace)

11 Cho Ben Thanh (Ben Thanh Market)

10 Chua Ba (Sri Mariamman Hindu Temple)

8 Bao Tang Chung Tich Chien Tranh (War Remnants Museum)

9 Nha Hat Mua Roi Nuoc Rong Vang (Golden Dragon Water Puppet Theatre)

TAO DAN

Bao Tang My Thuat Thanh Pho (Fine Arts Museum)

Chua Xa Loi

Thich Quang Duc

PHU NHUAN

18 Chua Vinh Nghiem (Vinh Nghiem Pagoda)

Ga Sai Gon (Railway Station)

QUAN 10

QUAN 1

QUAN 3

Lang Truong Vinh Ky (Lexicographer's Mausoleum)

Nha Hat Hoa Binh

Chua Viet Nam Quoc Tu

26 Bao Tang PHHTG (Museum of Vietnamese Traditional Medicine)

Nha Tho Tan Dinh (Jeanne d'Arc Church)

Chua An Quang

QUAN 5

Nha Van Hoa

see above

Hoi Quan Tam Son

Tay Ninh

Nha Hat Hoa Binh

Phu Tho (Race Track)

CHO LON

Chua On Lang

Hoi Quan Tue Thanh

Nha Tho Phanxico Xavie (Cham Tam)

QUAN 11

Chua Khanh Van (Nam Vien)

Cho Binh Tay

22 Chua Ong Nghia An (Ong Pagoda)

23 Thanh Duong Hoi Giao Cholon (Cholon Jamail Mosque)

24 Hoi Quan Tam Son (Tam Son Temple)

21 Chua Ong Lang (Quan Am Pagoda)

22 Hoi Quan Tue Thanh (Thien Hau Pagoda)

Medicine Street

CHO LON

Chua Ong Bon

20 Nha Tho Phanxico Xavie Cha Tam Church

19 Cho Binh Tay (Binh Tay Market)

27 Chua Giac Lam (Giac Lam Pagoda)

27 Boa Thap Xa Loi (Tower)

Chua Giac Vien (Giac Vien Pagoda)

29 Chua Phung Son

25 Cong Vien Van Hoa Dam Sen (Dam Sen Park and Water Park)

200 m
200 yds

Tan An, My Tho

independent states: communists in North Vietnam and non-communists in the Republic of South Vietnam.

Saigon subsequently suffered from poor leadership, corruption, demonstrations and coups – in addition to communist attacks from the north. The US supported South Vietnam's regime, and during the Vietnam War Saigon became the nerve centre of US military operations. The North Vietnam Army arrived in Saigon and, on 30 April 1975, overthrew the government, leading to reunification of the North and South. Saigon was renamed Thanh Pho Ho Chi Minh in 1976, after the founder of the modern Vietnamese state.

Shutting its doors to the outside world, southern Vietnam was economically restructured in line with the North and large-scale political repression followed. It took until the 1980s and the *doi moi* ("economic renovation") for the city's fortunes to improve. Northerners moved south to grab official posts and residences. Widespread turmoil, inflation and poverty ensued. Fearing communist reprisals, re-education camps,

conscription and abject poverty, many thousands of Saigonese fled the country.

In 1997 the Asian economic crash left many buildings and projects half-built or abandoned for years and prompted disgruntled foreign businesses to pull out, slowing down but not completely derailing progress.

CHANGING ECONOMY

Dynamic and increasingly cosmopolitan, HCMC has wasted no time catapulting itself into the 21st century and is now Vietnam's main commercial and economic hub. Always noted for its savvy business acumen, the city now enjoys feverish commercial enterprise and development, and exudes a tangible air of confidence. With massive multi-national investments and business pouring in, the only "exploding booms" nowadays come from the omnipresent construction work. The skyline over the last decade has dramatically changed from a low-rise cityscape to a downtown dotted with glitzy high-rises of international five-star hotels, corporate offices and

Cityscape at dusk.

luxury apartments. As a result, some real-estate prices are now higher than in Tokyo's notoriously expensive Ginza district. The emerging *nouveaux riches* and middle classes with their high incomes are all too evident, seen in the flashy cars, flashy restaurants, buzzing nightspots, chic boutiques and shopping malls selling all manner of international designer goods.

HCMC hasn't succumbed to full-scale globalisation quite yet and in some ways lags behind other more sophisticated regional hotspots. Most development is concentrated in the centre, contrasting with other parts of the city where general day-to-day living hasn't changed much. Although a legacy of its strife-torn past, the city still clings to its impressive colonial architecture and romantic Gallic-oriental charm, as well as its unique Saigonese identity.

ORIENTATION

Sprawling across 2,090 sq km (807 sq miles), with a population approaching 8.5 million, HCMC is Vietnam's largest city, and one of the densest urban areas on earth. The city is divided into 19 urban districts plus five outer districts, although the main points of interest are mostly found in Districts 1, 3 and 5.

District 1 is the city centre, where most of the main shops, upmarket hotels, restaurants, bars and tourist attractions are located. It contains the original French Quarter, dissected by the city's main tourist magnet, Dong Khoi Street. The magnificent buildings constructed by the French house some of the city's major attractions. Fortunately, most tourist sites and entertainment venues are concentrated in a compact area and are eminently walkable. Also in District 1 are the backpacker haunts along Pham Ngu Lao Street. With more tourists than Vietnamese, the area can be hectic and noisy, but it does have more foreign restaurants and travel agents than anywhere else, too. The main nightlife area for visitors is also here.

North and west of District 1, the more sedate **District 3** also offers colonial architecture, parks and wide, tree-lined

Reunification Palace facade.

boulevards interspersed with a few dining and shopping diversions.

To the southwest of the centre is sprawling **District 5** (which overlaps into Districts 6, 10 and 11), incorporating bustling **Chinatown** (Cholon) with its vibrant markets, pagodas and temples, and restaurants.

Except for a few other attractions scattered further afield in Districts 10 and 11, visitors don't usually travel beyond these areas. **District 7** and, across the river, **District 2** have developed as expatriate and middle-class suburbs.

CENTRAL DISTRICT 1

REUNIFICATION PALACE

Prominently located in the centre of District 1 at 135 Nam Ky Khoi Nghia Street is the former Presidential Palace of South Vietnam, now known as **Reunification Palace ❶** (Dinh Doc Lap; tel: 08-3822 3652/3808 5038; www.dinhdoclap.gov.vn; daily 7.30–11am and 1–4pm). To the communists, this piece of ostentation – sometimes referred to as the Reunification Hall

– will forever symbolise the decadence of the Saigon regime.

Surrounded by extensive gardens, this monolith of a concrete building stands on the site of the Governor-General of Indochina Residence, or Norodom Palace, which dates back to 1871. After the French left in 1954, the new president of the Republic of South Vietnam, Ngo Dinh Diem, installed himself here. In 1962, the left wing was bombed and damaged beyond repair during an air raid; Ngo ordered the palace to be demolished, and a new edifice was constructed on top, although he never lived to see its completion as he was assassinated in 1963.

The new Presidential Palace was the headquarters of South Vietnam's President Nguyen Van Thieu from October 1967 to 21 April 1975. In one of the most enduring images of the Vietnam War, communist tanks stormed the city on 30 April 1975 and crashed through the palace's front gates (these tanks are now displayed on the front lawns). This was *the* defining moment of the fall of Saigon, resulting in reunification

Little has changed inside the Reunification Palace, which used to house the president of South Vietnam. It survives as a museum and "historical relic".

District 1 street food.

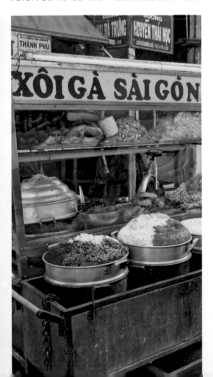

⊙ WHAT'S IN A NAME?

When the newly formed Socialist Republic of Vietnam compelled Saigon to take the name of Ho Chi Minh City in 1976, it was like rubbing salt into the wounds of its inhabitants. Today, most locals still defiantly refer to their city as Saigon as a matter of principle (they also prefer to call themselves Saigonese). At the very least, people use the name Saigon for downtown District 1, one of the first sectors of the city to be built and the original French Quarter. One reason might be that 'Saigon' is just so much easier to say than 'Thanh Pho Ho Chi Minh', the full Vietnamese name for the metropolis.

Although great measures have been taken – even to this day – to extinguish the Saigon name in most official capacities (some publications, for example, are not allowed to use the Saigon title), it is still, confusingly, allowed to be used in some forms: notably, the river winding its way around the city remains Saigon River, the main city newspaper is the *Saigon Times* and the city's state-owned tour company is Saigontourist (www.saigon-tourist.com). Place names like Saigon Zoo, Port of Saigon and Saigon Railway Station are still in use, and the three-letter ticket code for the city's Tan Son Nhat International Airport is SGN. No wonder visitors get confused.

and the subsequent creation of the Socialist Republic of Vietnam.

The former palace's multiple floors and nearly 100 rooms resemble a time capsule with everything left largely unchanged. The first floor houses the cabinet meeting room, used for military briefings (the 35 chairs equalling the number of the Saigon cabinet members). The president's reception rooms and private residential quarters, complete with Catholic chapel and bedrooms, are on the second floor, while the third floor features a private cinema and gambling room, plus a helipad. This and the top floor offer excellent views over **Le Duan Boulevard** (Dai Lo Le Duan).

The fascinating bomb-proof basement yields an eerie warren of tunnels and rooms, including a war command room with original war maps, a communications room and the president's combat duty bedroom. The ground floor features a photo gallery with frequent screenings of a documentary film. After a total makeover of the exhibition throughout the site in 2013, there

Notre Dame Cathedral.

are 35 red informative panels in Vietnamese, English and French allowing visits to the palace without tour guides. Directly in front, a small park offers a shaded oasis, edged by several cafés.

NOTRE DAME CATHEDRAL

Heading northeast and walking across the park, you'll come to Cong Truong Cong Xa Paris (Paris Commune Square) and one of Ho Chi Minh's most iconic landmarks, **Notre Dame ❷** or officially, Basilica of Our Lady of The Immaculate Conception (Nha Tho Duc Ba; tel: 08 3829 4822; open 5.30am–5pm; seven Masses on Sun, at 9.30am in English).

The French colonial architect Jules Bourad designed the neo-Romanesque structure to represent the glory of the French empire. Inaugurated in 1880, making it the oldest church in Vietnam, this was one of France's most ambitious projects in Indochina at the time; bricks used in the construction were shipped from Marseilles in France.

The Catholic cathedral has two main central bays and an interior that features stained-glass windows, Stations of the Cross in marble relief and Gothic vaults. A small square at the far end of the church is anchored by a white marble statue of the Virgin Mary.

GENERAL POST OFFICE

Adjacent to the cathedral, at 2 Cong Truong Cong Xa Paris, is the **General Post Office ❸** (Buu Dien Saigon; tel: 08-3824 4244; daily 6am–10pm), an impressive salmon-hued colonial-era building. Also known as Saigon Central Post Office, the city's main post office is also a tourist attraction in its own right, and certainly the loveliest place in HCMC to post a letter or postcard.

This classic colonial building, based on the design of the French architect Gustav Eiffel, appears little changed since its completion in 1891, with green wrought-iron work, handsome arched ceilings, colourful tiled floors – even old-fashioned pots of glue for stamps. The cavernous main hall, complete with over 30 service counters and old-style phone booths, is dominated by a huge portrait of Ho Chi Minh, plus two original map-murals dated 1892 and 1936. Full postal and telephone services are available here, as well as a gift shop. The post office and cathedral are hugely popular for fashion photo shoots and weddings, as both buildings provide perfect backdrops.

DONG KHOI STREET

Running about a kilometre from Le Duan Street to the Saigon River through the heart of District 1 and original French Quarter, **Dong Khoi Street** (Duong Dong Khoi) is the city's main commercial drag. This wide, tree-lined boulevard is home to shops, galleries, trendy cafés and luxury hotels. During French colonial times, this was known as the elegant Rue Catinat, the epicentre of colonial life and where the French built some of their most important buildings.

With France's departure in 1954, Catinat became Tu Do Street (Freedom Street), later notorious for its sleazy bars, clubs and massage parlours catering to American GIs seeking R&R. North Vietnamese communist tanks rolled down this street during the fall of Saigon. Following the south's "liberation" in 1975, it was renamed Dong Khoi (Popular Uprising) Street and for a time went to seed. Today, Dong Khoi and its offshoots reflect the city's accelerating economic boom, increasingly dominated by international designer boutiques and upmarket shopping malls. Yet despite its prominence, Dong Khoi Street still yields a surprisingly languid, amiable air and is eminently walkable.

MUNICIPAL THEATRE

At the junction of Le Loi and Dong Khoi streets at **Lam Son Square** (Cong Truong Lam Son) stands the **Opera House** ❹ (Nha Hat Thanh Pho; tel: 08-3823 7419; www.hbso.org.vn). It was designed by French architect Eugène Ferret, and features a grandiose, neo-classical pink facade, white classical statues and a domed entrance. It was opened in 1899 to keep the colonial French entertained. Post-1954, this became the Republic of South Vietnam's National Assembly headquarters for the next two decades. Following reunification, the authorities returned it to its municipal theatre function. Restored to its former glory to celebrate the city's 300th anniversary in 1998, it received a complete face-lift, modern lighting and sound systems, a rotating stage and an 800-seater hall. Today, it presents classical music and dance performances as it is a seat of the Ho Chi Minh City Ballet and Symphony Orchestra.

OLD-WORLD HOTELS

Lam Son Square is sandwiched between two historic hotels. The first is the **Hôtel Continental** (http://conti

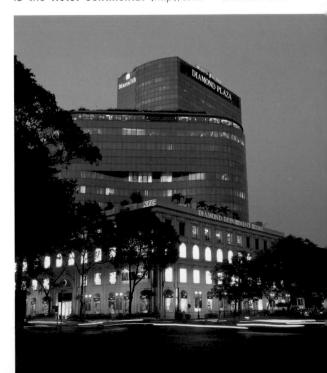

Diamond Plaza.

THE FRENCH FACTOR

The French may have gone from Ho Chi Minh City but they left behind some elegant colonial architecture and a café culture that encapsulates its spirit.

Among the fascinating melange of architectural influences, it's the mark of the French that is most evident – the legacy of nearly a century of colonial rule in Indochina. Many parts of HCMC, especially central District 1, still bear the French architectural stamp.

When Saigon was declared the capital of French Cochinchina in the 1860s, the French filled in the ancient canals, drained the marshlands and reclaimed land. They then created leafy parks, built wide, tree-lined boulevards and introduced steam-powered trams. Impressive new edifices were constructed to serve the city's administrative role and to accommodate its burgeoning expatriates. Grandiose public buildings included hotels like The Majestic (one of Southeast Asia's classic colonial hotels), the GPO, the Cochinchina Governor's Palace (now HCMC Museum), Hôtel de Ville (People's Committee Building) and Ben Thanh Market (known then as Les Halles Centrales),

Colonial buildings bear witness to French influence on the city.

among others. Norodom Boulevard (now Le Duan) developed as – and still is – a diplomatic and residential enclave with rows of pastel-hued villas. This French-designed quarter evolved as the playground of the French during Indochina: cafés and bars, boutiques, the Opera House and Botanical Gardens were established to keep the French amused. Cultivated by them into a mini-French metropolis, Saigon was christened the "Paris of the Orient".

Other French influences go deeper than bricks and mortar. French missionaries were responsible for the spread of Catholicism in the country, and a number of Catholic churches, including Saigon's own Notre Dame, were built in Saigon. It was a French Jesuit priest, Alexandre de Rhodes, who came up with the idea to translate the Vietnamese into its Romanised form, Quoc Ngu, in the 17th century. It was first used by the Catholic Church and the colonial regime's administration before it gradually replaced two Chinese systems of writing at the beginning of 20th century. Although only some 7 million of Vietnam's 92.7 million population are Catholics today, the country still has the largest Catholic population in Southeast Asia after the Philippines.

The Westernised idea of drinking coffee and socialising in sidewalk cafés was introduced by the French – and embraced wholeheartedly by locals. Cafés are found all over town, fuelled by the Vietnamese love of coffee (*ca phe*) and *tête-à-tête*.

Naturellement, the French also left their hallmark on local cuisine: baguettes, pâtés, pastries, *jambon* (ham) and yoghurt are now part of daily life. The national dish *pho* (rice noodle soup with slices of beef) allegedly originated from the Gallic dish *pot-au-feu*. The French also successfully introduced European produce like cauliflowers, artichokes, berries and roses, in the cool-climate highland region of Dalat – itself founded by a Frenchman, Alexandre Yersin.

Other notable contributions include the Pasteur Institute, a foundation dedicated to the research of viruses, vaccination and bacteria. Inaugurated in 1891 and named after its founder, Saigon hosted the first foreign Pasteur Institute, initiating an international network. The Fine Arts University (formerly L'Ecole de Dessin; http://hcmufa.edu.vn) was established in 1913 by two Frenchmen and continues today in the same role.

entalsaigon.com), built in 1880. In the early 20th century, this was where the cream of French high society gathered. The hotel was also a meeting point for a motley assortment of diplomats and spies, high-society people and journalists. During World War II, the Continental was dubbed "Radio Catinat", as many American press corps had their bureaux operating here. In the 1950s, British novelist Graham Greene resided in Room 214, where he wrote much of *The Quiet American*, the hotel and its surrounds finding their way onto the pages of Greene's acclaimed book.

On the opposite side is the glitzy five-star **Caravelle Hotel** (www.caravellehotel. com). The hotel's older 10-storey wing was home to the offices of the Associated Press, NBC, CBS, the *New York Times* and the *Washington Post* during the Vietnam War. The rooftop bar (now the Saigon Saigon Bar) was a favourite watering hole for many war correspondents, some recording the action without ever vacating their bar stools.

Further south down Dong Khoi Street, at the junction of the waterfront Ton Duc Thang Street, stands the aptly named **Majestic Hotel** (www.majestic saigon.com.vn). Built in 1925 by the French, the Majestic is one of Southeast Asia's classic colonial hotels. Despite several extensive renovations and now state-run, the elegant building still radiates an old-world colonial charm, with its Art Deco stained-glass windows, a grand, marbled lobby with crystal chandeliers, and its helpful dapper bellboys. The rooftop bars afford wonderful views of the Saigon River.

PEOPLE'S COMMITTEE BUILDING

If the Reunification Palace symbolises the former South Vietnam regime, then the **People's Committee Building** ❺ (UBND Thanh Pho), at the northern end of Nguyen Hue Street, is one of the strongest symbols of colonial rule. The Hôtel de Ville was completed in 1908, after 16 years of ferment over its structure and style. Its Baroque yellow-and-white facade encloses an equally ornate interior of crystal chandeliers and wall-sized murals. Now the headquarters of the HCMC People's

The General Post Office.

⊙ Tip

Crossing the road in HCMC is not for the faint-hearted. The sheer amount of traffic, particularly the 7.6 million motorbikes, can be daunting, but if you wait for traffic to stop, you could be kerb-side all day. The trick is to take a deep breath, walk out slowly, constantly looking left and right, and continue walking across (don't suddenly freeze), and the traffic will generally flow around you. Take care on the pavements – motorbikes sometimes ride up here too.

The historic Rex Hotel.

Committee, visitors are not permitted inside. One of the city's loveliest landmarks, the building is beautifully illuminated at night.

REX HOTEL

Situated on Nguyen Hue Street and overlooking both plazas, the legendary **Rex Hotel** (Khach San Rex, www.rexhotelvietnam.com) is part of Saigon history. Originally a French garage and American Cultural Centre, it became headquarters for the US Information Service and home to billeted US servicemen during the Vietnam War. The US military also hosted daily press briefings here, which came to be known as the "Five o'Clock Follies". The building only opened as a hotel in 1976, after reunification.

BITEXCO FINANCIAL TOWER (SAIGON SKYDECK)

HCMC's loftiest building is a stunning, 68-storey creation, designed to resemble a lotus bud. The **Saigon Skydeck** ❻ (36 Ho Tung Mau; tel: 08-3915 6156; daily 9.30am–9.30pm; www.bitexcofinancialtower.

com), Vietnam's third-tallest structure after Hanoi's Landmark 72 Tower and Lotte Center, gives panoramic views and features a touch-screen monitor that allows visitors to call up information on major landmarks. The helicopter pad that juts out 22 metres/yds on the 52nd floor includes a bar and restaurant. A lift whisks visitors up at a rate of 7 metres (23ft) per second. A small exhibition explains how the tower was constructed using 6,000 individually cut glass panels.

HO CHI MINH CITY MUSEUM

One block west of the People's Committee Building, at 65 Ly Tu Trong Street, is the **Ho Chi Minh City Museum** ❼ (Bao Tang Thanh Pho Ho Chi Minh; tel: 08-3829 9741; www.HCMC-museum.edu.vn; daily 7.30am–6pm). The neoclassical exterior is impressive, completed in 1890 and cleverly blending Western and oriental styles. Its faded interiors feature high ceilings, a sweeping staircase and chandeliers.

Spread over two floors, the displays are slightly less appealing but include handicrafts and an exhibition of southern beliefs and wedding rituals. The collection of war items upstairs with exhibits such as an old Vespa scooter and an accordion and banjo used to play propaganda songs, is more interesting. Underneath is a network of reinforced bunkers, built by Ngo in 1962, though they are not open to the public. The underground shelter comprises six rooms with 1-metre (3ft-thick walls, including a living room and communications centre. Ngo and his brother hid down here during a coup in November 1963, before fleeing to Cholon. At the rear of the museum is a collection of classic cars.

To the northwest of the museum, the mustard-yellow building on Nam Ky Khoi Nghia Street is the **City People's Court** (Toa An Nhan Dan Thanh Pho; www.tand.hochiminhcity.gov.vn, Vietnamese only), another impressive remnant of colonial-style architecture.

WEST OF DISTRICT 1

WAR REMNANTS MUSEUM

Two blocks north of the Reunification Palace at 28 Vo Van Tan Street is the **War Remnants Museum** ❽ (Bao Tang Chung Tich Chien Tranh; tel: 08-3930 5587; daily 7.30am–noon and 1.30–5pm; http://warremnantsmuseum.com or www.baotangchungtichchientranh.vn). A visit here is a sobering reminder of the heavy toll of war. Occupying the former US Information Agency, this was hurriedly opened as the Museum of American War Crimes after reunification in 1975. Its controversial name was changed in 1997 as part of conditions dictated by the US government over trade pacts.

A series of numbered exhibition halls displays the horrors of the French and American wars; these include graphic photographs, bell jars of deformed foetuses showing the effects of US-sprayed chemical defoliants, plus a guillotine used by the French and mock-up of the notorious "tiger cages". The poignant Requiem Hall features a large collection of photos taken by 134 photojournalists from 11 nations, themselves killed during both conflicts, and shows a rare, non-North Vietnamese war perspective. Although the exhibits are distressing to see, this is one of the city's biggest tourist attractions.

GOLDEN DRAGON WATER PUPPET THEATRE

Moving south, one block west of the Reunification Palace at 55B Nguyen Thi Minh Khai Street is the **Golden Dragon Water Puppet Theatre** ❾ (Nha Hat Mua Roi Nuoc Rong Vang; tel: 08-3930 2196; daily performance 5pm, 6.30pm and 8.30pm). Water puppetry *(Mua Roi Nuoc)* is unique to northern Vietnam's Red River Delta – where rice farmers for centuries practised this recreational art form in flooded rice paddies. Wooden puppets manipulated by bamboo sticks hidden beneath the water play out original stories based on folk tales and daily events, accompanied by traditional Vietnamese music.

Exhibit in the Ho Chi Minh City Museum.

Classical and modern styles: the Municipal Theatre, with the Caravelle Hotel on the right.

Hindu religious image at the Sri Mariamman Temple. The temple caters to the city's small Tamil population, but is also used by local Vietnamese.

Seeking blessings at Sri Mariamman Hindu Temple.

SRI MARIAMMAN HINDU TEMPLE

Several blocks southwest from the museum is the **Sri Mariamman Hindu Temple** (daily 7am–7pm) at 45 Truong Dinh Street. The temple caters to the city's small population of Hindu Tamils and has a stunning multi-tiered *gopuram* (ornate tower) over the main entrance. Built in the late 19th century, the ground-floor open complex has statues of the Hindu gods Mariamman, Maduraiveeran and Pechiamman in the sanctuaries. The Hindu temple is also frequented by a number of ethnic Vietnamese – the influence of local customs and practices apparent in the use of incense sticks placed in Chinese-style bronze urns.

BEN THANH MARKET

A few blocks southeast, at the intersection of Ham Nghi, Le Loi, Le Lai and Tran Hung Dao streets, is **Ben Thanh Market** (Cho Ben Thanh; daily 6am–6pm; www.ben-thanh-market. com). Opened in 1914 by the French and covering 11,000 sq metres (118,400 sq ft), its distinctive pill-box-style clock over the main entrance tower on Le Loi Street has iconic status. Under one roof is practically every conceivable product sold at countless stalls, located along alleys leading off a main central aisle. The market is busy but not so crowded that it's uncomfortable.

Predominantly still a market for locals, selling basic necessities like household wares, fabrics and foodstuffs, Ben Thanh is increasingly geared towards the lucrative tourist market, with some specialist goods on sale. Situated at the rear are food and drink stalls, plus an open-air fresh produce market.

Once the main market shuts, the **Ben Thanh Night Market** springs into action, operating until late at night along the streets immediately surrounding the building. The main attraction is the open-air makeshift food stalls serving authentic – and cheap – Vietnamese fare.

HO CHI MINH CITY FINE ARTS MUSEUM

On the other side of the intersection, at 97A Pho Duc Chinh Street, is the

Ho Chi Minh City Fine Arts Museum

⑫ (Bao Tang My Thuat Thanh Pho Ho Chi Minh; tel: 08-3829 4441; Tue–Sun 9am–5pm). Although the museum has displays of some interesting Vietnamese art, this is somewhat of a disappointment and a poor cousin to the infinitely superior Fine Arts Museum in Hanoi. Housed in a vast space, the actual collection is quite small and poorly displayed.

More riveting is the building that houses the museum. A fine example of colonial architecture, the building was constructed in the early 20th century as the residence of a Chinese businessman. It bears typical Asian-European characteristics of the era, and the original Art Deco stained-glass windows and antique elevator are still in place.

LE CONG KIEU STREET

Across from the HCMC Fine Arts Museum, narrow **Le Cong Kieu Street** (Duong Le Cong Kieu) has long been known as "Antique Street". One of the city's most atmospheric quarters, the row of narrow, open-fronted dwellings along this small stretch is devoted to selling a chaotic jumble of Asian and colonial-era bric-a-brac, furniture and home decor.

Formerly Rue Reims, this quiet residential street was home to Saigon's small Arab community, most of whom fled when the communists invaded in 1975. Today, the houses have been turned into shops that sell oriental mother-of-pearl mahogany chests, Art Deco bronze lamps, old *piastre* coins and black-and-white photographs. It used to be antique-hunting grounds, but not anymore: most goods today are massproduced reproductions.

DAN SINH MARKET

A few blocks southwest, on the corner of Yersin and Nguyen Cong Tru streets is **Dan Sinh Market** **⑬** (Cho Dan Sinh; daily 7am–6pm), also known as the "War Surplus Market" for obvious reasons. The back of this run-down building houses several stalls selling a vast jumble of armed forces clothing and goods, as well as wartime

The clock tower is a well-known feature of the bustling Ben Thanh Market.

Military hardware at the War Remnants Museum.

⊙ Tip

The signs at Ben Thanh Market say "fixed prices". Don't believe a word of it: always try to barter for a better price and you could easily come away with a bargain. If you aren't getting anywhere, simply walk away. If your price is anywhere near the one the trader wants, he or she will soon call you back and strike a deal.

Ben Thanh Market at night.

memorabilia. While some stock is genuine vintage, most is new surplus or massproduced stuff.

HO CHI MINH MUSEUM

The striking **Ho Chi Minh Museum** ⑭ (Bao Tang Ho Chi Minh; tel: 08-3845 5435; Tue–Sun 8–11.30am and 2–4.30pm) is easily visible just across the bridge in **District 4**, where Ben Nghe Canal (Rach Ben Nghe) enters the Saigon River. Oriental dragons slithering across the rooftop explain its alternative name, **Dragon House** (Nha Rong). One of the first buildings constructed by the French in Cochinchina in 1863, this was originally the head office of a French shipping company. It was from this wharf that Ho Chi Minh, using his real name, Nguyen Tat Thanh, left Vietnam in 1911 on a French merchant ship for 30 years of self-imposed exile. There are over two floors of photographs, documents, artefacts and Ho's personal items. You can even buy a Ho Chi Minh bust at the museum shop. The large, airy building, set in pleasant riverside gardens, offers wonderful river views and cooling breezes.

NORTHEAST OF DISTRICT 1

FORMER US EMBASSY

Head eastwards from Notre Dame Cathedral to 4 Le Duan Boulevard, the site of the **US Consulate**, which was built over the **former US Embassy**, a highly symbolic building of the US involvement in Vietnam. During the 1968 Tet Offensive, in an event marking a turning point in the war, Viet Cong guerrillas broke into the embassy grounds where a running battle ensued for several hours. The building had another starring role seven years later: on 30 April 1975, as North Vietnamese communist troops advanced on Saigon, the US ambassador and remaining troops were airlifted from the rooftop by helicopter. In 1999, the embassy was pulled down to make way for the new US Consulate – viewed as another step in eradicating the physical evidence of more turbulent times.

MUSEUM OF VIETNAMESE HISTORY

At the end of Le Duan Street, along Nguyen Binh Khiem Street, is the **Museum of Vietnamese History** ⑮ (Bao Tang Lich Su; tel: 08-3829 8146; http://baotanglichsuvn.com; Tue–Sun 8–11.30am and 1.30–5pm), housed in another stunning example of French-Chinese hybrid architecture, with a distinctive pagoda-style roof. Formerly the Musée Blanchard de la Brosse under French rule, the museum today gives an excellent introduction to Vietnamese history and culture from prehistory to the founding of the Democratic Republic in 1945.

Exhibits are displayed in a series of numbered rooms in historical sequence starting on the ground floor and covering relics, artefacts, dioramas, photographs and art-works. Highlights include outdoor displays of 18th- and 19th-century cannons, a 2,500-year-old bronze drum, ancient sandstone sculptures from the Champa and Cambodian civilisations and the preserved mummy of a woman who is thought to have died in 1860.

SAIGON ZOO AND BOTANICAL GARDENS

Adjoining the museum are the expansive grounds of **Saigon Zoo and Botanical Gardens** ⑯ (Thao Cam Vien; tel: 08-3829 1425; www.saigonzoo.net; daily 7am–6pm). Established in 1864 by two Frenchmen for the benefit of the colonials, the shady landscaped gardens are vast. The Zoo and Botanical Gardens house some 800 specimens from 120 species (many endangered), as well as 2,000 trees, and various cactus, orchid and bonsai plants. Among the celebrity animals on show are tigers, Asian elephants, giraffes and leopards, though animal-lovers may feel their enclosures are rather small and basic. Try to visit during animal feeding times (usually 3–5pm) and special events, like weekend elephant shows. A children's zoo features goats, sheep and hippos.

Dan Sinh Market is well worth a visit even if you are not intending to buy anything.

Ho Chi Minh City Fine Arts Museum.

The Ho Chi Minh Museum is a must-see for those wanting to find out more about the extraordinary life of Vietnam's famous founding father.

Antiques, Le Cong Kieu Street.

MILITARY MUSEUM

Close by the Botanical Gardens is the rather bare **Military Museum** (Bao Tang Quan Doi; 2 L St; Tue–Sun 7.30–11am and 1.30–4.30pm; www. baotanghochiminh-nr.vn). However, it is worth dropping by to see the collection of war-related items in its front yard. These include anti-aircraft guns, armoured vehicles and the mangled remains of US military hardware.

JADE EMPEROR PAGODA

One of the city's most colourful and captivating places of worship is the **Jade Emperor Pagoda** ⑰ (Chua Ngoc Hoang; daily 8am–5pm; free), located on Mai Thi Luu Street, on the northern fringes of District 1. Built in 1909 by Cantonese Buddhists who settled in Saigon, its unique interior architectural style is heavily influenced by southern Chinese elements. A dense fog of smoke from spiral incense coils suspended from the rafters envelops a fascinating array of weird and wonderful elaborate statues – some Buddhist, others Taoist-inspired. The ornately robed Jade Emperor surveys the main sanctuary from his central altar, while to his right, the triple-headed, 18-armed statue of Phat Mau Chau De, mother of the Buddhas of the Middle, North, East, West and South, looks out in three directions from her encasement. Left of the Jade Emperor's chamber, the Hall of Ten Hells features intricately carved wood reliefs portraying the fate awaiting those sentenced to the diverse tortures found in the 10 levels of hell.

WEST TO DISTRICT 3

VINH NGHIEM PAGODA

Heading west to **District 3**, the **Vinh Nghiem Pagoda** ⑱ (Chua Vinh Nghiem; http://vinhnghiemvn.com; daily 8am–5pm) on Nam Ky Khoi Nghia Street opened in 1971, and is one of the city's newest pagodas – and also the largest. Built with aid from the JapanVietnam Friendship Association, this striking Buddhist pagoda bears distinct Japanese and Zen elements. The large main hall is dominated by a huge golden Buddha perched on a lotus and flanked by disciples. Behind are altars consecrated to the dead, where funerary tablets and their corresponding photographs are placed for the first 100 days after their deaths.

An elevated terrace runs from the hall to a seven-storey tower containing Quan Am statues on each level. The large bell opposite was presented as a gift from Japanese Buddhists during the Vietnam War, as the embodiment of prayers for an early end to the conflict. The three-storey repository tower behind the main temple houses neatly stacked ceramic burial urns containing the ashes of deceased souls. The busy pagoda is home to numerous monks as well as a Buddhist college for nuns.

CHINATOWN (CHOLON)

About 5km (3 miles) west of downtown, HCMC's sprawling Chinatown, or Cholon, is a bustling place packed with Chinese shops and French architecture. "Cho Lon" translates as "big market", and aptly describes this endlessly buzzing maze of streets and alleyways. Ethnic Chinese (Hoa) originating from southwest China first settled here in the late 18th century. Once Cholon became entrenched as a successful trading area, Chinese immigrants arrived in droves, reaching a peak during the early 20th century. Today there are half a million Hoa here, making it the largest Chinese community in Vietnam.

Evolving as a separate municipality, Cholon was officially established as a Chinese community in 1879 by the French governor of Cochinchina. Despite thousands of Chinese fleeing Vietnam after 1975, exacerbated by the country's increased tensions with China, over half a million Hoa still reside here – the largest Chinese community in Vietnam. With the city's boundaries being constantly expanded, Cholon now spills over into Districts 6, 10 and 11.

Cholon, which is largely contained within District 5, is a great place simply to wander around, taking in the sights and smells, particularly along Trieu Quang Phuc Street, where all manner of herbs are sold. As with all of HCMC, though, development is coming. Some of the historical Chinese shophouses and colonial edifices are being demolished or have fallen into disrepair. The once atmospheric canal where trading and cargo boats sailed in is being widened, and characterless modern buildings are appearing. Despite such development, Cholon is still a fascinating and authentic working and living area, offering the visitor bustling markets and commerce, excellent Chinese food and richly decorated Chinese temples and pagodas (the latter are noticeably different from their Vietnamese counterparts). Listen out for the blaring Mandarin pop coming from shops and look out for the stores selling all manner of colourful ritualistic items. There are a handful of three-star hotels but most choose to make it a half-day trip from District 1.

A bust of Ho Chi Minh on display at the Museum of Vietnamese History.

Ho Chi Minh Museum.

Shophouses in Cholon have a unique blend of French and Chinese Baroque architecture.

The Golden Dragon Water Puppet Theatre.

Eating options include a handful of bakeries, offering everything from dim sum to custard tarts. Trung Nguyen Café (www.trungnguyen.com.vn) is the perfect place to sip their fantastic iced coffees and people-watch. The main points of interest in Cholon are found principally in the southwest.

BINH TAY MARKET

Binh Tay Market ⑲ (Cho Binh Tay; daily 6am–7.30pm) at Thap Muoi Street is Cholon's biggest market and epitomises its vibrant commercialism.

Built in 1928, its exterior is a fine example of early 20th-century Chinese-influenced French architecture: oriental-style multi-tiered roofs stalked by serpentine dragons blend with distinctive French mustard-yellow walls and a clock tower with four faces.

Although predominantly a wholesale market, Binh Tay is far less commercialised than Ben Thanh Market and thus offers a more authentic cultural experience. Spread over a vast 17,000 sq metres (183,000 sq ft) on two levels, the market is divided into organised sections, with more than 2,300 stalls. Not surprisingly, its goods have a more Chinese leaning than other city markets, with stalls crammed with joss sticks, herbs and dried goods used for traditional Chinese medicine and an array of Chinese food stalls. In the middle of the ground floor is a statue of the market's founder, Quach Dam.

CHA TAM CHURCH

Several blocks northeast of the market, at 25 Hoc Lac Street, is the Catholic **Cha Tam Church** ⑳ (Nha Tho Phanxico Xavie; www.chatamvn.com; daily 7am–6pm). A brilliant example of architectural styles, it initially looks French in style, but there is a pagoda-style entrance gate and Chinese characters around the stained-glass windows and altar crucifix. Cha Tam is infamous as the place where the Catholic president of South Vietnam, Ngo Dinh Diem, and his brother took refuge on 1 November 1963 after fleeing Gia Long Palace during a coup sanctioned by the US government. Having surrendered, they were

⊘ ACTIVITIES FOR CHILDREN

Ho Chi Minh City is particularly good for those travelling with children. The range of activities here will keep even the fussiest youngster entertained. In the heart of the city, **Saigon Skydeck** (see page 288) gives incredible views from the 49th floor of the new Bitexco building, and has interactive features to occupy young fingers. The **Golden Dragon Water Puppet Theatre** (see page 289) is a great 50-minute spectacle near the Reunification Palace, while **Saigon Zoo and Botanical Gardens**, with giraffe-feeding and a children's zoo among the highlights, is a good way to spend an afternoon. Also in town is **Diamond Superbowl** (34 Le Duan Street; http://diamondplaza.com.vn; daily 9.30am–10pm) on the fourth floor of the Diamond Plaza shopping centre. It has computerised scoring and some fluorescent lanes. Outside of the city, **Dam Sen Park** (see page 299) has a host of rides and activities, including a roller-coaster, monorail and dinosaur park, while **Dam Sen Water Park** has more than a dozen rides designed to soak and amuse. About an hour outside HCMC is **Suoi Tien** (www.suoi-tien.com), a US$150 million theme park. Among the 50-plus attractions on this 105-hectare (250-acre) site are a roller-coaster, cinemas, crocodile kingdom, bumper cars, the Space Drop Tower and an array of mythical statues.

assassinated on their way to central Saigon. A small plaque on a rear pew indicates where Ngo awaited his fate before being escorted away.

The adjacent **Tran Hung Dao Street** is the main artery linking Cholon to the city centre. This street's western section is known as "garment district" due to its continuous succession of open-sided garment workshops and wholesale warehouses stacked with rolls of textiles.

QUAN AM PAGODA

Heading east along Tran Hung Dao Street and then north along Luong Nhu Hoc Street takes you to **Quan Am Pagoda** ㉑ (Chua On Lang or Chua Quan Am; daily 8am–5pm), located on Lao Tu Street. This is one of the city's most stunning pagodas. Built in 1740 by Chinese Fukien immigrants, it's also probably the oldest.

Dedicated to the Goddess of Mercy (Quan Am), not surprisingly, the two statues of Quan Am dominate. Many of the 16 deities that are worshipped here are festooned with flashing fairy lights in the large open courtyard area at the back. Constantly busy with worshippers, the burning votive paper offerings and hanging spiral incense coils result in a permanent smoky haze.

The pagoda is a heady riot of red and gold, with decorative details and striking relief wall murals. The show-stopper is the entrance; its ridged roof and wall edged with exquisite ornamental glazed ceramic figurines and sculptures. Opposite the pagoda is a small pond with terrapins and fish.

THIEN HAU PAGODA

South along Nguyen Trai Street at No. 710 is **Thien Hau Pagoda** ㉒ (Hoi Quan Tue Thanh; daily 8am–4.30pm; free), one of Cholon's most important pagodas. Cantonese immigrants established this temple-pagoda in 1760, dedicating it to Thien Hau (Tin Hau), the Goddess Protector of Seafarers,

and giving thanks for a safe passage across the perilous South China Sea. The entrance is dark and imposing but beyond this the second open-air courtyard has three statues of Thien Hau standing one behind the other. To the left is a bed with feather-like fans to keep her cool.

A festival in Thien Hau's honour is held here in March, on the 23rd day of the lunar calendar. Thien Hau is also known as the **Women's Pagoda** (Chua Ba) because local women make offerings and prayers to Me Sanh, the Goddess of Fertility, and Long Mau, the Goddess of Mothers and Babies, statues of whom are displayed on other altars.

TAM SON TEMPLE

Diagonally across from Thien Hau, at 118 Trieu Quang Phuc Street, is the **Tam Son Temple** ㉓ (Hoi Quan Tam Son; daily 8am–5pm). Built by Fukien migrants in the 19th century, this temple is less elaborate in terms of architecture and sees fewer tourists. Instead, the temple is hectic with a

Tip

The Ho Chi Minh City Association for Victims of Agent Orange has an office at 331 Trung Hung Dao Street in Cholon. There is a simple, yet disturbing, display of images showing the effects the chemical weapon had on people, with captions in English. More photographs show how some offer help – if you wish to contribute as well, donations are welcome.

Vinh Nghiem Pagoda.

⊘ Eat

Cholon (District 5) offers excellent authentic Chinese food, but restaurants are not generally geared to tourists. Hardly any English is spoken by staff, and menus are often written in Chinese. That said, they are well worth exploring – best if you can take a guide with you. Chinese food outlets are everywhere in Cholon, but reliable introductions are food stalls in covered markets like Binh Tay (see page 296), plus restaurants in large shopping centres.

Spiral coils of incense at Quan Am Pagoda.

constant flow of women in search of blessings to improve their chances of conceiving children. The deities worshipped here include Me Sanh, Quan Cong and Thien Hau.

ONG PAGODA

Back on Nguyen Trai Street at No. 678 is Thien Hau Pagoda's counterpart, **Ong Pagoda** (Chua Ong Nghia An; daily 8am–5pm), also known as the Men's Pagoda. An intricate carved wooden boat stands over its entrance and a statue of Quan Cong (a famous Chinese military general) with a ruddy face, long black beard and ornate regalia presides over the main altar, flanking General Chau and the mandarin called Quan Binh.

CHOLON JAMIAL MOSQUE

The minimalist blue-and-white **Cholon Jamial Mosque** (Thanh Duong Hoi Giao Cholon; daily 8am–5pm), nearby at 641 Nguyen Trai Street, sits in sharp contrast with the area's highly decorative Chinese pagodas and temples. It was built by Tamil

Muslims, most of whom fled the country around 1975.

HAI THUONG LAN ONG STREET

Head south down Trieu Quang Phuc Street to get to **Hai Thuong Lan Ong Street** ㉔, or "Medicine Street". This lengthy street is named in honour of Lan Ong, an 18th-century physician, mandarin and master of Vietnamese herbal medical practice. Shops specialising in traditional Chinese and Vietnamese medicine have long proliferated here; nowadays they are mostly located in a concentrated hub in the eastern section of the street, around the intersection with Trieu Quang Phuc Street. From here, the shops run along both sides of Hai Thuong Lan Ong Street, especially between Nos 43–61 and opposite, Nos 70–108 and 134–142.

These old, open-fronted shophouses, some of which date back to French colonial times, are stocked full of weird concoctions purported to cure all sorts of ailments. Huge hessian sacks overflow with odorous fungi, strange dried plants and gnarled roots spill out onto the pavements, and dried sea horses are packed into plastic bags. Unfortunately, also for sale are preserved animal parts, like powdered rhino horn and ivory, flagons of coiled snakes and sharks' fins.

NORTH OF CHOLON

GIAC VIEN PAGODA

From Cholon head north to District 11, where a bright red-and-yellow entrance gate at 247 Lac Long Quan Street will lead you down a long alley to the **Giac Vien Pagoda** ㉕ (Chua Giac Vien; daily 8am–5pm). Built in 1803, Giac Vien was previously known as Earth Pit Pagoda (Chua Ho Dat), due to the vast amounts of earth required to fill the site before the pagoda – said to be frequented by Emperor Gia Long of the Nguyen dynasty – could be constructed.

Within its dimly lit and cluttered interiors enveloped in joss-stick haze are 153 beautifully carved wooden statues, with many Buddhist and Taoist deities located on the multi-tiered altar in the main sanctuary. The front hall has rows of old dark-wood tables, flanked by funerary tablets and time-worn photographs of the deceased. Monks here are not the only residents; bats have made the wooden rafters their home. As it is quite far removed from the city centre, about 6km (4 miles) away, the pagoda has a refreshingly tranquil feel and does not see many tourists.

DAM SEN PARK AND WATER PARK

Bordering Giac Vien Pagoda with two entrances nearby (319 Lac Long Quan Street and 3 Hoa Binh Street) lies the enormous **Dam Sen Park** ㉖ (tel: 08-3963 4963; daily 9am–9pm). One of the largest and most modern theme parks in Vietnam, it covers 50 hectares (124 acres) of landscaped parkland and offers an array of attractions for families, including a haunted castle, 3-D and 4-D cinemas, roller-coaster, Ferris wheel and several other theme-park rides. There is also a boating lake, crocodile farm, bird and animal enclosure, plus an "explore the

The Cha Tam Church was used as a hiding place by Ngo Dinh Diem, former president of South Vietnam.

Binh Tay Market in Cholon.

○ **Tip**

Tourists get followed in HCMC – there is just no avoiding it. Taxi drivers, postcard sellers, massage ladies all want your attention. A firm but polite refusal usually does the trick.

jungle" section. Visitors get around by mini-electric cars and monorail. It isn't quite Disneyland, but it is a good option if travelling with children. It has been a huge hit with the locals since its opening in 1999. For Vietnamese middle-class families, it represents the epitome of modern recreational activity.

Part of the sprawling grounds is given over to **Dam Sen Water Park** (tel: 08-3858 8418; www.damsenwater park.com.vn; Mon–Sat 9am–6pm, Sun 8.30am–6pm; access at a separate main entrance next to Dam Sen Park). It offers a multitude of water-based fun rides and slides, including the Boomerang, Wild River, Kamikaze Ride, and Space Bowl Slide. Gentler options for younger children include the Wave Pool and Wandering River. Weekends at both parks are packed, and they offer a good chance to see Vietnamese families at play.

GIAC LAM PAGODA

Heading north into Tan Binh District, about 7km (4 miles) from the downtown area at 118 Lac Long Quan Street, is **Giac Lam Pagoda** ㉗ (Chua Giac Lam; daily 8am–5pm). It is recognised as the city's second-oldest pagoda and is an important historical site. Built in 1744 (and reconstructed in 1909), Giac Lam's design reflects the typical architectural style of pagodas in south Vietnam. The large complex incorporates several sections, including monks' living and study quarters. Although larger than Giac Vien (see page 299) and receiving more visitors, there are many similarities between the two mustard-hued pagodas.

Giac Lam is supported by 98 carved ironwood pillars, inscribed with gilded *Nom* characters, an ancient Vietnamese script based on Chinese ideograms. Amongst its dark, well-worn interiors are around more than 100 statues, some over 250 years old. The large front hall, or Altar of Patriarchs, is filled with ancestral altars, portraits of monks from previous generations and rows of funerary tablets.

A small adjoining courtyard is edged by exquisite wall decorations and roof

A recreation of an apothecary's shop at the Museum of Vietnamese Traditional Medicine.

edges studded with blue-and-white porcelain saucers – these contrast with gruesome paintings of the 10 Buddhist images of hell. The main sanctuary at the opposite end houses beautifully carved, gilded wooden statues of the Buddha, reincarnations of the Buddha as well as judges and guardians of hell. The 49 oil lamps balanced on a tree-shaped wooden frame symbolise the 49 days the Sakyamuni Buddha meditated under the Bodhi tree to attain enlightenment.

The extensive grounds feature several tombs of monks and a seven-storey tower, Bao Thap Xa Loi, which can be climbed for excellent views of the city.

MUSEUM OF VIETNAMESE TRADITIONAL MEDICINE

Heading east back towards the city centre, at 41 Hoang Du Khuong Street in District 10, is the **Museum of Vietnamese Traditional Medicine** ㉘ (Bao Tang; tel: 08-3864 2430; www.fitomuseum.com. vn; daily 8.30am–5pm). The city's newest museum, it is a refreshing alternative to

the war and Ho Chi Minh-themed offerings elsewhere. The privately owned enterprise was founded in 2007 by FITO, a Vietnamese manufacturer of traditional medicinal products. The building alone is worth seeing as it's a remarkable replica of a traditional northern house, complete with dark-wood interiors and authentic furnishings.

Ranged over six floors and 18 exhibition rooms, the origins and chronology of time-honoured traditional Vietnamese medicine are explained. Meticulously displayed and labelled in English, there are around 3,000 items sourced by the owner – many dating back centuries – including ancient Vietnamese *Nom* script books and encyclopaedias of traditional Vietnamese medicine, plus various implements used for the preparation and storage of medicines, such as stone pestle-and-mortars and foot-powered grinding machines. Life-size dioramas include a 19thcentury Chinese-style medicine shop. The free guided tour and short introductory film will take about 45 minutes to complete.

◉ Tip

Ho Chi Minh City has two distinct seasons: the dry season, running from November/December to April/May, and the rainy season through the remainder of the year. During the latter, there are frequent heavy downpours (usually in the afternoon), so it's worth carrying a raincoat or umbrella at all times. Highest temperatures occur in April at the end of the dry season.

Thien Hau Pagoda.

Cao Dai followers at the temple in Tay Ninh.

AROUND HO CHI MINH CITY

There are numerous interesting sights within striking distance of Ho Chi Minh City. Pick from the Cu Chi tunnels, the gaudy Cao Dai Church, a national park and the beaches at Vung Tau, Mui Ne and Con Son Island.

The area surrounding **Ho Chi Minh City ❶** encompasses a diverse landscape. To the northwest are the flat plains that contain the tunnels of Cu Chi and the town of Tay Ninh, the birthplace of the Cao Dai cult. Northeast is the lush expanse of forest designated as Cat Tien National Park, while the coastline to the east is lined with sandy beaches extending from Vung Tau through Phan Thiet and on to the mountains that overlook Ca Na Beach. The Cham towers near Phan Thiet represent the southern reaches of the ancient Champa kingdom, with other areas east of Ho Chi Minh City once controlled by the Khmer and ancient Funan empire (in Vietnam referred to as "Oc Eo").

Religious diversity (Cao Dai, Muslim Cham and whale-worshipping fishermen), the military history of Cu Chi and the beach resorts of Mui Ne and Con Son Island (and, to a lesser extent, Vung Tau) are the main highlights of the area.

CU CHI TUNNELS

Located 70km (44 miles) to the northwest of Ho Chi Minh City is **Cu Chi ❷** (daily 7am–5pm; http://diadaocuchi. business.site), famous for its extensive network of underground tunnels. The tunnels were first used by the Viet Minh against the French in the 1940s, and

Military tank, Cu Chi tunnels.

later became hideouts for the Viet Cong, who reportedly extended the labyrinthine network until it reached beneath the Mekong Delta headquarters of the US Army's 25th Division.

From these hiding places, the Viet Cong were able to spring devastating surprise attacks on their enemies. In fact, by the mid-1960s, it is believed that over 200km (124 miles) of tunnels laced the region around Cu Chi. Located at the end of the Ho Chi Minh Trail, and straddling both Highway 1 and the Saigon River (both heading to

ⓞ Main Attractions
Cu Chi Tunnels
Cao Dai Great Temple
Vung Tau
Cat Tien National Park
Phan Thiet
Ta Cu Mountain
Mui Ne Beach
White Sand Dunes
Con Dao Archipelago

Map on page 306

⊘ Tip

Due to the sensitive political nature of Cu Chi, you will probably receive conflicting versions of the site's history from your tour guide and from the museum film and displays.

The Cu Chi Tunnels offer a fascinating experience.

Saigon), the tunnels were of vital strategic importance.

Individual tunnels ran up to 10 metres (33ft) deep, each with a breadth of between 0.5 to 1 metre (1.5–3ft), and stacked up to three levels. The top tier could support the weight of a 50-tonne tank, the middle layer could withstand moderate mortar attacks, while the lowest level was virtually impregnable.

The ground through which the tunnels burrowed is red clay, well suited to this kind of excavation. To avoid detection, the earth that had been removed was often dumped in bomb craters, rice fields or the Saigon River. The Americans often used trained dogs to sniff out the tunnels, but the Viet Cong would deflect them by scattering pepper at the tunnel entrances and vents. It is said that they would even use the same soap as Americans to confuse the dogs.

While the tunnel system included kitchens, meeting rooms, barracks, makeshift hospitals and storage for supplies, the tunnels were not intended for long-term accommodation (contrary to what is often written), as conditions inside them were quite deplorable. Likewise, a number of war anecdotes, including accounts of how doctors performed surgeries at the underground hospitals and administered blood transfusions via bicycle pumps, are highly implausible and probably concocted by overzealous government officials bent on glorifying the accomplishments of the Viet Cong.

Nevertheless, the tunnels are a vivid testament to the ingenuity and perseverance of the Vietnamese that eventually helped them win the war against the vast technical superiority of the Americans. Numerous tactics were used by the US troops to eliminate the tunnels' effectiveness, but with little long-term success until the B-52s began their relentless carpet-bombing. Although the Americans eventually destroyed much of the subterranean network, it was a temporary and Pyrrhic victory. The tunnels had already fulfilled their function by giving the Viet Cong not only the advantage of

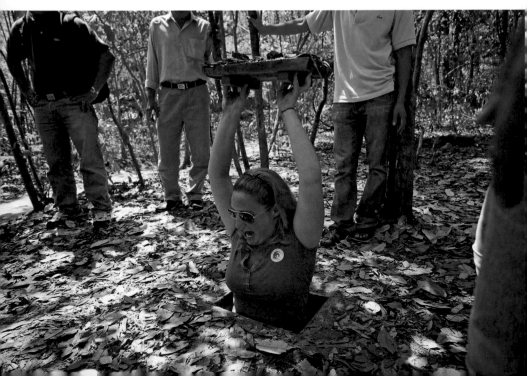

surprise but also the control of many surrounding villages.

Visitors often shudder when they crawl through a small section of tunnel, which has been enlarged and "improved" for the benefit of tourists. Reforested eucalyptus trees attest to the area's recovery from the ravages of chemical defoliants and carpet-bombing.

TAY NINH

Further to the northwest, Highway 22 passes through Tay Ninh province before continuing on to Cambodia. From the 7th to the 14th centuries, this area belonged to the powerful Funan empire before being absorbed into the Chen La kingdom, the forerunner of the Khmer kingdom. In the early 18th century, the Nguyen Lords defeated the last of the Champa people here and assumed control.

During the war against the French, Tay Ninh was a hotbed of anti-colonial sentiment, and in the 1950s a hero of the armed resistance forces made Black Lady Mountain (Nui Ba Den) his hideout. The mountain went on to become an important strategic point of bloody confrontations in the war against America.

CAO DAI GREAT TEMPLE

Tay Ninh's greatest attraction is found approximately 100km (60 miles) northwest of Ho Chi Minh City, in the township of **Tay Ninh** ❸ itself. Here, in all its resplendent gaudiness, stands the **Cao Dai Great Temple** (Thanh That Cao Dai). Cao Dai was founded in 1926 by Ngo Minh Chieu, and its followers believe that all major world faiths offer pieces of the truth, but that Cao Dai arose in a third age to unite them all. While Cao Dai borrows saints and divinities from other religions and philosophies, it is principally a repackaging of Buddhism, Confucianism and Taoism with a new liturgy and leadership hierarchy.

Adherents believe in one ultimate deity with many subordinate divinities, and also believe that the faithful receive divine revelations from a variety of spiritual entities, including their principal saints: Sun Yat-sen, Victor Hugo and Nguyen Binh Khiem. Today, there are an estimated 4 million Cao Dai followers in Vietnam and 400 temples, all with a similar design.

Most tours arrive at the temple for the noon prayer ceremony, though there are also daily ceremonies at 6am, 6pm and midnight. Followers in their colourful ceremonial gowns of azure, red, yellow and white cut striking figures in their procession towards the altar, entering from opposite sides.

The temple blends Buddhist and Catholic architectural conventions. The Holy See is oriented with the entrance facing the west, so that the congregation faces the east. The general shape is longitudinal, as in a basilica. Unlike a cathedral, the temple is not built on an axis but it does have a central domed tower built where a cathedral transept would normally be.

⊙ Tip

Visitors may observe the Cao Dai services from the upper balconies of the temple. They may not cross in front of the temple until services are completed, however. Shoes must be removed when entering the building.

The Cao Dai Great Temple is akin to a fantasy movie set.

Southern Vietnam

Nha Trang
Phan Rang
Thap Cham
Co Be, Ma

Phuoc
Vinh Hao
Lien Huong
Thon Lac Nghiem

Nui Hon Diep 1532

Di Linh
1864

Lam Dong

Ap Thanh
Huong
Da Thanh
Loc

Gia Bac
20
Dinh Diep
Dak Marong

Cho Lau
Phan Ri
Ap Long Hoa
Ap Phan Ri
Bau Trang (White Sand Dunes)
Ap Thien Ai
10 Mui Ne

Binh Thuan

Da Hoa
Ap Phuong
Ham
Xa Hieu
La Nga
Dak Marong
Ham Thuan
Bac
Ham Thuan Nam
Muong Man
Tanh 132
7 Phan Thiet
Thap Poshanu
Vinh Phan Thiet

Dong Nai

Dinh Quan
Ho
Xa Gia Kiem
Dau Giay
Long
Xuan Loc
8 Ta Cu Mountain Nature Reserve
9 Khe Ga
Ham Tan

6 Vuon Quoc Gia Nam Cat Tien (Cat Tien National Park)

Nui Ba Bang 986 **4**

3

Tay Ninh

Binh Phuoc

13
14

Nui Ba Den

Dong Xoai
Loc Ninh

Chon Thanh

Ap Bau Bang

Bet Cat

Binh Duong

Cu Chi (Tunnels) **2**

Thu Dau Mot
Bien Hoa
Thu Duc

Ho Chi Minh City **1**

1 Ho Chi Minh City

Long An

Tan Uyen

Nha Be

Ap Vam Vung
Ganh
Rai

Ba Ria–Vung Tau
55
51
Long Le
Phuoc Tuy
Long Dat
Cho Phuoc Hai
Vung Tau **5**

Trang Bang
Moc Hoa

Tien Giang
Cai Lay
My Tho **12**
Ben Tre **13**
Ben Tre

12 Trai Ran Dong Tam Snake Farm
San Chim Van Ho Bird Sanctuary **14**

Tan Chau
Hong Ngu
Dong Thap
Tran Chim Tam Nong (Stork Sanctuary) **19**

Cao Lanh
Sa Dec
15
Vinh Long **16**
Vinh Long
Tra Vinh **Tra Vinh**

Chau Doc
Long Xuyen **21**
An Giang
Oc Eo **20**
23
Rung Tram Tra Su (Bird Sanctuary)

Can Tho
Can Tho **17**

Hau Giang

Soc Trang
Soc Trang **18**

Bac Lieu
Bac Lieu

Kien Giang
Rach Gia **26**

22
Hang Mo So **25**
Ha Tien
Hon Chong **25**

Ca Mau
Ca Mau
Rung Duoc U Minh (Mangrove Forest)

CAMBODIA

Phnum Penh

11 Vuon Quoc Gia Con Dao (Con Dao National Park)
Con Dao

BIEN DONG

Gulf of Thailand

N

0 ─── 50 km
0 ─── 50 miles

Phu Quoc

Rach Gia, Ha Tien

Bai Thom
Bai Bung
Day Nui Ham Ninh
Ham Ninh

Phu Quoc

Vuon Quoc Gia Phu Quoc (Phu Quoc National Park)
Chua 538
Khu Tuong
Suoi Da Ban
Khai Hoan Fish Sauce Distillery
Phu Quoc Pearl Farm

Bai Sao
Bai Khem (Cream Beach)
An Thoi

27 Duong Dong
Ong Lang
Duong To
Ba Keo
Bai Truong (Long Beach)
Nha Lao Cay Dua (Coconut Prison)

28 An Thoi

Ganh Dau
Bai Dai
Cua Can

Set

Gulf of Thailand

0 ─── 10 km
0 ─── 10 miles

The temple also has striking twin towers at the front, and a smaller tower at the east end. On the outside a large eye symbolising the Cao Dai religion guards the entrance.

The interior has a blue, starstudded vaulted ceiling and an altar supporting a giant orb gilded with an all-seeing eye. The inner Church hall is divided into a nave with an aisle on either side, separated by columns encircled by Buddhist dragons. The ceremony is usually completed in less than 30 minutes, after which visitors are free to explore the temple.

NUI BA DEN

The most outstanding natural feature around Tay Ninh is **Nui Ba Den** ❹ (Black Lady Mountain), at 996 metres (3,268ft) the loftiest mountain in southern Vietnam. It has been a strategic military stronghold through every major conflict. Its name centres around the story of a principled lady who chose death over dishonesty a common theme in Vietnamese folklore. Although heavily scarred by war, over the past decades nature has made something of a comeback and the slopes are now protected as a nature reserve where many species of birds as well as primates thrive.

Visitors can hike from a temple at the base or take the cable car (daily 8am–5pm; charge) to a series of three cave temples halfway up the mountain, featuring numerous Buddhas in a variety of forms. However, while Nui Ba Den makes a pleasant outing, most will find Ta Cu Mountain (see page 312) near Phan Thiet a more convenient alternative, with similar features.

VUNG TAU

The port city of **Vung Tau** ❺ is situated 125km (80 miles) southeast of Ho Chi Minh City (HCMC). Located on a peninsula straddling two mountains, **Nui Nho** (Small Mountain) and **Nui Lon** (Big Mountain), Vung Tau offers some of the most stunning coastal scenery anywhere in Vietnam. The city has maintained its status as a popular weekend getaway for residents of HCMC, despite falling out of favour in the past decade with foreign visitors, who prefer the charms of Phan Thiet further down the coast.

Vung Tau is a modern city, with all the conveniences of HCMC, including Western fast-food chains, high-rise shopping centres and other trappings of 21stcentury life. Despite its popularity as a domestic vacation spot, the offshore oil industry dominates the local economy and actually owns many of the hotels.

THE STATUE OF JESUS

At the far end of the peninsula, perched on top of Nui Nho, is a 30-metre (100ft) **statue of Jesus**, arms outstretched to the sea and reminiscent of the famous *Christ the Redeemer* image of Rio de Janeiro in Brazil. The statue was erected by the Americans in 1971. Park your vehicle at the foot on Ha Long Street and hike

Vung Tau Lighthouse sits atop Nui Nho (Small Mountain).

View of Vung Tau.

up the path for about 30 minutes for incredible views of the coast.

Many locals enjoy their evening walks up the other side of Nui Nho via Hai Dang Street (across from the wharf) for unmatchable views of **Front Beach** (Bai Truoc), **Back Beach** (Bai Sau) and the cityscape between. Back Beach is the only sizeable sandy beach around the city. It is largely denuded of trees and has suffered from small oil spills in the past, but it's still a pleasant – albeit somewhat urban – place to swim and sunbathe.

Taking both left-hand forks on Hai Dang Street will lead about 1km (0.6 miles) to the very top of the mountain and the blinding-white **Vung Tau Lighthouse** (daily 7am–5pm), originally built by the French in 1910. Taking a left and then a right fork will lead you to an old **abandoned military bunker**, dating from the same period. You can freely explore the crumbling fort, whose walls are being torn apart by the roots of young Tung trees (*Tetrameles nudiflora*). Already the bunker is starting to look like a mini

version of the famous Ta Prohm Temple at Angkor Wat in Cambodia.

Alternatively, the other favourite evening hike leads you up Nui Lon peak via Vi Ba Street, past numerous Buddhist and Taoist temples, as well as one devoted to the Cao Dai faith. Big Mountain's premier landmark is **Villa Blanche** (Bach Dinh; daily 7am–5pm), built at the end of the 19th century for the French governor-general, Paul Doumer. Doumer was called back to France before the villa was completed, and never actually resided there. A new cable car (daily 8am–5pm; charge) runs from the base of the mountain, on the north side of the harbour, to the peak.

One of the Nguyen emperors, Thanh Thai, was held in Villa Blanche for some time before his exile to Reunion Island off Africa in 1909. Later, it became the residence of presidents Ngo Dinh Diem and Nguyen Van Thieu. Beautifully set above a forest of frangipani trees, the house contains ceramics and other items recovered from a Chinese junk shipwrecked off Cau Islet in the Con Dao Islands in 1690.

⊙ THE WHALE WORSHIPPERS

In coastal communities of southern Vietnam there is a little-known festival called Cau Ngu, celebrated by local fishermen who follow an ancient whale-worshipping cult. In the Cau Ngu (Fish Prayer) Festival, fishermen pray to whales, dolphins and even sharks, asking their spirits to watch over them in the coming year. The festival usually includes the Nghinh Ong procession: when a whale or dolphin dies and is washed ashore, there is an elaborate funeral to welcome its spirit, with performers dressed in traditional costumes, stilt walkers, musicians and dragon dancers. After the funeral, the remains of the creatures are then buried at the local fishermen's temple near the beach. Three to five years later, the bones are exhumed and carried around the town in a similar procession until they are finally returned to the temple to be worshipped. In communities where there are several temples, the temples may share a single skeleton, and take turns hosting Cau Ngu.

The practice manifests in other ways. Fishing boats are adorned with eyes and fins, both to honour the whales and ward off sea monsters. There are also additional holidays and festivals tied to individual temples.

The most important whale temples are located in Phan Thiet (see page 312) and Vung Tau (see page 308), but smaller versions are found in many fishing communities along the south-central coast.

WHALE TEMPLE

Like many coastal towns in southern Vietnam, Vung Tau has a fishermen's temple devoted to whale worship, **Lang Ca Ong** (also referred to as **Dinh Than Thang-Tam**, the Whale Temple; daily 8am–5pm; free). Dating from 1911, it is situated on the corner of Hoang Hoa Tham and Xo Viet Nghe streets, halfway between Front and Back beaches.

In this region, whales are highly revered by local fishermen, who see the mighty creatures as man's saviour from the perils of the high seas. Whales are depicted in beautiful murals with dragons and sea monsters, and skeletons of beached whales – some of them measuring 4 metres (13ft), and dating back to the

1860s – are displayed in glass cases. The Vietnamese adopted the whale cult from the people of Champa, who worshipped the whale deity. Cham people believed that a powerful god called Cha Aig Va assumed the form of a whale in order to rescue fishermen in peril. Every year, from the 16th to the 18th day of the eighth month of the lunar calendar, the Cau Ngu Festival is held at the temple.

OTHER TEMPLES AND PAGODAS

A large number of Buddhist temples are scattered around town and across both Nui Nho and Nui Lon mountains. **Hong Ba Pagoda** is located on an islet below the statue of Jesus and reachable only at low tide. **Quan Am Bo Tat Tu**, to the northwest on Tran Phu Street at Dau Beach, has a giant statue of the female Buddha (at odds with the statue of the taller Virgin Mary and Baby Jesus next door). About 3km (2 miles) away, **Thich ca Phat Dai** is notable for its beautiful pagoda, seen from Tran Phu Street on the north side of Big Mountain.

CAT TIEN NATIONAL PARK

About halfway between Ho Chi Minh City and Dalat lies **Cat Tien National Park** ❻ (tel: 061-366 9228/366 9330; www.namcattien.org; daily daylight hours), one of Vietnam's best areas for wildlife. The large expanse of forest shelters some 107 species of mammals, 360 species of birds and 120 species of reptiles and amphibians. There are significant populations of yellow-cheeked gibbons, green peafowl, hornbills, civets, sambar deer and gaur, as well as a few tigers, elephants, Asian black bears and sun bears. Tragically, the last Javan rhinoceros in mainland Southeast Asia was killed by poachers in Cat Tien in 2010. The park has 14 excursions and hiking trails, with more under development. These include a variety of hikes through rainforest, grassland and wetland habitats as well as nighttime safaris, and visits to S'Tieng minority tribes in Ta Lai village. The government no longer permits foreigners to visit the ancient temple ruins beside the park.

Phan Thiet Water Tower is a city landmark.

A mural of whales and dragons at Vung Tau's Whale Temple.

DRAGON FRUIT AND FISH SAUCE

Southern Vietnam is a land of plenty, typified by its luscious fruit and the national staple, *nuoc mam*.

While tourism and its associated activities in Mui Ne are an important engine of growth in Phan Thiet's economy, the other two pillars of local commerce – dragon fruit and fish sauce, which existed long before the first pleasure-seeking tourists appeared, have an even greater significance to the country as a whole.

DRAGON FRUIT

Dragon fruit comes from an enormous creeping cactus *(Hylocereus undatus)*, native to Central and South America, where it is known as *pitaya*. With a preference for dry climates, it grows extraordinarily well in Binh Thuan and Ninh Thuan provinces, where it is known as *thanh long*, and produces some of the highest yields of the fruit in the world.

Phan Thiet's famous fish sauce.

The bright-green cactus grows much like a vine. If left uncultivated it will climb trees and rock faces, anchoring itself with sturdy tendrils. Farmers keep them manageable by fastening plants to rows of short posts, continuously re-grafting hundreds of arms back into the base. The result looks like a writhing Medusa's head.

The plant's enormous, white, trumpet-like flowers bloom only at night, and are easily stimulated by manipulating light levels. Thus farmers place lights at the base of the plant every evening to induce multiple harvests in a single year. The peel of the fruit is pink, with green scale-like protrusions. The fruit is white with thousands of tiny black seeds, which can be eaten. The taste and texture are often compared to a kiwi, although dragon fruits are much larger, often reaching the size of an ostrich egg.

FISH SAUCE

Fish sauce, known in Vietnam as *nuoc mam*, is the foundation of Vietnamese cuisine. It's used as a seasoning, salt substitute, the base for broths and soups, and also a condiment. The best variety comes from Phan Thiet and Phu Quoc island. *Nuoc cham*, a mix of fish sauce, water, lime juice, sugar, chilli and garlic, is the most common dipping sauce in Vietnam.

Fish sauce is made from fresh anchovies – it is important to use fish that are about the same size – and sea salt, which are allowed to ferment. The mixture of one part salt to two or three parts fish is placed in large vats. A bamboo mat is placed over the slurry and weighted down to keep the fish from floating to the top as the mixture liquefies. The jars are then covered and left in direct sunlight for nine months to a year. Periodically the lids are removed to ventilate the sauce and allow sunlight to stimulate further fermentation. Once the mixture is sufficiently reduced to an oily liquid, it is either siphoned or drained through a spigot in the bottom of the vat. The fluid is poured into clean jars and allowed to air for a few more weeks to reduce the fishy smell. Meanwhile the leftover fishy solids are sold as fodder for pigs.

Top-grade fish sauce is always a clear amber colour, without any sediment, and has a fragrant and briny aroma (although it will always retain some of that inimitable fishy smell).

The crown jewel of the park is **Crocodile Lake** (Bai Sau). Getting here involves a drive and a long trek, but it's well worth it for the chance it gives to see some of the park's wildlife, including the Siamese crocodiles that were reintroduced in 2000.

It is possible to explore the park on your own, but trained English-speaking guides (who add to the experience) as well as cars and bicycles are available for hire. Air-conditioned bungalows can also be rented at the park headquarters, or you may opt to stay in a tent. Be sure to tell someone when and where you'll be hiking if you go it alone, as people have been known to get lost along the trails.

A **rescue centre** (open daylight hours) run by Wildlife at Risk or WAR (www.wildlifeatrisk.org) houses sun bears and wild cats, and is open to the public. Additionally, the Endangered Asian Species Trust (www.go-east.org) has built the new Dau Tien Endangered Primate Species Centre, which cares for rescued gibbons, langurs and slow loris. It too is open to the public.

Despite being recognised as a Unesco Biosphere Reserve, Cat Tien's future was jeopardised by plans to build two hydroelectric dams within the park. Fortunately, the government abandoned the project under pressure from its own environment ministry and international organisations.

PHAN THIET

Phan Thiet ❼, 200km (125 miles) from Ho Chi Minh City on the Ca Ty River, was once a sleepy little fishing port known only for its pungent *nuoc mam* (fish sauce) and dragon fruit. As tourism developed on the nearby beach of Mui Ne, however, the economy of Phan Thiet quickly grew. The riverfront is a lovely place to walk both day and night, offering the best views of colourful wooden fishing boats in the harbour and **Tran Hung Dao Bridge**, as well as **the

mountains to the north. The **Phan Thiet Water Tower** – at the eastern end of Le Hong Phong Bridge – designed by Prince Souphanouvong of Laos in the 1930s, is the symbol of both the city and the province. The tower, no longer in use as a receptacle to collect and store water, is lit up in the evenings until about 10pm.

Be sure to stop at **Nguyen Viet Vui's Butterfly Shop** (daily 8–11am and 5–8pm) on Trung Trac Street next to the Tran Hung Dao Bridge. Vui is one of Vietnam's leading naturalists, and an authority on native butterflies. He holds the national record for the largest collection of butterflies. Some of his 7,000 specimens are more than a century old and worth about US$20,000.

About 250 metres/yds further down Trung Trac Street, past the Le Hong Phong and Duc Thanh bridges, sits **Duc Thanh School**, where Ho Chi Minh himself taught in 1910 before "finding the road to national salvation". Across the street sits the **Ho Chi Minh Museum** (Tue–Sun 7.30–11.30am and

Chinese temples often commemorate New Year festivities with dragon dancing, which is thought to bring good luck and prosperity.

The Jesus statue above Vung Tau.

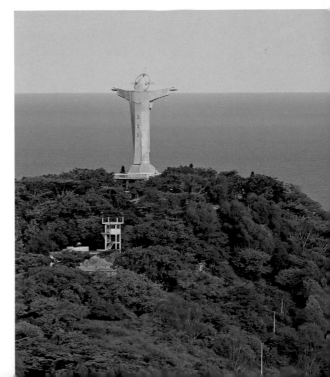

1.30–4.30pm), at the site of his former home. The museum is of little interest other than to view some of Ho Chi Minh's personal effects, which are of questionable authenticity (unless he really had a hat, cane and shirt for every museum in Vietnam).

On the other side of the town market is **Duc Thang Temple** (daily 8am–5pm; free), built in 1847. The jagged roof is decorated with numerous undulating dragons, and phoenixes and lions. Inside is a collection of ancient wooden scripture panels.

Van Thuy Thu Temple (daily 7am–5pm; charge) at 20A Ngu Ong Street is the oldest temple (built in 1762) dedicated to whale worship in Vietnam (see page 308). The temple contains over 100 whale skeletons, but the main draw is a restored specimen more than 22 metres (72ft) long – the largest in the country. Like all such temples, Thuy Thu was originally built by the edge of the sea, but as water levels have changed over the centuries, this temple is now stranded in the middle of a busy neighbourhood. Fishermen can be seen mending nets and building boats in the temple, which is thought to bring them luck.

TA CU MOUNTAIN

The **Ta Cu Mountain Nature Reserve** ❽ (Mon–Fri 6.30am–5pm, Sat–Sun 6.30am–6pm) towers high above the town of Ham Tan, about 30km (19 miles) west from Phan Thiet, along Highway 1A. Take a ride on the **gondola** to the top, or hike the forest trail for a better glimpse of the local birdlife. The old pagoda that nestled on the other side of the peak for over 130 years was torn down in late 2007 and replaced with a more kitschy, theatrical version complete with dragon-head pillars and an ornate Chinesestyle curved roof. The temple is surrounded by a cluster of stupas (relic shrines), a trio of smaller Buddha statues and – the main attraction – Vietnam's largest reclining Buddha, some 49 metres (161ft) long. A small cave is hidden in the boulders far to the right of the statue. Legend says that a boy once followed the cave

Over 440 species of butterfly are found at Cat Tien National Park.

all the way to the sea, 20km (12 miles) away.

KHE GA LIGHTHOUSE

Heading southwest of Phan Thiet, the coastal road passes through the **Landing Zone Betty**, a former American base, and straddles an enormous canyon along the beach.

Further down the coast is the **Khe Ga Lighthouse ❾**, located on a small island off Tien Thanh Beach, the longest continuous beach in the province. This is the tallest lighthouse in Vietnam, built by the French in 1897. It's still a beautiful spot, with large orange-and-red striated boulders jutting out of enormous windswept dunes. Just don't look to the west, where the beach is usually piled with rubbish, or at the resorts that are scheduled to be torn down to build a new port which will ship bauxite to China and deposit toxic red mud behind the beach.

MUI NE BEACH

In 1995, when it was declared to be the best spot in Vietnam to view the solar eclipse, **Mui Ne Beach ❿** caught the attention of resort developers looking for fresh territory to stake out. Within a few years, this obscure little fishing community nestled in a coconut grove had morphed into the premier beach-resort capital of southern Vietnam, and it continues to be one of the country's fastest-growing tourist areas, with dozens of major new hotel properties under development.

In 2004, when the Boxing Day Tsunami struck Southeast Asia, it initiated another turning point for Vietnam: the Russian invasion. Scores of Russian tourists, who used to vacation in Thailand, suddenly came to Vietnam instead. Henceforth Mui Ne became a favourite spot of Russian tourists, many of them from Vladivostok.

Mui Ne is located 10km (6 miles) north of downtown Phan Thiet. The unique geography of Binh Thuan Province has endowed it with not only one of the driest climates in Southeast Asia, but also one of the

Altar, Duc Thang Temple.

A wakeboarder in action off Mui Ne Beach.

Small fishing boat at Mui Ne.

windiest. With an average of 229 days per year with winds above 12 knots, it didn't take long for the world's kiteboarding and windsurfing community to discover its attractions. One drawback to having dozens of kiteboarding centres along the beachfront is that swimming or sunbathing can be a bit hazardous in the afternoons when the bay is crowded with enthusiasts, along with newly introduced jet-skis and illegal fishing nets.

Not to be outdone, the golfers are the next group to have arrived in force, following the construction of the 18-hole **Sea Links Golf & Country Club** now rebranded "Sea Links City" to incorporate a private beach, highrise condos, a shopping centre, villas and an upscale hotel-resort.

Mui Ne Beach, a name actually coined by the tourism industry, is made up of several wards within Phan Thiet City. Ham Tien Ward, and its Rang Beach, is the central tourism area where the bulk of resorts, restaurants and bars are located. This is the area most mean when they say Mui Ne Beach. The west end has the best beach and the most upscale venues, with the associated higher prices. The east end is prone to greater erosion and pollution. The cape on the east end is the "real" Mui Ne Village. The quaint hilltop community retains much of the original fishing-village charm that has evaporated from Ham Tien with development. Further north, on the way to the dunes, are lessvisited resort areas at Ganh and Suoi Hong Beaches, Hon Rom Village, and a newly invigorated resort area of Suoi Nuoc Beach.

THAP POSHANU CHAM TEMPLE

While the beach itself is the main draw in Mui Ne, there are a few other sights worth visiting, too. The three Cham towers of **Thap Poshanu** (daily 8am–5pm; charge) at KM5 Nguyen Thong were built in the 8th century to honour Shiva and other deities. The primary tower (usually locked) contains a pair of phallic *linga-yoni*. The tower beside is devoted to Agni, the fire deity, and the smallest tower to Nandi, the

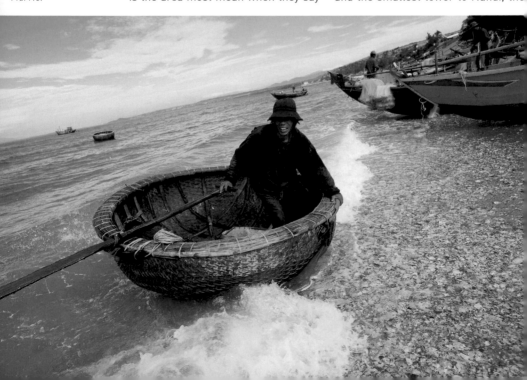

buffalo deity. The site offers the best view of Phan Thiet City, the Phu Hai River and Song Len Mountain. A new pagoda, abandoned French military outpost and a shop selling Cham crafts and local gemstones are all located on site.

WHITE SAND DUNES

The **White Sand Dunes** (also known as Bau Trang or "White Lake") are an immense Saharan-like series of gold-and-snow-white dunes, located around 45 minutes' drive, 30km (19 miles) northwest of Mui Ne village. Nestled in the dunes are two large reservoirs and a series of smaller lakes, which offer excellent opportunities to observe local birdlife, including four species of heron, the red-wattled lapwing and several species of bee-eaters (contact Vietnam Birding, www. vietnambirding.com, in HCMC for guided, expert tours). There are always village kids standing by, waiting to rent sleds to visitors for a spot of "dune surfing". Be sure to bring plenty of water, sunscreen and a hat – the glare is intense. The best time to visit is early in the morning or late in the afternoon to avoid the intense heat and also to take advantage of the dramatic lighting for photos. At night when there is a full moon the dunes are particularly impressive, but watch for snakes, scorpions and bandits.

On the way to the dunes, it's hard to miss the **titanium mining** operations along the highway. Some of the world's richest deposits are located along the coast of Binh Thuan province. This is a frequent source of unhappiness for resort owners, who fear the noise and known radioactive pollution that the mining operations bring.

Other than fishing, goatherding has been the traditional vocation for many locals in the surrounding villages. They are raised for their meat rather than milk – goat hotpot and grilled goat meat are local specialities here. With the rising demand for lizard meat, however, many residents are switching to lizard-farming (lizards are said to be delicious stir fried with lemongrass and chilli). Both

Southern Vietnam has notable Indian and Khmer influences, as seen in the Thap Poshanu towers.

Reclining Buddha at Ta Cu Mountain Nature Reserve.

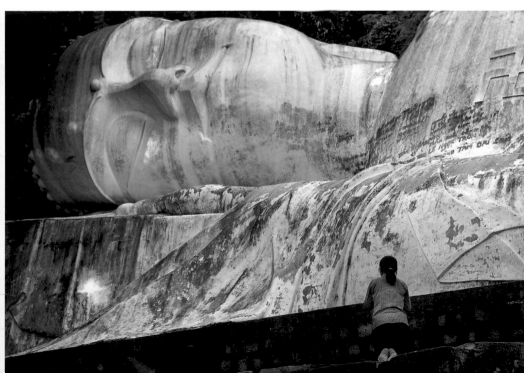

⊙ Tip

Efforts to protect sea turtles on Con Dao are undermined on mainland Vietnam where they are still served in restaurants and their lacquered carcasses are sold in souvenir shops. You can support efforts by not buying these products and reporting sellers to authorities.

White Sand Dunes.

goat and lizard pens can be seen amid the dunes.

Quad bikes (four-wheelers) have begun to dominate the once peaceful dunes. It can be a fun way to traverse them, but be mindful that neither the safety nor the wisdom of this activity is ensured.

RED SAND DUNES

The **Red Sand Dunes** are another popular sight on the way, but are not as impressive as the white dunes. The **Fairy Stream** (Soui Tien), however, that flows through the dunes is a lovely walk (30 minutes each way) through layers of blood-red, gold and silver sand dunes undulating through the countryside. Leave your shoes at the shop near the last bridge before Mui Ne village, as you'll be wading in ankle-deep water all the way to the small waterfall at the other end. An ostrich farm (a local fad) has been set up along the way. A crocodile farm sits out of view, above the small waterfall at the end of the stream, and across the road.

CON DAO ARCHIPELAGO

Once a feared prison known as "Devil's Island", **Con Son Island**, the largest of 14 islands that make up the **Con Dao Archipelago** ⑪ , is now the heart of a national park famous for its hawksbill and green marine turtles as well as the dugong – a relative of the manatee. The World Wildlife Fund has been actively involved in programmes here to protect these amazing creatures. Since 1995, more than 300,000 baby turtles have been released into the sea and around 1,000 mature turtles have been tagged.

Originally known as Poulo Condore, Con Son, which covers about 20 sq km (8 sq miles), was first settled by the British East India Company in 1703, but the Bugis mercenaries from Sulawesi, hired to build the garrison, murdered all their employers. Due to the remoteness of the island, the French used it later as a prison for Vietnamese anti-colonial protesters. The island became notorious for torture and death, but the full extent of the horrors – which continued under the South Vietnamese government – were not fully known until the end of the war in 1975. Prisoners were kept in 11 prisons on Con Son, and often held in tiny underground boxes with metal grille roofs, known as "tiger cages". Grisly dummies now shackled together in the prisons shed light on the horrors the inmates endured.

Hang Duong Cemetery holds the remains of the many prisoners who died here – most in unmarked graves. One of the best-known graves belongs to nationalist heroine **Vo Thi Sau**, in 1952 the first female to be executed here, at the age of 18. Her grave is decorated with offerings of mirrors and hairbrushes, a tribute to her gender and youthful age.

Occupying the former French governor's residence and overlooking the main bay is a small **Revolutionary Museum** (daily 7.30–11am, 1.30–5pm). The four rooms cover Con Dao's history, most of which revolves around the penal colony.

Con Son is mountainous and covered in rainforest, with great hiking trails for viewing endemic wildlife. The best information source is the **National Park Headquarters** (tel: 064-383 0669; www.condaopark.com.vn) at 29 Vo Thi Sau Street.

There are several good beaches on Con Son – like **Bai Dat Doc Beach** and **Bai Nhat Beach** – and also on some of the smaller islands, such as Bai Canh, which is also a major nesting area for turtles.

The waters around the Con Dao Archipelago encompass the country's most pristine and varied dive sites. Con Dao is also the only place in the country with an officially diveable wreck. That being said, the waters here have not entirely escaped the destructive fishing practices that have obliterated reefs in other parts of Vietnam. Things are not quite as untouched as they were a few years

ago, and many divers suggest that the last dugong was sold on the butcher block in the market, some years ago. Still, there are over 1,000 hectares (2,500 acres) of pristine coral reefs and over 1,300 marine species identified thus far. It is possible to see turtles, manta rays and reef sharks around Con Dao, and others such as devil scorpionfish, cowfish, giant moray eels, clownfish and many more are still very common.

The weather in this area is at its best from February to May, while the turtle-nesting season is May to September, overlapping with the prime diving between June and September. Rainbow Divers and Dive!Dive!Dive! (www.dive-condao.com) are recommended shops/diving centres operating on the island. The latter is also an invaluable source of information on Con Dao.

Traffic is mercifully light on Con Son's few roads, and the main resort hotels are found between the principal coastal road and Con Son Bay, including the luxury **Six Senses** resort.

Con Son Island vista.

Using water buffaloes to till the land in Ba Chuc.

THE MEKONG DELTA

Known as Vietnam's rice bowl, the Mekong Delta is a region of lush green fields, traditional villages and floating markets, connected by countless canals that are fed by the mighty Mekong.

Travelling through the serpentine, sleepy canals of the Mekong Delta is like taking a trip back in time. Its patchwork of fields and canals creates a scenic landscape, while its people are so relaxed and welcoming that the Delta often detains visitors for longer than they had expected.

The Vietnamese name for the Mekong is **Song Cuu Long**, meaning the River of Nine Dragons, in reference to the nine principal tributaries that empty into the South China Sea. The vast Mekong Delta is formed as the river fans out and deposits alluvium along its many smaller channels, creating a fertile landscape rich in agriculture.

The Mekong descends from its source high in the Tibetan Plateau and follows a 4,500km (2,800-mile) course through China, Myanmar (Burma), Laos, Thailand, Cambodia and southern Vietnam before emptying into the sea. For years it was nothing more than vast marshland, but by the end of the 18th century, two huge canals – the Thai Hoa, which linked Rach Gia and Long Xuyen, and the Vinh Te, linking Chau Doc and Ha Tien – were in use. Today, the region covers almost 40,000 sq km (15,400 sq miles) and its inhabitants include Khmer, Chinese and Cham.

Phu Quoc womenfolk.

TRAVELLING AROUND

An adequate road network serves the delta's 13 provinces, and, until recently, more than 100 ferries also operated. Now only few remain as the myriad of canals and bamboo bridges are slowly being upgraded into cable bridges and four-lane highways. In larger cities, the paved roads are in good condition, but in more rural spots, the "roads" are often little more than a series of loosely connected potholes. This can add hours onto journey times (particularly in the wet season), but also

Map on page 306

Main Attractions

My Tho
Vinh Long
Can Tho
Kh'leng Pagoda
Doi Pagoda
Chau Doc
Ha Tien
Hon Chong
Phu Quoc Island

My Tho Market, a typical Mekong Delta produce market.

allows travellers to fully appreciate the charming palm-thatched wooden huts and lush green landscape around them. The river and its network of tributaries carry a busy and varied flow of traffic, and jumping in a boat to explore the islands' narrow waterways is a key part of any trip to the delta.

AGRICULTURAL HEARTLAND

During the Vietnam War the region was thick with Viet Cong, and so was heavily bombed with chemical defoliants. Today, you would never know this – the delta is the most densely populated area in Vietnam, and markets here overflow with fish and other produce yielded by the delta's rich alluvial soil: sesame, peanuts, cashews, pineapples, pumpkins, tangerines, melons, cabbages, coconuts, sugar cane, dragon fruit, durians and rice are just a few of the crops produced here. Most grow year-round, but the end of the rainy season in March is a good month to visit and sample the enormous variety of seasonal fruits. The flat, moist land is perfect for rice cultivation; in many

places there are three full harvests during the year, and the delta produces enough rice to feed the whole nation, with a sizeable surplus exported to provide a substantial percentage of the country's earnings. However, climate change and rising sea levels pose an imminent danger to low-lying areas of the Mekong Delta and its agriculture. Saline intrusions and inundations, more frequent now than ever, destroy rice crops and force farmers to switch from rice to shrimp farming. Every year the government allots more land to shrimp farming, which in 2016 alone brought Vietnam a healthy profit of more than US$3 billion and is expected to bring US$10 billion by 2025.

As well as fields, there are good beaches on the western coast, the most popular of which is Hon Chong. Sand-worshippers can fly direct from HCMC to Phu Quoc Island, with its beautiful beaches and lush forests, just off the Hon Chong coast.

Despite the march of development across the rest of Vietnam, life in the Mekong Delta remains virtually unchanged – agriculture is still the dominant industry and the landscape is a tapestry of green paddy fields, mirror-like pools and expansive fields of exotic fruits, all fed by the life-giving brown waters of the river that snakes between them.

MY THO

My Tho ⑫, about 70km (43 miles) from HCMC through Long An province, is the gateway to the Mekong Delta. The sleepy capital of Tien Giang province, it was founded in 1680 by political refugees fleeing China at the end of the Ming dynasty, afraid that their affiliation to the Chinese would translate into a death sentence under their new masters. With a population of about 220,000, this provincial town lies on the left bank of the My Tho River (Song My Tho), the northernmost branch of the Mekong. Along the waterfront are

---

⊘ DOING THE DELTA

Getting to the heart of the Delta means taking to the water. Boat tours run all around the region, most following a similar trail. From My Tho, a four-hour trip will visit some of the four islands closest to the town. After stopping briefly at a fish farm and beehive, tourists are usually taken to listen to a performance of traditional music, before moving on to see women making candy coconut (a mixture of coconut milk, coconut cream, malt syrup and sugar) – something that Ben Tre is famous for. A horse and carriage await in Ben Tre along with a brief bicycle ride past rice fields, followed by the chance to feed crocodiles on Phoenix Island before catching the boat home. The cost is about US$15, but this can change depending on numbers. If this seems a bit touristy for your tastes, another option is to find local boat owners who can make a tailor-made itinerary that tends to be cheaper than the tour companies. Other trips involve visiting the floating markets in Can Tho, some include breakfast on the boat and stops at the flower or fruit gardens; these tours can easily be booked in Can Tho itself. All tours start early to avoid the heat. To reach the picturesque town of Tra Vinh you can go by bus or hire a motorbike driver for VND500,000, stopping at villages and rice fields along the way.

the main hotels and restaurants, along with a large tourist information centre that houses several companies. Thu Khoa Huan Park is a popular place to hang out in the evenings, as food traders set up stalls and children play on fairground rides. There are a couple of good cafés here too, making it an ideal place to people-watch.

The Catholic **My Tho Church**, on Ly Thuong Kiet Street, was built at the end of the 19th century, and there is still a Catholic congregation of more than 7,000 followers. At 60 Nguyen Trung Trac Street is the **Vinh Trang Pagoda** (Chua Vinh Trang; daily 9am–11.30am and 1.30–5pm). Built in 1849 and the largest in the province, the temple is an eclectic mix of French, Chinese, Vietnamese and Khmer architectural styles.

My Tho's busy **Central Market** on Trung Trac and Nguyen Hue streets is a great place to flex your bartering skills and haggle over succulent fruits plucked fresh from the trees. Fishing is one of the mainstays of the local economy, and although fish are sorted for wholesale at night, during the day the market is a great source of dry fish products, including the pungent kho muc, or dried squid, often eaten with shrimp paste. Be sure to sample the town's famously tasty pork and vermicelli noodle soup, *hu tieu* My Tho, and beef meatballs, *bo vien*, from one of the busy stalls outside. A more sanitised, but not necessarily sanitary, undercover market is also here inside a three-storey building, but most traders prefer to operate outside. Still, if you do go upstairs they sell fake perfume for US$2, which may just eradicate all those fishy smells.

From HCMC, My Tho is often the first stop for those embarking on a delta adventure. Scenic six-hour trips run by river ferry, chugging alongside boats carrying fresh produce to the city or manufactured goods from it. The province has a more than adequate road network, and a new cable bridge connects My Tho to nearby Ben Tre township.

MY THO'S ISLANDS

My Tho is the ideal spot from which to reach the natural canals and

> **⊙ Tip**
>
> A phenomenal number of fruits grow in the Mekong Delta. Look out for roadside stalls selling coconut, mangosteen, mango, pineapple, rambutan and durian – although the latter is so smelly most hotels won't let it through their doors.

Ha Tien.

mangrove-covered inlets of the neighbouring islands. They are known locally as the "Coconut Islands" due to the huge concentration of the trees cultivated by locals. The fruit is sold for consumption, while its wood is used for handicrafts and the fibre for rope and mats. **Unicorn Island** (Con Lan) is the largest, with a population of 7,000, followed by **Phoenix Island** (Con Phung) and **Dragon Island** (Con Long), and then the tiny **Turtle Island** (Con Qui). Most of the boat tours from HCMC will include visits to small coconut candy factories and handicraft workshops, which have been set up solely for tourists. Note: Phoenix and Turtle islands are a part of Ben Tre province.

DONG TAM SNAKE FARM

Some 12km (7 miles) to the west of My Tho is **Dong Tam Snake Farm** (Trai Ran Dong Tam; tel: 073-385 3204; http://trairandongtam.com.vn; daily 7am–5.30pm). Converted from a former US army base, the pythons, cobras and king cobras reared here yield a variety of substances used in traditional

medicines. Snake meat is believed to be an effective remedy against a number of ailments ranging from mental disorders to rheumatism and paralysis, and snake gall is combined with other drugs to treat coughs and migraine. Most Vietnamese men believe snake to be a virility enhancer, and an intriguing tonic is obtained by steeping three varieties of snake in alcohol – if you need a boost, it's sold at the gift shop.

BEN TRE

The Rach Mieu cable bridge immediately put Ben Tre on the tourist radar when it opened in 2008. As well as providing easy access to Ben Tre from My Tho, crossing the bridge also shows visitors just how vast the waterways here are.

Crisscrossed by many small canals, **Ben Tre province** has perfect conditions for rice-growing, but is also prone to flooding during the rainy season. Competing with the area's extensive rice fields are coconut plantations: more coconut palms are grown in Ben Tre than in any other province in the

Dong Tam Snake Farm.

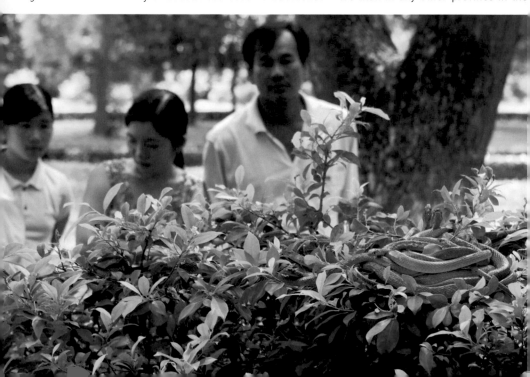

country. Look out for banh dua, a sticky rice and banana combo that is beautifully wrapped in banana leaves and is unique to Ben Tre. The provincial capital, **Ben Tre** ❸ ("Bamboo Boat Port"), is 10km (6 miles) from the My Tho ferry dock on the Ham Luong tributary, and is named after the little wooden vessels that used to dock there. A boat trip along the Ba Lai–Ham Luong waterway is the ideal way to get a feel of everyday life on the river. Bee farms and fruit orchards are scattered all over the area, and can be reached by the network of small canals.

Ben Tre town has a modest museum (daily 7–10.30am and 1.30–4.30pm; free) that focuses on the conflict with America but does also house a giant crocodile skull, from the time when tigers and elephants roamed these parts. The **Vien Minh Pagoda** (Chua Vien Minh; daily 7–11am and 1–9pm; free) is the head office of the province's Buddhist association and the town's main centre of worship. Rebuilt in 1958, it is thought to be around 100 years old.

AROUND BEN TRE

Located 70km (44 miles) from Ben Tre town is **Ba Tri** ❹, where the Nguyen Dinh Chieu Temple (daily 7.30–11.30am, 1.30–7pm) is dedicated to a 19th-century poet born in the town. The bird sanctuary of **San Chim Vam Ho** (daily 7am–6pm; charge), 38km (24 miles) southeast of Ben Tre or 15km (9 miles) northwest of Ba Tri, has a good collection of storks. Many visit here hoping to get that classic photo of Vietnam: a stork on the back of a water buffalo. The best time to visit is at dusk, when the birds fill the skies as they return to roost.

VINH LONG

The fruit-laden islands and floating market around Vinh Long make it a popular stopping-off point. West of Ben Tre province and 66km (41 miles)

from My Tho, **Vinh Long** ❺ has several islands ripe for exploration. Boats leave regularly from in front of the **Cuu Long Hotel** for trips to nearby **An Binh Island** and **Binh Hoa Phuoc Island**; both are 5km (3 miles) from Vinh Long. The official booking office is at **Cuu Long Tourist** (tel: 070-382 3616; http://cuulongtourist.com) at 1 Duong Thang 5 Street, but it is often cheaper to organise a trip privately with a local boatman. Mekong Travel Company (tel: 070-383 6252; www.mekongtravel.com.vn) has great staff who can also arrange bicycling tours in nearby countryside, or you can rent a bike for about US$3 a day.

The boat trip is a treat for fruit-lovers, as the excursion takes in villages with gardens and orchards heavy with juicy seasonal fruits. Visitors are also taken to see several cottage industries, such as potteries and rice-paper making, before strolling through well-tended bonsai gardens or staying overnight with one of a dozen local families on the islands. Many of the homes here are built on stilts, due to

Nguyen Dinh Chieu Temple in Ben Tre.

An exhibit at Can Tho Museum depicting a Chinese herbalist selling traditional medicine.

Coconut candy factory in Ben Tre.

the constant threat of flooding. Boat trips can also include Cai Be floating market on the other side of An Binh. The market operates from 5am to 5pm daily, but the mornings are best, when the market is at its busiest. If time is short, private jeeps can be hired for a swifter journey to the market. For the truly frugal, a ferry crosses to An Binh.

The town itself has several Chinese pagodas but the main action is around the day market. Several cafés, notably Hoang An, have pleasant riverside views.

TRA VINH

Leafy, sleepy **Tra Vinh** 16 is a beautiful town filled with strong Khmer influences. Some 40km (25 miles) southwest of Ben Tre, Tra Vinh province is bordered by the Tien and Hau rivers and washed by over 65km (40 miles) of coastline. Well off the tourist path, Tra Vinh is known locally as Go Do ("City in the Forest") after its ancient trees. A fifth of Tra Vinh's 131,000-strong population are ethnic Khmer who make their living from farming. Around 140

Khmer pagodas are dotted throughout the province.

The town is easy to walk around and has a couple of attractions, including a day market that runs along the Long Bing River. Ong Pagoda, in the centre of town, is a wonderfully dramatic-looking Chinese pagoda, while 200 metres/yds north is Ong Met Pagoda, which has Khmer carvings on the main wall and a more Thai style main hall. About 5km (3 miles) out of town is Ho Chi Minh Temple (daily 7am–5pm; free), which was built in 1971 and features a simple memorial at its centre and a patriotic exhibition of Ho Chi Minh's life all around it. Tree-fringed **Ao Ba Om** (Ba Om Lake) is a recreational area about 7km (4 miles) southwest of Tra Vinh town which also has a Khmer pagoda and museum nearby. Some 58km (36 miles) southwest of town is Co Pagoda (Chua Co) or Stork Pagoda, a Khmer pagoda that shelters hundreds of storks after sunset each day.

CAN THO

Can Tho 17 is the capital of Can Tho province and the largest and most modern city in the delta, with a population of nearly 1.3 million. Situated 34km (21 miles) southwest of Vinh Long on the banks of the Hau River (Song Hau), it is an important commercial centre and river port, bustling with energy.

As the hub of the Mekong Delta, Can Tho is a prosperous and vibrant city, best for strolling around and soaking up the atmosphere. One of the few places to visit in town is the **Can Tho Museum** at 1 Hoa Binh Street (Tue–Thu 8–11am and 2–5pm; Sat–Sun 8–11am and 6.30–9pm; free), with exhibits detailing local history. A short walk from here on 6 Hoa Binh is the Military Museum (also called Army Museum; daily 8–11am and 2–5pm; free) packed with American weapons left from the war, including a Hue chopper and a fighter jet.

The **Munirangsayaram Pagoda** at 36 Hoa Binh Street (daily 8am–5pm), built in 1946, is a centre of worship for the area's small Khmer community. This Hinayana Buddhist temple is similar to those found in Cambodia. Missing are the Taoist spirits and *bodhisattvas* found in Mahayana Buddhist temples that are more typical of Vietnam.

The city's **Central Market** is the largest fruit market in the Mekong Delta region, and although the main building is at the intersection of Hai Ba Trung and Nam Ky Khoi Nghia streets, the market hustle stretches along the length of Hai Ba Trung Street. Several restaurants on the waterfront serve regional specialities: frog, turtle, snake and many kinds of fish.

CAN THO'S FLOATING MARKETS

Boat trips on the Hau River are one of the highlights of Can Tho, and it is probably the best place in the Mekong Delta from which to tour the floating markets. Trips can be booked with the local tourism office, but a better option is to explore the markets by small motorboat; enquire along the dock or in guesthouses about chartering a boat (3-hour trips start from about US$19, twice as much for a 7-hour tour). Rise early for the 10km (6-mile) ride southeast to lively **Cai Rang**, the largest floating market in the delta. Here, all manner of boats and sampans gather, their occupants busily engaged in buying or selling a wide variety of fruit, fish and vegetables. Photo opportunities at this wholesale market are endless.

For a different experience, head to **Phong Dien**, about 20km (12 miles) southwest of Can Tho. This is a much smaller, and some say more authentic, floating market, thanks to the fact that fewer tourists bother to travel this far. Here, ladies in conical *non la* hats are happy to select, peel and slice fresh *buoi* (pomelo) or *xoai* (mango) for tourists from the mountain of fruit stacked high on their boats.

Clay figurine at Dat Set Pagoda.

Fresh fish, My Tho Central Market.

⊘ ÓC EO CIVILISATION

Some 40km (25 miles) southwest of Long Xuyen, in the hilly area of Ba The, are the ruins of Óc Eo, a major trading port during the first few centuries AD. Óc Eo lay submerged for many years until it was rediscovered in the 1940s after a French archaeologist took an aerial photograph of the area. Remnants of architectural structures and other finds made by researchers indicate that it was a city closely linked with the ancient pre-Angkor Indianised kingdom of Phu Nam (Funan), which dates back to the 1st century AD and was at the peak of prosperity during the 5th century.

It is possible to visit the ruins, but there's little to see, as the artefacts have been moved to museums throughout Vietnam. The museum in Long Xuyen has some exhibits from the site.

Floating market, Can Tho.

SOC TRANG

The Khmer-influenced province of Soc Trang is about 35km (22 miles) south of Can Tho. It is home to over 300,000 Khmer people and its capital, **Soc Trang ⑱**, has a number of interesting Khmer temples and pagodas. The best of these is the luridly painted **Kh'leng Pagoda** (daily 8am–5pm). Originally constructed more than 400 years ago, this pagoda was rebuilt in 1907 and is richly decorated on the outside with carved griffins, snakes and statues of dancing maidens. Inside, a gilded bronze statue of Sakyamuni Buddha presides over the main altar. About two dozen monks are in residence and 170 monks attend the Buddhist College on the premises. The ancient Dharma (Buddhist scripture), written on palm leaves, is one of the pagoda's most treasured relics. Opposite the pagoda is a small Khmer Culture Museum (23 Nguyen Chi Thanh, Mon–Fri 7–10.30am, 2–4.30pm) which displays costumes, artefacts and photographs as well as holding occasional Khmer dance and music shows.

DAT SET PAGODA

Near the centre of town, along 68 Mau Than Street, is the fascinating **Dat Set Pagoda** (Chua Dat Set; daily 8am–5pm; free), or the Clay Pagoda. Made entirely of clay, this Chinese pagoda houses statues and figurines sculpted from the same material by the monk Ngo Kim Tong. Look out for the intricately sculpted Bao Thap tower with its small Buddha figurines that rest on every lotus petal. There are also six giant paraffin candles, two of which have been burning in honour of the artist since 1970, when they were first made.

DOI PAGODA (BAT PAGODA)

On the outskirts of town, just 4km (2 miles) away, is **Doi Pagoda** (Chua Doi; daily 8am–5pm; charge), a popular stopping point for tourists. Less ornate than Kh'leng Pagoda, this Khmer temple is more famous for the thousands of screeching fruit bats residing in its gardens than for the colourful murals of the Buddha's life decorating the walls. It is said that while these bats may attack the fruit trees in other orchards, they know not to eat from the trees that shelter them. The best time to visit is around dawn and an hour before sunset, when the bats swoop out from the trees in a dense black cloud as they go hunting for food.

DONG THAP

Bordering Cambodia in the north, Dong Thap province is one of the three provinces lying in the marshy area known as **Dong Thap Muoi** ("10 Tower Field"). The province takes its name from the 10-storey Thap Muoi tower that was built in ancient times in the commune of An Phong. The tower, which no longer stands, was used as a lookout by the resistance forces against the French during colonial times. The area is populated primarily by people of Chinese, Khmer, Cham and Tai origin. Agriculture has always been the dominant industry, but recently industrial parks at Sa Dec, Song Hau and Tran Quoc Toan have been attracting business from around the delta.

AROUND CAO LANH

The provincial capital of Dong Thap province, **Cao Lanh** ⑲, has little of interest for tourists. More interesting are the sights around it. About 1km (0.6 miles) south of Cao Lanh is the **grave of Nguyen Sinh Sac**, Ho Chi Minh's father, who lived from 1862 to 1929.

About 20km (12 miles) southeast of Cao Lanh and accessible only by boat is **Rung Tram**, a forested area that harboured an underground Viet Cong camp called **Xeo Quit Base** (daily 7am–5pm) during the Vietnam War. For nearly 15 years, key Viet Cong personnel lived here in underground bunkers while planning strategic attacks against the American forces just 2 km (1.2 miles) away from the US military base.

Tran Chim Tam Nong is a stork sanctuary located 45km (28 miles) north of Cao Lanh in the Tam Nong area. This wildlife reserve is home to rare red-headed cranes, lots of fish and innumerable water chestnut trees, all best seen by boat (approx. VND100,000 per hour).

AN GIANG

To the west, **An Giang province** ("Splitting River") borders the Cambodian province of Takeo. Here, the Mekong enters the province and divides into two branches, forming the Tien and Hau rivers, which every year deposit millions of cubic metres of alluvial soil in the adjacent areas.

This prosperous region, intersected by numerous natural canals and small rivers, is rich in natural resources and fertile land, and produces many varieties of fruit trees and crops of rice, soya bean, tobacco, groundnut and mulberry; it's also known for its silk industry.

An Giang is home to a sizeable number of Vietnam's ethnic minorities, of which Khmer Krom (southern Khmer) is the largest. It is believed that An Giang was once an important centre of the ancient Oc Eo culture.

Reclining Buddha, Doi Pagoda.

The fishermen of Chau Doc live in houses that float on the Hau Giang River.

LONG XUYEN

Ang Giang province's capital, **Long Xuyen** , in the east of the province 190km (118 miles) from HCMC and 45km (28 miles) from the Cambodian border, is a thriving commercial town, the streets lined with cafés and motorbikes. The town's name refers to the shape of the river and literally means "dragon running through". Home to over 260,000 people, the predominant industries are rice production and the processing of fish (mainly catfish) for export, which have made the town the second-most prosperous town in the delta, after Can Tho.

Long Xuyen was home to the Hoa Hao sect, the region's major military force and army until 1956, and was the birthplace of Vietnam's second president, Ton Duc Thang.

Dominating the town with its tall bell tower at Hung Vuong Street is the greystone Catholic **Long Xuyen Cathedral**. Built between 1963 and 1973, the church can seat 1,000 worshippers and is the largest in the Mekong Delta. At 77 Thoai Ngoc Hau Street is the small

Khmer-style Kh'leng Pagoda.

An Giang Museum (Bao Tang An Giang; Tue–Sun 7–11am and 1.30–5pm). Displayed here are a few exhibits on the **Oc Eo** as well as personal effects of Ton Duc Thang and pictures of Long Xuyen in the 1930s.

CHAU DOC

A stone's throw from the Cambodian border, this town is situated on the right bank of the **Hau Giang River** (Song Hau Giang) and is the usual entry or exit point for people on a boat tour between HCMC and the Cambodian capital Phnom Penh. With a population of 120,000, **Chau Doc** has a lively feel, and there is plenty to see and do on day trips from the town.

The **Chau Phu Temple** (Dinh Than Chau Phu; daily 8am–5pm; free) in the middle of Chau Doc town at the junction of Tran Hung Dao and Nguyen Van Thoai streets was built in 1926. Here, the locals worship Thai Ngoc Hau, the man responsible for building the nearby Chau Doc Canal, which opened the frontier between Cambodia and Vietnam. Thai was a high-ranking and important official during the time of the Nguyen dynasty.

Across the river in nearby Chau Giang is the **Chau Giang Mosque**, which serves the district's Muslim Cham community, as well as ethnic Vietnamese who have returned from Malaysia and Indonesia. The Cham number around 20,000 in the Chau Doc area, and typically live in stilt houses on the water, making their living from fishing and weaving.

Chau Doc is renowned for its quaint **floating villages**. Living in houses built over empty metal tanks to keep them afloat, many villagers make a living from fishing. Metal nets under the houses allow the families to farm and catch fish, which are then sold at local markets and transported all over the region. The houses stay stationary, anchored to poles sunk deep into the river bed by rope.

AROUND CHAU DOC

Some 4km (2 miles) away from Chau Doc is the 230-metre (755ft) -high **Sam Mountain 23** (Nui Sam), named after the sea cucumbers that once thrived nearby. Buddhist and Taoist shrines scatter the mountain slopes, visited by ethnic Chinese and pilgrims from Vietnam and abroad. You can climb up the south side of the mountain or get a motorbike to take you to the summit (the road is on the east side). Either way you will be greeted by spectacular views of the surrounding countryside at the summit. On a clear day even Cambodia is visible. A military outpost with a few soldiers is found at the top; the latter are more interested nowadays in their badminton games than the prospect of possible military incursions from Cambodia. The outpost is a legacy of the days when the Khmer Rouge would cross the border and slaughter Vietnamese civilians.

At the foot of the mountain is the tomb of Thai Ngoc Hau (the Nguyen-dynasty architect of the Chau Doc Canal), which also holds his two wives and some of the workers who died during the construction of the canal.

TAY AN PAGODA AND TEMPLE OF LADY XU

Sharing the base of the mountain are the Indian-style **Tay An Pagoda** (Chua Tay An) and **Temple of Lady Xu** (Mieu Ba Chua Xu). Famous for its numerous finely carved religious figures, Tay An Pagoda was established in 1847 by a Buddhist monk from Dong Thap province named Doan Minh Huyen, who wanted to help feed and heal the province's poor people.

Nearby, the Temple of Lady Xu reputedly marks the spot where looting Siamese troops left her granite statue after carrying it down from its original seat at the top of the mountain. According to folklore, Lady Xu came from the sky and helped the locals cultivate rice and develop their agriculture and fishing industries. Worshippers, including many Chinese from HCMC, Hong Kong and Taiwan, regularly visit bearing money, gifts and food, making it one of the richest temples in Vietnam. Every year on the 22nd day of the fourth lunar month, a large procession of followers begins a week-long series of festivities to celebrate their pilgrimage.

RUNG TRAM TRA SU

The vast bird sanctuary of **Rung Tram Tra Su** (daily 7am–7pm), covering 845 hectares (2,088 acres), is along the road to Sam Mountain, around 30km (19 miles) southwest of Chau Doc and 10km (6 miles) from the Cambodian border. This area around the Hau River became a protected forest reserve in 2005, and is home to many different animals and over 70 species of birds, notably the Indian crane, which is listed in the Vietnamese *Red Book* as a rare and endangered species.

Scientific research is a key component of the sanctuary, and of the 140 types of plants found in this reserve, 79

The remains of the Khmer Rouge genocide victims at Ba Chuc.

Long Xuyen rural scene.

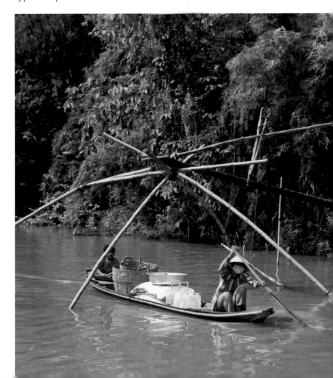

Tip

With its reasonably flat terrain, the countryside around Ha Tien lends itself very well to bicycle touring. Several of the hotels in Ha Tien rent bikes by the day at modest rates.

reportedly have medicinal properties. Rangers here offer hour-long motorised sampan rides along the waterways to visit hides elevated above the forest canopy.

BA CHUC

About 40km (25 miles) southwest of Chau Doc en route to Ha Tien are Vietnam's killing fields, **Ba Chuc**. For two weeks in April 1978, Khmer Rouge soldiers from Cambodia tore through this small border commune, mercilessly hacking adults to death with machetes and ripping young children limb from limb. In total, the raiding forces massacred 3,157 civilians, reducing the population of Ba Chuc to only two. A pagoda built in 1991 contains the skulls and bones of 1,159 victims. On display in the temple are some graphic photos depicting the aftermath of the slaughter.

KIEN GIANG

Kien Giang province, in the southwest of the Mekong Delta, shares a common border in the northwest with

Cambodia. In the west, it is washed by waters from the Gulf of Thailand. The border crossing from Ha Tien into Kampot in Cambodia is now open, but would-be travellers must hold a visa before entering Cambodia (it can be obtained at the border). Forests, plains, offshore islands and a 200km (124-mile) -long coastline make Kien Giang one of the delta's most geographically diverse and scenic provinces.

HA TIEN

Nestling in a cove formed by the **Gian Thang River** (Song Gian Thang) is the town of **Ha Tien** , with a population of about 50,000. Only 10km (6 miles) from the Cambodian border, Ha Tien's natural beauty, easy-going atmosphere and hospitality attract many visitors. To the east of Ha Tien, scenic **East Lake** (Ho Dong) – actually a sea inlet – is usually the first sight to greet visitors. The town is well known for its plentiful seafood and abundant black pepper plantations. It does a lively trade in items handcrafted from the shells of sea turtles, although it is best not to buy such goods as it only encourages this unfortunate trade.

MAC CUU FAMILY TOMBS

Ha Tien town has several temples dedicated to the legendary Mac family and an even greater number of tombs that rest on the eastern flank of **Binh San Mountain** (Nui Binh San). These 49 tombs are built of bricks and contain the remains of both Mac Cuu, a Chinese immigrant who founded the town, and his relatives. **Mac Cuu Family Tombs** (Lang Mac Chu), built in 1809 in a traditional Chinese architectural style, is the largest and is decorated with finely carved figures of the traditional Blue Dragon and White Tiger.

PHU DUNG PAGODA

If you only have time to visit one temple, head to 374 Phuong Thanh Street to see the **Phu Dung Pagoda** (Chua

Chau Phu Temple, Chau Doc.

ĐÌNH THẦN CHÂU PHÚ

1926

Phu Dung; daily 8am–5pm; free), founded by Mac Cuu's second wife, Nguyen Thi Xuan, in 1750. Her tomb is built on the hillside behind the pagoda's main hall, and the pagoda contains some interesting statues. In the centre of the main hall is one of the newborn Sakyamuni Buddha, in the embrace of nine dragons; on the main dais enclosed in a glass case is a bronze Chinese Buddha. Overcome by jealousy, Mac Cuu's first wife tried to kill her beautiful rival by placing her in an empty tank, intending her to drown as the rains slowly filled it up. Mac Cuu found and rescued her in time, and today visitors to Phu Dung Pagoda are predominantly women, intrigued by her story.

AROUND HA TIEN

Some 8km (5 miles) northwest of Ha Tien are the twin beaches of **Mui Nai** and **Bai No**, which flank the sides of a small peninsula. The beaches are unremarkable, but they are popular with holidaying Vietnamese; expect lurid plastic picnic seats, kayaks, souvenir shops, and plenty of company at weekends.

THACH DONG CAVE PAGODA

About 4km (2.5 miles) away, past scenic paddy fields filled with water buffalo, is **Thach Dong Cave Pagoda** (Thach Dong Thon Van), the "Grotto that Swallows the Clouds". The cave shelters a Buddhist sanctuary and several funerary tablets, while altars to Quan Am and to Ngoc Hoang, the Jade Emperor of Heaven, can be found in several of its chambers. Lookout points at the cave reveal breathtaking views of the surrounding rice fields and smaller offshore islands. Near the grotto is a mass grave where 130 people massacred by Khmer Rouge troops in 1978 are buried; they are commemorated by a stela known as **Bia Cam Thu** – the Monument of Hatred – to the left of the sanctuary's entrance.

HON CHONG AND SURROUNDINGS

The road from Ha Tien southeast to the provincial capital, Rach Gia, is

⊙ Tip

The best time to visit the Mekong Delta is between January and March, when temperatures are around 22°C to 34°C (72°F to 93°F). From May onwards, the rainfall and humidity increase. During the wettest months – July to October – some provinces are flooded and travel is restricted.

*View from
Sam Mountain.*

⊙ Tip

Homestays are a great way to experience what life is really like around this region. A growing number is now available, and they tend to offer basic accommodation but also the chance to cook, fish and live like locals for a few days.

generally good, and passes many small farms and picturesque villages. About 20km (12 miles) from Ha Tien, a detour off the main road in Ba Hon leads to the seaside town of **Hon Chong** ㉕. Unlike much of the pancake-flat Mekong Delta, this area is studded with impressive towering limestone formations. They are slowly becoming slightly less towering these days as these mountains are a prime source of quality limestone for the cement factories near Hon Chong, so are continually blasted with dynamite.

Once you pass the factories on the main road out to the beach, Hon Chong itself is relatively peaceful and beautiful. The best is **Duong Beach** (Bai Duong), which takes its name from the *duong* (casuarina) trees growing beside it. Its clear waters and picturesque surroundings make it an ideal spot to break the journey with a swim.

At the tip of the beach, a toll gate leads to **Chua Grotto** (Chua Hang). The grotto is entered from behind the altar of the main pagoda, which is set back into the base of the hill. Small shrines

line the cave, and a short walk through the rock leads you to the beach on the other side. For a small fee, tour boats here take you on a 20-minute cruise around the three islands, known locally as a mini Halong Bay.

Looking out to sea, you will see the famous **Father and Son Rocks** (Hon Phu Tu), the grottoes of which are a favourite haunt of sea swallows. A lightning strike in 2006 "killed" the father, knocking the stone column into the sea, so now only the son remains.

You can take a boat out to the islands, and then on to stalactite and stalagmite-riddled **Tien Grotto** (Hang Tien), or Coin Grotto. The cave is named after the zinc coins found buried within it by Nguyen Anh – the future Emperor Gia Long – and his troops, who camped here while battling the Tay Son rebels. A boat runs from a tiny dock on the beach from 7am to 4pm; the ticket costs VND9,000, but the boat only leaves once it has 25 passengers.

Leaving Hon Chung, around 3km (2 miles) before Ba Hon on the main

Street scene, Chau Doc.

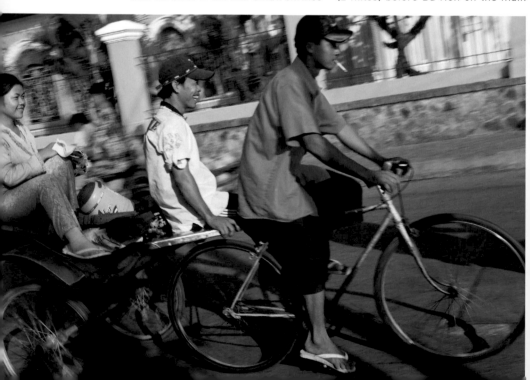

road is **Mo So Grotto** (Hang Mo So). Open to the sky and encircled by sheer stone walls, a torch and a local guide will come in handy when exploring the labyrinth of tunnels beyond the three main caverns.

RACH GIA

Ken Giang province's capital town is **Rach Gia** ㉖, located 100km (60 miles) southeast of Ha Tien. It is an active fishing port with a population of nearly 250,000, and is bordered by marshlands, many of which have been drained for rice cultivation. Well known for its seafood, Rach Gia has a good selection of restaurants serving both Chinese and Vietnamese food. The town also has a few interesting temples and pagodas, but does not offer as much as other delta towns; it's mainly used as a jumping-off point for travellers taking the ferry or plane to Phu Quoc Island.

PHU QUOC ISLAND

Vietnam's largest island, **Phu Quoc** ㉗, is a mountainous retreat with 150km (94 miles) of sandy coastline. Situated 45km (28 miles) west of Ha Tien and part of Kien Giang province, the mountainous forest-island is 50km (30 miles) long and covers 1,300 sq km (500 sq miles). In the 18th century, Nguyen Anh (who later became Emperor Gia Long of the Nguyen dynasty) was sheltered here from the Tay Son rebels by French missionary Pigneau de Behaine, who himself used the island as a base between the 1760s and 1780s.

In 1869 the French occupied the island, establishing rubber and coconut plantations and also a notorious prison. During the Vietnam War, the South Vietnam government reopened the penal centre and incarcerated nearly 40,000 Viet Cong between 1969 and 1972.

In the past decade tourism has exploded here and things are about to get even bigger – a plan has been approved to build a US$4 billion casino and resort with a five-star hotel on 130 hectares (321 acres), while the government aims to attract up to 3 million visitors a year by 2020.

Oysters are cultivated for pearls at Phu Quoc Island.

Hon Chong is often referred to as a mini Halong Bay.

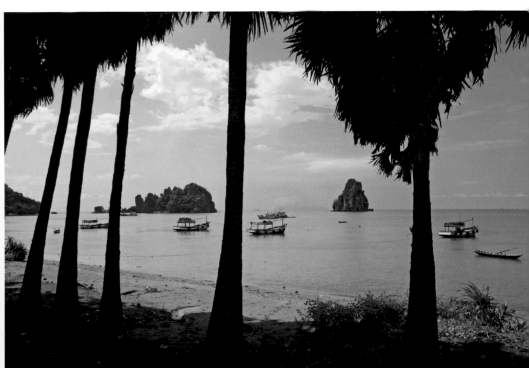

⊙ Eat

For the best and cheapest seafood in Phu Quoc, head to Dinh Cau Night Market in Duong Dong town. Here, along Vo Thi Sau Street, is a string of eateries serving fresh seafood and local Vietnamese dishes at low prices. There are English menus, as these places are well patronised by foreign tourists.

Thach Dong Cave Pagoda.

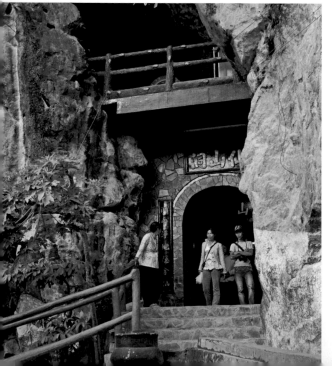

MAIN SIGHTS

Today, the old prison near **An Thoi** port at the southern end of Phu Quoc Island has been turned into a museum. Called **Coconut Prison** (Nha Lao Cay Dua; http://phuquocprison.org; Tue–Sun 7am–5pm; free), it displays photographs of torture techniques and escape attempts, and lays bare the brutal conditions experienced by the inmates.

Phu Quoc has bountiful fishing grounds, black pepper trees and high-quality *nuoc mam* (fish sauce). Mats covered with fish drying in the sun can be seen (and smelt from afar) all over the island, and there are a number of local factories, including one of the island's best distilleries, **Khai Hoan Fish Sauce Distillery** (daily 8–11am and 2–5pm; free), where you can brave the stink to see how fish sauce is made. The factory is located at Hung Vuong Street, near the main port and town of **Duong Dong**, on the west coast of the island.

The island's pristine waters also provide perfect conditions for the cultivation of pearl-bearing oysters. The **Phu Quoc Pearl Farm** (tel: 077-398 8999; daily 8am–5pm), just south of Duong Dong along Truong Beach (Bai Truong), most of all provides an interesting opportunity to buy pearls and gain some insight into the world of pearl cultivation.

Half a kilometre from Duong Dong's main market, on a tiny spit of land at the mouth of Duong Dong River, is **Cau Castle** (Dinh Cau; on Truong Beach, daily 8am–6pm). This is not really a castle but a temple-cum-lighthouse that acts as a spiritual beacon for Phu Quoc's fishermen. Built to honour the Goddess of the Sea, local fishermen and their families pray for her protection every time they put out to sea.

Phu Quoc can be accessed by a 2.5-hour boat ride from Rach Gia, Ha Tien or Hon Chung, or more easily via Vietnam Airlines flights from Ho Chi Minh City or Rach Gia. The best time to visit Phu Quoc is during the dry season from May to November.

PHU QUOC'S BEACHES

The real draw here is the coastline and its virtually uninterrupted fringe of spectacular white-sand beaches, washed by clear waters. **Dai Beach** (Bai Dai) in the northwest offers the perfect vantage point to enjoy the sunset, while remote **Thom Beach** (Bai Thom) in the northeast is usually deserted. **Truong Beach** (Bai Truong), better known as **Long Beach**, runs 20km (12 miles) along the western side of the island, stretching from Duong Dong almost to An Thoi Port in the south. This is where most of the island's resorts are located, so finding a bite to eat or an ice-cool cocktail to sip under coconut palms is never a problem.

Locals will tell you that **Sao Beach** (Bai Sao), also known as Star Beach, and **Khem Beach** (Bai Khem), or Cream Beach, 25km (16 miles) from

Duong Dong town on the far south-eastern coast, are the island's most beautiful stretches. They are correct, and super-fine white sand and crystal waters await those who make the trek there, but these beaches are also the most undeveloped.

PHU QUOC NATIONAL PARK

Established in 2001 in the hilly north-eastern part of the island is **Phu Quoc National Park**. The highest of the 99 peaks in the island, **Chua Mountain** (Nui Chua) is found within the confines of the nature reserve. Little is known about the biodiversity of the park's 37,000 hectares (91,427 acres) of lowland evergreen forest, which covers two-thirds of the island. Check with your hotel about jungle-trekking tours of the reserve.

A few kilometres east of Duong Dong in the middle of the island is **Suoi Da Ban** (Stony Surface Spring), which flows through rocky pools pleasant enough for a swim. About 5km (3 miles) south, **Suoi Tranh** (Picturesque Stream) flows down from

Ham Ninh Mountain (Nui Ham Ninh) to form an inviting waterfall called Ben Tranh. About 20 km northeast of Duong Dong is the picturesque Ham Ninh village, renowned for its breathtaking natural scenery and pristine waters. It lets tourists peer into a peaceful life of local fishermen and makes for a perfect place to try some of the local staples including ginseng-seaweed water, "Tram" mushrooms, boiled flower crab and sea-horse liquor.

AN THOI ARCHIPELAGO

To the south of the island is the **An Thoi Archipelago ㉘**, a group of 15 islands, the largest of which is Hon Thom, that has become enormously popular with divers and snorkellers. The surrounding waters are home to the endangered dugong as well as leatherback and hawksbill turtles, although underwater enthusiasts are more likely to see a huge variety of small, colourful reef and coral fish, many of which are endemic to Vietnamese waters.

Long Beach is on the western side of Phu Quoc Island.

Quang Cong Temple detail, Hoi An.

VIETNAM

TRAVEL TIPS

TRANSPORT

GETTING THERE

By air

Flying into Vietnam

Vietnam receives a small amount of air traffic compared with major Southeast Asian hubs such as Singapore and Bangkok. The main international airports are in Ho Chi Minh City (HCMC), Hanoi and Danang. Less important ones include Can Tho and Cam Ranh international terminals. HCMC is the prime gateway to the country, with fewer international flights going to Hanoi. Danang receives international flights from Hong Kong, Bangkok, Kuala Lumpur, Taipei, Chengdu, Seoul, Siem Reap, and Singapore.

While Vietnam Airlines still has the largest number of international flights, as part of the country's WTO obligations (signed in 2006), the country has opened up the aviation industry to a number of international carriers. As a result, new carriers are flying in to HCMC and Hanoi all the time, including budget favourite Air Asia (from Bangkok) and JetStar Airlines (from Singapore).

From Europe, it is possible to fly to Vietnam direct from several countries, including France, Germany and UK, while many Asian countries now offer direct routes. Flight time from Europe is about 12 hours.

Other carriers from Europe and the USA have to fly through Bangkok, Hong Kong, Kuala Lumpur, Singapore, Seoul, Tokyo or Taipei to reach either HCMC or Hanoi.

Flight time from the USA (via Taipei or Tokyo) to Hanoi or HCMC is around 19 hours.

From Australia, there are nonstop flights from Sydney and Melbourne to either Hanoi or HCMC. Flight time from Sydney to HCMC is approximately 8 hours.

Hanoi

Noi Bai International Airport (http://vietnamairport.vn) is about 45km (28miles) north of downtown Hanoi. After Ho Chi Minh City's airport, it is Vietnam's main domestic and international hub serving flights from Europe, Australia and Asia. Aside from Vietnam Airlines (www.vietnamairlines.com), there are some 29 international airlines serving Noi Bai Airport. The main international destinations are Bangkok, Kuala Lumpur, Seoul, Siem Reap, Singapore, Taipei and Tokyo.

The airport has two terminals: Terminal 2 (T2), inaugurated in January 2015, handles international traffic while Terminal 1 (T1) deals with domestic flights. The former currently has a capacity of up to 10 million (to increase to 15 million by 2030) and the latter of 9 million passengers a year. Designed by a Japanese company, T2 is a slick building featuring two wings with large glass walls, taking full advantage of natural light and saving daytime energy. The arrivals hall is located on the first and second floors while departures are on the third floor. A business lounge and commercial services area as well as restaurants are situated on the top floor, while duty-free shops and other facilities can be found on the first and third level. Both terminals (T2 and T1) are connected by a free shuttle bus operating every 10–15 minutes between 6am and midnight.

For flight information, call the Operation Control Centre, tel: 04-3587 6101.

Ho Chi Minh City

HCMC's **Tan Son Nhat International Airport** – just 7km (4 miles) from the city centre – is Vietnam's busiest airport hub, and accounts for nearly two-thirds of international arrivals and departures into

Vietnam. Currently, more than 40 airlines operate out of Tan Son Nhat International Airport. Built in the 1930s and developed with US help in the 1950s, it handled almost 22 million passengers in 2014.

Terminal 2, which services international flights, opened in September 2007 and with extension complete in 2015, is linked to the older Terminal 1 by a covered walkway. Terminal 2 has separate floors for Arrivals (first and second level) and Departures (third level).

Terminal 1 is used solely for domestic flights (namely Vietnam Airlines, Jetstar Pacific Airlines and VASCO). Both terminals have tourist information desks and food-and-drink outlets, but the larger, more upscale Terminal 2 has better facilities and swankier shops and restaurants. A new, $8 billion Long Thanh international airport is being constructed about 50km (31 miles) away from HCMC and is scheduled to become operational by 2020. When the final phase of the construction is completed by 2035, it will serve up to 100 million passengers annually.

For flight information, call the **Operation Control Centre**, tel: 08-3848 5383, 08-3844 6662.

Danang

Danang International Airport, the main hub for central Vietnam, is about 5km (3.1 miles) east of the city centre. The new terminal opened in 2011 and serves approximately 10,000 passengers per day with direct international flights to Hong Kong, Bangkok, Kuala Lumpur, Taipei, Chengdu, Seoul, Siem Reap, and Singapore. Vietnam Airlines and Jetstar Pacific also offer daily connections with Hanoi, Ho Chi Minh City and Nha Trang. For flight information call (0) 511 830338. The best way to get to the city centre from the airport is by taxi. Trusted companies include Mai Linh and Airport Taxi and are readily available outside the terminal.

From Danang, major places of interest like Hoi An and Hue are easily accessible by road.

By road

From **China**, it is possible to enter Vietnam at the Lang Son and Lao Cai border crossings in the north and at Mong Cai near Halong Bay, where you can enter from Dongxing.

One can also enter Vietnam from several border points in **Laos** including **Sop Hun (Laos)/ Tay Trang (Vietnam), Nam Xoi/Na Maew** (also spelled **Nao Meo**), **Nam Can/Nam Khan, Nam Phao/Cau Treo, Dansavanah/Lao Bao, Bo Y/ Ngoc Hoi**, and **La Lay (Quang Tri)**. Painfully slow buses bring passengers to the central towns of Lao Bao and Cau Treo.

Travellers can also enter Vietnam by crossing the border with **Cambodia** at Moc Bai, only a few hours by road from HCMC, or at Vinh Xuong (Kaam Samnor in Cambodia), located about 30km (18 miles) north of Chau Doc in south Vietnam and at Xa Xia (Prek Chak in Cambodia).

GETTING AROUND

From major airports

Hanoi

The best way to get to cover the 35km (21-mile) distance from **Noi Bai International Airport** to downtown Hanoi is by an **airport taxi** (tel: (0)-2432-668218; www.hanoiairporttaxi.org). The trip into town can take 40–60 minutes, depending on traffic and the actual destination. The taxi stand is directly outside the Arrivals area. Airport taxis charge a fixed rate of US$15–25 (depending on the vehicle's size and company), payable in US dollars or the dong equivalent, and are exempt from tolls. It is advisable to use only reputable and reliable companies such as Hanoi Group Taxi, Mai Linh Taxi and Thanh Ga as scams and 'fixed' meters are quite common. As the airport is located in Hanoi's northernmost Soc Son District, private vehicles heading to Hanoi from Noi Bai are subject to a road toll of US$2.60. Although taxis have meters it is often more economical to agree a price first.

⊘ Key airline offices in HCMC

Air Asia, 254 De Tham St, District 1, tel: 08-3838 9811, Call Centre: 04-3928 8282; www.airasia.com
Air France, 130 Dong Khoi St, District 1, tel: 08-3829 0981/2; www.airfrance.com.vn
British Airways, 2/F, Travel House, 170–172 Nam Ky Khoi Nghia St, District 3, tel: 08-3830 2933; www.ba.com
Cathay Pacific Room 502, 5th Floor, Centec Tower, 72–74 Nguyen Thi Minh Khai Street, District 3, tel: 08-3822 3203; www.cathaypacific.com
Emirates Airlines, Room 1409 Sun Wah Tower, 115 Nguyen Hue Boulevard District 1, tel: 08-3911 3099; www.emirates.com
Lufthansa, A&B Tower, 23rd Floor, Room 7A, District 1, tel: 08-3829 8529; www.lufthansa.com

Qantas, HT&T Travel Vietnam#, Mezzanine Floor, Resco Building, 94-96 Nguyen Du, District 1, tel: 08-3910 5373; www.qantas.com
Singapore Airlines, G/F, Suite 101, Saigon Tower Building, 29 Le Duan St, District 1, tel: 08-3823 1588; www.singaporeair.com
Thai Airways, G/F, Saigon Tower Building, Ground Floor Suite 101, 29 Le Duan St, District 1, tel: 08-3822 3365; www.thaiair.com
Tiger Airways, Nguyen Trai, P-NCT, Q 1, TP HCM, tel: 08-3920 5999; http://tigerair.vn
United Airlines, 4th Floor Travel House, 170-172 Nam Ky Khoi Nghia Street Ward 6 District 3, tel: 08-3930 6613; www.unitedairlines.com.vn/
Vietnam Airlines, 49 Truong Son, Ward 2, Tan Binh Dist, tel: 08-3844 6667; www.vietnamairlines.com

Upmarket hotels tend to offer an airport pick-up service; ask in advance if this is available and the cost. Occasionally, some smaller guesthouses will say they do free airport pick-ups, but will then try to charge for the trip. Establish in advance if the service really is free. Airport minibuses cost US$2 but only leave once full. They drop passengers off in the heart of the Hoan Kiem District.

Public buses (daily 5am–10pm) are slow and crowded, so forget about this option unless you are travelling light. The yellow and red No. 07 or **No. 17** buses connect Noi Bai Airport with Hanoi's downtown. The bus stop is on the right side of the terminal exit. Bus fares are 5,000–10,000 VND per person depending on the final destination and the trip to the city takes about an hour. Passengers are dropped off on the edge of the Old Quarter (No.17) not far from Hoan Kien Lake, the destination of most tourists, or in the western part of the town (No.07) – about an hour's walk from the historic centre.

Ho Chi Minh City
Tan Son Nhat International Airport is only 7km (4 miles) northwest of the centre, but the ride into town can take 30 or 40 minutes. The airport offers few transport options: there are no airport shuttle buses,

and it can be quite overwhelming for visitors, especially with unlicensed taxi "reps" hassling arrivals for business. Many hotels, especially 5-star establishments, offer pre-arranged transfer services, and, although sometimes costly, these are recommended.

Otherwise, your best option is an **airport taxi**, outside both Terminal 1 and Terminal 2. When leaving the international terminal, turn right and walk 200 metres/yds to the domestic terminal for more taxi options. Alternatively, turn left when leaving international terminal and head straight to find a taxi rank of a recommended company. There are no pre-arranged fixed rates, so be sure to establish the fare before departing (US$8–10 for a ride to downtown HCMC is reasonable). Note: if you agree to go by meter, some taxi drivers may take long, circuitous routes into town; and if you're heading to the backpacker area (around Pham Ngo Lao and De Tham streets), a common scam is to try to convince you that your hotel closed down recently. The taxi driver will then offer to take you to an alternative hotel where he will get a commission from the owner. There are some reputable firms, such as Mai Linh, Vinasun and Airport Taxi, but there are also copycat taxis with exactly the same name but displayed in a different font.

Alternatively, public air conditioned bus **No. 152** travels into District 1, stopping at convenient places like Dong Khoi and Nguyen Hue streets, the backpacker area, and Ben Thanh Bus Station; it operates from outside Terminal 1 (6am–6pm); tickets, VND5,000 (plus extra 5,000 for bags).

Domestic travel

By air

Vietnam Airlines (www.vietnamairlines.com) operates domestic flights to the following destinations: Buon Ma Thuot, Ca Mau, Con Dao, Dalat, Danang, Dong Hoi, Haiphong, Hue, Nha Trang, Phu Quoc, Pleiku, Quy Nhon, Rach Gia, Tam Ky, Tranh Hoa, Tuy Hoa and Vinh – as well as Hanoi and HCMC.

Jetstar Pacific Airlines (www.jetstar.com) is a budget airline that flies to Buon Ma Thuot, Chu Lai, Dalat, Danang, Dong Hoi Haiphong, Hanoi, HCMC, Hue, Nha Trang, Phu Quoc, Pleiku, Quy Nhon, Tanh Hoa, Tuy Hoa, and Vinh.

VASCO Airlines, a former subsidiary of Vietnam Airlines, connects HCMC with Ca Mau, Can Tho, Con Son Island (Con Dao archipelago), Dien Bien Phu, Hanoi, as well as Phu Quoc, Rach Gia and Tuy Hoa.

Flying is by far the best way to travel if you intend to visit only a few cities in Vietnam. A Vietnam Airlines flight from Hanoi to HCMC costs under US$180 return (with taxes and fuel charges included). Vietnam Airlines also flies to out-of-the-way places like Phu Quoc Island.

You can use credit cards to buy airline tickets in Hanoi and HCMC, but in other cities you may be asked to pay cash. Tickets are sold by most travel agents in the big cities, or book directly with the airline office at HCMC and Hanoi.

By train

Train travel, operated by **Vietnam Railways** (www.vr.com.vn) in Vietnam, is very slow. Due to the existence of just a single track along the coast, train travel can often be hit by delays. The fastest express train from Hanoi to HCMC (called the *Reunification Express*), the SE4, covers 1,730km (1,073 miles) in 29 hours, with the slower ones (like the TBN) taking up to 41 hours because of the numerous stops they make. If you need to

get somewhere fast, forget about the train. However, if you want to soak up the Vietnamese countryside the train has a lot to offer, including a chance to take in the beautiful scenery and – with long-distance trains being such a sociable means of travel – an opportunity to interact with Vietnamese people.

There are five classes of train travel in Vietnam: hard seat, soft seat, hard sleeper, soft sleeper and soft sleeper with air conditioning – this last option is only available on certain trains. Expect to pay at least US$90 for a berth in a four-person compartment on the fastest express train from Hanoi to HCMC (or vice versa). There are five trains that make this run every day, and berths are reserved quickly, so try to make reservations early. There is a dining car on most trains, or you can buy snacks from the vendors that service the train at local stops.

There are also local train services on the Hanoi–HCMC line that branch out to various coastal cities. Lines also run from Hanoi northwest to Lao Cai, east to Hai Phong, and north to Lang Son. Overnight trains, with a sleeper ticket, can be a good way to travel as you save on a night's accommodation and wake up at your destination.

Note: hardly any English is spoken at local train stations, so do yourself a favour and get a travel agency to organise this for you for a small, but worthwhile, fee.

Hanoi

Hanoi's Railway Station is at 120 Le Duan St, tel: 04-3825 3949 (located at the far western end of Tran Hung Dao St). The ticket office is open daily from 7.30am to 7.30pm. Another ticket office to the right of the station entrance is for north-bound trains. Book ahead if you want to guarantee a sleeper carriage.

Ho Chi Minh City

Trains leave HCMC for the northern coastal towns from the railway station, which is located at 1 Nguyen Thong St, District 3 (tel: 08-3843 6528). The ticket office is open daily from 7.30am to 7.30pm.

At the railway station forecourt is the private joint-venture **Golden Trains**, which operates more upscale carriages connected to SNT1 and SNT2 trains in the south offering better services, security

and facilities. These comprise daily overnight services between HCMC and **Nha Trang** (10 hours 20 minutes). Features include LCD TVs, air conditioning, luxury cabin berths and recliner chairs with power points.

Hanoi to Sa Pa

From Hanoi, the trip to Sa Pa requires an overnight train trip to Lao Cai, followed by a 45-minute bus ride from Lao Cai up to Sa Pa. Train tickets and transportation are best arranged through a travel agent in Hanoi as they get discounts on ticket purchases and will also arrange the final leg of the journey from Lao Cai to Sa Pa.

The Hanoi–Lao Cai train runs three times a night and once during the day. The daytime route doesn't have cabins with sleeping berths or air-conditioning, and so is best avoided. Evening trains have a selection of soft and hard sleepers, both with air-conditioning. A soft sleeper with air-conditioning costs about US$40 if you book tickets yourself at the station. More luxurious trains are on offer (www.sapatrain.com), which can be arranged via travel agents, and offer stylish carriages and superior service from US$80 return.

Transfers from Lao Cai are easy as numerous minibuses ply the road up to Sa Pa for US$4 (one way). Drivers wait until the bus is full, which sometimes takes a while.

The best and fastest way to get to Sa Pa from Hanoi is catching a bus plying the motorway between Hanoi and Lao Cai. A 5-hour trip on Sapa Express (http://sapaexpress.com) costs US$16 per person. The bus leaves Hanoi at 7am.

By bus

Bus travel in Vietnam can be gruelling, so it's best to opt for the more comfortable "Open Tour" air-conditioned express services. Departing every day, the bus allows you to get on or off anywhere along the route from either Hanoi or HCMC (for example, in Hue, Hoi An, Danang, Nha Trang, Dalat or Mui Ne) with few restrictions. The buses make stops every couple of hours for food and bathroom breaks. In contrast to standard local buses, you are guaranteed a seat to yourself and space to stretch your feet. The bus will pick you up from your hotel and drop you off at any hotel at your destination. The buses often work in partnership with sister travel agencies and hotels, but there is no undue pressure to stay at one of their recommended hotels. The ticket remains good for a month, but the clock starts ticking from the day you buy it, not when you first use it.

With a HCMC–Hanoi ticket costing about US$60 (including stops in between) this is one of the cheaper ways of getting around, but also one of the more time-consuming.

To book tickets, visit the offices of **Sinh Café** in Hanoi (66 Hang Than St; www.sinhcafe.com), or call at: 04-3836 4212/3756 8868. Alternatively, your hotel can make all the arrangements for a fee.

If you're feeling adventurous and want a truly "local" experience, you could take local public buses. Expect to get overcharged (at three or four times the local rates) and be stuck in an overcrowded deathtrap with a suicidal driver. It might be "authentic", but the fun tends to wear off quickly so these rides are better for short-distances only.

Mekong Delta

The best place to access the Mekong is from HCMC, and the easiest way to do it is to book yourself on an organised tour. Local travel agents will pick up from your hotel and a day trip typically costs from US$25 including lunch.

To blaze your own trail, head for the **Mai Linh** buses (64–68 Hai Ba Trung St; tel: 08-3939 3939) in HCMC, which offer express bus services to the Mekong Delta that always depart on time and go straight through without stopping to pick up more passengers. Book in advance to guarantee a seat. Ticket prices vary from US$3–7, depending on distance travelled. The local bus station is based in Cholon.

By car and minivan

In Hanoi, HCMC and the other major cities, you can hire cars and minivans to go on day trips or week-long excursions. Hiring a driver and vehicle in Vietnam is good value if your travelling party is large enough to share the cost. Ask to go for a test ride before making a commitment to a driver to see if the car is running properly. Expect to pay a minimum of US$60 a day (US$35 for half-day)

for a good car (with driver). The best way to arrange this is to book through an established travel agency as it is required to take responsibility for your safety. If you need an English-speaking guide, the travel agency can also arrange this.

Sometimes, drivers from one part of the country are reluctant to drive to another. Drivers from HCMC, for example, are usually hesitant to drive to Hanoi. Licence plates on cars denote what province the car is from, and drivers often fear that the police will give cars from outside the region trouble. A driver in HCMC might agree to take you as far as Danang, for example, and then help you find another driver to take you further.

Think very carefully about whether you should drive yourself. With the crazy road conditions and the near absence of traffic rules, you are better off hiring a car with a driver. In any case you will be hard-pressed to find car rental companies that cater to tourists in Hanoi and HCMC. Car rentals start from around US$30 per day.

Motorbike rentals

Motorbike rental is available, especially from mini-hotels and in tourist hubs: prices range from around US$5–10 per day for a reliable 100–110cc bike, although weekly and monthly rentals are available. Driving in Hanoi and HCMC, however, is really only for the more experienced (or crazy) driver. Apart from the sheer volume, traffic in Vietnam has its own unique rhythms and "logic". Always wear a helmet and buy accident insurance.

For those who want to explore Vietnam by motorcycle, contact Hanoi-based **Offroad Vietnam** (tel: 04-3926 3433; www.offroadvietnam. com), which has the best bikes and guides. Owner Anh Wu is a wealth of information on biking and trekking in the north. **Motortours Asia** (tel:04-979 900 800; www.mototoursasia.com) can arrange for bikers to pick up their machines in Sa Pa, Hue, Danang or HCMC for an extra fee.
Dalat and the Central Highlands are a popular place for hiring motorbikes, given the beautiful scenery, pleasant roads, and little traffic. They can be rented from Phat Tire Ventures (109 Nguyen Van Troi St, tel: 06-3382 9422;

mobile tel: 098-384 7217; www.ptv-vietnam.com) and Groovy Gecko Adventure Tours (65 Truong Cong Dinh St, tel: 063-383 6521; www.groovygeckotours.net).

Cycling

Cycling around parts of Vietnam is possible thanks to tour companies who can provide good-quality bikes. Just as importantly, they can also provide guides who can suggest the best routes and attractions along the way. The most popular rides are near Halong Bay, through the Mekong Delta, or around Hoi An and Hue. Cycling can also be a good way of getting around the cities, particularly Dalat.

Boats

Mekong Delta

No tourist can leave Vietnam without spending at least a day on a boat, preferably on the Mekong River. Boat tours organised by numerous companies in HCMC usually start at about US$20 per day but may easily reach over US$200 for a two days/ one night programme aboard a luxurious boat

Viet Bamboo Travel (tel: 08 3811 6800; www.mekongriverboattrips.com) have boats that take guests from My Tho to Chau Doc, Long Xuyen and Can Tho over three days. Other trips start in HCMC and take in Vinh Long, Can Tho, Chau Doc and then finish back in HCMC. The construction of several new bridges in the Mekong Delta as well as a motorway around HCMC has resulted in fewer commercial boat services (regular services to Can Tho and My Tho-Ben Tre no longer exist, for instance). This means more previously remote towns, such as Tra Vinh, are now relatively simple to access. Moreover, after a serious fire and numerous breakdowns, Vietnamese authorities suspended cruises of the Soviet-era hydrofoils between HCMC and the popular seaside resort of Vung Tau in 2014. They were resumed at the beginning of 2015 once the fleet operated by Vina Express company (tel: 08-3825 3333/3829 7892; www.vinaexpress.com.vn) had been upgraded or replaced altogether by modern and much safer high-speed boats. Currently, 3 operators: Petro Express, Greenlines and Vina Express operate the route.

Hydrofoils operating between HCMC and **Vung Tau** (around 80 minutes) terminate and depart at 10B Ton Duc Thang. There are several services on weekdays and five at weekends with several more during Tet (Lunar New Year).

Cat Ba Island

The best way to get to Cat Ba Island is by booking a tour through an agency in Hanoi, as it will arrange the rather complicated transportation links.

For those doing it on their own, travel from Haiphong or Halong Bay (Bai Chay) to Cat Ba Island via hydrofoil or ferry; the hydrofoil will take an hour and the ferry at least twice as long. The ferry and hydrofoil schedules change according to the season, but at least one hydrofoil departs from both Haiphong and Halong Bay to Cat Ba daily, and there are at least two ferries. Confirm hydrofoil and ferry schedules at your hotel or the pier.

City transport

Hanoi

Taxis

Taxis are omnipresent and are, on the whole, a cheap and quick way to get around. The majority are air-conditioned, and those operated by the more reputable companies are in fairly good condition. Taxis charge by the meter with a flagfall rate that ranges from VND9,000–16,000 for the first 2km (1.2 miles), followed by about VND12,000–16,000 for every kilometre travelled. Note: the taxis with the more expensive base rates often work out cheaper (and less stressful) overall, as they are highly regulated and the meters are likely not to have been tampered with. If you know where you're going and how far your final destination is, it might be a good idea to negotiate a flat fee for the cruise rather than use the meter.

There are dozens of different taxi firms that have cars out cruising the streets, but to guard against being ripped off, travellers should try to stick to the major recommended taxi companies: **Taxi Hanoi Group**, tel: 04-3853 5353; **CP Taxi**, tel: 04-3826 2626; and **Mai Linh Taxi**, tel: 04-38 616161 /3833 3333.

The operators at these major taxi companies speak English

and will dispatch a cab to almost anywhere in less than 15 minutes. Few drivers speak English, but most will recognise the English names of the popular tourist sites. Be sure to take a card from your hotel to show your taxi driver the hotel name and address (on your return trip), and the name of your destination in Vietnamese.

If you find yourself in a taxi that obviously has a rigged meter (the fare will rise very quickly), demand the driver stop, tell him the meter is broken and get out of the cab.

Motorbike taxis (Xe om)

Xe om, the Vietnamese phrase for motorbike taxis, are the most popular and prevalent form of public transport, but they do require nerves of steel and a slice of good fortune. *Xe om* can be found on almost every street corner and they generally charge VND 10,000 per kilometre. Settle the price beforehand and make sure the driver has an extra helmet for you – Vietnam's helmet laws have been in place since December 2007 and many drivers still go without, especially in Hanoi.

For short distances, *xe om* can be the best way to get around, but there is some risk to life and limb, so be aware of this. Some *xe om* drivers drive very aggressively. Women should never take a *xe om* anywhere alone at night, especially if leaving a bar or club. Day or night, never accept a ride from an inebriated *xe om* driver.

Cyclos

Hanoi's front-seater cyclos *(xich lo)* are three-wheeled rickshaws pedalled by drivers. By far the most fun way to travel, Hanoi's cyclos are unique in that they can carry two passengers instead of one (unlike in HCMC). Cyclos are the perfect way to take in the city's wide, tree-lined streets, so take a ride on one at least once.

There is persistent talk from the government that cyclos will eventually be banned, so visitors to Vietnam should not miss an opportunity to experience this most enjoyable form of transportation. Hiring a cyclo is no problem in Hanoi's Old Quarter; the drivers will try to get the attention of passing tourists. Generally, an hour's tour around the Old Quarter or Truc Bach Lake will cost about US$7, although cyclo drivers will press you to pay a higher price.

Cyclos can also be hired for short rides to specific destinations, though the price will have to be decided on first before you clamber onboard.

Buses

Hanoi's large Korean-made city buses ply most major streets. The network is quite extensive (there are about 80 routes) and fares vary between VND5,000–7,000 per person/trip. The Hanoi Urban Transport Management and Operation Centre (TRAMOC; 16 Cao Ba Quat, Ba Dinh Dist, Hanoi; tel: 04-3747 0029; www. tramoc.com.vn/) hands out a free map outlining the city's bus routes.

Despite the efficient network, few foreign travellers use the public buses as the routes are not clearly indicated on the outside and taxis are so affordable. Buses can also be very crowded and slow during rush hour, and most stop running by 8pm. Avoid buses if you are carrying a lot of luggage.

Ho Chi Minh City

Taxis

Taxis are the safest and most comfortable way of getting around. Most are air-conditioned, and fares are relatively cheap. The usual flagfall rate should not exceed VND15,000 for the first 1.5km (1 mile), followed by VND12,000–15,000 for each additional kilometre travelled. Stay clear of unlicensed taxis (especially around the airport and backpacker area); these either have rigged meters, or tend to quote over-inflated prices. Whenever you find the meter spinning wildly, stop the cab and leave it immediately! Although taxis can be easily flagged down anywhere, especially downtown, stick to taxis operating outside upscale hotels or use the companies listed here: **ML** (Mai Linh Taxis/M taxis; www.mailinh.vn), tel: 08-3829 8888/08-3838 3838; **Vina Taxi** (http://vinataxi.vn), tel: 08-3811 1111; **Vinasun** (www.vinasuntaxi. com), tel: 08-3827 7178; and **SASCO Airport Taxis** (www.sasco.com.vn), tel: 08-9014 93366).

Carry small notes, as drivers always claim they don't have enough change. As English is not commonly spoken, have your destination down in Vietnamese to show to the driver.

Motorbike taxis

The more adventurous may opt for motorbike taxis, known locally as

☉ Street mayhem

The streets of Vietnam's two largest cities, Hanoi and HCMC, are a crowded maze of bicycles, motorbikes, taxis, SUVs and trucks, all competing with thousands of pedestrians. Crossing the street can be a daunting prospect. To add to the chaos, the drivers of cars and motorbikes (there are thousands of the latter on the roads) use their horns incessantly – beeping to indicate a turn or to let you know they're overtaking. Driving the wrong way up one-way streets and on the pavements, plus ignoring red lights, are all par for the course. Traffic in Hanoi's Old Quarter area and HCMC's Dong Khoi Street is simply overwhelming.

As a pedestrian, remember that the Vietnamese are adept at manoeuvring around obstacles. As long as you don't make any sudden or abrupt movements when crossing busy roads, the traffic will flow around you like water. Be mindful but bold when crossing streets and never dash across the street.

xe om (literally translating as "to embrace"). Drivers invariably hang round at most street corners and call out "Motorbike?". Most are friendly and speak basic English, although increasingly many are from the countryside and do not. Xe om are a cheap, quick and adrenaline-packed means to beat the traffic jams, but they are more susceptible to accidents. Since 2007 all riders in Vietnam have been required to wear helmets; this is strongly enforced in HCMC with fines for offenders. The driver should supply you with a helmet; if he doesn't, find another driver. Always agree a price, preferably in writing, beforehand: short hops around town should cost around US$1–2. Motorbike taxis are not advisable after dark, especially for women.

Cyclos

Cyclos have traditionally been a novelty transport option for tourists, a uniquely Vietnamese, unhurried (and cheap) way to see the sights. Unfortunately, with increasing noise, pollution and traffic, cyclos

are not such an attractive option any more. In HCMC, cyclos were officially banned by the city authorities in 2008. Some cyclos still ply the streets, but you have to search hard. They can be found in the backpacker area, Cholon and Ben Thanh Market, or book through your hotel.

Many tour companies invariably use cyclos as part of city tours, so this is another option. Never take a cyclo after dark (for security and safety reasons) and always agree on the price (about US$2 per hour) beforehand in writing so there are no misunderstandings.

Buses

HCMC's fleet of buses are modern and offer an extensive city network with well-marked bus stops and the average price of VND5,000 that takes you anywhere in the city. Be aware though that few buses operate after 6pm. This is also one of the speediest forms of city transport – buses plough through traffic like Grand Prix drivers with little regard for anything in their path. Unfortunately, signs or instructions are only in Vietnamese and drivers can't speak English. As the city's main public transport mode, buses are often jam-packed during peak hours.

The main bus station for local routes is **Ben Thanh Bus Station** (Ben Xe Ben Thanh; tel: 08-3821 4444; www.huyttphcm.com.vn), located opposite Ben Thanh Market, junction of Tran Hung Dao, Le Loi and Ham Nghi streets, District 1; bus maps are available here. Another city bus hub is **Cholon Bus Station**, on Le Quang Sung St, District 6, near Binh Tay Market.

Useful bus routes include No. 1 (Ben Thanh Market and Cholon Bus Station, Cholon); No. 13 (Cu Chi); No. 44 (Binh Quoi tourist area); No. 11 (Dam Sen Park); and No. 152 or No. 152 (airport).

Local transport elsewhere in Vietnam

Sa Pa

Sa Pa is a small town best explored on foot. To get from one end of town to the other takes a maximum of 10 minutes, and there are a number of ethnic minority villages within walking distance.

Many visitors to Sa Pa choose to rent motorbikes to explore the surrounding mountains. Most

guesthouses and hotels rent motorbikes for about US$4-7 a day. Renting a bike from independent operators could be a hassle as the owners usually demand a passport as a guarantee or a US$250 deposit. Always make sure to wear a helmet and take notice of the fact that there'll be no one to help you if the motorbike breaks down in the middle of nowhere.

Cars, vans and 4WDs are also available for hire through hotels, guesthouses and travel agents. Rates will vary depending on the destination, distance and time of year. Most Sa Pa hotels can easily recommend reliable vehicles with a driver and guide.

Haiphong

Haiphong has a number of taxi companies that use reliable, metered, air-conditioned vehicles. The best are **Haiphong Taxi**, tel: 031-383 8383; **Mai Linh Taxi**, tel: 031-383 3833; and **Hoa Phuong Taxi**, tel: 031-364 1641. Rides within the city shouldn't cost more than US$2. There are plenty of motorbike taxis – don't pay more than US$1 for short hops, and always wear a helmet. Cyclos often cruise around town looking for customers. Short trips around town cost under US$1; an hour's tour of the city should cost about US$6.

Halong City

When travelling in Bai Chay, metered taxis are a good option. **Mai Linh Taxi**, tel: 033-362 8628, and **Halong Taxi**, tel: 033-362 6262, are reliable companies. Rates begin at VND14,000 for the first 1.4km (0.9 mile).

Motorbike taxis are probably the best way to get around in Bai Chay and Hon Gai. The drivers are also an excellent source of information on where to find good restaurants and hotels. Expect to pay about US$1–2 for rides around the city, depending on your bargaining skills.

Cat Ba Island

Cat Ba Town is tiny and can easily be covered on foot. For local transportation, xe om are the best bet.

Many visitors to the island rent motorbikes (large smoky Russian Minsks) for about US$6 a day and tour the island independently. Motorbikes can be rented from any number of shops and guesthouses along the main street.

Hue

Taxis, *xe om* and cyclos are found throughout the city and around all the major tombs. **Mai Linh** (tel: 054-389 8989) is one of the best companies, with new, comfortable cars, but even their drivers have been known to cheat their customers as much as any other company by rigging the meters and driving around in circles. Always be wary, and if you think the fee is climbing too steeply, simply stop and find another ride.

Hue is a fairly safe city to ride a bicycle. It's also an ideal mode of transportation to explore the royal tombs. Most hotels rent bicycles for US$1–2 per day. Motorbikes cost US$5–7 per day, while a car with driver runs to about US$40-60 per day.

Tourists who go alone by bicycle and motorbike tend to be targeted by local scam artists. Strangers will approach offering to show travellers the way to tombs and villages that are off the beaten path. All are ultimately looking to make money from you; some may actually rob victims once they are lured to a remote location. If you need a guide, ask your hotel to arrange one for you.

Danang

Motorbike taxis wait on every street corner. **Mai Linh Taxis** (tel: 0511-356 5656) are recommended. Motorbikes can be rented from most hotels for around US$5 per day.

Hoi An

Everything within the Old Town is reachable by foot. In fact, a motorbike or bicycle would be more of a hindrance than a help, and they are banned during the Full Moon festivals. Cars are banned from the Old

Boat trip in the Mekong Delta.

Town at all times. For trips to My Son, Cau Dai Beach or the Marble Mountains, rent a motorbike from any hotel for US$5–10 per day. Longboats for up to 8 people can be hired along the riverfront for US$5 per hour.

Quy Nhon

Mai Linh (tel: 056-354 6666) is the best choice for taxis in Quy Nhon. Local transport costs here are a bit out of touch with the rest of the country. Expats here have traditionally been big spenders and have driven up the costs. Expect to pay as much as US$10 per day to rent a motorbike, and double the normal rates you'll find elsewhere for other forms of transport and tours. Another good way to explore the nearby beaches and temples is to rent a bicycle (some hotels are willing to lend them) or buy a used one in case of longer stays.

Quang Ngai

Rent a motorbike from almost any hotel for US$6 per day. **Mai Linh Taxis** (tel: 055-383 8383) are also available.

Dalat

Motorbikes can be rented for about US$5 per day. A *xe om* for short distances around the city will cost about US$2. A taxi ride for quick trips around town will cost under US$5. **Mai Linh Taxis** (tel: 063-351 1111) is one of the more reputable taxi companies, but always double check the rate on the meter.

Dalat can be a fun place to ride a bicycle, but casual riders may find it challenging due to the many hills.

Nha Trang

Bicycles can be rented from most hotels for around US$2. All the major sights are within riding distance. Taxis, cyclos and *xe om* are found everywhere; drivers of the last two will pester you as you walk down the streets. Motorbikes can be rented from most hotels for around US$5. **Mai Linh Taxis** (tel: 058-3838 3838) offer the best taxi service, but keep your eye on the meter to make sure the numbers all add up correctly.

Phan Thiet

Motorbike rentals and **Mai Linh** taxis (tel: 062-389 8989) can be arranged through your hotel. Cyclos are not

common in Phan Thiet, and it's not advisable to ride bicycles here because of the chaotic traffic.

Mui Ne

Xe om and **Mai Linh Taxis** (tel: 062-3838 3838) are very common in Mui Ne. Motorbikes can be rented from most hotels for US$5–8 per day and bicycles for US$2–3 per day. Cyclos are not available. Most tour companies can arrange jeep tours to the Sand Dunes (US$25–30), Ta Cu Mountain (US$50) and other local sights. Great care should be taken when exiting the beach and heading west to Phan Thiet. Locals as well as tourists are killed in traffic accidents on an almost weekly basis, so go carefully.

Mekong Delta

To sightsee locally in the Mekong Delta area, sign up for a bus tour at a local agent, or hire a car or *xe om*, making sure your itinerary is clear and the price has been fixed before you set off. For a *xe om*, a good guide is US$2.50 per hour, or US$12 per day.

Xe dap loi, a bicycle hitched to a carriage and the Mekong's version of the cyclo, should cost around US$6 an hour. A *xe loi* (carriage with motor bike instead of a bicycle) should be the same price as a *xe om*, but expect to pay more for two or more people.

The Mekong's diverse tracks are made for touring by motorbike. Enquire at your hotel. Rates are usually US$7–10 a day. Riding a bicycle is another possibility – self-pedalling will cost US$2 a day.

As much as exploration is best done by boat, particularly the floating markets and tiny Mekong River islands, ask a local to ferry you around. Small motorboats can be hired from US$3 an hour.

Vung Tau

Most hotels can rent motorbikes for US$6–9 per day and bicycles for US$2–3 per day. Stand on any street corner, and a taxi, *xe om* or cyclo will stop right under your nose.

Con Dao Islands

There are no taxis or *xe om* on the island, although it's possible to rent a motorbike (less than US$10 per day) or bicycle (US$2–3 per day) from one of the hotels. Boats may be rented from the park service for about US$75 per day.

A

Accommodation

Choosing a hotel

Until the mid-1990s, Vietnam's hotel infrastructure, particularly in the north and centre of the country, was far below international standards. Rooms were often under-equipped or kitted out with fixtures and appliances that did not work, and there were frequent power cuts. Room rates were also relatively high.

Demand for accommodation often outstripped supply, but following a hotel boom in the mid-1990s onwards in Ho Chi Minh City and Hanoi, today's rooms offer far better value. Hotel development in the country is flourishing and visitors are spoilt for choice. International chains, with service standards and prices to match, can be found in all the major cities. Luxury hotels and resorts with business centres, high-speed internet access and/or Wi-Fi, and spas and fitness centres, are the norm these days, but there is also plenty of choice in the budget lodgings category, where a room can go for US$10 a night.

The easing of restrictions on foreign investment has resulted in a boom in upmarket accommodation. The Hyatt, Sheraton, Hilton and Sofitel chains are well represented in Ho Chi Minh City and Hanoi, and along the coast the Six Senses and GHM (which is linked to the high-end Aman chain) hotel groups have opened luxury properties in Vietnam.

Hotel staff are generally friendly and helpful, and adequate English is spoken in the major tourism and business centres. In more remote areas, communication in English can be a real problem. State-run hotels tend to have indifferent staff and low standards of service, which is a pity because some of Hanoi and HCMC's most atmospheric historic hotels are state-run enterprises.

Mini hotels and homestays

If you're on a tight budget, try the so-called "mini hotels", small, often family-run hotels with fairly modern (but modest) facilities. These abound in Hanoi and HCMC, but are also increasingly common in popular resort towns.

There are smaller family-run guesthouses that offer homestay accommodation. These are mainly found in the Mekong Delta area and offer a more personal touch (you will probably have dinner, go fishing or end up singing karaoke with the family). In the northern highlands, it's possible to arrange a stay with hill-tribe minority communities, particularly in and around Sa Pa. These would have to be booked with a travel agency that specialises in trekking tours.

Rates and bookings

When booking your accommodation, always check the hotel website first to see what the best rates are. If it's a smaller outfit without a website, call directly to ask. Hotel-booking websites should be your next port of call; these companies can often get you better rates because of the volume of business they bring in.

As disposable income increases, more and more Vietnamese are travelling. During the school holidays (June–August) the beaches get very crowded, and during the annual Tet festival (in late January or early February) buses and trains are packed to the rafters with domestic travellers. On those days that the lunar calendar indicates as auspicious for weddings, you'll also find many honeymooners flocking to Dalat. Hotel rates also spike during the Christmas and New Year periods. If you are making a trip during any of these times, it would be a good idea to book ahead.

Note: archaic communist-era Vietnamese laws insist that all hotel guests be registered with the local police. This could mean leaving your passport with the reception for the entire duration of the stay or just overnight. In Hanoi and HCMC, the practice is either to make a photocopy or to record details from your passport and landing card.

Addresses

Finding a residential or business address can be surprisingly tricky in Vietnam. Streets often change names when they run through different neighbourhoods, and in rural areas some won't have names at all. Street prefixes include "D" for Duong, "P" for Pho, and "DL" for Dai Lo. For the sake of clarity, we have added the suffix St to all street names; therefore Duong Tran Hung Dao is referred to as Tran Hung Dao St.

When a street number includes a slash, such as 98/6, your first task is to find number 98, go down the alley, and then hunt for building number 6. When a number is followed by a letter, such as 48C, it means a whole block of buildings is numbered 48, and you must find the third office in the block. Odd and even numbers are typically on opposite sides of the street and do not necessarily correlate with each other, so don't expect 31 to always be close to 32. To make matters worse, sometimes houses have no numbers at all. Be thankful you're not a postman in Vietnam.

CLIMATE CHART

Hanoi

Danang

Ho Chi Minh

■ Maximum temperature
□ Minimum temperature
— Rainfall

Budgeting for your trip

While still inexpensive for most Western travellers, Vietnam is not as cheap as it was a few years ago.

Accommodation in Vietnam can be cheap, but is generally more expensive than many other Southeast Asian countries. The US$6 rooms of old, with a bed, fan and little else, are now rare. Hostels with dorms only began to appear recently, and are still uncommon. Most guesthouses in the cities will cost around US$15–25 per night, which will get you air conditioning, a TV, fridge, hot water, up to two beds, and Wi-Fi. Mid-range beach hotels cost between US$30 and US$60. Service improves considerably as the price rises to US$100. Above that, you are in five-star territory.

Street food is cheap and convenient, with meals costing between US$1 and US$3. Mid-range Vietnamese and backpacker restaurants will charge US$4–6 per dish. A typical restaurant catering to tourists will cost US$8–15 for three courses and drinks. There are few truly high-end restaurants outside of Ho Chi Minh City and Hanoi, where the top tables can easily top US$25 per person.

Budget travellers can realistically get by with as little as US$25–30 per day for food, drinks, room, transport and sightseeing. A mid-range budget is about US$40–60 per day. Beyond that the sky is the limit if you have cash to burn.

It is common practice for Vietnamese to charge different rates for foreigners and locals. This was once mandated in government-run establishments, but has largely been abolished. Despite this, most Vietnamese see foreigners as an opportunity to make extra profit and so continue to charge above the norm. One should generally assume that a quoted price, especially when shopping, is at least double the normal rate (although more than four times is not uncommon), and bargain the price down. Knowing the street price can help, but it doesn't mean the seller will be willing to agree to it.

Note: it's not uncommon for restaurants to have an expensive English menu and a cheaper Vietnamese one. If you're watching your dong, ask to see the Vietnamese version too to compare prices.

Business hours

Most banks, public services and state-run offices work from Monday to Friday between 7.30 and 8.30am, and 4 and 5pm, with a lunch break between 11.30am and 1.30pm. Museums roughly follow the same hours, but many close on Mondays (sometimes Fridays). Tourist-orientated shops open daily from 9am to 7–9pm, and may close for lunch. Markets open as early as 5.30 to 6.30am, and are finishing up come lunch time. Markets in tourist areas (or during festivals) may open again in the evening. Only very large markets in city centres stay active all day. Pagodas and temples are open daily from early morning until the evening. There are no fixed hours, however, and sometimes the door may be shut because there is a special event going on inside – or the caretaker is away.

C

Children

Bringing children to Vietnam is not a major issue, as they will be welcome everywhere and there is plenty for them to enjoy. Most big cities have a water park and/or a zoo of some description. There are also good beaches along the entire coast and excellent national parks to explore. Be sure to leave the buggy at home as footpaths in most Vietnamese cities and towns are not pedestrian-friendly; a chest-mounted baby carrier is far more practical. Children should be warned never to approach dogs, monkeys and other small animals; those wandering the streets tend to be feral, and rabies is a risk.

The tropical sun is intense, so high-factor sunblock and hats are essential. Make sure children keep their hands clean; those who frequently suck their thumbs can easily pick up stomach bugs.

Climate

Given Vietnam's length – it stretches 1,650km (1,000 miles) from north to south – its topography and the effect of the monsoon tropical climate, temperatures and rainfall patterns can vary widely from one region to another. In the north, temperatures can dip to as low as 10°C (50°F) and be accompanied by a biting winter wind. In the south, however, it is hot all year round.

The south has two seasons, wet and dry. During the rainy months between May and November, it rains fiercely for about 30 minutes a day (but some days not at all), normally in the afternoon or early evening. The dry season runs from December to April, with the hottest months stretching from March to late April, with temperatures well over 30°C (86°F) and with high humidity levels. Seasons are extreme along the coast between Vung Tau and Phan Rang – one of the driest spots in Southeast Asia, where it almost never rains during the dry season.

The north experiences four seasons. The summer months from May to September are almost always hot and humid, with the most rainfall occurring during this period. Winter, from late December to early March, is often grey, drizzly and cool.

Central Vietnam from Danang to Nha Trang has its own weather patterns due to the monsoons: the dry season is from February to September, with the most rainfall from October to December. The seasons are not as pronounced here, however, and it can rain at any time of the year, but the hottest months are June/July while the coolest months are December/ January.

It's near-impossible to find a time of the year when the north, centre and south have equally good weather, but the safest bet – if you're travelling the length of Vietnam – is between March and April. The rains will have abated, humidity levels are still bearable, and it will be relatively warm and dry throughout Vietnam. However, if you are just visiting north and south Vietnam and skipping the centre, November and December are good months too.

Clothing

Bring casual, lightweight clothing of natural fabrics, which offer the most comfort in the humidity and heat. If you plan to spend time in the highlands, then a light jacket or fleece and long trousers – especially in winter – are advisable. Rain gear, including a small foldable umbrella, is a good idea, as it's always raining somewhere in Vietnam.

Sandals or footwear that can be easily slipped off are best. Shoes should be removed before entering homes, and even some shops.

Crime and security

In general, Vietnam is a safe country to travel in and violent crimes against foreigners are rare, though they do happen. Petty theft and robbery, on the other hand, are very common. In big cities, especially Ho Chi Minh City, tourists are often the victims of pickpockets and snatch-and-grab thieves.

Always leave valuables in a hotel safe, and when you must carry cash, put it in a money belt worn inside your clothes. When walking, or travelling in a cyclo, keep one hand firmly on handbags and cameras. When travelling on buses or trains, always stay with your bag. If you travel by train, bring a cable lock to secure your bags to your bed frame when you are sleeping.

Be careful of pavement vendors selling maps, books and souvenirs or people begging for money, especially in Hanoi and HCMC. They can easily distract you while a friend slips a hand into your pocket, grabs your wallet and vanishes. Mobile phones are easy prey, and it's not uncommon to have laptops and even sunglasses snatched by passing motorcyclists. Pickpockets could be children and women with babies as well.

The Vietnamese are extremely friendly and generous, but caution must be taken when making casual acquaintances. Vietnam has its fair share of con artists who hustle everything from Cambodian gems to "genuine" bones of missing American servicemen. Beware of people who suddenly approach you in tourist areas (especially in HCMC) and engage you in conversation, or try to persuade you to go somewhere with them. This is almost always a scam.

Women travellers

Women should take extra precautions when travelling alone, as some Vietnamese men can be very aggressive. Their behaviour may range from following you to your hotel room to physically touching you (usually after being egged on by their male friends).

Also, Vietnam can be a very difficult country for an Asian woman, or a woman of Asian descent, travelling with a white male companion. Some Vietnamese men mistakenly assume such women to be Vietnamese and prostitutes (the same is true for a younger Asian man travelling with an older Western man), and can often be verbally abusive.

Women staying alone in budget hotels may want to consider using an extra lock on the door at night. Quiet streets and isolated beaches should also be avoided late at night. It's a good idea to travel in

groups or to arrange transportation ahead of time. Paying a little extra to have a driver wait for you after a late night out is better than having to find a way of getting home late at night.

Police registration

By law, all tourists are required to be registered with the local police station. When checking in at hotels and guesthouses at the smaller and more remote towns, the staff will take your passport to the police for registration. They will normally return it to you the next morning, although sometimes

⊘ Big brother

In an archaic throwback to old-style communism, movements of "suspicious" foreigners may be monitored by the local police. Tour guides have been known to be instructed to report the activities of their clients, while some private tour companies, and certainly state-owned ones, are said to employ members of the country's internal security apparatus.

In reality, most tourists will never come in direct contact with police. However, visitors who spend more than a few days off the beaten path may receive visits from inquisitive policemen and even be followed. Persons suspected of engaging in criminal or politically sensitive activities will also be closely watched. Likewise, any mail or parcels sent or received in Vietnam may be searched for political or religious materials. Don't put your new Vietnamese friends in jeopardy – leave your political views at home.

Censorship is a way of life in Vietnam. Every form of media – including pop songs, newspapers, TV shows and children's books – must be submitted for prior approval before being printed, broadcast or performed. Internet websites with content deemed dangerous to the communist authorities are blocked. Even churches must submit their sermons and song lists for prior approval.

the staff may insist on holding your passport for the entire duration of your stay. In Hanoi, HCMC and the bigger cities, the staff generally only ask to see your passport and landing card, from which they will fill in details in a book and then return it. If you must turn over your passport, make sure that the correct one – and the landing card – are returned to you. Hotel staff are prone to misplacing passports; don't wait until you are at the airport before you check.

If you plan on staying with family or friends then you should visit the local police station to avoid any late-night visits by the police, as nosy neighbours often report suspicious foreigners. Although you may consider this a nuisance, you will be saving your hosts quite a bit of trouble from authorities.

Be aware that in some remote areas in the central highlands, internal travel permits are required for travel. Tourists have reported being arrested by provincial police in the central highlands and Mekong Delta for travelling in restricted areas. Occasionally, innocent tourists walk unknowingly into sensitive border areas and military installations unaware that they are breaking the law. The best advice is to play it safe in very remote areas and always contact the police. Spending your holiday under house arrest is not much fun.

Customs regulations

Entry formalities

Visitors to Vietnam are required to fill in a detailed customs declaration in duplicate upon arrival. Customs may inspect your luggage to verify that you have made a correct declaration. Currency in excess of US$5,000 should be declared. Books, reading material and videos are supposed to be declared, but it doesn't seem to be expected. Your items may be inspected to check for anything considered culturally or politically sensitive (including religious items), but this is usually only a concern for mailed parcels.

You must keep a copy of the customs declaration form to show customs officials upon leaving Vietnam. They may check to see if you are leaving with the items declared.

Exit formalities

Official authorisation from the Ministry of Culture is required to take antiquities out of the country. Visitors are not allowed to take ancient artefacts, Buddha images, antiques or "items of value to Vietnamese culture". An antique is defined as anything more than 30 years old. Travellers have reported problems in trying to leave with items that appear to be antiques, even if they are reproductions. It is a good idea to take a detailed receipt from the shop with a description of the item.

When leaving Vietnam, you may be stopped to have film, video and reading materials inspected. Usually this is just an annoyance, but if you are a journalist, your equipment may be seized unless you have express permission to take them out from the government's Foreign Affairs Press Department.

D

Disabled travellers

With all the traffic, the scarcity of lifts, clogged pavements, squat-type toilets and the sheer amount of people out and about on the streets, Vietnam is not designed for disabled travellers. The roads are extremely treacherous and traffic doesn't tend to stop, even for disabled Vietnamese people, especially in the major cities. It's a contentious issue that a country with so many disabled citizens hasn't done more to accommodate them. Thankfully, it's not impossible for adventurous disabled people with an easy-going attitude to get by. Make sure you plan well ahead and find out about hotel access. Generally the bigger hotels have wheelchair access, toilets and lifts for the disabled.

E

Eating out

Hanoi

Years ago, eating in Hanoi involved munching on simple rice or slurping down a bowl of noodles while balanced on a plastic chair by a dusty sidewalk. While that option still exists, there are now dozens of excellent restaurants, serving a variety of cuisines, including a fusion of French and Vietnamese dishes. Hanoi's culinary scene is as cosmopolitan as it gets. Unlike in Ho Chi Minh City, the capital's best eateries are well spaced out; the largest concentration is in the central Hoan Kiem District.

Coffee shops are an integral part of life in Hanoi. Simply cradling a latte isn't enough for Hanoi's trendy residents, though; more and more off-beat, arty and chic cafés are catering for the discerning customer. The coffee itself remains cheap and high quality, which isn't surprising as Vietnam is one of the world's largest producers of coffee.

Northwest Vietnam

In the northwest, travellers eat where they can, and food is merely a fuel to push onwards into the mountains. At pit stops along the way, restaurants mainly serve ethnic minority delicacies heavy with grilled pork, beef and vegetables. Not to be missed is the region's famous rice wine (ruou), served warm and flavoured with sour apples.

Northeast Vietnam

It's not surprising that northeast Vietnam offers up great seafood given its proximity to the South China Sea. What's amazing is just how good it is. In Haiphong and Halong, check out the street stalls and crack open some freshly caught crabs and prawns. Deeper in the interior, wild mushrooms, roots and pungent spices augment the local Vietnamese and Chinese dishes. In these areas, don't expect anything more than basic (but decent) restaurants.

The Tonkin Coast

South of Hanoi and down towards the central coast, restaurants cater to busloads of domestic tourists wanting to reach the beach. Some of the least desirable places here serve wild game meat, and some of the best offer Vietnamese standards with a unique Tonkin Coast twist that includes twice the normal amount of chillies. Along the coast itself, restaurants serving all manner of dried and fresh seafood are found.

Banh khoai.

Hue

Hue's famous cuisine is regarded as the food of the emperors – so you know it must be good. A meal in Hue is not complete if you haven't sampled some of its famous delicacies. *Banh khoai* is a rice-flour, egg and taro-based pancake, pan-fried with a filling of bean sprouts, pork and shrimp, then topped with *nuoc leo* (a local peanut sauce). *Banh beo* are tiny dishes of steamed rice flour, topped with spices and pork rinds, and then dipped in *nuoc mam* (fish sauce). *Bun* are noodle dishes that come with a variety of meats: *Bun Bo Hue* (Hue-style rice noodle soup with beef) and *Bun Bo Nuong* (rice noodles with grilled beef, mint and lettuce, topped with peanut sauce) are the most common.

Dalat and surroundings

With a tiny expat community and more domestic than foreign tourists, Dalat has fewer outstanding restaurants catering to foreigners than other tourist destinations in Vietnam. Some of the best food can be bought in the evenings from street vendors on the ramps and stairs leading into the **Central Market**, as well as the second floor of the middle building, at any time of the day.

Ho Chi Minh City

Ho Chi Minh City is Vietnam's culinary capital, with a diverse range of both Vietnamese and international cuisines. The city's economic boom and expat population, coupled with rising affluence, has created a cosmopolitan range of culinary choices and chic eateries. With cheap and excellent street fare available, Western fast food has yet to make a major impact. Most restaurants are clustered in District 1, the main tourist hub.

The café culture in Ho Chi Minh City is a throwback to French colonial times and is an integral part of life here. Caffeine connoisseurs don't need to look far to find a cup; there's a café on almost every corner. There are also some chain cafés: Trung Nguyen Coffee (www.trungnguyen.com.vn), Highlands Café (www.highlandscoffee.com.vn), Gloria Jean's Coffee or Starbucks (http://en.starbucks.vn).

The Mekong Delta

Given that the Mekong Delta is largely water, it's no surprise that it serves up some of the best seafood in Vietnam. Certain towns have dishes with strong Khmer or Chinese influences, while much of the food takes advantage of the coconuts that grow so abundantly here.

Electricity

The voltage in the cities and towns is generally 220V, 50 cycles, but sometimes 110V in the rural areas. Electric sockets are standard European and/or American, but bring an adaptor just in case. If you bring a computer to Vietnam, you should consider using a surge suppressor to protect its circuit.

Embassies and consulates

Embassies in Hanoi

Australia, 8 Dao Tan St, Ba Dinh District, tel: 04-3774 0100; www.vietnam.embassy.gov.au.
Canada, 31 Hung Vuong St, tel: 04-3734 5000; www.canadainternational.gc.ca/vietnam.
New Zealand, Level 5, 63 Ly Thai To St, tel: 04-3824 1481; www.nzembassy.com.
United Kingdom, Central Building, 4th Floor, 31 Hai Ba Trung St, tel· 04-3936 0500; www.gov.uk/government/world/organisations/british-embassy-hanoi.
United States, 7 Lang Ha St, tel: 04-3850 5000; https://vn.usembassy.gov.

Consulates in Ho Chi Minh City

Australia, 20th Floor, Vincom Center, 47 Ly Tu Trong St., tel: 08-3521 8100; www.hcmc.vietnam.embassy.gov.au.
Canada, 10th Floor, The Metropolitan, 235 Dong Khoi St, District 1, tel: 08-3827 9899.
New Zealand, 8th Floor, The Metropolitan, 235 Dong Khoi St, District 1, tel: 08-3822 6907.
United Kingdom, 25 Le Duan St, District 1, tel: 08-3825 1380.
United States, 4 Le Duan St, District 1, tel: 08-3520 4200; https://vn.usembassy.gov/embassy-consulate/ho-chi-minh-city/.

Entry requirements

Tourist and business visas

Nationals from most Southeast Asian countries do not need a visa for stays of less than 30 days, while citizens from Korea, Japan, Russia, Norway and Finland can go visa-free for 15 days.

For all other nationals, getting a visa is fairly straightforward, but one important change is that unless you are from the countries mentioned above, you cannot just turn up in Vietnam and get a visa on arrival. Most travellers apply for a one-month, single-entry tourist visa beforehand that costs US$45. A multiple-entry tourist visa for one month is US$65.

The easy way of getting a visa is to use the travel agent from whom you buy your air ticket. There will be a commission charge on top of the usual visa processing fee paid to the Vietnamese embassy or consulate. In addition to the application form, you must submit a valid passport and one passport-size photo. Allow two-three working days for approval. A letter will be issued and visitors then need to present this when they arrive at any Vietnamese airport.

Individual travellers may also apply directly for a visa with the Vietnamese embassy or consulate in their home country, but this might prove tedious. For a list of Vietnamese foreign missions overseas, check the Ministry of Foreign Affairs website (www.mofa.gov.vn).

Another option is to apply for a visa online. This option is available for two years starting from February 2017, as part of a pilot electronic visa programme. You may apply for a single-entry visa for 30 days. The e-visa may be obtained at https://xuatnhapcanh.gov.vn or https://immigration.gov.vn.

Many travellers who stop over in Bangkok apply for visas there. Travel agents in Bangkok offer attractive round-trip flight and visa packages. The best place to acquire visas however, is Phnom Penh, where travel agencies can arrange to have both multiple-entry business and normal tourist visas issued in as little as 24 hours – depending upon how much you are willing to pay.

Other types of visa available include press, family visit and official visit. To enter Vietnam on business, technically you should contact your Vietnamese sponsor, who will then submit an application form and letter to the embassy. Such visas allow for multiple-entry and are valid from one to six months. In practice, however, business visas can be arranged easily, just like tourist visas, from most travel agencies in Phnom Penh

or in Bangkok. Processing business visas costs more, with prices starting at around US$120.

Most major tour agents are now able to offer pre-arranged visas when you arrive in Hanoi, Danang and HCMC airports, for US$50 or more. The agent will fax you an "invitation letter" which you will need to present to immigration on arrival.

Note: visas must be used within one month of their issue. The period of your visa begins on the date you specify on the application form – not on the date you actually enter the country. Postponing your visit by two weeks means that your month-long visa will only be valid for two weeks.

Extension and renewal of visas

Most travel agencies in Vietnam can arrange 30-day extensions of tourist visas for US$22–30. Often this can only be done once, without having to leave the country to apply for a new visa altogether. However, these rules change frequently, and it also depends on how well connected your agent is. Six-month multiple-entry business visas can be renewed in Vietnam for around the same price as the original visa.

Etiquette

Arguing in a loud and aggressive manner will get you nowhere very fast in Vietnam. Complaining about bad service in an international-standard hotel is one thing, but such actions will fall on deaf ears at a humble guesthouse. The very notion of service is alien to the majority of the Vietnamese, and vociferous complaining won't persuade them otherwise. On the other hand, a smile can go a long way, open doors and win favours. The Vietnamese prefer a cooperative rather than confrontational approach.

As with many other parts of Asia, Confucian attitudes remain strong, and seniority demands respect whatever the circumstances. The eldest male member of any group is invariably "in charge". At any party it is the eldest who is served first, gets to eat first and generally dictates the course of events.

During meals

Most meals are eaten "family style" with shared courses. It is considered polite for hosts occasionally to dish out the best morsels, using their

chopsticks, into the guests' bowl throughout the meal. In many dining establishments it is common to discard table scraps on the floor or even on the table itself. Observe what others do, and do likewise. You do not have to accept every food item or drink (especially alcohol) that you are offered, but you should empty your rice bowl. Do not leave chopsticks sticking upright in your bowl as it symbolises an offering to the dead.

At temples

Anyone visiting the inner sanctum of a Buddhist temple will be required to remove their shoes and hat. Temples administered by the government as "cultural relics" (tourist attractions) generally require men to wear shirt and trousers, and women to wear a modest top with skirt or trousers. Contrary to what is often written, however, such dress is not required to visit most pagodas, and Vietnamese men and women will often show up in shorts and T-shirts. Be respectful when inside and always point your feet away from any Buddha image.

F

Festivals

Nearly all of Vietnam's festivals coincide with the lunar calendar. For an extensive list of festivals with detailed information and precise dates, check www.vietnamtourism.com. *See page 260.*

H

Health and medical care

Vaccines

The only vaccination required is for yellow fever, a prerequisite for travellers coming from or transiting from an infected area. Immunisation against hepatitis (A and B), Japanese encephalitis and tetanus is strongly encouraged.

It is a good idea to consult a physician a month to six weeks before departing to leave enough time to obtain the immunisations.

Malaria and dengue fever are prevalent throughout Vietnam, but are rarely seen outside the central highlands and the Mekong Delta. The best protection is prevention. Sleep under a mosquito net at night when visiting rural areas, use potent DEET repellent on exposed skin at all times, and where possible try to wear long-sleeved tops and trousers. Malaria-carrying mosquitoes are most active during the night, but the mosquitoes that spread dengue are most active during the day.

If you are travelling in remote areas, consult with a knowledgeable doctor to determine what antimalarial drugs are best suited for your travels. For more information check the website of the Centre for Disease Control (CDC) in Atlanta, United States: www.cdc.gov.

Food and water

Food is often prepared in insanitary conditions. Ice is delivered to restaurants and hotels each day by motorbike and laid bare on the doorsteps. Market produce is doused with canal and river water to keep it looking fresh. Butcher shops hang meat along dusty streets for hours in the hot sun.

Fruit and vegetables should be peeled before eating. Cooking them is a better idea. Savvy travellers advise against eating the raw herbs and lettuce served with Vietnamese noodle soup (pho) and spring rolls. However, most tourists ignore these recommendations without consequences. Because most places do not have refrigeration, food is thrown away at the end of the day. If a place is crowded, it is a good sign that it serves freshly cooked food.

Do not drink tap water unless it has been boiled properly. It is safest to avoid ice in drinks as well. Imported bottled water is available in most cities, but beware of bottles that are refilled with tap water. Check to make sure the bottle has a seal. And don't forget to drink plenty of liquids to guard against dehydration.

Emergencies

Should you have an accident or an emergency health problem in Vietnam, you may want to consider evacuation to Singapore or Bangkok for treatment. Visitors to Vietnam should therefore have health insurance that includes repatriation (or at least travel to Bangkok or Singapore for emergency treatment).

Medication

Imported pharmaceutical drugs are available throughout the country, but it is best to bring a small supply of medicine to cope with diarrhoea, dysentery, eye infections, insect bites, fungal infections and the common cold.

Hospitals and clinics

Hanoi

Hanoi French Hospital, 1 Phuong Mai St, Dong Da District, tel: 04-3577 1100; http://en.hfh.com.vn. A full-service hospital that caters to French nationals and wealthy Vietnamese. The health-care services are expensive and of acceptable standards.
International SOS Clinic, 51 Xuan Dieu, tel: 04-3934 0666; www.internationalsos.com/en/about-our-clinics_vietnam_3534.htm. The most expensive clinic in Hanoi. Staffed with international doctors and nurses. Refers patients abroad to Bangkok or Singapore for hospital treatments.
Vietnam-Korea Friendship Clinic, 12 Chu Van An St, Ba Dinh District, tel: 04-3843 7231. Excellent Korean-run clinic that is both affordable and clean. Has new facilities, and patients can choose either a Korean or Vietnamese doctor.

Ho Chi Minh City

Columbia Saigon, 8 Alexandre de Rhodes St, tel: 08- 3823 8888; www.columbiaasia.com. Good reputation with international doctors and emergency evacuation.
HCMC Family Medical Practice, Diamond Plaza, 34 Le Duan St, tel: 08-3822 7848; www.vietnammedicalpractice.com. International doctors offering vaccinations, dental services and emergency evacuation.
International SOS Clinic, 167A Nam Ky Khoi Nghia St, D3, tel: 08- 3829 8520. The top choice in the city has international doctors and 24-hour emergency services. Refers patients abroad to Bangkok or Singapore for hospital treatments.

I

Internet

Most Vietnamese cafés with indoor seating have free Wi-Fi, as do many bars, restaurants and hotels that serve foreigners. Most hotels have one or two computers with free access to the internet for their guests.

L

Left luggage

Tan Son Nhat Airport (tel: 08-3848 5383), which services Ho Chi Minh City, has left-luggage facilities (daily 7.30am–11pm) at both terminals.

All hotels and guesthouses offer a left-luggage service; usually it is free, but some may levy a small daily fee for extended periods.

LGBTQ travellers

Travel in Vietnam is a relative breeze for gay people. Legally there is no law against homosexuality, but police are known to harass Vietnamese homosexuals observed loitering. Same-sex couples will not be questioned about sharing the same hotel room at first, but if guests stay for an extended period, there will be presumptions made.

It is quite common to see open affection between the same sexes in cafés or on the street among the Vietnamese. Men can often be seen holding hands, and women too, even though they are not homosexuals; it's just a sign of deep friendship. On the other hand, it is quite rare to see open affection between men and women.

In 2002, Vietnamese writer Bui Anh Tan won a literary prize for his novel A World without Women, which tackles the issue of homosexuality in Vietnam. However, the fact that one of the novel's main characters is suddenly "cured" of homosexuality and becomes attracted to women makes the whole premise of the novel somewhat laughable. Still, the very fact that a novel like this was published (and made into a television series in 2007) in Vietnam shows a measure of progress in attitudes. In 2015, after a prolonged debate which galvanised Vietnamese society, an amended Family and Marriage law came into effect allowing same-sex marriages. However, the new law doesn't provide a legal recognition or protection for the spouses in such unions.

For more information on Vietnam's gay scene, check the Asian-wide gay portal **Utopia** at www.utopia-asia.com/tipsviet.htm.

Lost property

If you lose or have any valuable property stolen, report it as soon as possible to the local police to receive an insurance statement. Travellers who are very vocal about lost or stolen wallets have reported that their wallets were returned, including passports and credit cards (but minus any cash). Similarly, some thieves and opportunists who find lost items may return them – in exchange for a small ransom.

M

Maps

Most travel agencies offer free maps of the city in which they are located. Popular bookstores like Fahasa (www.fahasa.com.vn) and Phuong Nam (http://www.pnc.com.vn) sell maps for the cities and provinces in which they are located. Large bookstores in HCMC and Hanoi sell maps and detailed atlases for most parts of the country. There is usually a free local map (with advertisements) available at popular hotels and restaurants in each city as well. Most cities and provinces also have their own guidebooks (printed in English) which are sold at local bookstores.

Media

All Vietnamese media, whether print, broadcast, recordings or performances, must undergo a lengthy government censorship and approval process before they go public. In recent years, however, government-run newspapers have begun criticising corruption and some government policies, albeit in a somewhat timid manner.

Foreign newspapers and magazines can be purchased in larger bookstores in downtown HCMC and Hanoi, as well as some upscale hotels (although they aren't always current). Street vendors in tourist areas often sell second-hand copies too.

Newspapers

Vietnam has several English-language government-run newspapers, including *Viet Nam News* (http://vietnamnews.vn), *Vietnam Investment Review* (www.vir.com.vn) and *Vietnam Economic Times* (www.vneconomy.vn), with its weekly supplement The Guide.

Magazines

Vietnam Pathfinder (www.pathfinder.com.vn) and *Vietnam Discovery* are free government publications developed for tourists. Both have decent listings and reviews.

Radio

Voice of Vietnam (http://tnvn.gov.vn), the official government radio station, began as a propaganda tool during the wars. Two stations transmit English-language programmes on a variety of subjects several times a day on FM radio.

Television

Most hotels, restaurants, bars and cafés now have cable or satellite television with access to CNN, BBC, Australia Network, Star TV, Discovery: Travel & Living, HBO, Cartoon Network, MTV Asia and more. The quality of transmission is generally poor in rural areas; it's not uncommon to be interrupted in the middle of a programme with a sudden switch to another channel.

Money matters

Vietnam's unit of currency, the dong (pronounced *dome*, and abbreviated as VND), currently circulates in bank-notes of 500,000, 200,000, 100,000, 50,000, 20,000, 10,000, 5,000, 2,000, 1,000, and now infrequently, 500, 200 and 100. Coins of 5,000, 2,000, 1,000, 500 and 200 denominations are common in cities but not small towns. Notes from 10,000 to 500,000 are now made of polymer plastic, which ensures a longer life span and is difficult to counterfeit. Care should be taken when exchanging money or receiving change. The old 20,000 notes and the 5,000 are the same size and colour (blue) and easily confused. The 100,000 and new 10,000 (both green) as well as the 500,000 and new 20,000 (both blue) are also easily confused, though of different sizes.

All transactions are supposed to be conducted in Vietnamese dong;

in practice, a dual-currency system exists. That is, most purchases can be made in US dollars as well as Vietnamese dong.

Vietnamese have an obsession with unblemished US dollars and larger dong notes. They will often refuse notes with tears or hand-writing on them, although they can usually be turned in at banks. Counterfeiting of US notes $5 and higher, as well as VND100,000 and higher, is very common. Most of it actually comes through the government banks.

At the time of writing US$1 = 22,800VND.

Exchanging money

Changing money on the street is never a good idea. Most money-changers on the street are scam artists who will try to cheat you by offering ridiculously poor exchange rates or attempt to slip counterfeit notes into wads of the genuine stuff. It's best to stick to a bank.

Apart from banks, establishments that cater to foreigners, like hotels, travel agencies, restaurants and cafés, will also exchange dollars at bank rates. It is also possible to change dollars at almost any jewellery or gold shop; sometimes the rate is slightly higher than the bank rate. Look for a shop with the sign *Vang* (gold). They are easily identifiable because the signs usually have bright, gold-coloured letters. Be prepared to be offered two exchange rates: one for denominations of 50 and 100 US dollars, and a lower rate for smaller denominations.

Traveller's cheques and credit cards

Traveller's cheques in US dollars are accepted in most banks and in major hotels, but not in shops and not in smaller hotels or any restaurants. Major credit cards are accepted at upscale hotels, restaurants, shops and many tour offices.

Note: fairly high commission rates – usually 3 percent – are tacked onto your bill when using credit cards.

Cash advances can be withdrawn using major credit cards (again with the 3 percent commission) from a few banks, including branches of Vietcombank and Sacombank. Vietcombank will also provide cash dollars for US dollar traveller's cheques – for a 2 percent surcharge. ATMs are becoming more common

ATMs are becoming more common.

in large cities and tourist destinations. A small fee (about US$1) is charged for cash withdrawals.

Photography

Everything the photographer may need is readily available in most cities. Camera shops and photo-development outlets are commonly found in the tourist areas, and all now offer digital transfers onto CD and hard-copy photos from digital memory cards. Traditional and digital equipment of all kinds are available. Cameras are often more expensive than in Western countries but accessories are usually cheaper.

Photographing government buildings, policemen and military installations is prohibited. Virtually any other subject matter is fine.

Postal services

Post offices are generally open every day from 7am to 8pm, and are the telecommunications hub of Vietnam. In the smaller towns, they often don't even identify themselves as post offices *(buu dien)* at all, but rather by the name of the cell-phone plans (Vinaphone or Mobiphone) they sell.

Post offices usually offer computers with internet access (although very slow), fax services, and courier

services like FedEx, UPS, DHL and EMS. However, these services are not as reliable in Vietnam as they might be in other countries. It is common for foreigners to be charged extra for postal and courier services, although there is usually no official reason given for this.

Central Post Offices

Dalat, 2 Le Dai Hanh St, tel: 063- 353 1300

Danang, 60 Bach Dang St, near Song Han Bridge, tel: 0511- 182 1877.

Hanoi, 75 Pho Dinh Tien Hoang St, tel: 04- 3825 5948 .

Ho Chi Minh City, 2 Cong Xa Paris, Ben Nghe, District 1 St, tel: 08-3822 1677.

Hoi An, 6 Tran Hung Dao St, tel: 0510- 391 1257.

Hue, 8 Hoang Hoa Tham St, tel: 054- 382 0555.

Nha Trang, 2 Tran Phu St, tel: 058- 382 1002.

Phan Thiet, corner of Nguyen Tat Thanh St, tel: 062-382 7892.

Public holidays

The most important celebration of the year in Vietnam is Tet, or Lunar New Year, which falls either in late January or early February each year (see page 71), on the day of the full moon between the winter solstice and the spring equinox. Officially, there are three public holidays, but in reality almost all of Vietnam shuts down for an entire week.

It is best to avoid being on the road during this period (relaxing at a beach hotel is fine). As the celebrations begin the week before the actual festivities, roads, trains and planes become clogged with local and overseas Vietnamese rushing home for their family reunions. It may be difficult to arrange transportation and book hotels during this period.

The dates of nearly all festivals vary from year to year because they follow the lunar calendar. By counting the days from a new moon, it's fairly easy to determine when, say, "the third day of the second lunar month" falls on the familiar Gregorian calendar. But it's easier to consult a Vietnamese calendar, which always comes with both systems.

1 Jan: New Year's Day

Jan/Feb: Tet

3 Feb: Founding of Vietnamese Communist Party

10th day of the 3rd lunar month: Hung Kings festival

30 Apr: Liberation/Reunification Day (fall of Saigon)

1 May: International Labour Day

19 May: Ho Chi Minh's Birthday

June: Buddha's Birthday (8th day of the fourth lunar month)

2 Sep: National Day/Independence Day

Public toilets

Most bus trips that cater to foreign tourists include scheduled stops at places that have Western-style toilets. Shopping centres, most hotels and the better restaurants and cafés also normally have Western-style toilet facilities. However, go off the beaten tourist track and you will come face to face with squat toilets that you may not be used to. Be sure to carry a pack of tissue paper as toilet paper is unlikely to be available.

R

Religious services

Foreigners are free in most cities to attend registered, government-authorised temples and churches, but their attendance may be noted by authorities, especially at churches. Foreigners who visit unregistered places of worship, or churches in remote areas, may be detained and questioned at length by the local police.

Buddhists and Catholics will have no difficulty finding convenient places of worship. Most large towns have at least one Protestant and one Catholic church each. Cities with large Catholic and Protestant populations, such as HCMC and Danang, have a dozen or more authorised churches. HCMC also has several mosques, Hindu temples, and at least one Chabad Lubavitch (Jewish centre). Outside of Hanoi and HCMC, it's best to ask your hotel receptionist for the address of the local place of worship, and then go there directly to enquire about times for services.

S

Shopping

Markets and malls

Prices are generally reasonable in Vietnam. Traditionally, you would be expected to haggle, and this is still the case in markets and backstreet antiques shops – but don't expect huge discounts, as the naturally astute Vietnamese are stubborn salespeople and a two-price system generally exists for foreigners and resident Vietnamese. By contrast, haggling is not expected – or accepted – in obviously fixed-price places such as the shopping malls.

Vietnamese shop for groceries early in the morning. Market shopping tends to be more relaxed in the afternoons when the traders have cooled off a little. In the cities, shopping hours are usually 7.30–11.30am and 1.30–6pm, but increasingly shops and malls stay open until 8pm or later.

What to buy

Traditional Vietnamese handicrafts offer a wide variety of wares to choose from. These include paintings (lacquer, oil, gouache and silk), mother-of-pearl, ceramics, pottery, carved wood, embroidery, bamboo and wickerwork, baskets, sculpture, jewellery, jade (often fake), silks and brocades. You might like to consider adding a *non la*, the ubiquitous Vietnamese conical hat, or an *ao dai*, the traditional costume worn by Vietnamese women, to your wardrobe.

Fake war souvenirs are common – especially Zippo lighters and US army dog tags. Enduringly popular and very reasonably priced, T-shirts featuring Vietnamese flags and socialist Realist designs are available just about everywhere. Clothing is comparatively cheap and local tailors can very quickly produce well-made garments to the design of your choice.

Antiquities are sold but often those found in shops in the centre of Ho Chi Minh City and the old quarter of Hanoi sell Vietnamese wood or Laotian bronze Buddhas, old porcelain, ivory carvings, items of silver, small jade statuettes and objects used by the various cults. It is forbidden to export certain objects and in principle clearance must be obtained before taking antiquities out of the country.

An unusual souvenir manufactured mostly in the south and available at Ben Thanh Market is a bamboo screen designed to hang across doorways. Made of hundreds of tiny bamboo cylinders strung on long threads, they are painstakingly painted to show a typical Vietnamese theme – girls dressed in *non la* hats and *ao dai*, for example, or a blossom tree. Considering the work involved, they are very reasonably priced.

T

Taxes

Vietnam has a standard 10 percent Value Added Tax. Usually this is

Area codes: cities

Buon Ma Thuot **050**
Can Tho **071**
Chau Doc **076**
Danang **0511**
Dalat **063**
Haiphong **031**
Hanoi **04**
Ho Chi Minh City **08**
Hoi An **0510**
Hue **054**
Long Hai **064**
My Tho **073**
Nha Trang **058**
Phan Thiet **062**
Quy Nhon **056**
Rach Gia **077**
Vinh **038**
Vung Tau **064**

already included in quoted prices for goods and services. However, upscale hotels and restaurants serving mostly foreign tourists may add it as a separate fee to the final bill.

Telephones

Calling home from abroad is a lot cheaper than it used to be. The exception to this is at 5-star hotels, where IDD calls are still prohibitively expensive.

When calling a city in Vietnam from overseas, dial the country code **84**, followed by the area code, but drop the prefix zero. When making a domestic call from one province or city to another in Vietnam, dial the area code first (including the prefix zero). Note: local calls within the same province/city do not require the area code. Since March 2015, Vietnam has been changing its area codes for most provinces.

Voice Over Internet Protocol is the standard method of placing overseas calls from Vietnam. Calls can be made via any telephone by first dialling 17100, followed by the country code and number. Rates average US$0.50 a minute. Or you can just Skype.

Mobile phones

Local mobile phone numbers are 10 digits, starting with the prefix 09 (the most common being 090, 091, 095 and 098, with more added from time to time).

Most mobile phone users from overseas who have signed up for roaming facility with their service providers back home will be able to hook up with the GSM 900 or 1800 network that Vietnam uses. The exceptions are users from Japan and North America (unless they have a tri-band phone). It's best to check with your service provider. Alternatively, cheap phones using prepaid cards can be purchased in Vietnam for a few hundred thousand dong, along with a local number for an additional VND75,000. These prepaid cards are available at VinaFone and MobiFone shops, post offices, or any shop that sells mobile phones. Sim cards can be bought for about $7. Three main operators: MobiFone, Vinaphone and Viettel also offer a cheap 3G mobile internet service from US$ 2.5 for 1GB data download and upload.

Time zones

Vietnam is seven hours ahead of GMT. Since it gets dark between 6pm and 7pm uniformly throughout the year, Vietnam does not observe daylight-saving time.

Tipping

Tipping is not part of the traditional Vietnamese culture, although it is becoming more common in areas that are frequented by foreign tourists. If you've received particularly good service, a tip of VND5,000 to 20,000 is reasonable; avoid giving excessive amounts. Upscale hotels and restaurants usually add on a 5 to 10 percent service charge to their bills.

Tourist offices

Vietnam's tourism industry lags behind other Asian countries (and for some travellers this may be a good thing). The official representative for Vietnam's tourism – domestically as well as overseas – comes under the purview of the government-operated **Vietnam National Administration of Tourism** (VNAT; www.vietnamtourism. com). However, it is more involved in the construction of new hotels and infrastructure development than in providing tourist services. State-run "tourist offices" under the VNAT are merely tour agents out to make money and are not geared towards meeting the requirements of most travellers. For tours, car hire and travel-related information, you are better off with privately run travel and transport agencies. Much more interesting information (albeit sometimes dated) on the country and tourism can be found at www. vietnamonline.com.

Websites

General
www.vietnamtourism.com
Vietnam National Administration of Tourism.
www.mofa.gov.vn/en
Ministry of Foreign Affairs.

Regional sites
www.dalattourist.com.vn
Government tourism office for Dalat.
www.haiphong.gov.vn
Government and tourism site for Haiphong.
www.halong.org.vn
Tourism site of Halong Bay.
http://tourism.hanoi.gov.vn/english
Government and tourism site for Hanoi.

https://tnhvietnam.xemzi.com Reviews of Hanoi's shops, restaurants and hotels along with classifieds.
http://hochiminhcity.gov.vn.

Special Interest
www.thingsasian.com
Travelogues, stories and recommendations for much of Asia, with a special focus on Vietnam.
http://wwf.panda.org
WWF Indochina's Greater Mekong Programme.
http://www.expat.vn
Informative website for expats in Vietnam.
www.visit-mekong.com
All you need to know when travelling in Mekong Delta and South Vietnam.

Weights and measures

Vietnam uses the metric system. Temperatures are measured in degrees Celsius. Measurements in this book are given in metric with the imperial equivalents in brackets.

⚲ Area codes as of 2017

CITY/PROVINCE	OLD CODE/**NEW CODE**
Dial country code before area code	
Quang Ninh	33/**203**
Bac Giang	240/**204**
Lang Son	25/**205**
Cao Bang	26/**206**
Tuyen Quang	27/**207**
Thai Nguyen	280/**208**
Bac Can	281/**209**
Phu Tho	**210**/Unchanged
Vinh Phuc	**211**/Unchanged
Son La	22/**212**
Lai Chau	231/**213**
Lao Cai	20/**214**
Dien Bien	230/**215**
Yen Bai	29/**216**
Hoa Binh	**218**/Unchanged
Ha Giang	**219**/Unchanged
Hai Duong	320/**220**
Hung Yen	321/**221**
Bac Ninh	241/**222**
Hai Phong	31/**225**
Ha Nam	351/**226**
Thai Binh	36/**227**
Nam Dinh	350/**228**
Ninh Binh	30/**229**
Quang Binh	52/**232**
Quang Tri	53/**233**
Thua Thien Hue	54/**234**
Quang Nam	510/**235**
Da Nang	511/**236**
Thanh Hoa	37/**237**
Nghe An	38/**238**
Ha Tinh	39/**239**
Hanoi	4/**24**
Dong Nai	61/**251**
Binh Thuan	62/**252**
Ba Ria Vung Tau	64/**254**
Quang Ngai	55/**255**
Binh Dinh	56/**256**
Phu Yen	57/**257**
Khanh Hoa	58/**258**
Ninh Thuan	68/**259**
Kon Tum	60/**260**
Dak Nong	501/**261**
Dak Lak	500/**262**
Lam Dong	63/**263**
Gia Lai	59/**269**
Vinh Long	70/**270**
Binh Phuoc	651/**271**
Long An	72/**272**
Tien Giang	73/**273**
Binh Duong	650/**274**
Ben Tre	75/**275**
Tay Nin	66/**276**
Dong Thap	67/**277**
Ho Chi Minh City	8/**28**
Ca Mau	780/**290**
Bac Lieu	781/**291**
Can Tho	710/**292**
Hau Giang	711/**293**
Tra Vinh	74/**294**
An Giang	76/**296**
Kien Giang	77/**297**
Soc Trang	79/**299**

ORIGINS AND INTONATION

Vietnamese, the national language, is spoken by nearly the entire population. Significant variations in pronunciation, some vocabulary, and even the tones themselves exist between northern, central and southern dialect. However, small differences can even be found between cities and surrounding villages. Through the centuries of Chinese occupation the Vietnamese adopted the Han characters. In the 13th century they developed their own written variation – Nom. In the 17th century, on the initiative of a French Jesuit priest, Alexandre de Rhodes, missionaries translated the language into its Romanised form, Quoc Ngu, which was first used by the Catholic Church and the colonial regime's administration. Gradually its use spread, replacing the old written form in the 20th century.

Although Vietnamese uses compound words frequently, individual word fragments are always monosyllabic (unless borrowed from another language). Each syllable (word) can be spoken with one of six different tones (central and southern dialects only have five tones), which could convey six unrelated meanings. These tones are expressed by five diacritical accents and one atonic, where the word has no accent. For example, the word bo can mean "a toilet for children", "father", "lover", "to chop", "impolite", or "a government ministry". While these tones are clearly important, their significance can be overstated. Context is equally important. If the person on the receiving end is patient, most meanings can be conveyed eventually, even if the tones are not entirely correct. After all, tones disappear entirely when Vietnamese is set to music, yet the meaning is still clear, due to context.

Thankfully, Vietnamese has no verb conjugations or tenses (instead, five modifier words are used to convey tense), no masculine or feminine, and no plural noun forms (a universal modifier word is used – cac). To compensate for such simplicity, Vietnamese employs numerous confusing pronouns and titles, mimicking family relationships (for instance, you might address a man as young, middle or older "uncle", younger or older "brother", "friend", or even "grandfather", depending upon his age and the formality of the situation).

Learners often fret over which dialect they should learn. Ultimately, you should learn the dialect of the area where you plan to spend most of your time. Beginners are often told they should learn the Hanoi accent of the northern dialect, because it is the linguistic standard. Indeed, most language courses teach this dialect. Reasons given include the idea that the Vietnamese culture (and thus the language) began in the north and moved southward, or that Hanoians pronounce the language exactly as it is written. However, it has been argued that these justifications tend to be based more on politics and elitism than logic and pragmatism.

PHONOLOGY

The Vietnamese alphabet has 29 letters, although it lacks the English letters **f**, **j**, **w** and **z**. Most consonants are pronounced as they are in English, with a few exceptions: **c** takes on the sound of *g* or *k*. A **ch** sound at the end of a word sounds like *k*. The letter **d** with a crossbar sounds like a *d* in English, but a **d** without a crossbar sounds like *z* in the north and a *y* in the south. A **g** normally has the same hard sound as in English, but when followed by an *i*, it sounds like a *z* in the north and a *y* in the south. When a word begins with **ng** or **ngh**, the letters sound like the *ng* in the English word

long. However, when a word ends in **ng**, the letters sound like *m*. The letter combination **nh** sounds like *ny* as in canyon. As in English, **ph** sounds like *f*. In the south, an **r** sounds as it does in English, but in the north, it sounds like a *z*. A **th** at the beginning of a word sounds like a strongly aspirated *t*. A **tr** at the beginning of a word usually sounds like *ch*, but can also sound like a very hard *tr*. Finally, an **x** always sounds like the letter *s*.

Vowels are a much more complicated affair. There are 12 vowels in the alphabet, and each can be altered by the addition of five different diacritic marks to change the tone of the word. Furthermore, vowels routinely appear in series of up to three letters per word, creating new sound combinations. With such extensive variability, it takes a lot of practice to learn all the possibilities. Beginners should not be deterred, however. Vietnamese pronunciation is very consistent (within each of the regional dialects), so once a pattern is learnt, it can generally be applied to every reoccurrence of that pattern.

Five of the six tones correspond to individual diacritic marks above and below the key vowel in each word. The mid tone does not have an associated diacritic mark.

Mid Tone: Voiced at the speaker's normal, even pitch.

Low Falling Tone: Pitched slightly lower than the mid tone and falls lower.

High Rising Tone: Pitched slightly higher than the mid tone and rises sharply.

Low Dipping-Rising Tone: Pitched lower than the mid tone, dips and then rises.

High Breaking-Rising Tone: Pitched slightly higher than the mid tone, dips and then rises sharply.

Low Falling Constricted Tone: Pitched lower than the mid tone, drops lower, and then stops abruptly.

NUMBERS

0 *khong*
1 *mot*
2 *hai*
3 *ba*
4 *bon*
5 *nam*
6 *sau*
7 *bay*
8 *tam*
9 *chin*
10 *muoi*
11 *muoi mot*
15 *muoi nam*
20 *hai muoi* (north), *hai chuc* (south)
50 *nam muoi* (north), *nam chuc* (south)
100 *mot tram*
1000 *mot nghin* (north), *mot ngan* (south)
1,000,000 *mot trieu*

DAYS OF THE WEEK

Monday *thu hai*
Tuesday *thu ba*
Wednesday *thu tu*
Thursday *thu nam*
Friday *thu sau*
Saturday *thu bay*
Sunday *chu nhat*

BASICS

Yesterday *hom qua*
Today *hom nay*
Tomorrow *ngay mai*
Yes *vang* (north), *da* (south)
No *khong*
Hello *xin chao*
Goodbye *tam biet*
My name is... *ten toi la*...
How are you? *ban co khoe khong?*
Thank you *cam on*
Thank you very much *cam on rat nhieu*
Sorry/Excuse me *xin loi*
Can you help me? *Ban co the giup toi duoc khong?*
No problem/you're welcome *khong co gi*
Do you speak English? *Ban co noi duoc tieng Anh khong?*
I don't understand *Toi khong hieu*

DIRECTIONS AND TRAVEL

Go *di*
Come *den*
Where *o dau*
Right *ben phai*
Left *ben trai*
Turn *re* (north), *queo* (south)

Straight ahead *phia truoc*
Stop here *ngung o day* (north), *dung tai day* (south)
Fast *nhanh*
Slow *cham*
Hotel *khach san*
Street *duong*
Lane *duong nho, con hem*
Bridge *cai cau*
Police station *don canh sat*
Ferry *pha*
Aeroplane *may bay*
Taxi *tac xi*
Train *tau lua* (north), *xe lua* (south)
Bus *xe buyt*
Cable car *cap treo*
Rickshaw *xich lo*
Pier *ben tau*
Bus station *noi do xe*
Train station *nha ga*
How do I get to... the bus stop? *Toi di den... tram xe buyt... nhu the nao?*
Can you show me on the map where I am? *Ban co the chi cho toi biet toi dang o dau tren ban do?*
Where's the... tour office? *Van phong du lich... o dau?*

ACCOMMODATION

The air conditioning doesn't work *May dieu hoa khong hoat dong.*
The light doesn't work *Den khong sang.*
There's no hot water *O day khong co nuoc nong.*
Do you have... toilet paper? *Ban co... giay ve sinh... khong?*

SHOPPING

How much? *Bao nhieu?*
Expensive *rat dat*
Do you have a cheaper price? *Ban co gia nao re hon khong?*
Can I try it on? *Toi co the thu no khong?*
Too big *rat rong*
Too small *rat chat*
I'll take it *Toi se mua no.*
I don't like it *Toi khong thich no.*
Do you have another colour? *Ban co mau nao khac khong?*

COLOUR

White *mau trang*
Black *mau den*
Red *mau do*
Yellow *mau vang*
Blue *mau xanh nuoc bien*
Green *mau xanh la cay*
Orange *mau cam*

EATING OUT

May I have the menu, please? *Lam on cho toi cai thuc don?*
Nothing too spicy, please *Lam on moi thu khong qua cay*
I'm vegetarian *toi an chay*
Hot (heat hot) *nong*
Hot (spicy) *cay*
Cold *lanh*
Sweet *ngot*
Sour *chua*
Delicious *ngon*
Water *nuoc*
Coffee *ca phe*

OTHER HANDY PHRASES

Can I hire a... bicycle? *Toi co the thue... xe dap... khong?*
Do you accept credit cards? *Ban thanh toan bang the tin dung?*
I'd like a cash advance *Toi lay tien mat.*
Where's the... toilet? *Nha ve sinh... o dau?*
I do not feel well *Toi cam thay khong khoe lam.*
Can you get me a doctor? *Ban co the goi bac si cho toi khong?*
Is it safe to swim here? *Noi day boi co an toan khong?*
Is it all right to take pictures? *Toi co the chup hinh khong?*

GLOSSARY OF TERMS

foreigner *nguoi nuoc ngoai*
map *ban do*
ticket *ve*
museum *tang*
market *cho*
holiday *ky nghi* (vacation), *ngay le* (festival)
pagoda *chua temple*
tomb *lang mo*
church *nha tho*
Buddhist *Nguoi theo dao Phat*
Catholic *Nguoi theo dao Thien Chua*
Protestant *Nguoi theo dao Tin Lanh*
restaurant *nha hang*
toilet *nha ve sinh*
ship/boat *tau/thuyen*
motorbike taxi *xe om*
beach *bai bien*
island *dao*
city *thanh pho*
village *lang/xa*
cave *thung lung*
mountain *nui*
river *song*
waterfall *thac nuoc*
clinic *tram xa*
pharmacy *nha thuoc*

FURTHER READING

peacetime office for the LA Times. His experiences with the two Vietnams are recounted in depth with great sensitivity.

Vietnam: Rising Dragon by Bill Hayton. A comprehensive overview of contemporary Vietnamese history.

The Will of Heaven by Nguyen Ngoc Ngan. A collection of memoirs by survivors of communist re-education camps.

COLONIAL HISTORY

A Dragon Apparent by Norman Lewis. Travels through Indochina in the waning days of the French empire.

The Smaller Dragon: A Political History of Vietnam by Joseph Buttinger. Prehistory to the French conquest by a pioneering writer.

The Lover by Marguerite Duras. A sensual tale of a love affair between adolescent French girl and her Chinese lover in the pre-war Saigon with the demise of the French colonial power as a backdrop.

WAR WITH AMERICA

Da Nang Diary by Tom Yarborough. An exciting autobiography of a pilot's secret missions.

Fire in the Lake by Frances Fitzgerald. A classic on the Vietnam War.

The Killing Zone: My Life in the Vietnam War by Frederick Downs Jr. Written by the recipient of four Purple Hearts, it tells the tale of the platoon of Delta One-Six and their struggle for survival.

A Vietcong Memoir by Truong Nhu Tang. The voyage of a scion of the Saigon bourgeoisie to the jungle, to the National Liberation Front, to victory and finally to escape as a boat person.

We Were Soldiers Once... and Young by Harold G. Moore and Joseph L. Galloway. A powerful account by the two journalists on the ground during a decisive battle, and the brave men on both sides whom they interviewed later.

POLITICS AND POST-WAR

Catfish and Mandala by Andrew X. Pham. Illuminates the Vietnamese-American experience as the author's childhood in Phan Thiet is interrupted by escape in a boat. The story chronicles his family's struggle to reach

America, their difficulties adjusting, and his eventual retur.

The Girl in the Picture by Denis Cong. The story of Kim Phuc, the nine-year-old girl burnt by napalm and immortalised in the tragic photo.

Paradise of the Blind by Duong Thu Huong. The writer has been imprisoned for her writings that included veiled criticisms of the government.

Vietnam Notebook by Murray Hiebert. An insightful collection by one of the first Westerners in Hanoi after the onset of *doi moi*.

Vietnam, Now: A Reporter Returns by David Lamb. A journalist in the south from 1969 to 1975, Lamb returned to Vietnam in 1999 to open the

⊘ Send us your thoughts

We do our best to ensure the information in our books is as accurate and up-to-date as possible. The books are updated on a regular basis using local contacts, who painstakingly add, amend and correct as required. However, some details (such as telephone numbers and opening times) are liable to change, and we are ultimately reliant on our readers to put us in the picture.

We welcome your feedback, especially your experience of using the book "on the road". Maybe you came across a great bar or new attraction we missed.

We will acknowledge all contributions, and we'll offer an Insight Guide to the best letters received.

Please write to us at:
  Insight Guides
  PO Box 7910
  London SE1 1WE

Or email us at:
  hello@insightguides.com

CULTURE AND GENERAL HISTORY

Champa and the Archaeology of My Son, Andrew Hardy, Mauro Cucarzi & Patrizia Zolese (eds). A detailed history of the Cham civilisation.

Dumb Luck: A Novel by Vu Trong Phung. A hilarious tongue-in-cheek satire of hip Hanoians in the 1930s who want to be "modern".

The Eaves of Heaven: A Life in Three Wars by Andrew X. Pham. The author tells his father's story as it unfolds through the French occupation, the Japanese invasion and the war with America.

Ho Chi Minh: A Life by William J. Duiker. An exhaustive biography of the man who fought for Vietnam's independence from the French.

The Unwanted, a Memoir of Childhood by Kien Nguyen. A mesmerising memoir of an American-Asian boy's life in communist Vietnam from 1975 till 1985 when he emigrated to the US.

STORIES AND TRAVEL IN MODERN VIETNAM

Hanoi Stories by Pamela Scott. Tales of people and everyday life in Hanoi.

To Vietnam with Love: A Travel Guide for the Connoisseur by Kim Fay. A collection of recommendations with anecdotal stories from expats, seasoned travellers and locals.

Phaic Tan: Sunstroke on a Shoestring by Tom Gleisner and Rob Sitch. A witty spoof guide to Vietnam that tells you everything the tourist authority won't.

COOKERY

Communion: A Culinary Journey Through Vietnam by Kim Fay. A beautifully photographed journey through Vietnam and Vietnamese cuisine.

Culinary Vietnam by Daniel Hoyer. The ultimate guide to Vietnamese cuisine.

CREDITS

Alamy 29, 135B, 242/243T, 242BL
Apa Publications 30, 32, 33, 35
AWL Images 243ML
Calvin Tan/Apa Publications 174
Corbis 39, 43, 44, 78
Derick Lim/Apa Publications 31
Exotissimo 20
Getty Images 1, 4, 37, 38, 45, 50, 52, 55, 65, 70, 76, 84, 85, 111, 113, 118B, 125, 138, 160/161T, 244/245, 349
iStock 19B, 152, 222B, 260BR, 261TR, 344, 358
Jim Holmes/Apa Publications 10T, 27, 119, 157, 161BR, 261BR
Julian Abram Wainwright/Apa Publications 11BC, 11BR, 46, 61, 63, 69, 77, 79, 81, 89, 91, 132, 179, 261ML
Mai Truong 93ML
New York Public Library Picture Collection 34
Peter Stuckings/Apa Publications 6ML, 6MR, 6BR, 6BL, 7TR, 7ML, 7MR, 7ML, 7BR, 7TL, 8T, 8B, 8/9B, 9BR, 11TR, 12/13, 14/15, 16/17, 18, 19T, 21, 22, 23, 26, 28, 36, 40, 47, 48/49, 51, 53, 54, 56, 57, 58, 59, 60, 62, 64, 67, 68, 71, 72/73T, 72BR, 72BL, 73BL, 73BR,

73TR, 74, 75, 82, 83, 86, 87, 88, 90, 94, 95, 96, 97, 98/99, 100/101, 102/103, 104, 105T, 105B, 108, 109T, 109B, 110, 112T, 112B, 115T, 115B, 116, 117, 118T, 120T, 120B, 121, 122T, 122B, 123T, 123B, 124T, 124B, 126T, 126B, 127T, 127B, 128T, 128B, 129T, 129B, 130, 131, 133, 134, 135T, 136T, 136B, 137, 139T, 139B, 140T, 140B, 141, 144, 145, 146, 147T, 147B, 148T, 148B, 149T, 149B, 150T, 150B, 151, 153, 154, 155, 156, 158, 159, 160BR, 160BL, 161ML, 161BL, 161TR, 162, 163, 164, 165, 166, 167, 168B, 168T, 169, 170, 171T, 171B, 172T, 172B, 173T, 173B, 175T, 175B, 176, 177, 178, 180, 181, 182B, 182T, 183, 184B, 184T, 185T, 185B, 186, 187T, 187B, 188B, 189B, 189T, 190, 191, 192, 193, 194/195, 196, 197T, 197B, 198, 199, 201, 203, 204T, 204B, 205B, 205T, 206, 207, 208/209, 210, 211, 212, 213, 215T, 215B, 216T, 216B, 217, 218, 219, 220, 221, 222T, 223T, 223B, 224T, 224B, 225T, 225B, 226, 227, 228, 229, 230, 231, 232, 233, 234B, 234T, 235, 236, 237, 238, 239, 240, 241, 243BR, 243BL, 243TR, 246,

247T, 247B, 248, 249, 250, 251, 252B, 252T, 253, 255T, 255B, 257, 258T, 259, 260/261T, 260BL, 262, 263, 265T, 265B, 266, 267T, 267B, 268T, 268B, 269, 270, 272, 273, 274/275, 276, 277T, 277B, 278, 279, 281, 282, 283B, 283T, 284, 285, 286, 287, 288, 289B, 289T, 290T, 290B, 291B, 291T, 292, 293B, 293T, 294T, 294B, 295B, 295T, 296B, 296T, 297, 298, 299B, 299T, 300, 301, 302, 303, 304, 305, 307T, 307B, 309B, 309T, 310, 311T, 311B, 312, 313, 314T, 314B, 315T, 315B, 316, 317, 318, 319, 320, 321, 322, 323, 324T, 324B, 325T, 325B, 326, 327, 328T, 328B, 329T, 329B, 330, 331, 332, 333T, 333B, 334, 335, 336, 338, 344/345, 353, 356
Photoshot 242BR
Primate Rescue Center 188T
Public domain 42, 80
Robert Harding 92BL, 92BR, 92/93T, 93TR, 93BL, 93BR
Shutterstock 9T, 66
Six Senses 258B
SuperStock 24/25
The Nam Hai 10B
Vietnam News Agency 41

Front cover: Halong Bay *iStock*
Back cover: Whale Island *Peter Stuckings/Apa Publications*
Front flap: (from top) China Beach, Danang *Peter Stuckings/Apa Publications*; Women in Bac Ha *Peter*

Stuckings/Apa Publications; Rower in Van Long Reserve *Peter Stuckings/Apa Publications*; Pho eaters *Peter Stuckings/Apa Publications*
Back flap: Ba Vi National Park *Peter Stuckings/Apa Publications*

INSIGHT GUIDE CREDITS

Distribution
UK, Ireland and Europe
Apa Publications (UK) Ltd;
sales@insightguides.com
United States and Canada
Ingram Publisher Services;
ips@ingramcontent.com
Australia and New Zealand
Woodslane; info@woodslane.com.au
Southeast Asia
Apa Publications (SN) Pte;
singaporeoffice@insightguides.com
Worldwide
Apa Publications (UK) Ltd;
sales@insightguides.com
Special Sales, Content Licensing and CoPublishing
Insight Guides can be purchased in bulk quantities at discounted prices. We can create special editions, personalised jackets and corporate imprints tailored to your needs.
sales@insightguides.com
www.insightguides.biz

Printed in China by CTPS

All Rights Reserved
© 2018 Apa Digital (CH) AG and
Apa Publications (UK) Ltd

First Edition 1992
Eighth Edition 2018

www.insightguides.com

Editor: Sian Marsh
Author: Maciej Zglinicki, Mark Beales, Adam Bray
Head of Production: Rebeka Davies
Update Production: Apa Digital
Picture Editor: Tom Smyth
Cartography: original cartography Lovell Johns, updated by Carte

CONTRIBUTORS

This new edition was edited by Sian Marsh and updated by Maciej Zglinicki.

The bulk of the Places section was originally compiled by four writers.

Covering Hanoi, Around Hanoi, Northwest and Northeast Vietnam plus the Tonkin Coast was Aviva West.

Adam Bray was responsible for the entire Central Vietnam region.

Making sense of frenetic Ho Chi Minh City and condensing it into a digestible read was Samantha Coomber.

Gemma Price researched and wrote the chapter on the Mekong Delta.

Bringing Vietnam to life with all its vivid colour and expression was the principal photographer, Peter Stuckings.

The book was originally copy-edited by Alyse Dar, proofread by Jan McCann and indexed by Penny Phenix.

ABOUT INSIGHT GUIDES

Insight Guides have more than 45 years' experience of publishing high-quality, visual travel guides. We produce 400 full-colour titles, in both print and digital form, covering more than 200 destinations across the globe, in a variety of formats to meet your different needs.

Insight Guides are written by local authors, whose expertise is evident in the extensive historical and cultural background features. Each destination is carefully researched by regional experts to ensure our guides provide the very latest information. All the reviews in **Insight Guides** are independent; we strive to maintain an impartial view. Our reviews are carefully selected to guide you to the best places to eat, go out and shop, so you can be confident that when we say a place is special, we really mean it.

Legend

City maps

	Freeway/Highway/Motorway
	Divided Highway
	Main Roads
	Minor Roads
	Pedestrian Roads
	Steps
	Footpath
	Railway
	Funicular Railway
	Cable Car
	Tunnel
	City Wall
	Important Building
	Built Up Area
	Other Land
	Transport Hub
	Park
	Pedestrian Area
	Bus Station
	Tourist Information
	Main Post Office
	Cathedral/Church
	Mosque
	Synagogue
	Statue/Monument
	Beach
	Airport

Regional maps

	Freeway/Highway/Motorway (with junction)
	Freeway/Highway/Motorway (under construction)
	Divided Highway
	Main Road
	Secondary Road
	Minor Road
	Track
	Footpath
	International Boundary
	State/Province Boundary
	National Park/Reserve
	Marine Park
	Ferry Route
	Marshland/Swamp
	Glacier Salt Lake
	Airport/Airfield
	Ancient Site
	Border Control
	Cable Car
	Castle/Castle Ruins
	Cave
	Chateau/Stately Home
	Church/Church Ruins
	Crater
	Lighthouse
	Mountain Peak
	Place of Interest
	Viewpoint

INDEX

INSIGHT ⊙ GUIDES

OFF THE SHELF

Since 1970, **INSIGHT GUIDES** has provided a unique perspective on the world's best travel destinations by using specially commissioned photography and illuminating text written by local authors.

Whether you're planning a city break, a walking tour or the journey of a lifetime, our superb range of guidebooks and phrasebooks will inspire you to discover more about your chosen destination.

INSIGHT GUIDES

offer a unique combination of stunning photos, absorbing narrative and detailed maps, providing all the inspiration and information you need.

PHRASEBOOKS & DICTIONARIES

help users to feel at home, when away. Pocket-sized with a free app to download, they go where you do.

CITY GUIDES

pack hundreds of great photos into a smaller format with detailed practical information, so you can navigate the world's top cities with confidence.

EXPLORE GUIDES

feature easy-to-follow walks and itineraries in the world's most exciting destinations, with our choice of the best places to eat and drink along the way.

POCKET GUIDES

combine concise information on where to go and what to do in a handy compact format, ideal on the ground. Includes a full-colour, fold-out map.

EXPERIENCE GUIDES

feature offbeat perspectives and secret gems for experienced travellers, with a collection of over 100 ideas for a memorable stay in a city.

www.insightguides.com

Hanoi

0 _____ 500 m
0 _____ 500 yds

N

Old Quarter

0 _____ 2
0 _____ 200

TAY HO

Chua Phu Tay Ho
(West Lake Pagoda)

Xuan Dieu

Au

Sheraton
Hanoi Hotel

Chua Kim Lien
(Golden Lotus Pagoda)

KIM LIEN

Intercontinental
Westlake Hotel

Yen Phu

Nghi Tam

An Duong

Nghi Tam

An Duong

Ho Tay

(West Lake)

Sofitel Plaza

Pho Duc Chinh
Truc Bach

Nghia Dung

Co Xa

Yen Phu

Phuc Xa

Phuc Xa

Chua Tran Quoc
(Tran Quoc Pagoda)

Chua Ngu Xa
(Ngu Xa Pagoda)

Thanh Nien

*Ho Truc
Bach
(White
Silk Lake)*

Ngu Xa

Chau Long

Cua Bac

Nguyen Khac Nhu

Pham Hong
Thai

Tan Ap

Den Quan Thanh
(Quan Thanh Temple)

Tran Vu

Nguyen Truong To

Chua Noe Nhai

Bao Tang Dai Toc Hoc Viet Nam
(Vietnam Museum of Ethnology),
Cputra International City

Thuy Khue

Hoang Hoa Tham

Nha San
Bac Ho
Chi Minh
(Ho Chi
Minh House)

**CONG VIEN
BACH THAO
(BOTANICAL
GARDEN)**

Quan Thanh

Cua Bac
(Catholic Church)

Hang Dau

Ga Long Bien
(Station)

Cau Long Bien

Phu Chu Tich
(Presidential
Palace)

Hoang Van Thu

Phan Dinh Phung Chi Minh

Lang Chu Tich Ho Chi Minh
(Ho Chi Minh
Mausoleum)

**Ba
Dinh
Square**

**OLD
CITY**

Bac Son

Chua Mot Cot
(One Pillar Pagoda)

Bao Tang
Ho Chi Minh
(Ho Chi Minh
Museum)

B-52 Lake

Doi Can

Chua Mot
Cot

Le Hong Phong

**CITADEL
Military Area
(Restricted Access)**

Cua Dong

see above

Voi Phuc

Son Tay

Lenin

Cot Co
(Flag Tower)

Bao Tang Lich
Su Quan Su
(Military History
Museum)

Ly Nam De

Phung Hung

Bat Dan

**PHO PHUONG
(OLD QUARTER)**

HOAN KIEM

Giang Vo

Tran

Nguyen

Bao Tang My Thuat
(Fine Arts Museum)

Dien Bien Phu

Cau Go

Den Ngoc Son
(Temple of the
Jade Mound)

Tran Quang Khai

Bach Dang

Ngo Bai

Cat Linh

Thai Hoc

Nha Tho Lon
(St Joseph's
Cathedral)

*Ho
Hoan
Kiem*

Dinh Tien Hoang

Van Mieu
(Temple of Literature)

P. Nguyen Khuyen

Hai Ba Trung

Trang Thi

H. Khay Trang Tien

former
Bank of
Indochina

Bao Tang Cach Mang
Viet Nam (Museum of
Vietnamese Revolution)

Hang Bot

Ga Ha Noi
(Station)

**Hanoi
Towers**

Ba Tang Nha Bao Hoa Lo
(Hoa Lo Prison/Hanoi Hilton)

Sofitel Legend
Metropole Hotel

**FRENCH
QUARTER**

Bao Tang Lich Su
(National Museum of
Vietnamese History)

Chua Quan Su
(Ambassadors'
Pagoda)

Ly Thuong Kiet

Hilton Hanoi
Opera Hotel

Nha Hat Lon
(Municipal Theatre/
Opera House)

La Thanh

Kham Thien

Cung Van Hoa
Huu Nghi
(Cultural Palace)

Tran

Hung

Dao

Dai Hoc Tong
Hop Ha Noi
(University)

*Ho
Linh
Quang*

Le Duan

Tran Quoc Toan

Ham

Nguyen Du

Nha Hat
Tuoi Tre

Ho Duc Thang

Ng.
Thuong
Hien

*Ho Thien
Quang
(Thien Quang
Lake)*

Nha Hat
Dai Nam

Nha Hat Rap Xiec
(Circus Theatre)

Tran Nhan Tong

Nha Hat Cheo
(Cheo Theatre)

Tue Tinh

Den Hai Ba Trung (Hai Ba Trung Temple)

Go Dong Da

**CONG VIEN
THONG NHAT
(REUNIFICATION
PARK)**

Old Quarter (inset)

Cho Dong Xuan
(Dong Xuan Market)

Thanh Ha

Hang Chieu

Quan Chuong
(Old East Gate)

Nhat Duat

Den Bach Ma
(Bach Ma Temple)

Nguyen Sieu

Hang
Gia

Buom

Nha Hat Kim Do
(Memorial House)

Nha Hat
Chuong Vang
(Golden Bell Theatre)

**PHO PHUONG
(OLD QUARTER)**

Hang Bac

Cho Hang Be
(Hang Be Market)

Hang Quat

Cau Go

Nha Hat Mua
Roi Thang Long
(Thang Long
Water Puppet Theatre)

Dinh Tien Hoang

Den Ngoc Son
(Temple of the
Jade Mound)

Huc
(Rising Sun
Bridge)

Tran Nguyen

Nha Hat
Kim Dong

Chua Ba Da
(Ba Da
Pagoda)

*Ho
Hoan Kiem
(Hoan Kiem
Lake)*

LY THAI TO
(LY THAI TO PAF

Govern
Guest

Thap Rua
(Turtle Tower)

Buu Dien Ha Noi
(Hanoi General Post Office)

H. Khay Trang Tien